# The Ethnic Experience in Pennsylvania

*This volume was published with the cooperation and support of the Pennsylvania Historical and Museum Commission in its continuing attempt to preserve the history of the people of the Commonwealth.*

# The
# Ethnic Experience
# in Pennsylvania

*Edited and with an Introduction by*
John E. Bodnar

*Lewisburg*
**BUCKNELL UNIVERSITY PRESS**

Associated University Presses, Inc.
Cranbury, New Jersey 08512

Library of Congress Cataloging in Publication Data

Bodnar, John E        1944-
   The Ethnic experience in Pennsylvania.

   Includes bibliographies.
      1. Pennsylvania—Foreign population—Addresses,
   essays, lectures.   2. Minorities—Pennsylvania—
   Addresses, essays, lectures.   I. Title.
   F175.A1B62        917.48'06        72-3257
   ISBN 0-8387-1155-3

Printed in the United States of America

Quotation on page 252 from Philip M. Rose, *The Italians in America* (New York: George H. Doran, 1922), p. 82. Used with permission of Doubleday and Company, Inc.

# Contributors

John E. Bodnar, Associate Historian, Ethnic Studies Program, Pennsylvania Historical and Museum Commission

Caroline Golab, Department of Housing and Urban Development, Philadelphia

Richard N. Juliani, Assistant Professor of Sociology, Temple University

Maurice Mook, Professor of Anthropology, Lycoming College, Williamsport, Pennsylvania

Carl Oblinger, Assistant Professor of History and Humanities, Missouri State University, Maryville, Missouri

Bohdan P. Procko, Professor of History, Villanova University

George J. Prpić, Professor of History, John Carroll University, Cleveland, Ohio

James P. Rodechko, Associate Professor of History, Wilkes College

Clement Valletta, Associate Professor of English and American Civilization, King's College, Wilkes-Barre, Pennsylvania

Walter C. Warzeski, Chairman, Department of History, Kutztown State College

Michael P. Weber, Assistant Professor of History, Carnegie-Mellon University

Maxwell Whiteman, Consulting Archival Historian, Union League of Philadelphia

# Contents

# Acknowledgments

In bringing this volume together, many individuals have provided me with invaluable encouragement and assistance. Dr. Sylvester K. Stevens, former Executive Director of the Pennsylvania Historical and Museum Commission, and his successor, Mr. William Wewer, supported the project enthusiastically from its inception. Dr. Donald H. Kent was equally as enthusiastic and encouraged the project unfailingly. Mrs. Mae L. Kruger of the Commission's Ethnic Studies Program worked endlessly on correspondence, proofreading, and typing parts of the manuscript. Carl Oblinger provided some extremely valuable suggestions and criticisms. Dr. James Carens of the Bucknell University Press supported the publication from the very beginning. Finally, my wife Donna tolerated me through the compilation of this volume and the simultaneous writing of a dissertation.

John E. Bodnar
Pennsylvania Historical & Museum Commission

# Editor's Introduction

The late Louis Adamic, an immigrant himself from Yugoslavia, observed in *A Nation of Nations* that there were two ways of looking at our history. One could view the United States as an Anglo-Saxon country with a "White-Protestant-Anglo-Saxon Civilization" struggling to preserve itself against inflation and adulteration by other civilizations brought here by Negroes and hordes of "foreigners." On the other hand, Adamic noted, the pattern of American history could be viewed as essentially not Anglo-Saxon, although our language is English, but as a blend of cultures from many lands: "Diversity itself is the pattern, is the stuff and color of the fabric."[1]

However, until quite recently the cultural pluralist approach to the American past has been relatively neglected. Michael Kane, for instance, in a recent investigation of the treatment of minorities in social studies textbooks, found that a significant number of texts today continue to present a principally white, Protestant, Anglo-Saxon view of America's past and present, while the nature and problems of minority groups are largely neglected.[2] Indeed, Rudolph Vecoli has chided American scholarship for discouraging ethnic studies. "How many graduate students have shied away from research topics," Vecoli asks, "for fear they would be suspected of ethnic chauvinism?"[3]

Much of this neglect, of course, can be attributed to the persistent symbol of the "melting pot." As Israel Zangwill expressed it in *The Melting-Pot, A Drama in Four Acts* in 1908, "America is God's

Crucible, the great Melting-Pot where all the races of Europe are melting and re-forming."[4] Americans from Crevecoeur in his *Letters from an American Farmer,* to Ralph Waldo Emerson, to Frederick Jackson Turner all expressed similar variations of the symbol that was finally crystalized in Zangwill's play.[5] Even recent scholarly works such as Humbert Nelli's volume on the Italians of Chicago, suggest that ethnicity rapidly disintegrated in America after the end of mass immigration.[6]

What the traditional stress on assimilation rather than pluralism did was to omit the study of minority cultures and problems from our historical literature. Thus, J. Cutler Andrews, as president of the Pennsylvania Historical Association in 1966, was forced to make a plea for more studies of ethnic groups in the state.[7] The necessity of this plea is even more striking when one considers the richness and importance of ethnic history in a state like Pennsylvania. William Penn himself advertised for immigrants throughout Europe to come to his colony, regardless of race or religion. Benjamin Franklin, on the other hand, expressed nativist fears during the heavy immigration of Germans into the Commonwealth that Pennsylvania, which was founded by England, was becoming "a colony of aliens, who will shortly be so numerous as to Germanize us instead of our Anglifying them. . . ."[8] And stories of Irish miners who would draw chalk lines on the barroom floor and dare anyone to cross, and Jewish peddlers working their way through Pennsylvania's coal towns have yet to find their way into the accounts of the state's social history.[9]

Despite this general neglect of ethnicity, however, recent scholarship as a whole has been making a strong case for not only the importance of ethnicity in American history but its persistence. Students of American political history, such as Samuel Hays, have now concluded that ethno-cultural issues were far more important to voters than were tariffs, trusts, and railroads.[10] Lee Benson's provocative study of Jacksonian Democracy advanced the thesis that ethnic and religious differences have tended to be "relatively" the most important source of political differences since the 1820s. Michael Holt found that the major factor in the rise of the Republican Party in the 1850s in Pittsburgh was anti-Catholic sentiment among

native Americans. Samuel Lubel, of course, has suggested the importance of ethnicity in bringing the Democratic Party to power in
1932. And now John Allswang contends that ethnicity was a greater
determinant of voting behavior than socioeconomic forces in Chicago
in the early decades of this century.[11]

In addition to the interest in ethnic politics, ethnicity has been
found to be a crucial and persistent factor in many areas of American
history and life. Social historians and sociologists interested in occupational and geographical mobility have found differences in mobility
based upon lines of ethnicity.[12] Scholars now turning to the history
of the family in America have found ethnicity to be a vital element,
even a "system of order."[13] Virginia McLaughlin discovered that
the family organization of immigrant Italians remained essentially
intact in Buffalo because of the strength of ethnic (Italian) culture.[14]
And Martin Marty, claiming the story of the peopling of America
is only a half-told tale, has suggested that most scholars have failed
to account for the importance of ethnic consciousness in the development of American religion.[15]

Moreover, it is now not only recognized that ethnicity *was* a crucial factor in American society but that it still is. The United States
Census Bureau in a 1969 study entitled "Characteristics of the
Population by Ethnic Origin" reported that about seventy-five million
of the approximately two-hundred million persons in the United
States identified themselves as being of either German, English,
Irish, Spanish, Italian, Polish or Russian origin.[16] This does not
include about twenty million Afro-Americans and numerous other
ethnic groups.

Recent studies of personalities of ethnic groups provide additional
evidence of direct correlation between ethnicity and certain psychological and personal traits. Thus, despite the fact that the bulk of
Irish immigration terminated nearly a century ago, the Irish are
still relatively heavy drinkers and prove to spend more time with
their children than the Italians. Moreover, among Americans, the
Irish and the Jews appeared to be ahead of everyone else in their
support for black militancy and in their opposition to war.[17]

John M. Goering has even asserted that the declining importance of objective ethnic constraints—foreign birth, ethnic endogamy—does not necessarily imply complete assimilation, but rather operates as a condition for the emergence of a more subjective or ideological ethnic interest. In a study of three generations of Irishmen and Italians, Goering discovered that about one-half of his sample of the first and second generations thought of themselves as ethnic and thought it was important. However, almost seventy percent of the third generation thought of themselves ethnically.[18]

Thus, it is clear that ethnicity has not only permeated American life for generations but has persisted until today. Greeley has attributed this persistence to the fact that Americans have always had to live with diversity. America was religiously pluralistic from colonial times. Thus, despite considerable pressures put upon immigrants to Americanize, the pressures were not absolute. American society was not basically hostile to the persistence of ethnic groups. Moreover, Greeley argued, as does Milton Gordon, that there has been a powerful drive in man toward associating with those who, he feels, possess the same blood and same beliefs as he does. As Milton Gordon described it, it is the desire for a sense of "peoplehood."[19]

In the original essays presented here, ethnic groups are studied from a variety of viewpoints. Using one particular state and its cultural past as a focal point, the essays attempt not only to bring to light accounts of immigrant and racial groups that have been frequently overlooked, but they seek to reveal the varying perspectives to which scholars have subjected ethnic studies. Thus, Clement Valletta's study of the Italians of Roseto deals largely with their folk beliefs. On the other hand, Richard Juliani, a sociologist, looks at the social organization of Italians in Philadelphia, and Caroline Golab seeks to explain patterns of Polish settlement in the industrial city. Bohdan Procko and George Prpić attempt to trace the activities of Ukrainian and Croatian immigrants who settled in Pennsylvania.

Quantitative history adds an additional dimension to the methodological spectrum. In the essays of Carl Oblinger on Negro transient groups and Michael Weber on immigrant mobility in Warren, we discover the usefulness of statistical inquiry in revealing aspects of the ethnic experience. Oblinger, for instance, is able to establish the existence of an impoverished class of Negroes in Lancaster and Chester counties. Weber attempts to examine the extent ethnicity affected social mobility.

Some of the essays look at the internal workings of the ethnic community. Maurice Mook reveals the influence of the ethnic group over its members. Walter Warzeski, James Rodechko, and John Bodnar survey the difficulties that plagued certain ethnic groupings and attempt to state the consequences of this strife. Maxwell Whiteman examines the reception of Jewish immigrants in Philadelphia.

While these studies can in no way be construed as being definitive, they do provide case studies of the ethnic experience in one state. They adopt a range of methodological techniques, and they offer an extensive sampling of the source material available on Pennsylvania's ethnic history. Furthermore, taken collectively, they suggest the vitality of the ethnic community and significance of ethnicity as a variable in American history and life.

# NOTES

1. Louis Adamic, *A Nation of Nations* (New York: 1944), pp. 6–7.
2. Michael B. Kane, *Minorities in Textbooks, A Study of their Treatment in Social Studies Texts* (Chicago: 1970), p. 138.
3. Rudolph Vecoli, "Ethnicity: A Neglected Dimension of American History," *The State of American History*, ed. Herbert Bass (Chicago: 1970), pp. 79–83.
4. Israel Zangwill, *The Melting Pot, A Drama in Four Acts* (New York: 1919), p. 33.
5. Philip Gleason, "The Melting Pot: Symbol of Fusion or Confusion," *American Quarterly* XVI (Spring, 1964): 20–25.
6. Humbert S. Nelli, *Italians in Chicago, 1880–1930—A Study in Ethnic Mobility* (New York: 1970).
7. J. Cutler Andrews, "The Gilded Age in Pennsylvania," *Pennsylvania History* XXXIV (Jan., 1967): 4–6. See also Philip S. Klein, "Our Pennsylvania Heritage, Yesterday and Tomorrow," *Pennsylvania History* XXV (1958): 7–8.
8. Roy L. Garis, *Immigration Restriction* (New York: 1927), pp. 7–8; John Bigelow, ed., *Works of Benjamin Franklin* (New York: 1887–88) II: 223, 297–99.
9. See the particular interesting collection of oral history on the anthracite area in the George Korson Collection, King's College, Wilkes-Barre, Penna., especially reel 28, interview with Bruce Christ, August 23, 1957.

10. Samuel Hays, "Political Parties and the Community-Society Continuum," *The American Party Systems,* eds. William N. Chambers and Walter Dean Burnham (New York: 1967), chapter 6.

11. Lee Benson, *The Concept of Jacksonian Democracy: New York as a Test Case* (Princeton: 1961), p. 165; Michael F. Holt, *Forging a Majority: The Formation of the Republican Party in Pittsburgh, 1848–60,* (New Haven: 1969), p. 218; Samuel Lubell, *The Future of American Politics,* Third edition (New York: 1965); John Allswang, *A House for all Peoples: Ethnic Politics in Chicago* (Lexington, Ky.: 1971). See Walter D. Burnham, "Quantitative History: Beyond the Correlation Coefficient, A Review Essay," *Historical Methods Newsletter* IV (May, 1971): 62–66.

12. Clyde Griffen, "The Effect of Craft and Ethnic Differences in Poughkeepsie, New York, 1850–1880," *Nineteenth-Century Cities,* eds. Stephan Thernstrom and Richard Sennett (New Haven: 1969), p. 29; also see Thernstrom, "Men in Motion: Some Data and Speculations about Urban Population Mobility in Nineteenth-Century America," *Anonymous Americans,* ed. Tamara K. Hareven (Englewood Cliffs, N.J.: 1971), pp. 31–34; Paul Worthman, "Working Class Mobility in Birmingham, Alabama, 1880–1914," *ibid.,* pp. 172–213.

13. See Tamara Hareven, "Family Structure and Social Change in Boston," paper delivered at Organization of American Historians meeting, April 8, 1972, Washington, D. C.

14. Virginia Yans McLaughlin, "Patterns of Work and Family Organization: Buffalo's Italians," *Journal of Interdisciplinary History* II (Autumn, 1971): 299–314.

15. Martin E. Marty, "Ethnicity: The Skeleton of Religion in America," *Church History* XLI (March, 1972): 5–21.

16. U. S. Bureau of Census, Current Population Report, "Characteristics of the Population by Ethnic Origin," Series P-20, No. 221 (Nov., 1969). See also Michael Novak, *The Rise of the Unmeltable Ethnics* (New York: 1972); Peter Schrag, *The Decline of the WASP* (New York: 1972); Albert Nemi, "The Role of Immigration in United States Commodity Production, 1869–1929," *Social Science Quarterly* LII (June, 1971): 190–96.

17. See Andrew M. Greeley and William C. McCready, "An Ethnic Group which Vanished—The Strange Case of the American Irish," paper presented at the American Historical Association meeting, Dec. 28, 1971, New York.

18. John M. Goering, "The Emergence of Ethnic Interests: A Case of Serendipity," *Social Forces* LXIX (March, 1971): 379, 384.

19. Andrew M. Greeley, *Why Can't They Be Like Us. Facts and Fallacies about Ethnic Differences and Group Conflict in America* (New York: 1969), pp. 19–22. Milton Gordan, *Assimilation in American Life* (New York: 1964), p. 38.

1

# Irish-American Society in the Pennsylvania Anthracite Region: 1870-1880

## JAMES RODECHKO

*James P. Rodechko is Associate Professor of History at Wilkes College. He obtained an undergraduate degree from Hofstra University in 1961 and a Ph.D. from the University of Connecticut in 1967.*

Discussions of Irish-American life in the Pennsylvania anthracite region often focus too narrowly on Molly Maguire activities. The violence associated with the Mollies during the 1870s has involved long and often bitter controversy. There are some who claim that the Mollies were simply criminals and murderers who had little just cause for their actions.[1] Still other views hold that the Mollies were oppressed workers who initiated revolutionary tactics against an unjust capitalist system.[2] But arguments that stress criminal intent or capitalist oppression, while partially true, tend to ignore more complex reasons for violence. In particular, there has been little examination of the broad Irish-American community in the anthracite region.[3] In retrospect, the structural weakness of this community contributed to the sporadic violence and uncertainty that existed in the coal fields.

It is generally recognized that society in the anthracite region was disorganized during the Gilded Age. Historian Rowland Berthoff has argued that effective leadership was nonexistent and social conflict prevailed in the area throughout the better part of the nineteenth century. What is most interesting, however, is that this disintegration often operated within particular ethnic groups.[4] This is especially true of the Irish-American community in the 1870s. Although the anthracite Irish were conscious of common ethnic origins and problems, they were unable to form purposeful organizations. This set them apart from Irish immigrants in other areas who developed more effective organizational responses to American conditions. As a result, the anthracite Irish were particularly frustrated in their attempts to advance on the socio-economic scale.

Due to agricultural disaster in Ireland, massive numbers of Irishmen had been seeking refuge in America since the 1840s. Because Irishmen were either disillusioned with farming or were unable to afford land, they generally congregated in large urban areas like New York, Boston, and Chicago.[5] Since they lacked specialized training and usually had to seek employment as unskilled laborers, they also settled in Pennsylvania's anthracite region. By 1870, there were 44,122 Irish-born immigrants in Schuylkill, Luzerne, Carbon, Columbia, and Northumberland counties. In the two most productive anthracite counties, Luzerne and Schuylkill, there were 38,075 Irishmen. Since a large proportion of Irishmen in the region tended to marry within their own ethnic group, considerable numbers of second generation Irish-Americans increased the size of this community.[6]

Generally the anthracite Irish were on the bottom of the social and economic ladder. Historical opinion suggests that the majority of employed Irishmen were coal miners, a few served as policemen, and only a small number reached the professional and business classes. As miners, their pay was usually low. In fact, young boys often took employment in the mines or sought related work to supplement meager family incomes. In times of overproduction or national depression, salaries were even lower and unemployment widespread. The work itself was dangerous and physically exhausting, often resulting in injury or early death. Occupational problems, in turn, pervaded almost every aspect of the miner's life. In dingy houses, towns, and stores operated by mine owners, immigrants not only encountered health hazards, but found rents and prices carefully regulated to consume most of the miners' pay. The miserable conditions that existed in the towns, when combined with occupational hardship, often caused Irishmen to turn to alcohol for relief. Alcoholism, in turn, weakened family ties and accounted for considerable numbers of Irishmen who were arrested for disorderly conduct.[7]

Native Americans reacted to Irish social and economic problems with either indifference or open hostility. Many felt that Irish alcoholism and crime rates verified traditional stereotypes of the irresponsible and indolent Irish. Newspapers cited jokes and anecdotes that depicted the Irish as stupid, corrupt, and vulgar.[8] And since most Irishmen were Catholic, they were often stigmatized for "foreign" and "dangerous" religious values. Prejudice often contributed to the Irishman's poor economic condition. At times, a "no Irish need apply" attitude gripped the coal region. Welsh, English, and native American mine bosses preferred to hire fellow countrymen at the expense of Irish immigrants. In fact, Irishmen were sometimes fired to make room for others who desired employment.[9]

The Irish also encountered law enforcement authorities on unfavorable terms. Although Irishmen gained positions with town and village police departments, these local departments dealt severely with Irish offenders. In describing a St. Patrick's Day disturbance, Wilkes-Barre's *Record of the Times* noted that the "police had a very persuasive way of taking prisoners to the lock up, which was irresistible." Nevertheless, advocates of law and order were unwilling to entrust law enforcement solely to local authorities. In fact, the generally recognized authority was the infamous coal and iron police force, privately paid for and controlled by the mine owners. Although the coal and iron police had questionable legal authority, they were considered more reliable than local authorities. This was largely because they were composed of supposedly more "responsible" English, Welsh, and native American groups. When mine owners found the Irish particularly obstinate, as in the Molly Maguire incidents, they used the Pinkerton Detective Agency to bolster efforts by coal and iron police. Irish miners, in turn, looked upon all law enforcement agencies with suspicion and fear.[10]

While conditions were poor and prejudices apparent, there were those who anticipated better things for the Irish. Historian J. Walter Coleman suggests that by 1870 Irish-American numerical strength "aroused the fears of prior inhabitants of the older groups. . . ."[11] These fears seemed well grounded since Irishmen were highly conscious of their social condition and were prepared to initiate organized efforts to remedy the situation. Native Americans showed concern that anthracite Irishmen would follow the experience of the New York Irish and assert political control over the region. The supposed "natural aptitude" Irishmen had for politics and their alleged "clannishness" seemed suggestive of future success. Irish-American spokesmen also expected success in the anthracite region. They not only looked to future political and economic influence in eastern Pennsylvania, but claimed that the Irish there, as in other parts of the United States, would soon be strong enough to play a leading role in the crusade for Ireland's national independence.[12]

For a variety of reasons, however, the Irish did not achieve the influence many predicted for them. In retrospect, those who expected the development of powerful Irish-American organizations tended to overestimate Irish numerical strength in the region, particularly in comparison to the overall population. This tendency stemmed from the fact that the Irish were constantly in the public eye. Irishmen were involved in organized labor and were usually principal participants in labor-capital discord. The publicity given to the Molly Maguires, along with stories of their alleged political and economic influence, tended to suggest the idea of a powerful conspiracy involving large numbers of Irishmen. Then, too, the fact that Irishmen were more commonly found in statistics on crime and alcoholism than other elements of the population, not only suggested that Irishmen were a major social problem, but that they constituted a large numerical group.[13]

In point of fact, statistics indicate that the Irish community was not especially large when compared to the total anthracite population.

Whereas the Irish-born in New York constituted 21.3 percent of the city's total population in 1870, the Irish in Luzerne and Schuylkill counties constituted only 13.7 percent of the total population. In all five of the coal producing counties, 44,122 Irish immigrants amounted to only 11.7 percent of the total population. Furthermore, during the 1870s the number of Irish immigrants, which had risen rapidly in the 1860s, began to level off. By 1880 the Irish-born numbered 41,764 and constituted 8.8 percent of the population in all the anthracite counties. In the Luzerne, Lackawanna, and Schuylkill regions, Irishmen constituted 10.4 percent of the population. In short, percentages alone indicated that anthracite Irishmen would find it difficult to emulate the experience of the New York Irish.[14]

Geographic factors further affected the influence of the Irish. Although Francis Dewees argued that organized activities were facilitated by the "limited area of the anthracite coal-fields" and "rapid means of transit from point to point," it is apparent that he grossly exaggerated the situation.[15] The anthracite region actually entailed a broad area of some 400 to 500 square miles. This area was divided into several distinct coalfields: the Lehigh, the Wyoming-Lackawanna, and two fields in Schuylkill County. The fields were separated from each other by mountains and farm lands. Furthermore, geographic conditions and available transportation facilities caused mine owners to look to different market places for their coal. The Wyoming-Lackawanna area sent its coal mainly to New York, the Schuylkill fields turned to Philadelphia, and Lehigh looked to both New York and Philadelphia. This situation meant that the anthracite population was divided and localism prevailed. When broader contacts did occur, they existed between specific localities in the anthracite region and outside urban areas. Irish political, economic, and social efforts were consequently hindered by the same divisive geographic factors that lent to disorganization in the broader anthracite community.[16]

Irish efforts aimed at economic improvement naturally involved the organization of coal miners. The Workingmen's Benevolent Association, founded in 1868 to provide death and sick benefits to miners and their families, soon became the principal vehicle for labor protest in the anthracite region. By 1869 organizational expansion was so successful that the Workingmen's Benevolent Association (WBA) spoke for 85 percent of the anthracite miners and had a membership of 30,000.[17] But while membership increased, disunity was a pervasive problem. Although the Irish were the predominant ethnic group within the WBA, there were also English, Welsh, and German elements. Since representatives of the various groups accused the others of weakness and disloyalty, cohesion was difficult to maintain. John Powell, a Welsh miner writing in 1871, blamed the failure of a strike in Luzerne County on "spineless" Irishmen who were "weak in faith" and not nearly "as united as the Welsh."[18]

Aside from ethnic rivalries, the WBA was beset by regional divisions. These divisions resulted from differing management and mining practices throughout the anthracite fields. In the southern fields in Schuylkill County, mine shafts were old and deep, tunneling was expensive, and the margin of profit was consequently narrow. Since coal was more easily mined in the newer Wyoming-Lackawanna region to the north, profits were higher. As a result, wages were better in Wyoming-Lackawanna, there was less support for the WBA in that region, and miners there often ignored or opposed work suspensions. Wilkes-Barre's *Record of the Times* encouraged this mood with claims that Lackawanna workers had the "least right to accuse their employers of injustice" since "they were paid more than any other region received. . . ." In Schuylkill labor was more aggressive since wages were lower. But the willingness of Luzerne miners to terminate strikes quickly, inevitably caused bitterness among Schuylkill workers and lessened their enthusiasm for long strikes. Furthermore, since workers in Luzerne were disinterested and money was scarce in Schuylkill, it was difficult to build up WBA funds in order to withstand prolonged strikes.[19]

Leadership was also a problem for the WBA. John Siney, an Irishman who was instrumental in organizing the union, served as first president. He believed that labor should seek harmony with capital and that conflict with mine owners only damaged the miners' position. In keeping with his philosophy, Siney opposed strikes and used his influence to prevent aggressive WBA members from initiating them.

This usually meant that Siney enjoyed respect among Luzerne miners but suffered criticism in Schuylkill County. In 1873 many Schuylkill workers were delighted when Siney resigned the WBA presidency to devote attention to the broadly based National Miners' Association. When Siney subsequently tried to gain WBA support for the National Association, Schuylkill miners resisted. As a result, the WBA and National Association engaged in an exhausting struggle for membership in Schuylkill County. In Luzerne, however, WBA members worked with the National Association and exchanged membership cards.[20]

While workers were often dispirited and divided, management became increasingly aggressive during the 1870s. This was especially apparent in the Schuylkill region where the Reading Railroad exerted influence. The railroad's president, Franklin B. Gowen, vigorously opposed WBA activities and directed a steady propaganda barrage against the union. By identifying the union with Molly Maguire vendettas and communist doctrines, Gowen was able to arouse public opinion against the miners. Through his monopoly of transportation facilities, Gowen was also able to manipulate shipping rates and force coal operators in Schuylkill to take a hard line against the WBA. In an 1871 strike, when several coal companies seemed about to surrender to WBA demands, Gowen raised transportation rates to prohibitive levels and forced faltering companies to hold the line against the union. After the strike of 1871 was broken, Gowen began to buy coal lands for the Reading Railroad. Between 1871 and 1874, he purchased over 100,000 acres for the railroad, greatly strengthening its control over the Schuylkill fields and increasing its ability to deal directly with the union. In 1873 Gowen broadened management unity when he initiated a pool among all anthracite producers to fix prices and divide markets. The pool resulted in high profits for management, but did nothing to improve the miners' working situation.[21]

The struggle between the WBA and mine owners came to a head in 1875. At that time anthracite operators, due to Gowen's influence, introduced wage cuts throughout the coal region. In response, Joseph Welsh, the new WBA president, called a strike. As usual, the strike was not uniformly accepted throughout the fields. Northern miners, encouraged by Siney, remained at work while Schuylkill miners stayed out for some five months. The "long strike" exhausted and embittered Schuylkill miners and forced the WBA to give in and accept wage cuts.[22] The union was now discredited while Irish members faced discrimination. Since Irishmen had been powerful in the WBA and had been commonly identified with violence during the strike, mine operators often refused to rehire them after the strike ended. In the midst of a national depression, many Irishmen found themselves in especially dire economic straits.[23]

Some hope emerged in 1876 with the appearance of a new union in the coal fields. In that year the Knights of Labor began to organize Scranton miners. The Knights soon entered most of the anthracite fields and generally filled the void left by the WBA. The Irish, more than any other element, were attracted to the Knights. This was especially true after 1879 when Terrence Powderly, an Irishman, became Grand Master Workman. But the same conditions that had hindered the WBA also affected the Knights. Regional disunity persisted and employers were still extremely aggressive toward labor activity. Like the WBA, the Knights were popularly identified with the Molly Maguires. The Catholic clergy often opposed the Knights because of this identification and because prospective members had to take a secret oath.[24]

Since labor organizations were usually ineffective, Irishmen often sought alternative solutions to their problems through political action. The Irish in the anthracite region usually followed Irish-American voting patterns in other parts of the United States and adhered to the Democratic Party. Republican newspapers in Wilkes-Barre and Pottsville alluded to Irish influence in the Democracy and subtly suggested that Republicans drew support from more respectable Welsh, German, and English elements.[25] On occasion, particularly in Schuylkill County, the Irish were able to dominate the Democratic organization. At such times, it was assumed that Irish politicians gained strength through political favors and the manipulation of Irish votes. Reports abounded that unscrupulous Irish politicians had been responsible for tax collection frauds and had personally profited from improper administration of public charities.[26]

Generally, however, there was a tendency to exaggerate the Irish role in the Democratic Party and the political benefits they derived as a result of that role. On the state level the Republicans were usually victorious in the 1870s, thus minimizing Irish efforts to bring the state government to bear on anthracite problems.[27] Within the anthracite region, where the Democrats were more successful, Irishmen encountered formidable barriers to political dominance. Whereas large Irish populations in geographically confined urban areas found political control relatively easy, the smaller Irish community in the expansive coal regions found it impossible to achieve such political integration. It was also apparent that Irish politicians encountered strong opposition from fellow Democrats. In Schuylkill County in 1874, when Irishmen succeeded in nominating James B. Reilly for Congress, German-born and native American party leaders were highly indignant. The *Miners' Journal* indicated that Schuylkill Democrats were simply not used to the tactics Irishmen practiced in New York's Tammany Hall.[28]

Irishmen themselves were at times dubious about supposed benefits derived from close affiliation with the Democratic Party. Many thought that Democrats showed only slight concern for Irish problems. The fact that Franklin B. Gowen was a high-ranking Democrat convinced a number of Irishmen that uniform adherence to the Democracy was unwise. In 1875 large numbers of Irishmen voted Republican. Although it was alleged that the Republican gubernatorial candidate, John F. Hartranft, bargained for Irish votes by promising pardons to convicted Molly Maguires, renewed Republican concern for labor was more responsible for the shift in political loyalties.[29] At other times, when both major parties seemed indifferent to Irish needs, a few Irish spokesmen called for third party action. In 1872 and 1873, John Siney unsuccessfully urged Irishmen to support the National Labor Reform Party. After 1875, when the Greenback-Labor Party penetrated the eastern United States, a considerable number of Irishmen felt inflation could solve Irish problems.

In 1878 Terrence Powderly ran on the Greenback-Labor ticket and was elected mayor of Scranton. Although Powderly had considerable Irish support during the campaign, he made little effort to deal with basic social and economic problems. Powderly thought it enough to appoint "friends of labor" to the Scranton police force.[30]

In addition to political and economic activities, Irishmen sought comradeship and relaxation in a land where they were commonly disliked. Societies, clubs, and informal groups appeared that enabled Irish-Americans to meet with people having similar interests and backgrounds, and at times to help them deal more favorably with the new and strange society they confronted. Occasional literary societies, scientific organizations, and musical groups attempted to inculcate cultural values. For Irish miners, however, the tavern was a more significant center of social life. The tavern not only provided a chance for relaxation and relief from daily problems, but offered an opportunity to initiate political and economic activities. Aside from the tavern, Irish miners formed numerous baseball clubs that competed with each other and with teams representing the broader anthracite community. Irish fire brigades often engaged in rivalry with other companies in demonstrating swiftness and efficiency.[31]

The most notable Irish social organization in the anthracite region was the Ancient Order of Hibernians (AOH). This was a fraternal and charitable organization that had branches throughout the United States. It provided poor Irish-Americans with opportunities for social contacts and helped to ease the poverty they endured. In the anthracite region, however, the Ancient Order was adversely affected by identification of leading members with the Molly Maguires. While the exact connections between the AOH and the Mollies are still unclear, rumors alone were enough to weaken the Hibernians nationally and especially throughout the coal region.[32] In Schuylkill County, where the Mollies were most active, an organization called the Emerald Beneficial Association gained support because it specifically opposed the AOH and advocated respectable nonviolent principles. In Luzerne County, where the Mollies were not particularly strong, branches of the AOH refused to recognize any connection with the Schuylkill branches. The national executive of the AOH also took action and denounced local organizations in Northumberland, Carbon, Columbia, and Schuylkill Counties. Extensive fragmentation and declining prestige, therefore, prevented the AOH from complementing Irish political and economic efforts in the anthracite fields.[33]

There were also Irish-American societies organized to secure Ireland's national independence. For the immigrant, the concern for Ireland was not just due to sentiment, but was closely related to the alienation he suffered in America. The Irishman related his degradation in America very closely to Ireland's degradation as a nation. He believed that the same Anglo-Saxon who had been responsible for Ireland's poverty, now attacked and defiled the Irish in America. He wondered, "What might not Irishmen have been under proper treatment and good government, instead of the despised and rejected of nations?"[34] Thus poor and depressed Irish-Americans who joined the Ancient Order of Hibernians found additional self-respect and comradery in nationalist organizations. Nationalist efforts, in turn, lent cohesiveness to the Irish-American community and strengthened political and economic efforts for advancement.[35]

While nationalist activities were common throughout urban America, they failed to gain momentum in the anthracite region. The anthracite Irish showed concern for Ireland, but devoted little time or energy to the national cause. The Clan-na-Gael, a leading nationalist society in America, penetrated the coal region in 1876. But the Clan's secrecy, its inclination to espouse revolutionary methods, and the fact that Clan members were often associated with the AOH, served to identify the Clan with the Molly Maguires.[36] This problem was compounded by the fact that leading nationalist organizers preferred to remain in New York and Boston where Irish populations were larger and funds more available. Furthermore, nationalist organizations in urban areas were closely affiliated with successful Irish-American political organizations. Whereas Tammany politicians in New York often gave nationalists financial aid and publicity in return for support during election campaigns, strong political contacts were unavailable in the anthracite region.[37]

Most of the organized Irish efforts involved religious considerations. Irish-Americans generally looked to the Catholic Church for spiritual guidance and for help and direction in their daily lives. The Church not only developed its own groups and agencies to promote immigrant interests, but frequently supported or condemned independent immigrant organizations. This had already become a recognizable pattern of development in other parts of the United States. In New York City, for example, Irish Catholic leadership was strong and forceful. There a succession of powerful Church leaders, notably Archibishop John Hughes, John Cardinal McCloskey, and Archbishop Michael Corrigan gave firm direction to the Irish Catholic community. They were so powerful that critics often complained about their broad political and economic influence. Because of their leadership, however, New York Irishmen could look for assistance in numerous Catholic schools, clubs, charities, and youth associations.[38]

In the anthracite region, Irishmen were acutely conscious of common religious ties. Clerical leadership, however, was divided and failed to give Irish-American organizations a clear sense of direction. Church directives came principally from two areas. Archbishop James Frederic Wood controlled a diocese that included Philadelphia and Schuylkill County. It was natural that Philadelphia absorbed most of his energies at the expense of the Schuylkill region. The northern anthracite fields, meanwhile, looked to Bishop William O'Hara of Scranton for religious direction. Aside from this different geographic focus, the two men held contradictory attitudes on Irish Catholic affairs. Archbishop Wood, for example, was of English ancestry and a convert to the Catholic Church. Like other American Catholics, he seems to have viewed the Irish, with their reputation for lawlessness and drunkenness, as a liability to the Church's progress in America. Feeling that the Irish had to be watched carefully, he was suspicious of societies and labor organizations that involved Irish participants. Bishop O'Hara, on the other hand, being of Irish extraction and more familiar with conditions in the anthracite region, was inclined to sympathize with and encourage organizational efforts.[39]

In the 1870s the main point of contention between Wood and O'Hara concerned the Ancient Order of Hibernians. Since Molly

Maguire activities occurred mainly in Schuylkill County, Wood was forced to consider the alleged connections between the Mollies and the AOH. For evidence of the Schuylkill situation Wood seems to have relied rather heavily on reports from those who found a close connection between the Mollies and the AOH, mainly Franklin B. Gowen and the Pinkerton Detective Agency. Acting on information they provided him and his personal dislike of the Hibernians' secret ritual, Wood criticized the order during the early 1870s and excommunicated it in 1875. Bishop O'Hara, however, was inclined to look more favorably upon the AOH. He generally tried to distinguish between individual members who were guilty of violence and the higher purposes of the order. Only in 1877, when available evidence increasingly identified the AOH with the Mollies, did O'Hara reluctantly take stronger action and excommunicate the AOH membership. But before the differences of opinion between Wood and O'Hara were resolved, they had a pronounced impact on Irish Catholic affairs. Parish priests cited either O'Hara or Wood to justify their own attitudes toward the AOH. While priests agreed that violence was intolerable, there was no such unanimity regarding the AOH.[40] This indecisiveness involved other societies as well. The Emerald Beneficial Association, professing strong Catholic sympathies, encountered clergymen who either supported the association unconditionally or who identified it with the AOH and suspected it of radical activities. As a result of clerical indecision, therefore, Irish-Americans approached their societies with uncertainty and half-hearted enthusiasm.[41]

The divisions among clergymen paralleled other Catholic problems. Because the anthracite Irish were generally poor and inhabited a broad geographic area, the Church found it difficult to raise sufficient funds to provide for its widely dispersed communicants. This difficulty was especially apparent since the AOH, which usually contributed to the Church, became increasingly ineffective during the 1870s. There was a constant need for more church buildings and Catholic schools. Additional priests were also needed to direct temperance efforts and charity work. And while resources were scarce, those that were available were not always used efficiently. It often occurred that Irish Catholic temperance societies and charities were more concerned with status and prestige than with social work. In fact they tended to compete with each other for social recognition. This was especially apparent when the societies invested money and effort in elaborate displays for St. Patrick's Day celebrations.[42]

The various weaknesses in Irish organizational activities were compounded by the lack of a strong Irish press. Since native American newspapers were more disposed to criticize the Irish than to give coverage and support to their organizations, an Irish-American press was extremely important to the development of the immigrant community. In New York and Boston immigrant newspapers supported various organizational efforts. Irish-American county associations, temperance societies, athletic clubs, and Catholic groups all received extensive coverage. Viewpoints were offered concerning labor grievances, living conditions, and politics. The press also encouraged self-respect and confidence by elaborating on Irish cultural achievements, recounting Irish history, and playing upon valuable Irish-American contributions to the United States. But most notably the press helped to reinforce an ethnic consciousness and cohesiveness that complemented organized responses to American conditions.[43]

In the anthracite region the only indigenous Irish newspaper of note was the *Emerald Vindicator,* published in Pottsville by John Boland. The *Vindicator* began publication in 1875 as the official organ of the Emerald Beneficial Association. As such, the paper continually praised the association's adherence to Catholic doctrines, publicized its efforts to find employment for members during hard times, and echoed its commitment to "Faith, Hope and Charity, and Brotherly Love. . . ." By supporting "literature, science and virtuous practices among all mankind," the paper essentially urged Irishmen to adhere to respectable self-help methods of advancement.[44] But in terms of Irish political affairs, organized labor, and societies other than the Beneficial Association, the paper offered little of value to Irishmen. In fact, the paper failed to account for Irish-American consciousness of ethnic origins or common problems and suggested that German-Americans and other Catholics should take a leading role in the Beneficial Association. Since Irish immigrants had little interest in this approach to their affairs, the paper had a small circulation and constantly issued appeals for new subscribers.[45] Whereas Irish-American newspapers in other areas were usually published on a weekly basis, the *Emerald Vindicator* had neither the funds or subscribers for more than a monthly issue.

The availability of Irish-American newspapers that were published in other areas hindered the development of a strong Irish press in the coalfields. Throughout the 1870s, the *Boston Pilot* and New York *Irish World* circulated in the anthracite region. These papers tried to attract a broad reading audience by including news items about Irishmen who lived throughout the United States. They also devoted attention to affairs in Ireland. In this manner, therefore, the anthracite Irish satisfied their longing for the Old Country and found sympathetic consideration of their own condition.[46] But the coverage of anthracite affairs was inevitably superficial. The advice and information provided held greater relevance for urban Irishmen than for the anthracite Irish.

The failure to develop effective organizations resulted from a combination of factors. Certainly an aggressive business community and limited economic opportunities adversely affected the Irish laborers' place in the anthracite region. But to place the blame for failure solely on prevailing social and economic arrangements would simplify a complex situation. Geographic divisiveness, for example, hindered any unified Irish response to anthracite conditions. It is also notable that ties to nearby urban areas prevented the development of Irish leadership that was more fully conversant with anthracite problems. Furthermore, rivalries with other ethnic groups and among existing Irish-American organizations served to expend Irish energies and limit organizational responses. Thus while anthracite Irishmen were intensely conscious of common origins and problems, they were unable to develop the kind of institutions that had been so effective elsewhere.

The inability to develop stable institutional arrangements caused frustration and despair within the Irish-American community. Political and economic weaknesses encouraged the Molly Maguires. Violence, in turn, created unfavorable public opinion and prompted

Catholic spokesmen to take a critical view of Irish activities. As a consequence, struggling organizations were discredited. Without representative organizations, many Irishmen found it desirable to seek opportunities in other areas. During the 1870s there was frequently a movement from the southern anthracite fields to the Wyoming-Lackawanna region, where salaries were higher. More usually, however, Irishmen were inclined to leave the coal region completely and seek employment in Philadelphia or New York. Some returned to Ireland, others went to the bituminous fields in western Pennsylvania, and still others sought land in the west.[47] Their places in the anthracite region were soon taken by Slavic newcomers. In the 1880s and 1890s these new immigrants, who came in more massive numbers than the earlier immigrant groups, were able to forge more effective labor organizations.[48] By that time, however, Irish-Americans like John Mitchell and John Fahy, who had learned from past failures, were often instrumental in organizing large numbers of new immigrants.

## NOTES

1. Francis P. Dewees, a writer who observed the Pennsylvania anthracite fields during the 1870s, argued that the Molly Maguires were Irishmen who, "without cause," transported the traditional conflict between England and Ireland to the coalfields. Allan Pinkerton, the detective hired to deal with the Mollies, condemned them as criminals and murderers who threatened law and order. See Francis P. Dewees, *The Molly Maguires; The Origin, Growth and Character of the Organization* (New York: 1877), p. 44; and Allan Pinkerton, *The Molly Maguires and the Detectives* (New York: 1877).

2. Anthony Bimba, *The Molly Maguires* (New York: 1932). There are also arguments that the Molly Maguires never existed and that coal mine operators provoked violence and created the myth of a criminal organization of Irish coal miners in order to discredit the struggling labor movement. But while operators certainly tried to associate the Mollies with organized labor, there is little convincing evidence that the Mollies never existed or that violence was contrived solely by conspiring businessmen. See Charles A. McCarthy, *The Great Molly Maguire Hoax: Based on Information Suppressed 90 Years* (Wyoming, Pennsylvania: 1969); and *Irish World*, March 3, 1877, p. 4; June 30, 1877, p. 4.

3. Works dealing with the Molly Maguires sometimes provide glimpses of Irish-American life, especially the labor movement, but fail to offer an integrated approach to the Irish-American community. Wayne G. Broehl,

for example, gives considerable information about the anthracite Irish, but inevitably devotes most of his attention to the activities, apprehension, and court trials of the Molly Maguires. See Wayne G. Broehl, *The Molly Maguires* (Cambridge: 1964).

4. Berthoff suggests that immigrant groups were sometimes hostile toward each other and were often alienated from the native American anthracite community. He notes that even within ethnic groups harmony was not a general rule and conflict often occurred. Victor Greene indicates that by the 1890s this situation had changed when Slavic newcomers were more unified and aggressive than earlier ethnic groups, and were thus better able to deal with the problems and conditions that confronted them. See Rowland Berthoff, "The Social Order of the Anthracite Region, 1825–1902," *Pennsylvania Magazine of History and Biography* LXXXIX (1965):261–291; and Victor R. Greene, *The Slavic Community on Strike: Immigrant Labor in Pennsylvania Anthracite* (South Bend: 1968).

5. William V. Shannon, *The American Irish* (New York: 1963), pp. 27–29; Carl Wittke, *The Irish in America* (Baton Rouge: 1956), pp. 23–31.

6. U. S. Bureau of the Census, *A Compendium of the Ninth Census, June 1, 1870* (Washington: 1872), p. 432; Berthoff, "Social Order," p. 270; and Broehl, *Molly Maguires,* p. 83.

7. Wittke, *Irish in America,* p. 221; *Record of the Times* (Wilkes-Barre), January 18, 1871, p. 3; *Ibid.,* June 19, 1872, p. 3; *Ibid.,* August 7, 1872, p. 3; Harold W. Aurand, "The Anthracite Strike of 1887–1888," *Pennsylvania History* XXXV (April, 1968):172–173; and *Irish World,* May 27, 1871, p. 2; *Ibid.,* June 3, 1871, p. 4.

8. *Miners' Journal,* May 7, 1870, p. 3; *Ibid.,* May 14, 1870, p. 3; *Ibid.,* May 8, 1874, p. 7. The *Pottsville Standard* and Pottsville *Evening Chronicle,* Democratic newspapers attempting to woo Irish votes, afforded the Irish more generous treatment than other anthracite publications. Even then, however, the *Standard* felt obliged to caution Irishmen to be responsible and law-abiding citizens. See *Pottsville Standard,* March 13, 1875, p. 2; and *Evening Chronicle,* November 14, 1877, p. 2.

9. Broehl, *Molly Maguires,* pp. 219, 251; Berthoff, "Social Order," p. 268; and J. Walter Coleman, *The Molly Maguire Riots: Industrial Conflict in the Pennsylvania Coal Region* (Richmond: 1936), p. 19. There were long-standing complaints that Irishmen lived in miserable shanties which they refused to repair. They were not only stigmatized for consuming large quantities of alcohol, but for selling it illegally. Landlords also found it difficult to convince Irish immigrants to sign leases because of the problems landlordism raised in Ireland. In general, there was a feeling that Irishmen could not be controlled. See: Dillon Yarington to G. M. Hollenback, May 29, 1856 and July 10, 1856 (G. M. Hollenback Papers, Wyoming Historical and Geological Society, Wilkes-Barre, Pennsylvania).

10. Sylvester K. Stevens, *Pennsylvania: The Heritage of a Commonwealth* (West Palm Beach: 1968), II, pp. 614–615; Broehl, *Molly Maguires,* pp. 251, 256; and *Record of the Times,* March 22, 1871, p. 3.

11. Coleman, *Molly Maguire Riots,* p. 20.

12. *Miners' Journal,* February 2, 1877, n.p.; Broehl, *Molly Maguires,* p. 323.

13. *Miners' Journal,* February 2, 1877, n.p.

14. U. S. Bureau of the Census, *Compendium of the Ninth Census,* p. 432; and U. S. Bureau of the Census, *Compendium of the Tenth Census, June 1, 1880, Part I* (Washington: 1883), pp. 527–528.

15. Dewees, *Molly Maguires,* p. 36.

16. Aurand, "Anthracite Strike," p. 169; Berthoff, "Social Order," p. 263; and J. Cutler Andrews, "The Gilded Age in Pennsylvania," *Pennsylvania History* XXXIV (January, 1967) : 16.

17. Philip S. Foner, *History of the Labor Movement in the United States, Vol. I. From Colonial Times to the Founding of the American Federation of Labor* (New York: 1947), p. 455.

18. John Powell to a Friend, June 20, 1871, in Alan Conway, ed., *The Welsh in America; Letters from the Immigrants* (Minneapolis: 1961), pp. 191–192.

19. *Irish World,* January 30, 1875, p. 4; *Record of the Times,* April 19, 1871, p. 2; *Ibid.,* May 10, 1871, p. 2; and Commonwealth of Pennsylvania, *Report of the Department of Mines of Pennsylvania, Part I, Anthracite,* 1916 (Harrisburg: 1917), p. 5.

20. Clifton K. Yearley, Jr., *Enterprise and Anthracite: Economics and Democracy in Schuylkill County, 1820–1875* (Baltimore: 1961), pp. 183–185; and Bimba, *Molly Maguires,* pp. 42–43, 56–57.

21. Foner, *History of Labor* I, p. 456; Yearley, *Enterprise and Anthracite,* pp. 197–213; Stevens, *Pennsylvania* II, pp. 616–617; and Broehl, *Molly Maguires,* pp. 114, 121–125, 171.

22. Philip Taft, *Organized Labor in American History* (New York: 1964), p. 70; and Foner, *History of Labor* I, pp. 457–459. Victor Greene suggests that "the booming coal production in the north irritated the other sections as it was obviously sabotaging their strike effort and seizing their share of the market." See Greene, *Slavic Community on Strike,* p. 67.

23. Broehl, *Molly Maguires,* p. 219.

24. Norman Ware, *The Labor Movement in the United States, 1860–1895* (Gloucester, Massachusetts: 1959), p. 35; Aurand, "Anthracite Strike," pp. 171, 174; and Greene, *Slavic Community on Strike,* p. 81.

25. *Record of the Times,* September 13, 1871, p. 2; and *Miners' Journal,* October 15, 1870, p. 2.

26. *Record of the Times,* October 4, 1871, p. 2; October 18, 1871, p. 2; and Coleman, *Molly Maguire Riots,* p. 63.

27. Frank B. Evans, *Pennsylvania Politics, 1872–1877: A Study in Political Leadership* (Harrisburg: 1966), p. 1.

28. *Miners' Journal,* August 7, 1874, p. 4; October 9, 1874, p. 4; *Record of the Times,* September 20, 1871, p. 2; July 31, 1877, p. 2; and *Pottsville Standard,* November 7, 1874, p. 2.

29. George P. Donehoo, ed., *Pennsylvania: A History* III (New York: 1926), p. 1487; and Evans, *Pennsylvania Politics,* pp. 226–227. J. Walter Coleman notes that while Irish corruption existed in the anthracite region, it was negligible when compared to what was happening in New York City or on the national political level. The large majority of Irishmen were unaware of political bargains and voted for the candidates they felt would support labor interests. See Coleman, *Molly Maguire Riots,* pp. 61–62, 173.

30. *Emerald Vindicator,* October, 1875, p. 4; *Ibid.,* November, 1875, p. 1; Evans, *Pennsylvania Politics,* pp. 227–228; Berthoff, "Social Order," p. 274; and Thomas R. Brooks, *Toil and Trouble; A History of American Labor* (New York: 1964), p. 54.

31. Broehl, *Molly Maguires,* pp. 84–85, 181; and *Emerald Vindicator,* October, 1875, p. 8; *Ibid.,* December, 1875, p. 8.

32. *Irish American* (New York), February 26, 1876, pp. 4, 8; and *Miners' Journal,* May 4, 1877, p. 4.

33. *Miners' Journal,* April 27, 1877, p. 3.

34. Philip H. Bagenal, *The American Irish and Their Influence on Irish Politics* (Boston: 1882), pp. 129–130. O'Donovan Rossa, an Irishman who spent a considerable part of his adult life in America, said: "I cannot feel that America is my country; I am made to feel that I am a stranger here, and I am made to see that the English power, and the English influence and the English hate, and the English boycott against the Irish-Irishmen is to-day as active in America as it is in Ireland." See O'Donovan Rossa, *Rossa's Recollections, 1838–1898* (Mariner's Harbor, New York: O'Donovan Rossa, 1898), p. 262.

35. Patrick Ford, editor of New York's *Irish World* between 1870 and 1913, indicated that Ireland's overthrow of English rule would be "conducive to the honor of the Irish race in all lands." Thomas N. Brown substantiates this view with the argument that Anglo-Saxon dominance was more apparent to Irishmen in America than in Ireland. In Ireland poverty was general and British oppression indirect, mainly through the agent of an absentee landlord. In America the contrast between the wealthy Anglo-Saxon native and the poor Irish immigrant was much more perceptible. In this atmosphere, the Irishman's feeling for Ireland and hostility to England was consequently more pronounced than in Ireland. See *Irish World,* January 3, 1874, p. 4; and Thomas N. Brown, *Irish-American Nationalism, 1870–1890* (New York: 1966), pp. 17–41.

36. Wayne G. Broehl notes that Clan-na-Gael officials had high hopes for Irish nationalist efforts in the anthracite region. But Irish-American and native American spokesmen in the anthracite fields often opposed revolutionary methods to free Ireland from British rule. The *Emerald Vindicator,* an Irish-American newspaper published in Pottsville, gave little coverage to the Irish national cause and specifically excluded coverage of violent Fenian efforts. The *Miners' Journal* suggested that Fenian leaders cheated Irishmen of the their wages. See *Emerald Vindicator,* April, 1875 to March, 1876; *Miners' Journal,* June 4, 1870, p. 2; October 15, 1870, p. 2; and Broehl, *Molly Maguires,* p. 323.

37. Irish nationalists in America often vied with each other to gain support from American political parties. During the 1880s, for example, Irish nationalists engaged in a desperate internal struggle for influence within the Republican party. See Wharton Barker to Benjamin Harrison, October 9, 1888; William Carroll to Wharton Barker, October 18, 1888; John Devoy to William Carroll, October 18, 1888; Howard M. Jenkins to Louis Michener, February 2, 1889; in Wharton Barker Papers (Manuscript Division, Library of Congress); *Irish Nation* (New York), April 14, 1883, p. 4; *Gaelic American* (New York), December 22, 1923, p. 8; January 5, 1924, p. 5; and John Devoy to John Roach, August 5, 1884, *Devoy's Post Bag, 1871–1928,* eds. William O'Brien and Desmond Ryan, II (Dublin: C. J. Fallon, Ltd., 1948), pp. 252–254.

38. The New York Catholic leadership was generally conservative. This was in part due to "the accidents of personality," but also stemmed from the fact that Irish Catholics in New York attained political and economic power more quickly than in other areas and thus had an interest in preserving the existing structure. As a result, the New York hierarchy disdained labor movements and had little reason to sever its close ties with Tammany Hall. Despite these attitudes, however, the hierarchy supported Catholic clubs and societies that aided distressed Irishmen. For a discussion of the New York hierarchy, see: William V. Shannon, *The American Irish* (New York: 1963), pp. 114–115; and Robert Cross, *The Emergence of*

*Liberal Catholicism in America* (Cambridge: 1958).

39. John J. Delaney and James Edward Tobin, *Dictionary of Catholic Biography* (Garden City: 1961), p. 1212; and Broehl, *Molly Maguires,* pp. 78–79.

40. *Irish American,* January 1, 1876, p. 5; January 8, 1876, p. 5; *Miners' Journal,* February 16, 1877, n.p.; April 27, 1877, p. 2; and Broehl, *Molly Maguires,* p. 178.

41. *Emerald Vindicator,* May, 1875, p. 1; September, 1875, p. 8.

42. *Irish American,* February 5, 1876, p. 8; and *Irish World,* October 14, 1871, p. 1; February 13, 1875, n.p. Ethnic rivalries also strained church funds as German and Irish Catholics demanded their own priests, schools, and societies. See Berthoff, "Social Order," p. 272; and Oscar Jewell Harvey and Ernest Gray Smith, *A History of Wilkes-Barre: Luzerne County, Pennsylvania* IV (Wilkes-Barre, 1929), pp. 1967–1968. The *Emerald Vindicator* noted friction among temperance workers and indicated: "We would like to see all the societies in Schuylkill County dwell in peace and harmony, as Temperance itself is peace. . . ." See *Emerald Vindicator,* June, 1875, p. 5.

43. James P. Rodechko, "An Irish-American Journalist and Catholicism: Patrick Ford of the *Irish World,*" *Church History* XXXIX (December, 1970): 524–540; Wittke, *Irish in America,* pp. 202–215; Florence E. Gibson, *The Attitudes of the New York Irish Toward State and National Affairs, 1848–1892* (New York: 1951).

44. *Emerald Vindicator,* September, 1875, p. 8; December, 1875, p. 2.

45. *Ibid.,* October, 1875, p. 4; November, 1875, p. 4.

46. *Irish World,* June 24, 1871, p. 4; August 12, 1871, p. 8; May 27, 1871, p. 2; June 3, 1871, p. 4; May 13, 1871, pp. 4, 8; and Broehl, *Molly Maguires,* p. 158. An *Irish World* correspondent living in the anthracite region noted: "The *Irish World* is an especial favorite here with the miners, the vast majority of whom are bold, vigorous Irish-Americans, not less on account of its sound, patriotic views, than for its genuine sympathy, at all times, for the poor man." See *Irish World,* April 22, 1871, p. 5.

47. *Miners' Journal,* May 4, 1877, p. 1; February 23, 1877, p. 3; *Emerald Vindicator,* April, 1875, p. 2; and Berthoff, "Social Order," p. 290. Irish-American spokesmen often encouraged Irishmen, without particular success, to seek land in the west and leave crowded industrial and urban areas. Agricultural life was deemed more respectable than factory work. The *Irish World* made pointed references to miserable anthracite conditions and called upon government to "open a refuge on the soil to those unhappy men and their families." See *Irish World,* May 19, 1877, p. 4.

48. Greene, *Slavic Community on Strike.*

# 2

# The Polish Experience in Philadelphia:
# The Migrant Laborers Who
# Did Not Come

## CAROLINE GOLAB

*Caroline Golab graduated from Georgetown University in 1966 and received her Ph.D. in American history from the University of Pennsylvania. She is currently with the Department of Housing and Urban Development.*

Almost one-half of [Pennsylvania's] population is of alien origin. It is found upon investigation that except for the usefulness of this one-half in our industries, the other half pays little attention to it.[1]

Fifteen cigars are made in Philadelphia every second of the working day. In every second of time there are also made . . . twelve loaves of bread, ten pairs of stockings, one steel saw, one man's hat, fifty newspapers, one and a half yards of carpet. Every hour a new dwelling house is completed and a new trolley is ready for the tracks.[2]

In an overriding sense, the history of the immigrant in the United States is the history of urban America; and the history of urban America is the history of the nation's industrialization. This is especially true of those decades following the Civil War, for in these years the overwhelming majority of America's immigrants chose to settle in cities, large and small, and these cities were the site of the nation's greatest economic and industrial activity. Immigration, urbanization, and industrialization walked hand in hand. Which came first, or which one precipitated the other, does not concern us here. The point to remember is that all three were intimate partners in the vast social change which was altering American life for ages to come.

I

The Polish experience in Philadelphia is a unique one, but one which, on the surface at least, appears to have little to offer students who wish to study immigration in those formative years of the American city, 1870–1920. In the first place, Philadelphia was not a major center of the new immigration. The city's foreign-born population never exceeded 27%, a peak which was reached in 1870 primarily because of the heavy Irish influx of earlier years. During this same period, however, other large northern cities were housing populations of which 35 to 50% were foreign-born.[3]

Secondly, Philadelphia's Polish population was small—very small. Eastern European Jews constituted the largest foreign-born group in the city, and they outnumbered the Italians by two to one. The Italians, in turn, outnumbered the Poles by four to one. The smallness of the Polish population was especially puzzling because Philadelphia was a major industrial center (second only to New York City) and a major port-of-entry (again second only to New York). Poles were disembarking in Philadelphia, but they were not staying in the city.[4]

Philadelphia's Polish population was small, not only when compared to other groups in the city, but also when compared to the Polish populations of other American cities. Father Wracław X. Kruszka, an early historian of the Poles in America, estimated that in 1903 there there 250,000 Polish immigrants and their American-born children in Chicago; 70,000 in Buffalo; 65,000 in Milwaukee; 50,000 in Detroit and Pittsburgh and 30,000 in Cleveland. He did not mention Philadelphia. In 1908 the Polish *Press* estimated the Chicago group to number 350,000 and the New York City group, 250,000. There were now 80,000 Poles in Buffalo and 75,000 in Detroit and Milwaukee. Again, Philadelphia was not mentioned. By 1920 Chicago's Polonia numbered 400,000; the Pittsburgh and New York groups each totalled 200,000 or more; and Detroit, Buffalo, and Milwaukee each housed 100,000 Polish immigrants and their children. Philadelphia's Polish community, finally mentioned, was listed at 50,000. This number reflects Polish migration into the city after 1915, a period of renewed industrial activity due to War orders which were pouring into the city's factories. Poles who settled in Philadelphia after 1915, however, did not come directly from Poland; they drifted into the city from northeastern and central Pennsylvania, New Jersey, Delaware, and southern New York.[5]

Although Philadelphia's Polish group was small, Pennsylvania's Polish population was enormous. In fact, Pennsylvania housed more Poles, Slovaks, Croatians, Slovenes and Ukrainians than any other state. There were twice as many Poles in Pennsylvania as in New York or Illinois. Nevertheless, only one-quarter to one-third of Pennsylvania's Poles resided in Philadelphia and Pittsburgh; the remainder lived in the smaller cities and towns of the state. This was in sharp contrast to the pattern in other states. In New York and Illinois, for example, the vast majority of Poles lived in New York City and Chicago.[6]

For some reason, the Poles were not settling in Philadelphia. Why were they, as a whole, avoiding the city? What characteristics or idiosyncracies did those who did settle in Philadelphia have which differentiated them from those who didn't come or from those who came but did not stay?

II

The answers are complex, but are rooted in the immigrants' process of adaptation to their new society, for ultimate distribution and place of settlement are very much a function of adaptation. People can react or adapt to a new situation only in terms of what they bring with them to that situations. Europeans who came to America (or to a particular city in America) confronted a society with established physical, political, social, ideological, and economic structures (the last of which, initially at least, was the most important). How they reacted or adapted to this structured environment depended in great measure upon the idiosyncracies of their culture (e.g., their urban or rural orientation; their preferences or dislikes for certain forms of work); their experiences in an industrializing Europe (e.g., exposure to factories, to new types of work, to new modes of living); and the particular nature of their emigration (was it voluntary or involuntary? permanent or temporary? were they immigrants or really migrants? did they come alone or with families?).

Too often in the past there has been a tendency to think of the immigrants' adaptation solely in terms of their experiences on this side of the Atlantic. Their experiences on the other side of the ocean tend to be forgotten. It is no coincidence that the very word "immigrant" (as well as the person) was apparently an American creation; the word did not exist in the English language until coined by Samuel Morse in 1789.[7] Preemigration experiences, however, are essential for understanding the immigrants' distribution and hence their adaptation to American society. The Poles are an excellent illustration of this fact.

The vast majority of Poles who came to America after 1870 were peasant-farmers, people of the soil who placed great stock in their traditional view of life. Such roles as merchant, artisan and craftsman were reserved for the Jews, a people with whom the peasants shared their daily lives. Nevertheless, long before they began to sail for America, the traditional life-style of the Poles had been undergoing subtle but irremedial change.[8]

Consider, for example, the institution of migration. For generations preceding the First World War migration was the Pole's accepted way of meeting the exigencies of the moment. From his point of view it was an outgrowth of his complex relationships with the soil. The peasant-farmer attached great importance to the land. Owning land meant economic security and independence, the freedom from want and hunger. Land was the source of social security: it determined status and delineated social position within the community. Ideally, land of one's own also represented emotional security—the beauty of the personality at peace with the environment, physically and spiritually. Because land was the primary organizing principle of economy and society, the Pole could not envision a life which was set apart from it. As Władisław Reymont said so well, "A man without land is like a man without legs: he crawls about and cannot get anywhere."[9]

In the middle decades of the 19th century the land began to fail the Polish peasant. There was too little of it, and it did not produce enough to support a wife and children. Moreover, the population was growing—too rapidly it seemed. Births were not necessarily increasing, but people were living longer and children were surviving to maturity. Too many sons were now claiming the property. Smaller and smaller divisions resulted in decreasing productivity and efficiency. Crops and plots had to be mortgaged; debts continued to mount. The Polish farmer was up against a wall: in order to save his land and the life which was wedded to it, he had to seek work elsewhere. Migration presented itself as the only solution.

Viewed from the local level, therefore, migration was the Pole's response to his immediate predicament. In a larger sense, however, migration was a response to the industrialization which was overpowering Central and Eastern Europe at this time. It was a changing and transitional Europe which created a "peasant proletariat roaming the countryside, indeed the world, for employment in agriculture and industry."[10]

Theoretically, the Pole who emigrated before World War I was leaving a country which did not exist. Poland had been wiped from the map of Europe in 1795 and was parcelled out among three powers, Austria, Prussia, and Russia. She was not fully reconstituted until Versailles in 1919. Because of this unique arrangement, each sector of Poland developed differently. These differences influenced which Poles emigrated, when they emigrated, and what became of them after their arrival in America.

The German sections of Poland—Poznań, Silesia, West and East Prussia[11]—sent the first Poles to the United States. Until 1890 these German Poles constituted at least 75% of all the Poles in the country; by 1920 they represented less than 10%. Irksome governmental policies rather than over-population or depressing agricultural conditions induced these first Poles to leave as early as the 1860s. By 1890 industrialization was in full swing, especially in Poznań and Silesia, and applications of scientific methods had raised agricultural productivity to new heights. Polish emigration from the German provinces diminished proportionately. Displaced or discontented Polish farmers no longer sailed for America. They bought land as part of the campaign against Bismarck's *Kulturkampf;* or, they headed for the coal mines, iron mills, and textile factories of Upper Silesia.[12]

Poles from Poznań, Silesia, and West Prussia landed in Philadelphia in the mid-1860s and early 1870s. Many were adventurers and free spirits, lone individuals who had come to see what the New World had to offer. More often, however, they were forward-looking, ambitious men with families in hand, who hoped to better themselves in the land of opportunity. Unlike the Austrian and Russian Poles who were soon to outnumber them by the tens of thousands, these German Poles came with the intention of staying permanently. They were also better educated than their Russian and Austrian counterparts, had some knowledge, rudimentary or otherwise, of the German language, and possessed crafts and skills as well as agricultural expertise. Finally, they had lived and worked in the towns and cities of German Poland, a region which was in the full force of its industrialization.

Austria was defeated by Prussia and thrown out of Germany in 1867. Because of her precarious position as a multi-national state, she was forced to reorganize herself economically as well as politically. The resulting creation, the Austrian-Hungarian Empire, decided to maintain a hands-off policy in Galicia,[13] its Polish province, and to sponsor industrial activity in Moravia and Bohemia. This represented an attempt by the government to placate its Polish people and at the same time use them to control another minority of the

Empire, the Ukrainians, who made up at least 40% of Galicia's population. This alliance, however, was made with Polish nobles at the expense of peasants, both Polish and Ukrainian. The nobility resisted industrialization in Galicia because it would upset their already tenuous relationships with the peasantry, relationships which were tied to the land. Galicia, therefore, was designated the agricultural provider of the Empire.

Land, or the lack of it, was the source of Galicia's problems. In 1890 77% of the people made their living from the soil. The percentage was the same in 1900 and barely declined to 73% by 1910. In 1848, the year in which the serfs were freed, the nobility owned 42% of the land; as late as 1902 they continued to control 37% of it. Peasant holdings, in contrast, were constantly divided and redivided. The resulting plots were economically disastrous. Of 1,100,000 peasant properties (1902) 77.5% were of less than 12.5 acres and covered only 26% of the province. The peasant population continued to grow rapidly. It was soon apparent that even the breakdown of the large noble land holdings would not ease the chronic shortage of land.[14]

Austria-Hungary not only ignored land reform, but also failed to develop Galicia's significant industrial potential. Although the province contained rich deposits of salt, potassium, potash, anthracite, and petroleum, little attempt was made to tap these resources. Greater efforts were made after 1910, but in that year only 7% of Galicia's workers were employed in industrial activity (as compared with 25% in German Poland). Moreover, most of this activity was of the cottage and artisan variety. Austria-Hungary's efforts to industrialize were too little and came too late for the people of Galicia. The paltry sum which had been or could be absorbed by industry meant that the vast majority of Galicians, deprived of or losing their lands, must seek work elsewhere—preferably outside of the province.[15]

Migration was not new to the peoples of Galicia. In times of crisis they turned to it as a means of survival. Four hundred thousand persons died of typhus following the potato famine of 1847–1849. Cholera carried off 74,000 in 1865 and 91,000 in 1873. These crises

POLAND: ADMINISTRATIVE DIVISIONS, 1912

—O—O— Frontiers of States

—·—·— Limits of Countries and
Provinces

———— Limits of Governments and
Regencies

Mitau

Kowno

Krolewiec  Gabin  Wilno

Gdansk

Kwidzyn  Olsztyn  Suwalkis

Bydgosztz  Grodno

Plock  Lomza

Poznan  WARSZAWA  Siedlce

Kalisz

Piotrkow

Lignica  Radom

Wroclow

Opole  Lublin

Kielce

Krakow

Cieszyn  Lwow

O   Chief town of Province

•   Chief town of Government
     and Regency

precipitated a heightened movement to the towns and cities of the province, especially to the two largest cities, Kraków and Lwów. When internal migration could no longer meet the needs of the people, emigration commenced. The decade of the 1870s was the first to witness a loss of population (1,997) due to external migration. Eighty-two thousand emigrated during the 1880s. Almost 341,000 departed during the 1890s; the exodus accelerated after 1900.[16]

By no means did all of these persons sail for America. The Poles, concentrated in the western half of the province, at first went as settlers to eastern Galicia and the Bukowina; some furtively crossed the Dnieper River into Russia. When these areas became saturated in the 1870s, they headed for the industrial regions of Bohemia, Moravia, Silesia, and lower Austria; thousands of others, the *Sachsengänger,* migrated yearly to the large agricultural estates of Prussian Poland and Denmark. Nevertheless, "increasing numbers reason, 'If we must leave home, why not go further, wherever wages may be the highest, and stay until we have earned what we need.' So the father goes himself to America or sends his son to get money to redeem or to enlarge the farm."[17]

In theory at least, "Poland" was restored by the Congress of Vienna in 1815. This semi-reconstituted "Kingdom of Poland" was a mere mite of its former self. Russia was to oversee the Kingdom's economic and political affairs, but in reality exercised total control over the area. In addition to the ten provinces or departments which made up the Congress Kingdom—Kalisz, Kielce, Łomża, Lublin, Piotrków, Płock, Radom, Siedlce, Suwałki, and Warszawa—Russia directly annexed the remaining parts[18] of what had once been northern and eastern Poland (see map). The Congress Kingdom sent by far the greatest numbers of Poles to the United States.

Unlike Austria, Russia had definite plans to industrialize her Polish provinces. The Kingdom was to be the major industrial center of the Russian Empire and was to be the main artery of transit between Russia and western Europe. The Dąbrowa coal basin, for example, supplied 25% of all coal mined in the Empire in 1900; 20% in 1913. The Congress Kingdom also produced substantial portions of iron and steel, granulated sugar, flax, hemp, cotton and woolen yarns, and fabrics.[19]

The czar freed the serfs after the abortive uprising of 1863; the agricultural reforms of the following year gave them full ownership of their lands. Shortly afterwards, the rural population began to increase very rapidly. The demand for land began to outstrip the supply. This problem, while acute, did not reach crisis proportions until the turn of the century. Until that time internal migration, not emigration, was the peasant's primary response to the situation.

The rapid growth in Congress Poland's cities reflected this increased internal migration. In 1872 there were seventeen cities with a population of 10,000 or more and two with 40,000 or more—Warszawa and Łódź. By 1913 there were sixty cities with 10,000 inhabitants and ten with 40,000 or more. Warszawa increased its population from 175,000 in 1860 to 345,000 in 1880 and 730,000 by 1900. Of all Poland's cities, however, Łódź represented the most notorious example of rampant growth. A provincial city of 28,000 in 1860, its population grew to 72,000 by 1880 and exceeded 325,000 by 1900—a fourteen-fold increase since 1860. In 1900, only 42 of every 100 persons in the city were natives.[20]

Congress Poland's total population increased by more than 75% between 1877 and 1910, but its industrial work force increased by 341%—from 90,767 to 400,922. Moreover, the population was redistributing itself within the Kingdom, and this redistribution was directly related to the increasing industrialization:

| Department | % total population increase, 1872–1913 |
|---|---|
| Piotrków | 221.7 |
| Warszawa | 146.0 |
| Lublin | 114.3 |
| Radom | 119.9 |
| Kielce | 92.7 |
| Kalisz | 91.7 |
| Siedlce | 86.5 |
| Płock | 45.3 |
| Łomża | 31.8 |
| Suwałki | 20.5 |
| 105.1 | Total Congress Kingdom |

Piotrków, the province which recorded the largest population increase, was the most industrialized area of the Kingdom. It employed 60% of all Polish working men and was the seat of the Dąbrowa coal basin, Łódź, and textile centers such as Częstochowa, Sosnowiec, Zgierz, Tomaszow, and Pabianice. Poland's largest and most productive steel mills and metal firms were also located in this province.[21]

Until 1900 it appeared as if Congress Poland, because of its industrialization, would be able to absorb most of its surplus agricultural population. The Russo-Japanese War of 1905, however, cut off essential outlets to Eastern markets, and the subsequent Revolution of 1905, with its strikes and other upheavals, prolonged the economic uncertainty. Trade ceased and production halted. These industrial convulsions, plus the fact that 80% of all the people in the Kingdom were farmers (one-half of whom owned no land of their own), left emigration as the only meaningful alternative. One hundred fifty-three thousand persons left the Kingdom in 1904; 268,000 left in 1908, and more than 360,000 left in 1912. The majority of these Poles migrated to Prussia, not to the United States, in search of employment.

Nevertheless, between 1900 and 1904 Congress Poland sent 30,000 persons, including Polish Jews, to the United States each year. Forty-eight thousand arrived annually from 1905 to 1909. Sixty-four thousand came in 1910 alone and another 112,000 in 1913. Fifty percent of all of these persons were landless agricultural laborers; another 27% were small land owners. Thirty percent subsequently returned to Poland. As these figures include Polish Jews, virtually none of whom returned to Poland, the actual repatriation of Polish migrants was much higher. According to Paul Fox, an early observer of the Poles in America, a minimum of 40% of all Christian Poles eventually returned to Poland.[22]

During the four decades preceding World War I, Poland in all her forms—German, Austrian, and Russian—was undergoing a profound demographic and economic transformation. Long before his trek to America, the Pole had been affected by industrialization, urbanization, and the concomitant migration. This migration took the form of movements from farms to villages, villages to towns, and towns to cities; seasonal migration to other parts of Europe; and finally, migration to places beyond the continent of Europe. Migration was such an integral part of life that it was rare to find a Polish farmer who had not migrated to some other place in Europe—Germany, Russia, Denmark, Hungary, or France—before going abroad to the United States, Canada, Brazil, or Australia. Indeed, America was one of many options available to the Polish peasant.[23]

There were many implications and ramifications to the Pole's experiences in an industrializing Europe. First of all, these experiences changed him from a peasant-farmer into a migrant-laborer. The Pole who came to America was not an immigrant. He was a migrant, a temporary worker. Always, his intention, if not his dream, was to return to Poland with his American (or Silesian or Brazilian) savings and to buy land or rescue his property from debt. If this were not so, the Pole would have made greater efforts to seek out land and farms in America. Why settle in the city, the very antithesis of Polish life? As noted, many returned to Poland, but others were intending to do the same had not World War I and economic opportunity intervened. The Pole became an immigrant only when he began to view his future in America and not in Europe.

Secondly, migration in search of work, especially long-distance migration, was confined mainly to the younger male segments of the population who, as a whole, possessed few skills and crafts. Throughout Poland such roles as tailor, blacksmith, carpenter, mason, etc., were performed by the Jews. Thus, because the Poles who migrated were unskilled, they had to seek industries which required that type of labor—coal mining, street and railroad construction, oil and sugar refining, tanning, and iron and steel making. Textile and garment manufacture, on the other hand, did not appeal to them. Such work required semi-skilled to skilled labor and tended to be low-paying and female-oriented. Moreover, in Polish peasant culture the "needle crafts" were the preserve of the womenfolk. This was in contrast to the Jews, for example, who not only migrated as families, but who also had a tailoring tradition fully compatible with both male and female participation.

Thirdly, because of his status as a migrant laborer, the Pole was very mobile. He was unencumbered with wife and children, preferring to travel alone; more likely, he was not yet married. Nor was he poverty stricken. He became a migrant precisely because he had known better times or at least still believed in them. If he sought work abroad he usually paid for his own passage. Thus, he was both willing and able to go wherever there was work. If this meant that must go to America, to Chicago, or to the small towns of Pennsylvania, then this is where he would go.

Finally, because he was accustomed to migrating in an urbanizing and industrializing Europe, the Polish farmer had been exposed to towns, cities, factories, and machines—to a constant array of new people, places, and things. He was not totally unprepared for the type of work he would find in America. The industries which employed him in America were of the same type, even identical, to those which employed him in Europe. In America, as in Poland, he headed for the cities and regions which supported heavy industrial activity.

The United States, like Poland, was a transitional society experiencing vast social change; both countries were at various stages in their industrialization. The Poles came to the United States only when European agriculture, and especially industry, could no longer provide openings for their labor. Of the Poles who settled in Philadelphia, virtually none came from Piotroków, the province which was experiencing the greatest industrial activity and urban growth. In contrast, most of Philadelphia's Poles came from areas which were the least industrialized and the least urbanized—eastern Galicia or the Russian provinces of Łomża, Suwałki, and Płock.[24] These had the fewest opportunities to offer surplus agricultural laborers who were in need of ready work.

## I I I

The Poles who came to the United States after 1870 (or to a particular piece of it, Philadelphia, for example) confronted a society with established physical, social, political, and economic structures. They could only react to this new society in terms of their culture, which included preferences and dislikes for certain forms of work, and their previous experiences in an industrializing Europe, experiences which had changed them from peasant-farmers into migrant-laborers. Because they were migrant laborers, the Poles came to America in search of work, but they came in search of work which was compatible with their qualifications (unskilled labor), their cultural predilections, and their temporary status. Thus, the economic structure of the receiving society becomes the most important variable influencing the Poles' ultimate distribution in the United States.

The great Eastern and Southern European migration to Pennsylvania began in the 1870s. Poles, Lithuanians, and Slovaks were the first to come. Russians, Magyars, Croatians, Slovenians, and some Italians followed in the 1880s. The Poles remained the leading group until 1901. In that year Southern Italians pushed them into second place. Immigration to Pennsylvania from 1899 to 1914 totalled 2,328,788. Italians represented 510,000 of this number; Poles, 337,000; Slovaks, 240,000; Croatians, 182,000; and "Hebrews," 150,000.[25]

The nature of immigration to the state had changed radically since 1876. Only 10% of the 184,438 immigrants who settled in Pennsylvania in 1914 came from Northern and Western Europe, whereas 85% came from Southern and Eastern Europe. Twenty-seven percent of the Southern and Eastern Europeans were Italian or Sicilian; 12% were Polish, 8% "Hebrew," 7% Ukrainian, 6% Slovak and 6% Croatian. Fifty years earlier the proportions were reversed: more than one-half of Pennsylvania's immigrants came from those countries which in 1914 represented only 10%. Indeed, English, Scotch, Welsh, Dutch, Scandinavian, German, and Flemish immigrants were now conspicuous for their scarcity.[26]

Pennsylvania was the home of such vast numbers of immigrants because it was truly a "titan of industry." The influx of Slavic and Italian workers coincided with the industrialization of the state. The consolidation of and technological advances in coal mining which enabled that industry to utilize large numbers of unskilled workers; the beginnings of iron and steel production and its innumerable manufactures; the incessant demand for railroads—and more railroads—to facilitate the inflow and outflow of coal and iron; the perpetual need to repair and to maintain these railways and to load and unload the freight cars; the manufacture of glass, cement, and chemicals: all these activities demanded huge armies of laborers whose qualifications were strength and availability rather than knowledge or skill.

Slavic and Italian workers had the ideal qualifications for these activities: they were unskilled, plentiful, available, and mobile. Moreover, the size of the state's enterprises—a Carnegie Steel Company, a Pittsburgh Plate Glass Company, a Pennsylvania Railroad, an H. C. Frick Coke Company, a Westinghouse Air Brake Company, a Pressed Steel Car Company—was enormous. They were able to employ tens of thousands of workers at a single point in space and time. If the majority of the Italians and Poles lived outside of Philadelphia and Pittsburgh, it was precisely because Pennsylvania's industry and the nature of immigration were directly related.[27]

Given this relationship, it is not surprising to find that the first Polish settlements in Pennsylvania were in Shamokin (1870), Shenandoah (1873), Excelsior (1875), and Mt. Carmel (1877), all in Northumberland County, and in Nanticoke (1875) in Luzerne County. Along with Lackawanna, Carbon, and Schuylkill Counties, Luzerne and Northumberland Counties, located in the northeastern part of the state, were the chief anthracite producers of the country.

Mining in all its varieties—anthracite, bituminous, and coke—employed more persons than any other Pennsylvania industry. In 1915, according to the Commissioner of Labor and Industry, 135 anthracite firms employed 159,170 persons; 672 bituminous companies employed 153,753 persons; and 125 coke companies employed another 13,345 persons. Sixty-four percent of the anthracite, 68% of the bituminous, and 50% of the coke workers were foreign-born. By the turn of the century the Poles were the largest single group employed in anthracite mining. In 1896, for example, the Philadelphia and Reading Coal and Iron Company, the largest anthracite firm in Pennsylvania, employed more Polish workers than any other group, including native-Americans. Foreign-born Slavs and Hungarians constituted 39% of all workers and 54% of foreign-born workers employed in anthracite mining in 1905. Bituminous mining, with its headquarters in the western part of the state (Fayette, Westmoreland, and Allegheny Counties), also depended heavily on Slavic labor. Slovaks were 20.3% and the Poles, 12.3% of all bituminous workers in 1910. In addition to their high concentration in the mining industry, the Poles were also over-represented in Pennsylvania's iron, steel, glass, and cement industries.[28]

Industry and the nature of immigration were also closely related in Philadelphia. Whereas the economy of central and western Pennsylvania stressed bigness, required large numbers of unskilled workers, and was devoted to the more primary forms of industrial activity, Philadelphia's economy stressed skill, diversity, precision, and quality.

In 1910 Philadelphia's 8,381 manufacturing establishments produced everything from "battleships to bon-bons." More specifically, they manufactured 211 of the 264 articles listed in the 1910 census and employed 252,221 wage earners and 33,473 clerks and salaried officials. Included among these 8,381 firms were the world's largest locomotive factory, carpet mill, car building works, leather plant, and publishing house; the nation's two biggest shipyards, largest hosiery mill, petroleum refinery, and sugar refinery.[29] Each of these firms employed more than 500 persons and constituted "the backbone of Philadelphia's industrialism. Yet, with their enormous plants and wonderful equipment, their tens of thousands of employees and their tremendous output, by far the greatest portion of the goods made in Philadelphia are produced in the more than 8,000 smaller establishments of the city."[30]

Between 1870 and 1920 textile and clothing manufacture employed more men and women than any other city industry—between one-quarter and one-third of all wage earners, and accounted for more than 30% of the total value of all products.[31] The most important branches were woolen and worsted goods; women's and men's clothing; hosiery and knit goods; carpets and rugs; and cotton goods. The manufacture of iron and steel products, Philadelphia's second major industrial bulwark for most of the period, included (in order of value): foundry and machine shop products, including machinery; locomotives; rolling mill products; electrical machinery and supplies; steel ships; saws; stoves; cutlery; hardware and tools; files; safes and vaults; agricultural implements; bolts, rivets and washers; and tin and terneplate. Printing and publishing vied with metal manufacture for second place. The city's output of books, magazines, and sheet music made Philadelphia the third largest printer and publisher in the nation. Leather manufacture, the city's fourth largest industry, included tanned and finished leather, boots, shoes, trunks, bags, belts, and purses; morocco or glazed kid products were a Philadelphia specialty. All of these industries—textiles, printing and publishing, metal goods, and leather—were long-established Philadelphia institutions which required large pools of skilled or semi-skilled labor. Only the leather industry, in its initial stages of processing and tanning, and certain branches of the metal industry employed substantial numbers of unskilled workers.

The areas of employment in Philadelphia open to unskilled laborers were not to be found directly within industry or manufacturing. Generally, unskilled jobs were those which required little training or skill but much strength and endurance: construction and repair of streets, roads, bridges, buildings, and railroads; the unloading and loading of ships and railroad cars; the cleaning of streets and sewers; the collection of trash and garbage. Three large railroads—the Pennsylvania, the Philadelphia and Reading, and the Baltimore and Ohio, had major trunk lines and acres of rail yards within the city as well as terminals on the Delaware River. As the second major port of the nation, Philadelphia Harbor, together with the Delaware River, also generated much work: deepening and widening channels; removing unnecessary islands; building dikes, wharves, piers, docks, and bridges. While important, however, these activities did not employ the vast numbers which were to be found in industry and manufacturing.[32]

Compared to central and western Pennsylvania, Philadelphia had few economic opportunities to offer Polish laborers. Not only did the Poles lack skills and crafts, but the city's major industry—textile and garment manufacture—did not readily appeal to them. Textile manufacture was primarily a woman's industry. Garment manufacture employed both men and women, but Polish men, unlike Italian or

Jewish men, had little background in the needle trades and hence were not inclined to seek their livelihood in this field. By its very nature the printing and publishing industry required large numbers of skilled persons—printers, pressmen, proofreaders, editors, etc. These persons had to read, write, and speak English efficiently. Consequently, this industry remained the preserve of native-Americans, or of native-born English-, Irish-, Scotch-, and German-Americans. Of the 11,935 workers employed in the printing and publishing industry in 1915, only 397 were foreign-born. The metal industry, because of its diversity and the nature of its products, also required skilled or trained individuals and thus, as a whole, had little to offer large numbers of unskilled workers. Two of the nation's largest steel rolling mills (Midvale Steel Company and Disston Saw Works) were located in the city. Excellent examples of successful vertical integration, these plants produced acid and open hearth steel ingots, not as final products or for general sale, but for use in the manufacture of their own products. Both these firms, especially in their rolling divisions, employed thousands of unskilled laborers. For this reason, and because they were basic steel producers, they were the exceptions within Philadelphia's metal industry. Needless to say, they were prime employers of Polish labor in Philadelphia.

The Philadelphia which confronted the Polish migrant was a city whose industries were highly diversified, small in size, and very demanding in the quality of products and skill of workers; comparatively, it was a city with very few firms and industries capable of employing large numbers of unskilled workers. Moreover, Philadelphia's major industries—textile and garment manufacture; printing and publishing; machine shop and hardware manufacture and leather production—had taken hold of the economy very early in the city's history. This meant that subsequent technologies, techniques and attitudes had to adapt themselves to preset economic conditions and to industrial institutions which were already fully formed and functioning. To a large extent, land, labor, and capital markets were saturated. New industries, especially those requiring large amounts of unskilled labor, often found it difficult to secure a place for themselves within the city. New industries which did move into the city—

"lace curtains," for example, did so only because of the skilled force of textile workers, mainly women, already there. The same was true of machinery manufacture:

> Not only is Philadelphia noted for the excellent workmanship, accuracy and the ingenuity of its machinery products, but it is also a great machinery center because of the diversity and variety of machines that are produced. . . . Philadelphia presents perhaps one of the best examples in economic history of the demonstration of the law which compels industries to follow labor. . . . Manufacturing enterprises have been drawn to Philadelphia because of the abundant supply of skilled and trained labor which could be secured in the city.[33]

In short, by the late 19th century Philadelphia's economy was old and rigid. No longer as malleable as it had been in its infancy, it lacked the fluidity and openness which characterized newer industrial centers like Buffalo, Cleveland, Detroit, or Chicago. For this reason, and because the nature of its industry was already firmly established, it could not, and did not need to, compete with central and western Pennsylvania for masses of unskilled laborers.

## I V

By 1915 the composition as well as the orientation of Polish immigration to Philadelphia had changed radically. Emigration from Poznań, Silesia and East Prussia had ceased. Poles from Austria and Russia now far outnumbered the pioneers from Germany. Western Galicia and the Russian provinces of Płock, Łomża and Suwałki sent the most representatives; substantial numbers also came from the provinces of Grodno, Kielce, Warszawa and Lublin. Unlike their predecessors from Germany, these Austrian and Russian Poles were migrants who had come in search of work. At first they had no intention of settling permanently in America. Time, however, was to alter their plans.

Many of these Poles were routed to Philadelphia by New York employment agencies at the request of foundries, tanneries, sugar and chemical refineries; others came directly to the city in response to invitations from friends and relatives already here. A large number, however, perhaps half or more, had originally settled elsewhere, usually in the central and northeastern portions of the state: Phoenixville, Shamokin, Mahanoy City, South Bethlehem, Shenandoah, Lebanon, and Reading, for example. For various reasons they eventually decided to leave central or northeastern Pennsylvania and to seek work and shelter in Philadelphia.[34]

The presence of this latter group is revealing because it indicates that, initially at least, the primary target of the Poles had been central or northern Pennsylvania and not Philadelphia. Moreover, the movement of Poles from central Pennsylvania to Philadelphia underscores the basic economic differences which characterized the two areas. The city shared a unique relationship with its hinterland. Each was dependent on the other for a distinct type of labor. In the early years of industrialization native-Americans were able to meet Pennsylvania's unskilled labor needs, but by the 1870s demand for such labor began to exceed the supply. As industrialization advanced westwardly across the nation, other states contributed to the shortage by draining Pennsylvania of its native supply. Iron and steel manufacturers and coal companies were forced to recruit unskilled labor in large eastern cities such as New York and Philadelphia. Philadelphia's chief role, therefore, was to serve as a recruitment center for unskilled labor. According to Pennsylvania's Department of Labor and Industry:

> One means taken to secure a working force was to send an official representative to the city of New York or Philadelphia with instructions to gather together a gang of laborers and bring them back to the plant needing employees. Special inducements in the way of wages were held forth and unusual opportunities offered to all those who were willing to leave the larger cities and help out the companies in the western section of the State. Once the stream of immigrant labor was started toward the State's industrial centers, it was comparatively easy to keep it moving. Immigrant laborers who found employment in the coal fields, in the iron and steel industries, and in other industrial activities, wrote to their friends, not only in this country, but in their native coun-

try, telling them of the unusual industrial opportunities and wages, and urging them to come to the State.[35]

In addition to this movement of unskilled labor out of the city, there was a movement of *skilled* labor *into* the city. Immigrant laborers who moved to Philadelphia from central or northeastern Pennsylvania were not newcomers to America. By the time they reached the city they were generally familiar with American industry and the American environment. They probably knew some English and perhaps had acquired a rudimentary skill or trade. The city attracted them because it offered improved economic status and job security. Because it was a recruitment and rerouting center, Philadelphia also attracted workers in times of strike or depression; in the city there was sure to be someone who would know of work, here or elsewhere. Thus, Philadelphia serviced the state by sending or rerouting unskilled laborers to the mines and steel mills. Pennsylvania serviced Philadelphia by initiating immigrants to American ways, familiarizing them with American industry, and then sending many of them to meet the labor needs of the city, needs which were biased in favor of the skilled, trained, or, at least, the acclimated worker.

An analysis of the occupations of Philadelphia's Polish workers provides additional insight into the nature of immigration to the city. It shows which occupations and industries attracted the Poles, and which did not, and hence illustrates the selectivity of the immigration process. In his 1915 Philadelphia *City Directory,* William Boyd records the occupations of 4,232 persons of Polish origin.[36] These 4,169 men and 63 women represented no less than 256 different occupations. Almost two percent were engaged in professional, executive or managerial activities. Ten percent were self-employed, operating a small store or manufacturing business, or providing a service for the immediate community, e.g., insurance agent, notary, restaurant or tavern keeper, etc. Eight percent were employed in general and public service occupations and transportation.

By far the largest portion, 80%, or 3,389 men and women, were engaged in some industrial activity. More than 1300 of these persons, or 31% of all Polish workers, performed some skilled or semi-skilled task. The metal, textile (but not the garment) and leather industries were their chief employers; the tobacco, paper, printing and publishing industries, on the other hand, employed very few skilled Polish workers. Almost two-thirds (217) of the Poles in the metal trades were highly skilled machinists, persons who used precision instruments to design and build machinery. Poles employed by the lumber industry were also skilled craftsmen—carpenters, cabinet makers, wood-workers, and joiners. Those in the leather industry tended to perform semi-skilled tasks.

Polish wage earners engaged in textile manufacture were most often dyers, weavers, spinners, and polishers; most of these were Poles—or the sons of Poles—from Poznań, Silesia, or West Prussia. Only 75 of 1,314 persons reporting skilled activities were employed by the garment industry; once again, most of these were German Poles. Evidently, the Poles were not a source of labor for clothing manufacture, an industry crucial to Philadelphia's economic welfare, employing thousands of its workers, and an industry which was the livelihood of the city's Jews and Italians.

One-half (2,075) of all Polish persons reporting occupations were unskilled. The vast majority (1,934) were general laborers. The remainder were iron and steel workers. Many of the 1,934 laborers were also metal workers; others were construction hands and rail-road employees. Greater numbers, however, worked in chemical factories, petroleum and sugar refineries, or loaded and unloaded rail-road cars and ships in Philadelphia Harbor. Thus, if unskilled, as was 49% of the total, the Poles were employed as general laborers in the metal, leather, chemical, and building industries, or as steve-dores and longshoremen. None of the unskilled found work in the textile or garment industries. If skilled, however, the Poles were likely to be employed by the textile (but not the garment) industry, or as machinists and related workers in the metal industry.

The relationship between immigration and economic structure is also reflected in the manner in which the Poles distributed themselves throughout Philadelphia. Despite the smallness of their numbers, the Poles did not confine themselves to one, or even to two, but settled in at least ten distinct areas of the city: Bridesburg/Frankford, Port

Richmond, Kensington, Nicetown, Callowhill, Northern Liberties, South Philadelphia, Manayunk, and Southwest Philadelphia. They distributed themselves in this fashion because Philadelphia's industries were decentralized. In an age when the automobile was still a luxury and efficient mass transit was not available, it was imperative that workers settle as close as possible to their place of employment. Indeed, in 1915 virtually all of Philadelphia's Poles walked to work.

Because Philadelphia was an old city by American standards, the central portions of the city were built up; space was at a premium. Moreover, most of the industries and factories which had established themselves in these areas had done so prior to the Industrial Revolution. Consequently, these sections were not always as able to absorb the larger and more primary forms of new industry as were the frontier or fringe areas of the city. These latter areas were more fluid in that their economic, industrial and housing structures had not yet been finalized. It is not surprising, therefore, to find that Polish settlements were most often found, not in the older, so-called "slum" areas, but along the city's frontier—in Nicetown, Port Richmond, Bridesburg, Manayunk, Northern Kensington and Southwest Philadelphia. Just as the Poles were attracted to the newer, industrializing centers of the state and the nation, so, too, were they attracted to the newer, developing areas of the city; the urban frontier had the most to offer unskilled migrant workers in terms of ready and appropriate employment.

No matter where they settled, in the older slum areas, or along the urban frontier, the Poles' occupations paralleled the economic and industrial structures of the areas in which they settled—a further indication of the close relationship between immigration, economy, and industry. Indeed, certain industries or factories symbolized the nature of the work offered in a particular area and hence the type of work which was expected of the immigrants. For the Poles these industries and factories were usually primary and basic ones. In Nicetown it was steel: the Midvale Steel Company, makers of armored plate and ordnance; the Budd Company, manufacturers of railway equipment; Link Belt Company, machinery manufacturers; Charles C. Davis Company, spike manufacturers; and the American

Pulley Company. In Manayunk it was PennCoyd Iron Works, structural iron specialists and bridge builders to the world. In Bridesburg it was metals, chemicals and leather: Henry Disston and Sons, Inc., one of the nation's foremost saw and file manufacturers, and Miller Lock (Yale-Towne) Company; Charles Lennig and Company and Barrett Manufacturing Company, chemical manufacturers; Gillinder and Son, glass makers; and Robert H. Foerderer, Inc., leather and glue manufacturers.

In Port Richmond it was acres of rail yards and river terminals, and Cramp's Shipyard. In Callowhill it was the Baldwin Locomotive Works, the largest one of its kind in the world, and the Freihoffer Vienna Baking Company. In Southern Kensington it was the textile and leather industries: John B. Stetson Company, the famous hat makers; John Bromley and Sons, rug makers; and Dungan Hood and Company, glazed kid manufacturers. In South Philadelphia it was the shipping, sugar and oil industries: Spreckels Sugar Refinery, Franklin Sugar Refinery; Baugh and Sons, manufacturers of oil, lubricants, fertilizers, grease and tallow products; and the Atlantic Refining Company. In Southwest Philadelphia it was the J. B. Brill Company, makers of most of the nation's street and trolley cars.


V


The ultimate distribution and settlement of Eastern and Southern Europeans in America's cities after 1870 were not random or fortuitous occurrences. Forces were at work directing certain groups in certain numbers to specific areas of the nation. For the Poles, work was the factor most responsible for determining ultimate distribution and place of settlement. By definition, the Pole was bound to the work he performed: an unskilled peasant-farmer turned migrant-laborer, the product of an industrializing and urbanizing society, he had definite preferences for certain types of work and a disinclination for others. Each American city possessed unique industrial and economic structures and offered a specific mix of jobs which required specific types of labor; each area of the city also had its peculiar

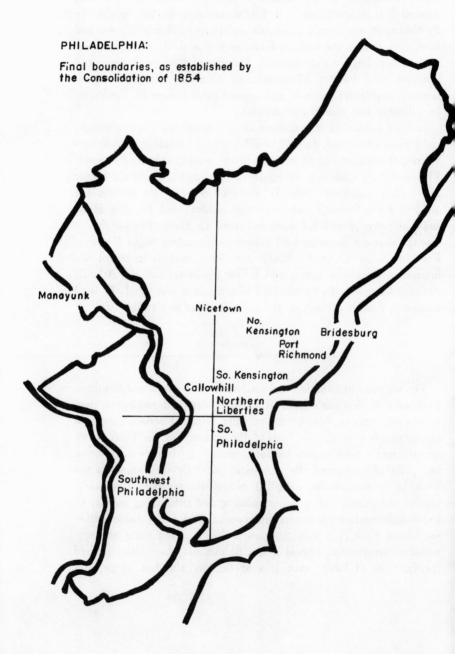

PHILADELPHIA:

Final boundaries, as established by
the Consolidation of 1854

Manayunk

Nicetown

No.
Kensington

Bridesburg

Port
Richmond

So. Kensington

Callowhill

Northern
Liberties

So.
Philadelphia

Southwest
Philadelphia

economic orientation and industrial needs. Where the qualifications of the Polish migrant met the needs of the urban economy, both nationally and locally, the immigrant and the city came together; communities could now be formed.[37]

As a whole, the Poles did not settle in Philadelphia because this city had little to offer them in terms of ready and appropriate work. The Poles who did settle in Philadelphia were those who were able to fit themselves into the peculiar structure of the city's economy. They were either skilled persons who had acquired their expertise in Europe or elsewhere in the United States, most often in central and northeastern Pennsylvania, or they were unskilled persons who were able to find jobs in the limited areas of employment open to such workers in the city. Because they were unskilled migrant-laborers, the majority of whom were young men traveling alone, and because their chief aim in coming to America was to find work compatible with their qualifications, they were willing to go wherever they must to find such work. Instead of Philadelphia, they headed for centers of heavy industrial activity—central, western, and northeastern Pennsylvania, or Chicago, Buffalo, Cleveland, and Milwaukee. Here could be found ample opportunities for workers whose primary offerings were the strength of their bodies and sincere devotion to hard work.

## GENERAL SUMMARY OF OCCUPATIONS: POLISH WORKERS, PHILADELPHIA, 1915

| | | | |
|---|---|---:|---:|
| I. | Professional | 57 | 1.30% |
| II. | Executive/Managerial | 16 | .37 |
| III. | Self-Employed | 405 | 9.59 |
| IV. | Service Occupations | 354 | 8.37 |
| V. | Skilled and Semi-Skilled | 1,314 | 31.06 |
| VI. | Unskilled | 2,075 | 49.03 |
| VII. | Other | 11 | .26 |
| | | 4,232 | 100.00% |

| I. PROFESSIONAL | | | |
|---|---|---|---|
| | | librarian | 1 |
| actor | 1 | musician | 8 |
| artist | 2 | music teacher | 2 |
| chemist | 3 | nurse | 1 (f) |
| clergy | 12 | optometrist | 1 |
| editor | 3 | orchestra conductor | 1 |
| lawyer | 1 | orderly | 1 |

| | | | |
|---|---|---|---|
| photographer | 10 | meat | 47 |
| physician | 3 | men's furnishings | 4 |
| publisher | 1 | milk | 5 (1f) |
| secretary | 1 | music | 1 |
| stockbroker | 1 | musical instruments | 1 |
| teacher | 3 (1f) | news | 1 |
| | ——— | novelties | 2 (1f) |
| | 57 | paints | 1 |

II. EXECUTIVE/
   MANAGERIAL

| | | | |
|---|---|---|---|
| | | poultry | 1 |
| | | pretzels | 1 |
| bookkeeper | 1 | produce | 5 (1f) |
| executive | 3 | shoes | 16 |
| manager | 10 | stationer | 1 |
| purchasing agent | 1 | trimmings | 1 |
| superintendent | 1 | varieties | 40 (6f) |
| | ——— | wagons | 5 |
| | 16 | f = female | |

III. SELF-EMPLOYED
A. Mercantile/Manufacturing

B. Community Services
   *Professional and*
   *Semi-Professional:*

| | | | |
|---|---|---|---|
| baker | 48 | | |
| baskets | 1 | insurance agent | 6 |
| birds | 1 | notary | 1 |
| bottles | 2 | printer | 4 |
| brooms | 1 | real estate agent | 5 |
| candy | 10 (4f) | steam ship agent | 2 |
| church goods | 1 | undertaker | 6 (1f) |
| cigars | 28 (3f) | *other:* | |
| coal | 1 | dining | 3 |
| druggist | 5 | liquors | 28 |
| drygoods | 20 (5f) | livery | 2 |
| florist | 1 | pool | 9 |
| flour | 1 | teams | 1 |
| fruit | 1 | | ——— |
| furnishings | 1 | | 405 |
| furniture | 4 | IV. SERVICE OCCUPATIONS | |
| grocer | 59 (3f) | A. General: | |
| hardware | 1 | barber | 39 |
| harnesses | 2 | bartender | 28 |
| home furnishings | 6 | bellman | 1 |
| horseshoes | 1 | bootblack | 4 |
| huckster | 7 | clerk | 35 |
| jewelry | 3 | cook | 10 |
| marble | 1 | elevator operator | 1 |

| | | | | |
|---|---|---|---|---|
| housekeeper | 1f | paperhanger* | 7 | |
| janitor | 2 | *plumbing and heating:* | | |
| meter reader | 1 | gas fitter* | 1 | |
| midwife | 19f | heater* | 1 | |
| porter | 2 | pipefitter* | 10 | |
| salesman | 16 | plumber* | 9 | |
| sexton | 2 | steamfitter* | 1 | |
| waiter | 19 | *roofer** | 9 | |
| watchman | 14 | *contractor** | 4 | |

B. Transportation

| | | | | |
|---|---|---|---|---|
| chauffeur | 4 | B. Chemicals and Allied Products (6) | | |
| conductor | 8 | gluemaker** | 2 | |
| conveyancer | 1 | paintmaker | 2 | |
| driver | 64 | soap maker | 1 | |
| engineer | 15 | temperer* | 1 | |
| fireman | 29 | C. Clay, Glass and Stone Products (42) | | |
| hostler | 1 | brickmaker** | 4 | |
| mariner | 1 | *glass:* | | |
| motorman | 19 | bottlemaker | 1 | |
| stoker | 3 | gasmaker** | 1 | |

C. Public Service:

| | | | | |
|---|---|---|---|---|
| collector | 3 | glassblower* | 2 | |
| police | 2 | glasscutter | 1 | |
| post office carrier | 3 | glass worker | 4 | |
| post office clerk | 1 | glazier* | 29 | |
| telephone operator | 1 | D. Food and Kindred Products (61) | | |
| US Army | 1 | baker** | 11 | |
| US Navy | 4 | brewer** | 1 | |
| | | bottler | 12 | |
| | 354 | butcher* | 16 | |

V. SKILLED AND SEMI-SKILLED

| | | | | |
|---|---|---|---|---|
| | | meatcutter** | 10 | |
| A. Building and Contracting (78) | | confectioner | 8 | (1f) |
| *Brick, cement and stone work:* | | icemaker | 1 | |
| bricklayer* | 10 | sausagemaker | 1 | |
| cementworker | 2 | sugarboiler | 1 | |
| marbleworker | 1 | E. Leather and Rubber Goods (181) | | |
| mason* | 1 | hosemaker | 1 | |
| stonecutter* | 3 | leatherworker | 99 | |
| *electrician** | 4 | moroccoworker | 6 | |
| *painting and decorating:* | | rubbermaker | 8 | |
| decorator* | 2 | shoemaker* | 62 | |
| painter* | 13 | | | |

shoe operator 1
tanner** 4

\* = skilled
\*\* = semi-skilled

F. Lumber and Its Remanu-
facture (123)
   cabinetmaker* 18
   carpenter* 76
   chipper 7
   cooper* 4
   handlemaker 1
   joiner* 1
   millwright* 1
   wagon builder* 3
   wagon maker 3
   woodworker* 9

G. Paper and Printing (44)
   binder 3
   boxmaker** 2
   engraver* 1
   lithographer* 1
   papermaker 16
   pressman* 3
   printer* 15
   stereotyper* 1
   tag maker 2

H. Textiles (232)
   buffer 1
   cordmaker 1
   dyer* 25
   finisher** 1
   ironer 1
   knitter* 4
   loom fixer* 5
   mill worker 20
   pattern maker* 3
   piecer 1
   polisher** 13
   presser** 2
   roller* 1
   rope maker 17
   spinner** 13
   stitcher 1

stripper** 1
textile worker 1
weaver* 121

I. Clothing Manufacture (75)
   dressmaker* 10f
   hatter 7
   hosiery operator** 3
   hosiery worker** 1
   milliner* 3f
   stocking maker 1
   tailor* 50

J. Metals and Metal Manu-
facture (347)
   blacksmith* 46
   boilermaker* 17
   brass worker** 3
   car builder** 2
   coppersmith* 6
   core maker** 1
   cornice maker* 2
   file cutter 1
   file maker 3
   grinder 1
   hammer man* 2
   harness maker* 1
   instrument maker 3
   locksmith* 4
   machinist** 217
   metalworker 3
   riveter** 8
   rivet maker 1
   saw maker 9
   shovel maker 1
   smelter* 1
   spring maker** 6
   tinsmith* 5
   watchmaker** 1
   wireworker** 3

K. Tobacco and Its Products (3)
   cigarmaker 3

L. Miscellaneous and Unde-
finable (122)
   bambooworker 1

| | | | | |
|---|---|---|---|---|
| basketmaker | 3 | rigger* | 7 |
| boxman | 1 | umbrellamaker** | 1 |
| broommaker | 2 | upholsterer* | 6 |
| buttonmaker | 20 | | |
| calker | 3 | | 1,314 |
| craneman | 1 | * = skilled | |
| crane operator | 6 | ** = semi-skilled | |
| designer* | 1 | VI. UNSKILLED | |
| driller* | 4 | foundryman | 1 |
| estimator* | 1 | ironworker | 110 |
| foreman* | 26 | laborer | 1,935 |
| inspector** | 6 | longshoreman | 1 |
| gasworker | 1 | steelworker | 28 |
| helper | 1 | | |
| machine operator | 4 | | 2,075 |
| molder** | 15 | VII. OTHER | |
| oilclothmaker | 4 | farmer | 4 |
| oiler | 1 | gardener | 3 |
| organmaker** | 1 | miner | 2 |
| packer** | 2 | student | 2 |
| reedworker | 3 | | |
| repairman | 1 | | 11 |
| | | GRAND TOTAL | 4,232 |

NOTE: The 4,232 persons reporting occupations in Boyd's 1915 *City Directory* were engaged in 256 different tasks. The schema used in classifying these occupations was constructed with the following aims in mind: (1) the schema must reflect the economic development and economic structure of the Polish people within the larger Philadelphia economy; such a classification, therefore, must give some indication of the skilled or unskilled nature of the occupations and must also locate these occupations within their proper industries; (2) the schema must reflect the internal structure of the Polish community itself; it must indicate the level of development of the various Polish settlements, their permanence or nonpermanence, and the extent to which the settlements were self-servicing and self-sustaining.

Occupations listed in Category V, SKILLED AND SEMI-SKILLED, have been classified skilled (*) or semi-skilled (**) in accordance with definitions provided by the U. S. Bureau of Labor, *Classification of Occupations* (Washington, D.C., 1918).

# NOTES

1. Pennsylvania Department of Labor and Industry, "Recent Immigration to Pennsylvania," *Monthly Bulletin* I, No. 5 (October, 1914):33.

2. *Philadelphia Yearbook 1917,* p. A 11.
3. Percent Foreign-born:

|  | 1870 | 1880 | 1890 | 1900 | 1910 | 1920 |
|---|---|---|---|---|---|---|
| Boston | 35 | 32 | 38 | 35 | 36 | 32 |
| Buffalo | 36.5 | 33 | 35 | 30 | 28 | 24 |
| Chicago | 48 | 41 | 41 | 35 | 36 | 30 |
| Cleveland | 42 | 37 | 37 | 33 | 35 | 30 |
| Detroit | 44.5 | 39 | 40 | 34 | 34 | 29 |
| Milwaukee | 47 | 40 | 40 | 31 | 30 | 24 |
| New York | 44.5* | 40** | 42** | 37 | 41 | 36 |
| Newark | 34.5 | 29.5 | 30.5 | 29 | 32 | 28 |
| Philadelphia | 27 | 24 | 26 | 23 | 25 | 22 |
| Pittsburgh | 32 | 28.5 | 31 | 26 | 26 | 20.5 |

* Manhattan only.   ** Does not include Brooklyn for 1880 and 1890.
*Source:* U. S. Census, 1870–1920.

4. According to the 1920 Census, Philadelphia's foreign-born population totalled 400,744. The leading groups were: Russians (95,744) ; Irish (64,500) ; Italians (63,723) ; Germans (39,766) ; Poles (31,112) ; English (30,886) ; Austrians (13,387) ; Hungarians (11,513) ; Rumanians (5,645) ; and Lithuanians (4,392). The vast majority of the Russians were Jews who had fled the Russian pale and the cities and towns of Western Russia and the Ukraine. The Austrians, Hungarians, Rumanians, Lithuanians, and, especially, the Poles also included very large numbers of Jews. The number of Eastern European Jews in Philadelphia, therefore, was more than 120,000, and the number of Poles was much less than the recorded 31,112. At best, the number of foreign-born Poles in Philadelphia was 5,000 in 1910 and 15,000 to 18,000 by 1920. These latter estimates are based on the records of Philadelphia's eight Polish Roman Catholic parishes and the listings of Boyd's *City Directory* for 1915.

5. W. Kruszka, *Historja Polska w Ameryce* (Milwaukee: 1937), II, 174; Emily Greene Balch, *Our Slavic Fellow Citizens* (New York: 1910), p. 264; Anonymous Estimate of the Chicago Polish *Press,* December 15, 1908; Paul Fox, *The Poles in America* (New York: 1922), p. 63. In an article entitled "Poles in Philadelphia," the Philadelphia *Bulletin,* August 11, 1920, reported that there were seven Polish colonies in Philadelphia totalling 75,000 persons (foreign-born parents plus native-born children).

6. U. S. *Census,* 1910, 1920; Balch, *Our Slavic Fellow Citizens,* p. 255; K. D. Miller, *Czecho-Slovaks in the United States* (New York: 1922), pp. 49–50; P. M. Rose, *The Italians in America* (New York: 1922), pp. 53–54; F. J. Warne, *The Tide of Immigration* (New York: 1916), pp. 223–224; F. J. Sheridan, *Italian, Slavic, and Hungarian Unskilled Immigrant Laborers in the United States,* U. S. Bureau of Labor *Bulletin,* No. 72 (September, 1907): pp. 412–415.

7. M. M. Mathews, *A Dictionary of Americanisms on Historical Principles* Vol. I (1951), p. 863.

8. For discussion of land, peasant culture, and conditions in Eastern Europe prior to emigration, see William I. Thomas and Florian Znaniecki, *The Polish Peasant in Europe and America* (Boston: 1918–1920), I; Balch, *Our Slavic Fellow Citizens;* U. S. Immigration Commission, 1907–1910, *Abstracts of Reports with Conclusions and Recommendations of the Minority* (Washington, 1911), p. 30; Victor R. Greene, *The Slavic Community on Strike: Immigrant Labor in Pennsylvania Anthracite* (University of Notre Dame, 1968), p. 26; Polish National Committee of America (Wydział

Narodowy Polski w Ameryce), *Polish Encyclopedia* (Geneva, Switzerland: Atar, Ltd., 1906), 3 vols.; William J. Rose, *Poland Old and New* (London: 1948), pp. 18–22; Roman Dyboski, *Outlines of Polish History* (London: 1924), pp. 213–229; Dyboski, *Poland* (London: 1933), pp. 45–49; Henryk Frankel, *Poland: The Struggle For Power 1772–1939* (London: 1946), pp. 56–63; F. E. Whitton, *A History of Poland From the Earliest Times to the Present Day* (New York: 1918); Francis Bujak, *Poland's Economic Development* (Cracow: 1926); *The Cambridge History of Poland,* eds. W. F. Reddaway, J. H. Penson, O. Halecki, and R. Dyboski (1941); Roger Portal, "The Industrialization of Russia," *The Cambridge Economic History of Europe,* eds. H. J. Habakhuk and M. Postan (1965): VI, Chapter IX; M. Erasme Piltz, *Petite Encyclopedie Polonaise* (Paris: 1916); Alexandre Woycicki, *La Classe Ouviere dans la Grande Industrie Du Royaume De Pologne* (Lovain, Paris, 1909).

9. Władisław Reymont, *Chłopi* [Peasants] (New York: 1925), II, p. 77.

10. Greene, *The Slavic Community on Strike,* p. 26. See also Frank Thistlethwaite, "Migration from Europe Overseas in the Nineteenth and Twentieth Centuries," *New Perspectives of the America Past* II, eds. Stanley N. Katz and Stanley I. Kutler (Boston: 1969), p. 65.

11. These are the Polish territories as defined by the Prussian Government. In traditional Polish nomenclature these areas were the provinces of Poznań (Posen), Bydgoszdz (Bromberg), Gdansk (Danzig), Kwidzyń (Marienwerder), Olsztyn (Allenstein), Gabin (Gumbinnen), Królewiec (Konigsberg), Opawa (Troppau), Opole (Oppeln) and Wrocław (Breslau).

12. *Polish Encyclopedia,* II, pp. 139–140, 165; Bujak, *Poland's Economic Development,* pp. 45–54; Stanislaw Posner, "Poland as an Independent Economic Unit," *Poland's Case for Independence,* ed. by Polish Information Committee (New York: 1916), pp. 151, 147; Richard Wonser Tims, *Germanizing Prussian Poland: The H-K-T Society and the Struggle for the German Empire, 1894–1919* (New York: 1941), p. 115.

13. Galicia was made up of two provinces, Kraków and Lwów (Lemberg).

14. *Polish Encyclopedia,* II, p. 143; *Cambridge History of Poland,* pp. 438ff; Bujak, p. 52.

15. Balch, pp. 138–139; Bujak, pp. 52, 53; *Polish Encyclopedia,* III, p. 239; *Cambridge History of Poland,* pp. 438, 450–451; Posner, pp. 148–150.

16. Bujak, p. 53; Balch, p. 132; *Polish Encyclopedia,* II, p. 142.

17. Balch, p. 139.

18. The provinces of Wiłno, Kowno, Witebsk, Grodno, Mohylow, Mińsk, Wolyn, Kijow, Podole, and Kurlandya.

19. *The Cambridge Economic History of Europe,* VI, II, pp. 818, 859; *Cambridge History of Poland,* p. 392; Bujak, p. 49.

20. Bujak, p. 4; *Polish Encyclopedia,* II, pp. 184–185ff; *Cambridge History of Poland,* p. 393; Posner, pp. 156–157.

21. *Polish Encyclopedia,* II, pp. 149–150; *Cambridge Economic History of Europe,* VI, II, p. 859.

22. *Polish Encyclopedia,* II, pp. 150–151; Fox, *The Poles in America,* p. 64.

23. Interviews with over 300 Polish immigrants have yet to reveal a single instance in which an immigrant had not migrated to other parts of Europe, or abroad, before coming to the United States.

24. Information as to birthplaces of Philadelphia's Poles was compiled from the records of seven of the city's Polish Roman Catholic parishes— St. Stanislaus, St. Josaphat, St. John Cantius, St. Laurentius, St. Adalbert, St. Hedwig, and St. Ladislaus.

25. Pennsylvania Department of Labor and Industry, "Report of Division of Immigration and Unemployment," *First Annual Report, 1913* (Harrisburg, 1914), pp. 232–233. NOTE: Pennsylvania's Bureau of Statistics and Information did not record the Jewish population by national group, i.e., Russian, Polish, Austrian, etc., but listed them in a separate category, "Hebrews."

26. Pennsylvania Department of Labor and Industry, "Report of Division of Immigration and Unemployment," pp. 233–235.

27. For discussion of Pennsylvania's industrial activity and the labor which supported it, see S. K. Stevens, *Pennsylvania, Titan of Industry* (New York: 1948), I; Guy C. Whidden and W. H. Schoff, *Pennsylvania and Its Manifold Activities* (Philadelphia: Twelfth International Congress of Navigation, 1912); Sheridan, *Italian, Slavic, and Hungarian Unskilled Immigrant Laborers in the United States;* Pennsylvania Department of Labor and Industry, "Report of Division of Immigration and Unemployment," pp. 240–255; Pennsylvania Department of Labor and Industry, "Racial Displacement in Pennsylvania Industries," *Monthly Bulletin* (November, 1914): 28–35.

28. Pennsylvania Department of Labor and Industry, *Annual Report, 1915* (Harrisburg, 1916); Sheridan, *Italian, Slavic and Hungarian Unskilled Immigrant Laborers in the United States,* p. 413; Greene, *The Slavic Community on Strike,* pp. 34–35; Pennsylvania Department of Internal Affairs, *Annual Report 1903* (Harrisburg, 1904); *Annual Report 1905* (Harrisburg, 1906), pp. 448–449; U. S. Immigration Commission, 1907–1910, *Abstracts of Reports* (Washington, D.C., 1911), p. 506.

29. In order, these firms were: Baldwin Locomotive Works; Hardwick and Magee; Brill Car Manufacturing Company; Foerderer, Inc.; Curtis Publishing Company; U. S. Naval Shipyard and Cramp's Ship and Engine Company; Berkshire Hosiery Mills; Atlantic Oil Refining Company; and E. C. Knight's Franklin Sugar Refinery.

30. *Philadelphia Yearbook 1917,* p. A 3; Whidden and Schoff, *Pennsylvania and Its Manifold Activities,* p. 227; H. L. Collins and W. Jordan, *Philadelphia, A Story of Progress* (New York: 1941), III, 59–76; and J. T. Scharf and T. Westcott, *History of Philadelphia 1609–1884* (Philadelphia: 1884), II, pp. 2226–2340.

31. There were 7,097 manufacturing establishments in Philadelphia in 1904. These employed 228,899 persons and produced $591 million worth of goods. One thousand, three hundred thirty-one firms, employing 80,310 persons, were engaged in textile manufacture and produced goods worth $170 million. In 1915 textile manufacture employed 103,976 persons out of a total of 313,783 wage earners; Philadelphia Department of Labor and Industry, *Annual Report 1915;* see also: Whidden and Schoff, pp. 209, 212–214; *Philadelphia Yearbook 1917,* p. A 3; Stevens, *Pennsylvania, Titan of Industry,* I, pp. 324–326.

32. For example, in 1915, of 313,783 total wage earners recorded by the Pennsylvania Department of Labor and Industry for Philadelphia, 15,396 were engaged in building and contracting; 3,404 in laundry work, and 33,709 in public service occupations. The remainder were employed in the manufacture of chemicals, clay, glass, store products, clothing, food, leather and rubber goods, paper, textiles, metal products, tobacco, etc.

33. *Philadelphia Yearbook 1917,* p. B 7.

34. Interviews with over 3000 Polish immigrants in Philadelphia, as well as the records of the Polish Roman Catholic parishes, clearly establishes the

fact that a very large, but indeterminable number, of Poles who settled in Philadelphia had first established themselves in communities in central or northeastern Pennsylvania.

35. Pennsylvania Department of Labor and Industry, "Report of Division of Immigration and Unemployment," pp. 231–232.

36. For a discussion of Boyd's *City Directory* and the method used to compile this list of names, see Caroline Golab, *The Polish Communities of Philadelphia, 1870–1920: Immigrant Distribution and Adaptation in Urban America* (unpublished Ph.D. dissertation, University of Pennsylvania, 1971), Appendix I.

37. In an attempt to explain immigrant distribution and adaptation in urban America, the economic factor has been emphasized very strongly throughout this essay; the importance of cultural variables has also been indicated. However, consideration of a *demographic* component is also necessary if a complete and balanced picture is to be obtained. The Poles shared positive and negative relationships with other groups. In Philadelphia they had to compete with others for the relatively few unskilled positions available: they had to compete with those already settled in the city—the Irish, Irish-Americans, and Blacks; and with those who arrived with them—the Italians and the Jews. How well they competed, of course, would depend on cultural and economic variables. For further discussion of demographic considerations, see Golab, *The Polish Communities of Philadelphia, 1870–1920*, Chapter I.

# 3

# The Old Order Amish of Pennsylvania

## MAURICE A. MOOK

*Maurice Mook received graduate degrees from Northwestern and the University of Pennsylvania. He has authored over fifty articles on the Amish. After "retirement" from Penn State, he became Professor of Anthropology at Lycoming College.*

The Old Order Amish people are one of the most interesting and important religiously centered ethnic groups in Pennsylvania. They are also one of the earliest. They first came to and settled in southeastern Pennsylvania in the early eighteenth century.[1] Their largest settlement in Pennsylvania is still in this area. The Lancaster County Amish community is the oldest Amish community in the world today. The Amish no longer live in Europe, where they originated, and there is no older Amish community elsewhere in the New World. The eastern part of Lancaster County has been continuously occupied by Amish people for two and one half centuries.

Some Old Order Amish people know their history in Europe and the history of their early settlement in America better than they know their more recent history. These people refer to the Lancaster County Amish settlement as the "Mother Colony." They are correct in their assumption that it is such a colony, for most Amish settlements elsewhere in the United States today either directly or indirectly derive from the Lancaster County group.[2]

74

Many people, including historians and other social scientists, talk and write as though all of the Pennsylvania Amish live in Lancaster County. There are, however, now twenty Old Order Amish communities in Pennsylvania. Before it is indicated where these are now located, it is necessary to distinguish between an Amish community and an Amish congregation. An Amish *congregation* is a group of Amish families that worship together, whereas an Amish *community* is a group of Amish families that live in the same area, whether or not they worship together. An Amish community is a settlement or "colony," and a settlement may include several or more congregations. What we call a congregation they call a "church," and a church to them is always the group that shares particular beliefs and worships as a unit. By church they never mean a building, for the Old Order Amish do not have special structures in which they worship. What we call a church in this sense, they call a "preaching place" or a "worship house." They worship in the downstairs rooms of their family farm homes. So the community to them is a geographical group, whereas the congregation or church is a ceremonial unit. This is the way these terms will be used in the present discussion.

The situation and terminology is further complicated by the fact that the Amish often have to divide their churches into "districts." When the worshipping group grows so large that all of the families can not assemble in the downstairs rooms of their farm houses, they divide the congregation on a geographical basis into districts. The geographical basis of these districts is shown by their names for them. A church may have North and South districts, or East and West; or the name may derive from a geographical feature of the district, or a town it is near, or a post office which serves it.[3]

These districts into which a church may be divided then become the ceremonial unit or worshipping group. Thus the Amish settlement near New Wilmington in Lawrence County has one church divided into eight districts. These districts are congregational divisions of their church. The district divisions of a church are in "fellowship" with each other, whereas Amish churches may or may not be in fellowship with each other. Churches in fellowship have the same *Ordnungen,* which are rules or regulations designed to control the conduct of members of a congregation. Churches that are not in fellowship are separated by differences in their *Ordnungen*. Such churches may share the same basic beliefs, but still differ in the specific regulations of conduct based on these beliefs. All Old Order Amish churches, wherever they are, have the same basic beliefs; but they may vary considerably in the customs that relate to and are based on these beliefs. This explains the wide range of differences in customs that distinguish Amish groups. They vary so much in their customs that one is wrong somewhere as soon as he generalizes concerning such customs. This variety in customs between even neighboring Amish groups will be shown later in this chapter when the Old Order Amish churches in Mifflin County are considered.

---

The location of Old Order Amish communities in Pennsylvania in 1972 is shown in the following table. The geographic communities are here listed in the approximate order of their size. There is, however, no data available on the exact size of present Amish communities. The number of Amish church districts (congregations) in each county is known, but the number of members of each congregation is no longer available. The annually published *Mennonite Yearbook and Directory* formerly indicated the approximate number of members in each congregation, but the practice was discontinued in 1967.

The following list of Pennsylvania Amish communities is based on Ben J. Raber's *Der Neue Amerikanische Calender Auf das Jahr 1972*. This calendar, compiled and published by an Old Order Amishman, is found in many Amish homes. The Raber list gives the name of each church district, and for each congregation indicates the names of the ministers of each district, with the post office address of each. It is by the use of these addresses that I have arranged the data according to geographic communities. The enumeration in the Table, derived from the *Calender,* is the most accurate information we have, by virtue of the fact that the compiler is an Amishman. The ministers of local Amish churches cooperate with a fellow Amishman more than they would with a non-Amish person who might attempt such an enumeration. The difficulty of assembling information from reluctant Amish respondents was one reason why the *Mennonite Yearbook and Directory* discontinued trying to compile information on Amish church membership. A similar situation, prevailing in other churches as well, also led the U. S. Census Bureau to discontinue its *Census of Religious Bodies* series in 1936.

In the following Table, column 1 indicates the county in which the Amish community is located; column 2 gives the name of the post office community *near* which (not in which) the Amish reside; and column 3 indicates the number of congregations, or church "districts," in each community.

### AMISH COMMUNITIES AND CONGREGATIONS IN PENNSYLVANIA IN 1972

| *County* | *Location* | *Congregations* |
|---|---|---|
| 1. Lancaster | east and south of Lancaster City | 49 |
| 2. Mifflin ("Big Valley") | Belleville | 9 |
| 3. Lawrence | New Wilmington | 8 |
| 4. Lawrence | Enon Valley | 1 |
| 5. Crawford | Atlantic | 1 |
| 6. Crawford | Spartansburg | 2 |
| 7. Juniata | north and east of Mifflintown | 3 |
| 8. Indiana | Smicksburg | 3 |
| 9. Centre (Brush Valley) | Rebersburg | 1 |
| 10. Centre (Penns Valley) | Aaronsburg | 1 |
| 11. Somerset | south of Meyersdale | 2 |
| 12. Snyder | Mt. Pleasant Mills | 1 |
| 13. Snyder | Winfield | 1 |
| 14. Mercer | north of Mercer | 2 |
| 15. Lebanon | Myerstown | 2 |
| 16. Adams | Littletown | 1 |

| 17. Bradford | LeRaysville | 1 |
| 18. Franklin | Dry Run | 1 |
| 19. Crawford | Townville | 1 |
| 20. Crawford | Conneautville | 1 |

The twenty present Pennsylvania Amish communities are located in fourteen counties. Although their early concentration was in southeastern Pennsylvania, communities are now found also in central, southwestern and northwestern Pennsylvania. The only Amish settlement in northeastern Pennsylvania at the present time is the congregation at LeRaysville in Bradford County. It is a recent settlement, having been established in 1966. In the early years of Amish migration to America, small Amish congregations were located in the vicinity of Reading. They soon became extinct, however, and none has been established in this area since.[4] The northernmost Amish community in southeastern Pennsylvania at the present time is the community, consisting of two church districts, near Myerstown in Lebanon County. The settlement was begun by families from the Lancaster County group that moved to Lebanon County in 1941.

Most of the earliest Amish congregations in southeastern Pennsylvania failed, but their remnants coalesced into the formation of the present thriving Lancaster County group.[5] This oldest and largest Amish community in Pennsylvania has sent out many families which have formed new Amish communities in other sections of the state. The second largest and third oldest community in Pennsylvania is the "Big Valley" concentration of Amish in Mifflin County. This group was established in 1791 and most of its original inhabitants came from Lancaster County.

In the 1750s and 1760s three Amish communities were established in Somerset County as a result of the trans-Alleghenian migration of Amish families deriving from Lancaster County. Two of these three colonies became extinct, largely as a result of the removal of their inhabitants to Ohio, but the colony in southernmost Somerset County has survived to the present day.[6] This colony is the second oldest in Pennsylvania, and until recently was the third largest in the state.

It has been marked by two interesting developments in the history of the Amish in the New World. The "Beachy Amish" (or "New Order" division, sometimes called the "automobile Amish") movement[7] began in this community, and the community is still unique as an Old Order group in that the members of both of its congregations worship in church buildings, rather than in the farm homes of its members. Both of its congregations are larger than most Amish districts elsewhere, because it is possible to assemble more families in a building built especially for worship than it is to accommodate an equally large number of families in most Amish homes.

As the "Mother Colony" the Lancaster community has also been the source of new congregations in other states. In 1940 the new Amish settlement near Mechanicsville in St. Marys County, Maryland, was established by families migrating from Lancaster County.[8] In 1941 the new Amish community in Lebanon County, Pennsylvania, derived from Lancaster County. The movement from Lancaster County still continues. In 1967 a new colony in Brush Valley in Centre County was established by families coming from Lancaster County. At the present time only two of its resident twenty-nine families did not come from Lancaster County. The motives for the Lancaster County families coming to Brush Valley were two-fold: land is cheaper in central Pennsylvania, and there was also the desire to escape the touristic exploitation of the Amish in Lancaster County. I have heard Brush Valley Amish people say that "you can sell one farm in Lancaster County and buy three farms up here."

Three of Pennsylvania's present twenty Amish communities were founded in the eighteenth century—Lancaster in southeastern Pennsylvania, Somerset in the southwestern sector of the state, and Big Valley (Mifflin County) in central Pennsylvania. Several new colonies were established in the nineteenth century, but most of them failed.[9] The only one that survived was the church established in 1847 in Lawrence County, near New Wilmington, by families migrating from Big Valley. This geographic community now consists of eight church districts or congregations.[10] The history of this community was disturbed a few years ago when U.S. Social Security officers at a forced sale sold a large part of the farm equipment and livestock of one of the Amish resident bishops. The community survived this experience, however, and continues to grow. One of its most visible cultural characteristics is that all of the buggies of its married members have yellow canvas tops. This is due to the fact that this community derived from the church now known as the "Byler District" in Big Valley, whose members also have yellow buggy tops. Both groups are known locally as the "Yellow Buggy Top People" on account of this easily visible symbol of their identity. Amish groups everywhere have customs and properties which serve as symbols of the differences among the Amish themselves, as well as those between the Amish and the "people of the world."[11]

All of the other communities and congregations of the Amish in Pennsylvania today were established in the twentieth century. (Numbers 4 through 10 and 12 through 20 in the foregoing Table.) More new Amish congregations have been established recently in Pennsylvania than ever before in their history. This is also true of all other states that have a large number of Amish people, such as Ohio, Indiana, Iowa, Missouri, and the Province of Ontario in Canada. There is also no indication of any decrease in the rate of increase of the Amish people. This recent rapid increase of Amish communities was embodied in a statement a young Amish minister made to me just a few weeks ago. He was helping me count and locate the Amish communities in the state at the present time. "We can do it if you want to," he said, "but the list will be out of date tomorrow."

Old Order Amish communities are one of the best examples in the modern world of what sociologists call a "sectarian society." A sectarian society is a people whose way of life is pervasively permeated by their basic religious beliefs. Such a people practices its beliefs; their beliefs both determine their customs and vindicate their lifeways. A sectarian group, as distinguished from most denominations, is also withdrawn from and in conflict with the world. According to this sociological typology a denomination is in accommodation to the world, but a sect is socially separate from and in conflict with the world.[12]

In a sectarian society is it impossible to understand the lifeways of a people without a knowledge of their basic religious beliefs. These will, therefore, be briefly stated for the Amish, especially as they relate to their basic patterns of life.

One of their most basic beliefs is their idea that they should not be conformed to the modern world. "Be ye not conformed to the world" is a recurrent motif of Amish preaching. To the Amish our modern world is a worldly world, and the worldly world is a wicked world. They are taught to believe, and the Amish very deeply believe, that they can not in conscience conform to our non-Amish ways of life. A similar belief is embodied in their "peculiar people" principle. Early Christians were told "Be ye a peculiar people," and the Amish believe that they too, as Christians, should be a peculiar people. They are peculiar in the clothes they wear, in the length of their hair, in the dialect they speak, and in many other ways. Pride is a sin to the Amish people, and they try hard not to be proudful. But if there is any respect in which they may be a little proudful, it is that they may be proud of being a peculiar people. For Christians are supposed to be a peculiar people, and the Bible tells them so.

The Amish also make much of the fact that the Bible enjoins Christians not to be "unequally yoked with unbelievers." They know that all non-Amish are not unbelievers, but they seize the "unequal yoke" idea as the basis of their social separation from non-Amish people. In spite of the fact that they are no longer geographically isolated from non-Amish neighbors, they have succeeded in maintaining a large measure of social separation from people not of their religious persuasion.

All of the three foregoing beliefs are based upon the Bible. It is their basic belief that that lives of Christians should be foursquarely based upon the Bible as the embodiment of Christian doctrine and practice. Amish bishops and preachers teach that "if it's Biblical it's good, and if it is non-Biblical it must be bad." Or they will say "if it's Scriptural it's good, and if it is non-Scriptural it can't be." Amish people read the Bible literally, interpret it fundamentalistically, and think that it means just what it says. *Das Buch* to them is the German Bible, not an English translation of it. An

Amish woman in northwestern Pennsylvania once told me "I think the Bible should be read in the language of Jesus, German."

The Amish are also much opposed to infant baptism, and one of their reasons for the opposition is their belief that it is non-Biblical. They claim that all references to baptism in the Bible refer to adult baptism. They therefore will only baptize adults. Amish girls are baptized in their late teens, and boys in their late teens or early twenties. Even transcending their belief in the non-Biblicality of infant baptism is their Anabaptist conception of "believers' baptism." Pre-Amish Anabaptists baptized only believers upon their confession of faith; and, of course, infants and children do not have the judgment to confess faith. If one is going to practice the baptism of believers upon their confession of their faith, this means that only adults may be baptized.

Among the Amish one joins the church by being baptized. And as soon as one has joined church he is, as an adult, a fully functioning member of his society. Baptized Amish individuals as adults are than ready to marry, and soon after baptism they do so. Marriage is endogamous among the Amish, and it is an "ordinance," an obligation.[13] The ceremony of marriage must be performed by a bishop of the church, and he also must perform the ceremony of baptism. An Amish bishop would never marry an Amish boy to a non-Amish girl, or vice versa. But "endogamy" to the Amish means that marriage must be within the larger Amish society, not necessarily within a single congregation or local community. Baptism and marriage are separate, but interrelated, ordinances. Not all baptized persons marry, but to be married one has to be baptized. The social symbols of Amish adulthood are baptism and marriage.

Another basic belief of the Amish is that the church must be kept pure. All churches, whether Amish or not, do this by having rules (*Ordnungen* to the Amish) intended to control the conduct of member of the church. The *Ordnungen* of each local Amish church are drawn up by its ministers and usually recorded in writing by the bishop of each church. Although the Amish do not publish their *Ordnungen,* each member of each Amish church well knows what the *Ordnungen* of his church are. They deal with most aspects of

Amish life and are to be adhered to by all members of the church.

If any member of an Amish church willfully and intentionally disobeys any one of the *Ordnungen* of his church, he is subject to *Meidung*. *Meidung* means two things to the Amish: that the person is disowned and excommunicated by his church, and that he is also to be shunned in most relations of life. The shunning of an errant member of an Amish church is the obligation of all other members of his church and by all members of churches in fellowship with his congregation. The Amish practice of shunning is one of the strictest agencies of social control that social scientists have ever found in any known human society. It is especially effective among the Old Order Amish, for it is applied in the home and in the community, as well as in the worship service and at the ordinance of communion. The proof of its effectiveness is the fact that Old Order Amish churches with the strict practice of *Meidung* lose fewer members by defection from the group than "New Order" Amish churches with less strict shunning practices.

The fact that the Amish believe that the church must be kept pure does not distinguish Amish churches from non-Amish churches; it is the way in which they try to keep their church pure that does so. Other churches have, or have had, practices of disownment and excommunication, but few have applied the practice of shunning as severely and effectively as the Amish always have and still do. The Amish are especially strongly committed to this practice, for it was the principal issue involved in their origin. The Amish originated by separating from the southern European Anabaptists (also called Swiss Brethren) in what is now the canton of Bern, Switzerland, in 1693. At that time the Brethren were applying a "light" *Meidung*, which was only applied in the worship service. But Jacob Ammon said that shunning should be applied in the home and in the congregational community, as well as at the worship service and communion table. Ever since the "Amish Division," based essentially on this difference, those who followed the practice advocated by Jacob Ammon have been called "Amish."[14]

The Amish want not only a "pure" church, but also a "free" church, by which they mean a church free from state control. They believe that the church and state should be strictly separate. The Amish recognize that government is necessary, but they also regard it as essentially evil. Therefore they feel that the less they have to do with government the better off they are. They have always been opposed to state-established churches and almost everything that such churches do. One of their objections to infant baptism was that it was a policy of such churches. The negativistic attitude of the Amish toward government has led to two practices, often regarded as evidence of poor citizenship on their part: they usually do not vote, especially in state and national elections, and they will not hold public offices. This attitude has also been a basis of their "nonresistant" practice of refusing to fight in wars.

The Amish church has been one of the historic peace churches, both in Europe in their early history and in the United States since their transplantation in this country. Their opposition to warfare is two-fold: it is an activity engaged in by political states or jurisdictions, and it is also unchristian. Their basic objection to warfare is the latter. They interpret the message of the New Testament as incontrovertibly pacifistic. However, they do not call themselves pacifists; they say they are "nonresistant." They never argue that warfare is a poor way of settling international disputes; they never contend that it is economically wasteful and nonproductive; they never even say that it makes for enmity and ill will among men. Their opposition to warfare is not primarily based on such practical political, economic, or psychological arguments as these. Theirs is a Biblically based pacifism, which they call "nonresistance." The Christian message is clear, and they act upon it accordingly. Warfare is to them simply unchristian, and that is all there is to it.

Another practice the Amish base on their religion is their opposition to pictures, especially photographs of persons. Their principal Biblical basis for this is "Thou shalt not make any graven image, or any likeness" (Exodus 20:4), but there are many other Biblical statements to the same effect.[15] This may seem to be a minor matter to many, but it is not so to most Amish. There are differences among Amish individuals with respect to this "witness." But it does show that small things can be large things to members of small groups, on a single sacred book.

It should be recognized, however, that the Bible is not the only basis of Amish life. The Amish believe that "if it's Biblical it's good"; but they also believe that if it is Anabaptist, or even that if it is old, it is also good. They appeal to the Bible, and to Anabaptism, and to historicity as the sanctions of their behavior and as the bases of what they regard as their Good Life.[16]

The Lancaster County Amish community is better known than any other Pennsylvania Amish community. This is unfortunate, for the Lancaster Amish are not typical of many other Amish communities elsewhere, even those within the state. The Amish of Lancaster County are more prosperous than most other Amish communities; they do not differ as much among themselves in Lancaster County as they do in some other areas; their farms are smaller in size than they usually are elsewhere; nowhere else do the Amish grow tobacco as extensively as they do in Lancaster County; no other Amish group relies as much on cash-crop farming as the Lancaster Amish do. There are many other ways in which the Lancaster Amish differ from other Amish communities, both in Pennsylvania and in the other states they now inhabit. For both of these reasons the final section of this chapter will emphasize the Amish of central Penn-especially to the members of sectarian societies who base their lives sylvania as distinct from the Amish of southeastern Pennsylvania.[17]

Both sociologically and culture-historically the most interesting Amish in the world today are the Amish who live in "Big Valley" in central Pennsylvania. The "world" in this case is eighteen states of the United States and one province of Canada, which is where most Amish now live. Over four-fifths of all Amish today live in Pennsylvania, Ohio, and Indiana. Although they settled in Pennsylvania, and Pennsylvania is still popularly known as "the Amish State," there are now many more Amish in Ohio. There are also

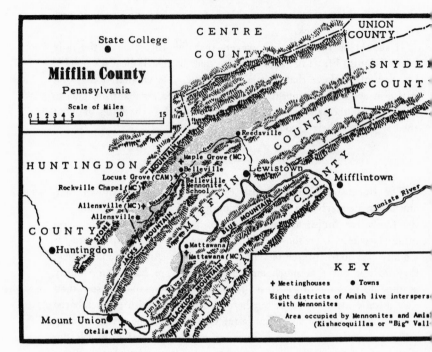

Courtesy of the *Mennonite Encyclopedia*

almost as many in Indiana as there are in Pennsylvania.

The Big Valley Amish are more interesting than most Amish elsewhere because they have divided so often and exist today as several separate groups. They share the same basic religious beliefs but differ in their customs based on these beliefs. They also vary in their material cultural properties. Thus, they exist as a community of cultural contrasts, and these contrasts are both more numerous and more varied in Big Valley than they are anywhere among the Amish.

One basic variation is between the "Old Order" and "New Order" Amish. The Amish seldom use these labels, however. They usually speak of the "House Amish" as distinct from the "Church Amish." Their words for these divisions embody one of the basic cultural contrasts found among them: the Old Order does not have meetinghouses; the New Order does. The Old Order Amish worship in the downstairs rooms of their farm houses. When the congregational group becomes too large to assemble in their homes, they divide the congregation into two groups or "districts," usually on a purely geographical basis. The districts then worship on alternate Sundays and the bishop of the original congregation can thus serve both districts. This is made possible by the fact that the Amish worship once every two weeks, rather than once every week as we "English" do. The Amish call all non-Amish people "English."

They will occasionally say that someone is "Mennonite, not English," for they know that they derived from and share basic beliefs with Mennonites and consequently feel closer to Mennonites than to other "English" people. When Amish individuals leave an Old Order congregation, they usually join a conservative Mennonite church. They are then known as, and sometimes call themselves, Amish Mennonites.

There are many contrasts between the House and Church Amish, but their basic differences may be listed as follows: 1) The Church Amish have church buildings, whereas the House Amish do not. 2) The Church Amish use electricity in their homes and barns, but the House Amish do not. 3) The Church Amish use tractors in the fields, while the House Amish use gasoline engines only as sources of stationary power. 4) The Church Amish own and use automobiles and trucks; the House Amish are not permitted to own them. 5) The Church Amish practice a light *Meidung,* and the House Amish apply a strict *Meidung.* The more conservative Old Order Amish churches apply the Meidung more strictly than more "progressive" Old Order churches do.

There are now nine House Amish congregations in Big Valley, and one Church Amish group. There are also three Mennonite churches in the Valley, all three of which originally derived from the House Amish. Not long ago there was still another House Amish congregation in the Valley, but within recent years, this group accepted electricity, the use of tractors and automobiles, and in 1962 built a church house. It thus became a Church Amish con-gregation.

An interesting difference among the Amish is related to whether they worship in their houses or in churches. Those who worship in the home serve a congregational meal after the fortnightly worship service, whereas the Church Amish usually do not do so. This meal after the worship service is practically the same among Old Order Amish churches everywhere. The menu consists of bread, apple or peach butter, pickles, red beets, "schnitz" pie, coffee for adults and milk for the children. In Big Valley schnitz pies are baked in the form of and are called "half-moon" pies. Men and women not only sit separately in the worship service but also eat at separate tables for the Sunday midday meal. Except for babies in arms they eat in order of age. The Ministers (irrespective of their ages) and older men and women eat first; young people and children eat later. All Amish meals begin and end with a short period of silent worship.

Many of the above differences between the House and Church Amish are not peculiar to the Amish in Big Valley. Many other Amish communities are divided into Old Order and New Order churches. But the Old Order churches in Big Valley differ more among themselves than they do elsewhere. Local Old Order churches are often known by the last name of their bishop. The Old Order churches in Big Valley are today known as the Yoder, Zook, Byler, Renno, etc. churches. The New Order church is the Speicher church. The four most conservative churches in the Valley are known as the "Old School" people. They are sometimes called "Nebraska" Amish by their English neighbors. However, this term has gradually ac-quired a tone of condescension, even of derision, and its use should therefore be avoided.

Big Valley Old Order churches differ in many customs and arti-facts, other than those that distinguish the House and Church Amish. Three of the most easily visible differences are the color of their buggy tops, the suspenders men wear, and the length of men's hair. Long hair is everywhere a symbol of Amishness to the Amish. But Amish churches differ in their definitions of what constitutes long hair. The "Old School" Amish men in Big Valley wear their hair to their shoulders; Byler men wear their hair to the lower lobe of the ear; Renno men have hair about half-way down the ear. Church Amish men wear their hair still shorter, and the men of this group also have quite short and well-trimmed beards. All baptized Amish men have beards, but no Amishman is permitted to grow a mustache. The Amish practice baptism of adults only, and most marry soon after they are baptized. This virtually, but not quite accurately, means that married men have beards and unmarried young men do not.

Amish women differ less in the length of their hair and the way they comb it than men do. All adult Amish women dress their hair the same way: they have a very sharp and straight part that runs from the middle of the forehead to the back of the neck. Their long hair is then pulled back on both sides of the head and ends in a knot on the back of the head. Little Amish girls may have braids and combs in their hair, but as they grow older they must put away such childish things.

Men of the Old School churches wear no suspenders; they keep their pants up with a puckering string in the back. All Amish men, and boys as well, must wear broad-fall trousers, which they call "barn-door britches." These have no fly in front; their trousers have four buttons across the waist and the flap falls down in front. Most Byler church men have but one suspender, which may be worn over either shoulder. Renno men wear two suspenders, but they must be homemade. The Church Amish men may wear "brought-in" or "store-boughten" suspenders. Lately stores have been selling plastic suspenders to liberal—and daring—Amishmen.

Stores in Amish areas usually stock plain cloth and certain articles of Amish clothing (hats, shoes, stockings, socks, suspenders, underclothing, and the "prayer veils" for Amish women) for the benefit of their Amish customers. If the Amish cannot purchase these articles at local stores, they buy them from mail-order houses, quite a few of which now cater to the needs of the members of various plain-clothes churches throughout the country.

There are many church differences in the clothing of Amish

women. One interesting detail is the half-moon shaped piece of cloth they wear sewn to their dresses in the sacral area of the back. These tend to be longer in conservative churches and shorter in more "liberal" Old Order churches. They also must be the same color and made of the same material as the dress. No one seems to know why they wear these, except that "we have always had them." They may be, and probably are, a survival from the time when all women wore bustles.

The Amish churches of Big Valley also differ in the color of their buggy tops. Old School buggies have white canvas tops, Byler buggies have yellow tops, and Renno buggies have black tops. (Old Order Amish buggy tops in Lancaster County are gray.) The large group of Amish in Lawrence County in Western Pennsylvania has been mentioned and here all church districts have yellow buggy tops. This group migrated to Lawrence County from Big Valley in the 1840s, but all districts here are still in "fellowship" with the Byler church in Big Valley. The recently established Old Order congregation in Penns Valley in Centre County and the Winfield congregation in Snyder County also have white buggy tops. Both of these groups derived from Old School churches in Big Valley, all of which use white buggy tops.

There are many other cultural differences among the Old Order churches of Big Valley. They differ in the tucks and pleats of the muslin or organdy head coverings (also called "prayer veils") that all Amish women must wear, in the colors permitted for men's shirts, in the kind of farm equipment each church allows, in whether or not they paint their barns and houses, and in many other ways. In all of these variations among Amish churches, one is strongly impressed with, and sometimes surprised by, the small details of life that the church can control in a sectarian society.

Although the casual visitor to an Amish community may see Amish culture as a curious compound of conservative customs, a closer perspective reveals a people committed to a way of life which may have certain values for non-Amish Americans. For one thing, they may be counted among the best—old-fashioned, one must say— farmers of the nation. A Pennsylvania jurist has reminded us that, in spite of their refusal to fight our wars, and in spite of their eschewal of our higher education, the Amish are "usually out of trouble and should be included among our best citizens." Their own most highly esteemed values are family, faith, and farming—"these three, but the greatest of these" for them is their faith, for it underlies the other two. It is fair to say that all else in their life is minor and marginal.

An Amishman and I once stood on Jack's Mountain, from the top of which we could see almost every Amish farm in Big Valley. The Amishman had lived in Big Valley all his life. "There you see our virtues," he said, "which are order, sufficiency, and peace." These virtues they have for us also to strive for. They are indeed, as they want to be, and as they say themselves, *Die Stillen im Lande*—the "quiet ones on the land," who as solid, substantial, successful tillers of the soil have made their unobtrusive contributions among us now for nearly three centuries.

As *Die Stillen im Lande* they want only to be left alone, and we should leave them alone. And may they prosper in Pennsylvania, in the future, as they have in the past.

## NOTES

In the following notes *M.E.* refers to *The Mennonite Encyclopedia,* vols. I–IV (1955–59). The excellent articles in this Encyclopedia are standard sources for Mennonite history, doctrine, and culture. The Mennonite Church has always regarded the Old Order Amish as one of the major divisions of American Mennonitism. There are articles in the Encyclopedia on all of the best established Pennsylvania Amish communities. See "Lancaster County," "Lancaster County Amish," "Lawrence County," "Mifflin County," "Somerset County," etc.

1. "The Amish came to Pennsylvania as early as 1727. Some families may have come earlier." John A. Hostetler, *Amish Society* (Baltimore: 1968), p. 38.

2. A few Amish colonists came directly from Europe to the middle west without passing through Pennsylvania. Also some early Amish settlers in Canada migrated from Europe directly to Ontario.

3. The conceptual distinctions between "community," "church," and "district" are discussed in "The Number of Amish in Pennsylvania," *Mennonite Historical Bulletin* vol. 16, no. 1 (January, 1955). There were ten Old

Order Amish communities in Pennsylvania in 1955; there are twenty in 1972.

4. For the history of these early, now extinct congregations, see Grant M. Stoltzfus, "History of the First Amish Mennonite Communities in America," *The Mennonite Quarterly Review* vol. 28, no. 4 (October, 1954) : 235–62.

5. Two of the early colonization failures in southeastern Pennsylvania are well documented. The failure of the Amish colony at Northkill, near present Hamburg, Pennsylvania, is dramatically recorded in the Introduction to Harvey Hostetler's *Descendants of Jacob Hochstetler* (Elgin, Ill.: 1912) ; the failure of an early Amish community in Chester County is analyzed in Maurice A. Mook, "An Early Amish Colony in Chester County, Pennsylvania," *Mennonite Historical Bulletin* vol. 16, no. 3 (July, 1955) : 1–3.

6. The history of the Amish in Somerset County is told in Ivan J. Miller's article "Somerset County, Pa.," *M.E.*, IV (1959), pp. 572–5 (map of Amish and Mennonite communities in Somerset County, Pa., and Garrett County, Maryland, p. 573) ; and in Alvin J. Beachy, "The Amish Settlement in Somerset County, Pennsylvania," *The Mennonite Quarterly Review* vol. 28, no. 4 (October, 1954) : 263–92. The history of the Conemaugh Amish congregation in northern Somerset County that failed is related in Maurice A. Mook, "The Amishman who Founded a City," *Christian Living* (July, 1955) : 4–7. Amishman Joseph Schantz founded "Schantz's Town," which became Johnstown. When the city began to grow the Amish left the urbanized area.

7. Alvin J. Beachy, "Beachy Amish Churches" and Erwin N. Hershberger, "Beachy Congregation," *M.E.*, I (1955), p. 254.

8. Dieter Cunz, *The Maryland Germans: A History* (Princeton, New Jersey: 1948), pp. 417–25 tells the story of the origin and early growth of this Maryland Amish settlement. There are, however, some extravagant statements with reference to Amish customs in Dr. Cunz's discussion.

9. I have discussed all fifteen cases of Amish colonization failures in Pennsylvania, with attention paid to the causes of these failures, in "Extinct Amish Mennonite Communities in Pennsylvania," *The Mennonite Quarterly Review* vol. 30, no. 4 (October, 1956) : 267–76. The best documented case study of Amish community failure in Pennsylvania is Professor John Umble's history of the nineteenth-century Amish colony in Union County. This Buffalo Valley congregation, a few miles northeast of Mifflinburg and northwest of Lewisburg, began in the 1830s and became extinct in the 1880s. Professor Umble's parents were members of this community. *Mennonite Quarterly Review* vol. 7 (1933) : 71–96 and 162–90.

10. Listed in Raber's 1972 *Calender,* p. 35, top of column 2.

11. On the symbolization of Amish cultural differences, see John A. Hostetler, *Amish Society,* ch. 6, "The Symbolic Community."

12. For the sociology of sectarian societies see H. Richard Niebuhr, "Sects," *Encyclopedia of the Social Sciences* vol. 13 (1934) : 624–31 ; Niebuhr, *The Social Sources of Denominationalism* (New York: 1929), Ellsworth Faris, "The Sect and the Sectarian," *The Nature of Human Nature* (New York: 1937), ch. 5, and Elmer T. Clark, *The Small Sects in America* (New York: 1949), especially chaps. 1 and 8.

13. "Ordinance" = "sacrament" as used in liturgical churches. See "Ordinances" and "Sacrament" in *M.E.* IV (1959), pp. 72–3 and 397–8.

14. Harold S. Bender, "Amish Division," *M.E.* I (1955), pp. 90–92. Milton Gascho's "The Amish Division of 1693–1697," in *The Mennonite Quarterly Review* vol. 11 (1937) : 235–66, is the best available discussion of the origin of the Amish, based on primary historical documents, with a full account of Jacob Ammon's activities.

15. B. Stevenson, *The Home Book of Bible Quotations* (New York: 1940), "Idol" and "Image," pp. 215–17.

16. I have stated many of the basic beliefs of the Amish people in "Our Neighbors, and Brothers—The Amish," *Lycoming College Magazine* vol. 24, no. 5 (1971): 28–30. This discussion is in terms of a dialogue with an Old Order Amish minister who outlined "some of our basic beliefs." All Amish beliefs are Anabaptist beliefs and the latter are outlined in Harold S. Bender, "The Anabaptist Vision," *Church History* (March, 1944) and in Franklin H. Littell's *The Anabaptist View of the Church* (Boston: 1958). An especially clear statement is John Horsch, *Mennonites in Europe* (1950), chaps. 33–47.

17. The literature on the central Pennsylvania Amish is not extensive. See *M.E.* III, "Mifflin County" (1957), pp. 683–4 for a brief indication of the groups there in the 1950s. Joseph W. Yoder's *Rosanna of the Amish* (Huntingdon, Pa.: 1940) is an interesting story of Amish life in Big Valley at the turn of this century. Maurice Mook and John Hostetler's "The Amish and Their Land," *Landscape* (Spring, 1957) is entirely based on the Mifflin County Amish. The most recent discussion is Maurice A. Mook, "The 'Big Valley' Amish of Central Pennsylvania: A Community of Cultural Contrasts," *Lycoming College Magazine* vol. 24, no. 5 (May, 1971): 1–5. A large part of the final section of the present paper is based on this article.

## 4

# Alms for Oblivion: The Making of a Black Underclass in Southeastern Pennsylvania, 1780-1860*

## CARL D. OBLINGER

*Carl Oblinger is a graduate of Franklin and Marshall College. He has held a Ford Foundation grant to complete his dissertation on Negro transient groups at Johns Hopkins University.*

George Washington Harvey Scott was a most unfortunate black man. Born and reared a slave with the John Barkley family of Drumore township, Lancaster County, Scott had expected he would be provided with the necessities for a new life upon freedom. He never realized his hopes; in 1830, John Barkley died intestate and his estate, in the confusion of probate, provided nothing for the nineteen-year-old Scott. The now freed man remained on with widow Barkley another three years before he moved to Lancaster City in 1833. There he married, rented a house from Robert Baty, and toiled as a carter for five years in the teeming, narrow streets.

* A Ford Foundation Fellowship in Ethnic Studies made the research for this article possible. I am grateful to Professors David Donald of Johns Hopkins University and David Katzman of the University of Kansas for many helpful suggestions regarding the presentation of my data.

Forced out of business by the Irish in 1837, Scott broke up house-keeping a year later and began a "wandering, roving existence." In and out of prisons and almshouses in southeastern Pennsylvania towns on charges of vagrancy and petty larceny in the 1840s and 1850s, he died in the streets of West Chester in 1859, racked with the pain of catarrh fever.[1]

Like George Scott, Rachel Ann Hinson spent her youth as a slave in New Castle County, Delaware. Freed and married in the same state in the 1830s, Rachel and his husband, John Hinson, worked for and lived with Quaker farmers in the vicinity of West Chester until some misfortune befell them and their three children in the 1850s. After numerous encounters with the constabulary of West Chester in the 1850s, John Hinson was arrested for stealing a horse and wagon in Montgomery County in 1856. He jumped bail and escaped, but Rachel and her three children remained in the custody of the authorities, who eventually sent them back to the Chester County Almshouse, where they had previously been lodged. Rachel tried desperately to keep the children with her, but the Almshouse authorities indentured the two boys and a girl to prosperous and frugal Quaker farmers in Chester and Lancaster County. She apparently never saw her husband and children again; the almshouse authorities buried her in the West Chester Potter's Yard on Union Street in 1866.[2]

These two short vignettes are remarkable for two reasons: they suggest how often blacks in southeastern Pennsylvania between 1800 and 1860 became transient paupers, and they illustrate an almost hidden dimension in the measurement of black vertical mobility in antebellum America. This essay summarizes some findings about the black poor which are part of a larger study of black communities in southeastern Pennsylvania towns during the antebellum period. An examination of the careers of over 15,000 black paupers in Lancaster and Chester counties between 1780 and 1860 furnished data with which to study the black poor, recreate their collective experiences, and determine what forces drove elements of this transient population into poverty.[3]

I

The black poor[4] in antebellum southeastern Pennsylvania were originally recruited from cast-off or disinherited slaves. As slaves became less a symbol of deference and more of an expense in the late colonial and early national periods, many wealthy and influential slave masters cast off or manumitted their bondsmen without making provision for their "victuals and clothing" or without teaching them a trade, as state law and Quaker tradition required.[5] These unfortunate could not secure a decent living. It took a court order in 1810 to persuade James Anderson of Donegal Township, Lancaster County, to provide sustenance for his former slave, Caesar Allen, after the latter had been found "wandering the countryside insensible to all things." Caesar had been free ten years, the court examination detailed, and had survived only because of the "benevolence of Conrad Ziegler in putting him up in the cold months."[6] Much earlier, Mingo, a former slave of William Lewis of Kennett Township, Chester County, was set free when he was no longer able to care for himself. Finding himself "in a starving condition" in November, 1777, the former bondsman appealed for aid and was promptly placed in the East Marlborough Township poor house on a court order.[7] Those not so fortunate as Mingo and Caesar in receiving relief from the County Court cleared a few acres in woodlands on the fringes of settlement and made homes.[8]

The vast majority of black paupers in late eighteenth and early nineteenth century Pennsylvania, however, were runaway slaves and indentured servants.[9] These bondsmen and indentured retainers, who were imported from the upper slave states after 1760 and who worked at milling, tanning, farming, tailoring, brazing, and a variety of other trades,[10] often ran away from their masters to seek their fortunes in the cities and towns of southeastern Pennsylvania and eastern New Jersey. Most found opportunity for employment in the towns closed. One such mulatto runaway was "Black Abraham" Johnston, "about twenty-four years of age, five feet seven or eight inches, well-made," who had been a slave blacksmith in Berks County; caught while returning to his master, he explained to his captors that he was coming back because "chances for my kind of employment" were dim indeed.[11] Most runaways, however, did not return. Charles Berry, a talented black indentured servant belonging to George Brinton of Thornbury Township, Delaware County, between 1790 and 1794, "absconded and eloped many times from his master's service" and was repeatedly recovered only because his master went to "considerable trouble and expense."[12] As most late eighteenth century newspaper advertisements testify, many masters did not go to much trouble or expense to recover their wards and seemed relieved to be rid of their impudent charges.[13] Finding skilled employment closed in the towns and domestic service monopolized by a mulatto elite and not desiring to reindenture themselves, these transients often drifted into the iron communities surrounding the forges and bloomeries which dotted the valleys of early national southeastern Pennsylvania.[14] There they discovered the existence of a unique class of indentured and slave iron workers specifically imported to work at skilled as well as at menial tasks in the charcoal iron industry.[15] In the nineteenth century, however, many of this class of black labor took on the attributes of the transients who joined their communities: they became increasingly mobile, sometimes moving to new jobs as often as six or seven times a year; they found themselves more often employed in the unskilled sectors of the charcoal iron industry rather than the skilled as previously; and, most importantly, they began to shun the exigencies of a settled married life, drawing strength instead from their irregular contacts with fellow transients.[16]

Without steady employment even in marginal jobs, these transients scrounged for a living. The career of Dabbo Ganges, a Negro imported from West Africa in 1808 and manumitted in Chester County in 1816, illustrates how a transient managed to survive in freedom. Like so many of his black contemporaries, Dabbo, upon securing his freedom, drifted among the farmers in southern Chester County hoeing, raking hay, and bleaching linen, and he moved between the iron communities of northern Chester County and lower Berks County chopping wood and driving teams. Despairing of a decent living in the winter months, Dabbo devised an ingenious stratagem for survival. Usually in January, as he found himself without means of support, the pugnacious black would enter a white's house at random, seat himself by the fire or stove, and announce his intentions to break bread and lodge there. More often than not he would receive a decent meal and bedding near the fire for the night. With the depression of 1837, Dabbo stayed with more frequency at the Chester County Almshouse, seldom moving more than a day's distance from there during his forays into the Pennsylvania hinterland.[17] Most black transients were never as fortunate as Dabbo; for a majority their fate lay in the potters' graves or the prisons and workhouses of late eighteenth and early nineteenth century Pennsylvania.[18]

I I

Between 1820 and 1860 wave on wave of freedmen and fugitive slaves from the border slave states poured into southeastern Pennsylvania. These newcomers were ill-equipped to handle the exigencies of migration and the radically changed conditions of freedom. Without friends or kin in Pennsylvania, many died within a few months of arrival.[19] Others merged with the black paupers already in the area to form a transient group that usually moved on every few months.[20]

Though manumitted border state slave groups fared well in antebellum Pennsylvania, individually freed blacks did not.[21] There were peculiar reasons why this was so. Some slaves owned in Maryland and Delaware gained freedom only by agreeing to serve prosperous southeastern Pennsylvania farmers as indentured servants for a limited number of years.[22] Upon fulfilling the terms of their indenture contracts they were abandoned without trade or livelihood. A warrant for the arrest of John Woodward of Philadelphia, issued upon the order of the steward of the Chester County Almshouse in 1841, details the circumstances of one such abandonment. William Reed, born a slave in Delaware, was indentured as a child in 1836 "for victuals, clothes, and schooling" to Woodward when he farmed near Kennett Square, Chester County. Finding a more profitable livelihood in Philadelphia in 1841, Woodward dismissed young William Reed from his service; two months later the directors of the Chester County Poor admitted William Reed to the house of employment.[23] Similarly, James Miller, upon the cognizance of his former master, Jesse Chandler of New Castle County, Delaware, was admitted into the Delaware County (Pennsylvania) House of Employment in June, 1841. Joseph Hannum of Concord Township, Delaware County, had mercilessly exploited Miller for two years but now found he had "no use for the scoundrel."[24] The directors of the poor for Lancaster and Chester counties recorded at least thirty other such cases during the 1830s and 1840s. Most border state freemen migrating to Pennsylvania, however, were never fortunate enough to hold an indenture and usually found employment only intermittently in the Keystone state. Their presence was recorded in the almshouse and death records for the two counties between 1825 and 1858.[25]

Other transients were fugitive slaves from the South Atlantic states who fared much worse in southeastern Pennsylvania than their manumitted contemporaries. Despairing of economic aid and decent living conditions in the towns and rural townships, they either built crude huts on the "Barrens"[26] or joined other transients in boarding houses.[27] Some of them managed to secure employment in intermittent domestic work and day laboring jobs. John Tillman's career typified the experiences of these casual laborers. Absconding from the employ of William Ralphwell of Smyrna, Delaware, and coming to Chester County in 1851, his biographer recorded twenty-five moves in the next ten years. Sometimes he lived alone, and sometimes he kept house with black domestics in the rural townships. Most of his employment was day labor of short duration with Quakers in the townships contiguous to West Chester and Downingtown.[28]

Other fugitives turned to less respectable, but oftentimes more realistic, action for survival. Elijah Yorke, an absconding bondsman from Virginia, stole a set of carpenter's tools in Lancaster City in 1856 in order to "set up his own shop to earn money for bread."[29] Likewise, fugitive John Craig forced his way into a blacksmith shop in West Chester in 1853. As he explained in court testimony: "If they won't employ me, I will get suited with a set of tools to do the job myself."[30] A few turned to organized crime. Most notorious was fugitive "Jimmy" Miller's chicken poaching operation in West Chester.[31] Crime records indicate, however, that most desperate and unemployed fugitives stole only items of wearing apparel, food, and maybe a little wood and coal during the cold winter months.[32]

# I I I

Other transients came from families which had once held positions of relative permanency and status in black communities. When the head of a black family was convicted of a crime, his dependents often became paupers.[33] For instance, the Hinson family, in the process of moving from Chester to Schuylkill County, was stranded in Norristown without transportation. With the prospect of starvation very real, John Hinson stole a horse and wagon "in which to convey his family northward." His subsequent arrest, imprisonment, and escape contributed to the family's disintegration, impoverishment, and also to the eventual death of his wife.[34] Other black working-class families stole food in times of depression. Washington Hannum, after observing his children's deformities caused by malnutrition during the depression of 1837–1838, stole a side of bacon while working in Philadelphia County and was sent to the Eastern Penitentiary for two years. His brother-in-law observed in almshouse testimony that if it were not for the elder Hannum's imprisonment "his family would never have entered the Delaware County Poor House and become wards of the County" in 1840. Washington Hannum never regained his previously enviable reputation and consequently his former level of employment among the straight-laced Quakers in Chester and Delaware counties. Other records show he never reunited with his family.[35]

More black paupers were offspring of families impoverished by the premature death of the head of the household. The death rate for black skilled and semi-skilled men between 1830 and 1860 was high.[36] When the father died young, it was hard, if not impossible, for his sons and daughters to maintain his status.[37] Young sixteen-year-old Sarah Benson found her way to the Philadelphia House of Employment in 1854 after both her parents had died in a cholera epidemic. On examination at the almshouse, Sarah revealed that her father had been a respected head waiter in Philadelphia and a friend of the influential Coates family in Coatesville, to which he commuted on weekends.[38] Both Rosanna Shorter and her mother became paupers in York after Rosanna's father, Adam Shorter—a York County hostler—died in Philadelphia.[39] A most tragic case was that of Francis Anderson, whose father worked steadily as a boatsman on the canal between Reading and Philadelphia in the 1830s. Foreseeing his own impending death (he had an incurable case of tuberculosis), Francis's father arranged with another canal boatsman, James Johnson, for the younger Anderson's care. After the canal froze over the winter after the elder Anderson's death in November of 1842, the parsimonious Johnson discharged Francis. Emmor Kimber, a Quaker, discovered the boy wandering about in Charlestown Township, Chester County, in January of 1843, and promptly sent him to the poor house directors.[40] To be sure, a few working class sons and daughters under employable age were spared impoverishment when their fathers died,[41] but, after 1835, more fell to the fate of Francis Anderson, Rosanna Shorter, and Sarah Benson.

The largest increase in the black poor population consisted of skilled and unskilled workers who were unable to maintain their economic and social position because of competition from white immigrants. The economic expansion in the 1840s and 1850s in the shoe and boot industry in Lancaster and Columbia, in iron and associated trades in Columbia in the 1830s and 1840s, and in light manufacturing in York in the 1840s and 1850s attracted a large influx of Irish and, to a lesser extent, Germans. These newcomers drove blacks out of some craft and building trades and sometimes even out of domestic labor.[42] In Lancaster, Columbia, and West Chester the Irish who moved into the iron trades, building trades, and boot and shoemaking in the 1850s replaced blacks whose families had been a generation in such occupations.[43] The decision of the wealthy mulatto shoemaker, Abraham Shadd, to move to Canada West from West Chester in the 1850s had as much to do with the economic pressure he felt from Irish immigrants as with the persecution he experienced for his abolitionist activities.[44] Less prestigious blacks than the Shadds were forced into poverty. One such man was James Gibson, who had been apprenticed as a paper hanger in York in the 1820s. He had lost his steady employment in the depression of 1837 and, feeling the occupational competition from skilled Irish in the building trades, he abandoned steady work in 1840 and, according to his own statement, "was variously employed in different places for different persons short periods of time following my trade. . . ."[45]

Irish labor pushed many blacks in semi-skilled and unskilled work out of positions they had held over a lifetime. Blacks who had been carters and waiters in the cities of southeastern Pennsylvania, laborers and boatsmen on the canals, and laborers in quarries, were increasingly replaced by Irish workmen in the late 1830s and early 1840s.[46] The case of John Coats, an itinerant black widower, typified the experience of many of these laboring blacks replaced by Irish. "Why with my quarrying job and a good wife," Coats testified to the Chester County Almshouse steward, "I paid twenty-five dollars rent a year, paid taxes, and voted at elections. . . . But I lost my job at the stone quarry on Nemans Creek last Christmas [December, 1841] and I have not worked any since. I got out of money and had to come to the poor house."[47] George Scott was more self-reliant than Coats. Forced out of his carting business in Lancaster City by the competition of the Irish and by the depression of 1837–1838, Scott did not immediately apply to the almshouse for relief. His continuing inability to find steady employment in jobs traditionally reserved for blacks, however, finally forced him, in 1843, to the same expedient as Coats.[48]

Consolidation of craft industries in antebellum Pennsylvania pushed other blacks into pauperism in the 1840s and 1850s. By the 1850s the large merchant manufacturers, who organized production instead of just buying products from craftsmen, who brought together large numbers of journeymen under one roof, who trained new journeymen for special tasks and hired other craftsmen to serve as foreman,[49] dominated the shoe and boot industry in Lancaster and Columbia,[50] the iron and associated trades in Columbia,[51] textiles in Lancaster,[52] brick and carriage making in West Chester,[53] the building industry in Lancaster and York,[54] and small agricultural implement production in York.[55] Black craftsmen could not compete with these new entrepreneurs; to do so they needed capital, mass labor, and an advanced education—items which they were repeatedly denied in southeastern Pennsylvania.[56]

Not being able to compete with the new manufacturing concerns, a large number of black artisans were squeezed out of traditional craft employment.[57] William Smith, a carpenter living in both Philadelphia and West Chester in the antebellum period, was one such artisan. Earning his livelihood in and around Philadelphia between 1821 and 1839, Smith found in the 1830s he could not profitably contract with prospective customers as previously. He was unable to compete with contractors who offered carpentry, paper hanging, bricklaying, and masonry, and could build an entire house more cheaply than Smith. The distressed carpenter could find only occasional small jobs. As his family faced the prospect of impoverishment, Smith grew intemperate and despondent, and he finally left his wife in 1841 at the Chester County Almshouse. He died later the same year.[58] Harriet Thompson told an equally distressing tale when she applied for admission to the almshouse. Her husband, George Thompson, had been a shoemaker in West Chester in the 1850s, but had lost his job with a Mr. Hague in 1858 when his employer could not compete with two other larger West Chester shoe firms.[59]

Even when black craftsmen were able to retain their jobs, they had difficulty in insuring that their sons could follow a skilled trade. In West Chester, for instance, black skilled workers could no longer make apprenticeship agreements for their sons in the mechanical trades—a necessary prerequisite for their son's occupational advancement—because a new group of employers had replaced older, more familiar, white townsmen.[60] These new entrepreneurs, influenced by increased racial prejudice in West Chester, more readily hired Irish transients than black skilled workers. Consequently, the number of blacks working in tailoring, tinsmithing, and blacksmithing in the 1850s was sharply reduced.[61]

## I V

The findings about black pauperization in antebellum, southeastern Pennsylvania confirm what other students of nineteenth century black history have discovered: high rates of black movement into disreputable poverty, especially in the two decades before the Civil War.[62] The importance of this study is that by tracing the careers of thousands of black transients it has measured the magnitude of that downward pressure and attempted to locate the forces which pushed black men and women into poverty in two antebellum Pennsylvania counties. Important differences probably existed in the number of black poor in southeastern Pennsylvania and in other areas of the antebellum North. Chester and Lancaster Counties bordered two slave states which sent large numbers of impoverished fugitives and freemen across the state line in the 1840s and 1850s. But it is apparent that historians cannot now ignore the tragic experiences of these transient and downwardly mobile men and women [when measuring black vertical mobility], especially when the black poor in southeastern Pennsylvania annually comprised a fourth of the black workers during the two decades before the Civil War.

*Table 1:* The Black Poor as a Percent of the Total Black Population in Lancaster and Chester Counties, Pennsylvania, for Select Years, 1790–1860

| Years | White Population [a] | Total Black Population [b] | Black Poor [c] | Percent of Black Total as Poor |
|-------|------------------|------------------------|-------------|-------------------------------|
| 1790 | 62,501 | 1,583 | — | — |
| 1800 | 73,341 | 2,301 | 146 | 6.8% |
| 1810 | 90,101 | 3,865 | 443 | 11.5% |
| 1820 | 107,479 | 5,872 | 904 | 15.6% |
| 1830 | 121,997 | 6,684 | 1140 | 17.1% |
| 1840 | 134,572 | 8,900 | 1754 | 19.5% |
| 1850 | 156,545 | 11,930 d | 3093 | 25.9% |
| 1860 | 181,525 | 11,168 d | 1802 | 16.1% |

a. Computed from the *Heads of Families at the First Census of the United States, taken in the year 1790: Pennsylvania*, p. 45; Original Returns of the Assistant Marshals for Lancaster and Chester Counties. Second United States Census (1800); *United States Census, Persons within the United States in 1810* . . . , pp. 37, 37 a; *Census for 1820, Published by Authorization of an Act of Congress*, pp. 18, 18*, 20*; Original Returns of the Assistant Marshals, schedules for Lancaster and Chester Counties. Fifth United States Census (1830); Department of State, *Compendium of the Enumeration of the Inhabitants and Statistics of the United States (1840)* (Washington: Thomas Allen, 1841), pp. 24–25; J. D. B. DeBow, Superintendent of the United States Census, *Compendium of the Seventh Census* (1850), pp. 166, 167, 296–297; Joseph C. G. Kennedy, *Population of the United States in 1860; Compiled from the Original Returns of the Eighth Census* (Washington: Government Printing Office, 1864), pp. 419, 426, 438.

b. Computed by adding the black population reported in the United States Censuses to the Negroes from the Black Poor Column.

c. Computed from the Admissions, Admissions and Examinations Books, and Hospital Reports of Lancaster and Chester County Almshouses, 1800–1860; vagrancy reports, 1800–1860; Prison Admissions and Discharge Books, 1800–1860; and, criminal indictments, 1800–1860 for Lancaster and Chester Counties.

d. In 1850 and 1860, a household enumeration by the United States Census enabled me to determine if the black poor appearing in Column C were also recorded in the United States Census. A 10% random sample check (circa 489 individuals) revealed that less than 5% of my sample (24 blacks) appeared in the 1850 and 1860 Census.

*Table II:* The Sources of Black Poverty in Antebellum Southeastern Pennsylvania: An Estimate of the Number and Percent of the Black Poor Recruited from Selected Categories by Decade, 1800–1860

|  | 1800–1810 | 1811–1820 | 1821–1830 | 1831–1840 | 1841–1850 | 1851–1860 |
|---|---|---|---|---|---|---|
| Total No. of Black Poor by Decade [a] | 438 | 1,491 | 2,582 | 3,413 | 5,134 | 4,328 |
| Pennsylvania Slaves and Indentured Servants | 375 | 500 | 800 | 800 | 500 | 300 |
|  | 85.6% | 33% | 31% | 24% | 10% | 7% |
| Freedmen from Border States | 13 | 300 | 500 | 700 | 1,000 | 1,200 |
|  | 2.9% | 20% | 19% | 21% | 20% | 27% |

| | | | | | | |
|---|---|---|---|---|---|---|
| Fugitive Border State Slaves | 40 | 200 | 400 | 600 | 1,000 | 500 |
| | 9.1% | 13% | 15% | 17% | 20% | 11% |
| Families of Imprisoned Slaves | 10 | 50 | 100 | 200 | 300 | 300 |
| | 2.4% | 3% | 4% | 6% | 6% | 7% |
| Families Impoverished by Head's Death | — | 450 | 800 | 800 | 1,000 | 1,000 |
| | | 30% | 31% | 24% | 20% | 23% |
| Downward Mobility— Irish and German Migration | — | — | — | 300 | 1,000 | 800 |
| | | | | 8% | 20% | 18% |
| Downward Mobility— Consolidation of Craft Industry [b] | — | — | — | — | 200 | 300 |
| | | | | | 4% | 7% |

a. Computed from the Admissions, Admissions and Examinations Books, and Hospital Reports of Lancaster and Chester County Almshouses, 1800–1860; vagrancy reports, 1800–1860; Prison Admissions and Discharge Books, 1800–1860; and, criminal indictments, 1800–1860 for Lancaster and Chester Counties. These figures include all black poor who appeared at least once in these records during the decade. The other figures are only rough estimates based upon examination reports of Chester and Lancaster Almshouses.

b. The totals for the 1840s and 1850s include blacks migrating to Chester and Lancaster Counties from Philadelphia who had experienced downward mobility.

*Table III:* Number and Percent of Black Workers in Occupations, 1850–1860—Southeastern Pennsylvania Towns[a]

| | Columbia Borough | |
|---|---|---|
| Occupation | 1850 | 1860 |
| Professions | | |
| Teacher | — | 1 |
| Clergyman | — | 1 |
| Total | — | 2 (1.2%) |
| Proprietors | | |
| Lumber Merchants | 2 | 2 |
| Shopkeeper | — | 3 |
| Total | 2 (1.0%) | 5 (2.9%) |

| White Collar | | |
|---|---|---|
| Railroad Car Agent | 2 | — |
| Conductor | — | 1 |
| Clerk | 1 | 1 |
| Hotel Host | — | 1 |
| Total | 3 (1.3%) | 3 (1.7%) |
| **Building Trades** | | |
| Brickmolder | 1 | — |
| Plasterer | 1 | — |
| Total | 2 (1.0%) | — |
| **Mechanics** | | |
| Blacksmith | 1 | 1 |
| Forgeman | — | 1 |
| Total | 1 (.5%) | 2 (1.2%) |
| **Service** | | |
| Barber | 10 | 7 |
| Shoemaker | 8 | — |
| Waiter | 2 | — |
| Total | 20 (8.9%) | 7 (4.0%) |
| **Unskilled** | | |
| Huckster | 2 | — |
| Gardener | 2 | — |
| Porter, Carter | 2 | 2 |
| Servant | — | 2 |
| Day Laborer | 191 | 150 |
| Total | 197 (86.6%) | 154 (88.5%) |

| | Lancaster City | |
|---|---|---|
| Occupation | 1850 | 1860 |
| **Professional** | | |
| Doctor | — | 1 |
| Clergyman | 2 | 2 |
| Total | 2 (4.4%) | 3 (5.4%) |
| **Proprietors** | | |
| Confectioner | 2 | — |
| Total | 2 (4.4%) | — |

White  Collar
   Railroad  Car  Agent — 1
                                   —

| | 1850 | 1860 |
|---|---|---|
| **White Collar** | | |
| Railroad Car Agent | — | 1 |
| Total | — | 1 (1.8%) |
| **Mechanics** | | |
| Coppersmith | 2 | — |
| Forgeman | 1 | 1 |
| Total | 3 (6.7%) | 1 (1.8%) |
| **Service** | | |
| Barber | 10 | 8 |
| Baker | — | 1 |
| Waiter | 2 | 1 |
| Coachman | 1 | 1 |
| Total | 13 (28.9%) | 11 (19.6%) |
| **Unskilled** | | |
| Gardener | — | 2 |
| Factory Hand | — | 1 |
| Day Laborer | 25 | 36 |
| Total | 25 (55.6%) | 39 (69.6%) |

| | West Chester | |
|---|---|---|
| Occupation | 1850· | 1860 |
| **Professions** | | |
| Clergyman | 1 | 1 |
| Gentleman | — | 1 |
| Total | 1 (1.0%) | 2 (1.4%) |
| **Proprietors** | | |
| Master Blacksmith | — | 1 |
| Confectioner | 1 | — |
| Oysterman | 3 | 2 |
| Total | 4 (3.6%) | 3 (2.1%) |
| **Building Trades** | | |
| Brickmaker | 1 | 3 |
| Total | 1 (1.0%) | 3 (2.1%) |
| **Mechanics** | | |
| Cooper | 1 | — |
| Blacksmith | 1 | 1 |
| Total | 2 (1.8%) | 1 (.7%) |

| Service | | |
|---|---|---|
| Barber | 2 | **3** |
| Shoemaker | 3 | **4** |
| Waiter | 7 | **3** |
| | ——— | ——— |
| Total | 12 (10.9%) | 10 (7.0%) |
| Apprentices [b] | | |
| Shoemaker | — | **1** |
| Tobacconist | — | **1** |
| Barber | — | **2** |
| | | ——— |
| Total | — | 4 (2.8%) |
| Unskilled | | |
| Carter, teamster | 2 | — |
| Huckster, trader | 3 | **1** |
| Hostler | — | **1** |
| Railroad porter | — | **1** |
| Servant, domestic | — | **2** |
| Farm laborer | — | **2** |
| Day laborer | 85 | **113** |
| | ——— | ——— |
| Total | 90 (81.8%) | 120 (83.9%) |

a. Computed from the Original Returns of the Assistant Marshals. Seventh Census of the United States: 1850. National Archives, Washington, D.C.; and Original Returns of the Assistant Marshals. Eighth Census of the United States: 1860. National Archives, Washington, D.C.

b. The United States Census MSS. population schedules did not record apprentices for West Chester in 1850.

*Table IV:* Comparative Occupational Mobility in Three Pennsylvania Towns, 1850–1860 [a]

Lancaster City—Manual Laborers

| 1850–1860 | Irish | Negroes |
|---|---|---|
| Upward mobility to white collar or above | 1.0% | — |
| Upward mobility within manual class (i.e. from unskilled or semiskilled to skilled) | 9.0% | 4.2% |
| No significant mobility | 90% | 83.3% |

Downward mobility within
manual class (i.e. from skilled to
semiskilled or unskilled)                    —              12.5%

|        | Number in Sample | 101  | 24   |
|--------|------------------|------|------|
| Total  | Percent          | 100% | 100% |

### Columbia—Manual Laborers

| 1850–1860 | Irish | Negroes |
|-----------|-------|---------|

Upward mobility to white
collar or above                      —              —

Upward mobility within manual
class (i.e. from unskilled or
semiskilled to skilled)            11.1%            2.8%

No significant mobility            88.9%            88.7%

Downward mobility within manual
class (i.e. from skilled to
semiskilled or unskilled)            —              8.5%

|        | Number in Sample | 54   | 71   |
|--------|------------------|------|------|
| Total  | Percent          | 100% | 100% |

### West Chester—Manual Laborers

| 1850–1860 | Native Whites | Immigrants[b] | Negroes |
|-----------|---------------|---------------|---------|

Upward mobility to white
collar or above                    22%            16.7%            —

Upward mobility within
manual class (i.e. from
unskilled or semi-skilled
to skilled)                         7%             5.6%            3.4%

No significant mobility            59%            64.8%           69.5%

Downward mobility within
manual class (i.e. from
skilled to semi-skilled
or unskilled)                       7%              —             6.8%

| | | | |
|---|---|---|---|
| Downward mobility from manual class to pauper class (i.e. from self-dependence to public support and vagrancy) | 5% | 12.9% | 20.3% |
| Number in Sample | 100 | 54 | 59 |
| Total     Percent | 100% | 100% | 100% |

a. Computed from the Original Returns of the Assistant Marshals. Seventh Census of the United States: 1850; Original Returns of the Assistant Marshals. Eighth Census of the United States: 1860. National Archives, Washington, D.C.

b. Includes German and Irish. There were too few Irish in West Chester for comparative purposes in the 1850s. Most upwardly mobile immigrants were German.

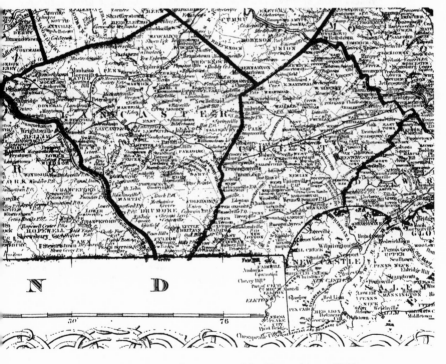

Lancaster and Chester Counties, with Townships, 1868.
From Colton's New Townships map of Pennsylvania, 1868.

## NOTES

1. I pieced together George Scott's life from copies of letters sent to the Chester County Almshouse in the Lancaster County Poor House Correspondence Book, entries for August 9 and 26, 1858, located in the basement of Conestoga View, the Home of Relief, Lancaster, Pennsylvania; Lancaster County Prison Admissions and Discharges Book, entries for March 3, 1854, March 31, 1856, August 18, 1857, and April 18, 1858, located at the Lancaster County Historical Society, Lancaster, Pennsylvania; Henry Fleming (Justice of the Peace), Docket Book, entry for May 9, 1857, Chester County Historical Society, West Chester, Pennsylvania (hereafter cited as C.C.H.S.); and, Chester County Public Offices, Coroner's Office, Inquisitions (all years), notations for March 13, 1859, File Box 12, Shelf 2, Cabinet B, C.C.H.S. (In this note, as in those that follow, the citations are to representative selections. I have made no attempt to exhaust the possible examples that might be cited.)

Blacks born of slave mothers could be held in bondage after 1780 only until they were twenty-eight years of age. See Stanley Kutler, "Pennsylvania Courts, the Abolition Act and Negro Rights," *Pennsylvania History* XXX (January, 1963), 14–27.

2. I pieced together Rachel Hinson's life from a page of "convicted for crime" inserted into the Original Returns of the Assistant Marshals, Schedules for West Chester, Seventh U. S. Census (1850), tabular returns located at C.C.H.S.; letters received at the Chester County Almshouse at Marshalton, Almshouse Folder, entries for May 13, 1856 (from Cockranville), May 10, 1856 (from Wilmington, Delaware), August 29, 1856 (Schuylkill Haven), March 12, 1856 (West Chester), March 4, 1856 (Cockranville), August 28, 1858 (Reading), and December 22, 1858 (Lancaster); and Chester County, Public Offices, Coroner, Pauper's Inquisitions (1841, 1849, 1866), entry for June 8, 1866, Folder 92, Shelf 4, Cabinet B, C.C.H.S.

3. The 15,000 represent the total population of black poor in Lancaster and Chester counties between 1780 and 1860 recorded in the two counties' Quarter Sessions Court Records (criminal court proceedings), coroner's inquests, vagrancy reports, newspaper descriptions, the United States Census, MSS. population schedules, 1790–1860, and poor house and prison records. Especially helpful have been the admissions and discharge books for the Chester and Lancaster County Almshouses, which recorded the name, age, sex, and dates of entrance and discharge for the black poor, and which enabled me to ascertain the approximate dates black paupers resided in the two counties and the reasons many found themselves in poverty. Very few of the black poor that I found in these records could be located in the manuscript population schedules of the United States Census. In Table I, I have tabulated the proportion of the total black population in Lancaster and Chester Counties that was in poverty between 1800 and 1860 and how this number varied over the sixty-year period. Table II suggests what percent of this total black poor population come from each of the various sources that I describe in this essay. I am well aware that the records of these inarticulate have limitations as well as strengths. See Carl Oblinger, "Like an Iron Fist: Black Communities in Southeastern Pennsylvania Towns, 1780–1860," (forthcoming Ph.D. dissertation, Department of History, Johns Hopkins University), Appendix A for a critical discussion of the sources used in this essay.

4. I have used the terms disreputable poor, poor, indigents, paupers, and transients interchangeably in this essay to connote the group of people at the bottom of the black social structure in southeastern Pennsylvania who were cut off from the more geographically and occupationally stable black community members by the insurmountable barriers of class interests and perceptions. For an excellent description of disreputable poverty in a comparative context see David Matza, "The Disreputable Poor" in *Social Structure and Mobility in Economic Development,* eds. Neil Smelser and Seymour M. Lipset (Chicago: 1966), pp. 310–339. This article correctly emphasizes the distinction between working and lower-class culture, a distinction which I use here and in my forthcoming dissertation, "Like an Iron Fist."

5. Most recorded manumissions occurred in the eighteenth century, while slave masters in the early nineteenth century usually abandoned their bondsmen without recording their freedom.

For those manumitted in the eighteenth century, see the fifty-one recorded manumissions in the Miscellaneous Deed Book (grantors) 1688–1852 and (grantee), 1688–1852, Chester County Clerk of the Courts Office, Chester County Court House, West Chester, Pennsylvania; the two folders of Pennsylvania Supreme Court Arbitrations on Negro slavery in Records of the Supreme and Superior Courts, 1799–1965, Record Group 33, Division of Public Records, Pennsylvania Historical and Museum Commission, Harrisburg, Pennsylvania; and the bundle of Habeas Corpus Papers on Negro Slavery, Prothonotary's Attic Vault, York County Court House, York, Pennsylvania. Of the twenty-five slaves whose manumissions were recorded with the Bradford Monthly Meeting between 1777 and 1783, only a few were provided with adequate "victuals and clothing." See Bradford Monthly Meeting Minutes, 1765–1800, *passim,* C.C.H.S. For a comparison of late eighteenth century manumission practices with those of the period between 1720 and 1758 in Pennsylvania, see Alan Tully, "Patterns of Slaveholding in Rural Southeastern Pennsylvania, 1720–1758" which appeared in the Fall 1972 issue of the *Journal of Social History.*

For abandoned bondsmen in the nineteenth century see the entries in the Chester County Almshouse Admissions Book, 1800–1826, for "Negro Phillis, who died," July 20, 1801; William Vanleer, "a lame Negro servant," who died April 1, 1807; Theopolis Ganges, "a blind Negro . . . who went to his old master," September 11, 1807; Shadrack Cole, April 13, 1816; and especially Exeter, "a very old slave of Custis Grubb," who died May 20, 1827.

6. See the Minutes of the Directors of the Lancaster County Poor (hereafter cited as Lancaster Poor Minutes), 1798–1826, entries for July 2 and October 1, 1810, located at the Lancaster County Historical Society, Lancaster, Pennsylvania. For another case of a slave abandoned by his master, see Lancaster Poor Minutes, entry for January 7, 1811 (Negro Poll Brinton).

7. "To The Overseers of the . . . ," Slavery File (1770–1779), C.C.H.S. For the cases of those freed earlier see "Negro Jack," Slavery File (1780–1799), C.C.H.S., and especially the case of "Negro Daniel," indentured "against his voluntary and free will," Historical Society of Berks County, MSS. 1790–A (June 1, 1790), as well as the fragments recorded in the material of *supra,* footnote 5.

8. "Redemptioners," Newspaper Clipping File, May 9, 1929, C.C.H.S.; and notes taken during an interview with Mrs. Robert Cummins of Villanova, December 13, 1971, on the careers of Humphrey Marshall's slaves, freed in 1805.

9. See Table II for an estimate of the number of black poor in Pennsylvania who had been indentured servants and slaves.

10. For evidence on the occupational skills of this class of slaves and their number, see Darold D. Wax, "Negro Imports into Pennsylvania," *Pennsylvania History* XXXII (1965) : 256–257, and "The Demand for Slave Labor in Colonial Pennsylvania," *ibid.* XXXIV (1967) : 339–340; Chesman A. Merrick, *White Servitude in Pennsylvania* (Philadelphia: 1926), pp. 74, 94; and Tully, "Patterns of Slaveholding," p. 16.

An idea of the fluid exchange of slaves and indentured servants occurring between Maryland and Pennsylvania may be gained by examining the bills of sale for slaves and black indentured servants made in York, Lancaster, and Chester counties, Pennsylvania, and Cecil, Harford, and Baltimore counties, Maryland, 1760–1800. Alexander, John, and Robert Galbreath of York County were particularly active in the black indentured trade, buying Maryland slaves' time and reselling them to prosperous gentlemen in York Town. See York County Deed Book 2X, 322, 351, 386 and Deed Book 2Y, 208, 213, 307.

11. *The Weekly Advertiser* (Reading, Pennsylvania), June 9, 1798.

12. Petition of George Brinton before the Court, Micajah Speakman and Caleb Peirce presiding (witnessed February 5, 1793) Slavery File, 1780–1799, C.C.H.S.

13. This conclusion is based upon the data in Darold D. Wax, "The Slave Trade in Colonial Pennsylvania" (unpublished Ph.D. dissertation, Department of History, University of Washington, 1969), *passim;* and my analysis of some 450 runaway slave and indentured servant advertisements in the *Pennsylvania Herald and York General Advertiser,* 1781–1800, the Lancaster *Journal,* 1794–1802, *The Weekly Advertiser* (Reading), 1790–1800, and the *Pennsylvania Gazette* (Philadelphia), 1779–1800. State law required the master to advertise; consequently, about half of the nearly 400 masters offered only a pence or a few cents for the return of their slaves and indentured servants.

14. See George Homan's article in the Philadelphia *Sunday Inquirer* magazine *Sunday Today,* p. 26, for September 24, 1966.

15. For information on this class of slaves, see Joseph E. Walker's pioneering works: "Negro Labor in the Charcoal Iron Industry of Southeastern Pennsylvania," *Pennsylvania Magazine of History and Biography* (hereafter cited as P.M.H.B.) XCII (1969) : 466–487; "A Comparison of Negro and White Labor in a Charcoal Iron Community," *Labor History* X (1969) : 487–497; and *Hopewell Village: A Social and Economic History of an Iron Community* (Philadelphia: 1966). Also see Tully, "Patterns of Slaveholding," p. 16; Wax, "The Demand for Slave Labor," pp. 342–345; Franklin Ellis and Samuel Evans, *History of Lancaster County, Pennsylvania* . . . (Philadelphia: 1883), p. 71; H. H. Hain, comp., *History of Perry County, Pennsylvania* (Harrisburg, Pennsylvania: 1922) p. 271; and especially the notations on Adam Solomon, a free Negro who worked at the Nanticoke Iron Works, Kent County, Delaware, and migrated to work at "a particular iron works in Lancaster County," in the Papers of Adam Solomon, 1767–1769, the John Pemberton Collection, MSS. 1036, Quaker Collection, Haverford College Library, Haverford, Pennsylvania.

16. This conclusion is based upon my analysis of data on 412 black iron laborers at Hopewell Forge, Codorus Forge, and Cornwall Furnace between 1791 and 1852. I borrowed the material on Hopewell Forge from

Professor Joseph E. Walker of Millersville State College, Millersville, Pennsylvania. His records are based in turn on the excellent Source Material Collections, which are organized into record groups at Hopewell Village National Historical Headquarters, Berks County, Pennsylvania. Material on Codorus Forge is located in the Business Records Collection, Division of Public Records, Pennsylvania Historical and Museum Commission, Harrisburg, Pennsylvania, and for Codorus Forge, Hopewell Forge, and Cornwall Furnace in the voluminous (89 volumes) Grubb Furnace and Forge Account Books, 1765–1880, at the Historical Society of Pennsylvania, Philadelphia, Pennsylvania.

Some dependents of these black iron workers found their way to the Lancaster and Chester County Poor Houses. See, for example, the experiences of Mary Ann and Betsy Morris, both of whom died at the Chester County Poor House in the winter of 1826. Mary Ann's ex-husband, Job Martin, had been employed at Ringwood Forge, West Fallowfield Township, Chester County. See the Chester County Almshouse Admissions Book, entries for February 21, 1826, and March 10, 1826, C.C.H.S.

17. See the extensive item on "Dabbo" in *Kennett Advance* (Kennett Square, Pennsylvania), October 8, 1892. Confirmation of the details in this newspaper reminiscence may be found in the Chester County Almshouse Admissions Book, entries for February 8, 1817; June 11, 1818; December 1, 1823; March 11, 1824; and, February 24, 1838.

18. This conclusion is based upon the Uwchlan Friends Observation Minutes of 113 Freedmen living in Chester County between 1777 and 1803, Slavery File, Miscellaneous Papers, C.C.H.S.; the miscellaneous entries recording the death of freemen in the Chester County Almshouse Admissions Book, 1800–1826, *passim;* and the nearly 400 coroner's inquest papers stored in Cabinet B, C.C.H.S. An informative article on the colonial potters field in Germantown, Pennsylvania, which served as a burial place for all "strange Negroes and Mulattoes as die in any part of Germantown forever," is Townsend Ward, "The Germantown Road and Its Associations," *P.M.H.B.* VI (1882) : 131ff.

19. Many contemporary observers noted the high death rate and poor health of fugitives fresh from slavery. The most descriptive accounts are: the report in the *Liberator,* II (April 7, 1832), p. 55; the commentary in coroner's inquest reports for Lancaster and Chester counties; the memoirs of Judge J. J. Lewis of West Chester, Pennsylvania, located in the Miscellaneous Papers, Slavery File, C.C.H.S.; and especially Judge Isaac Darlington's Docket Book located at C.C.H.S., which records the examinations and testimony of hundreds of fugitive slaves, 1821–1839.

20. This merger was inevitable, for to survive, these fugitives and freemen—untutored in the traditions of disreputable poverty—had to adjust to their degraded condition and adopt new habits of work, sex, and family living. For the theory behind this influence see Matza, "The Disreputable Poor."

21. I traced a sample of one hundred border state freemen drawn from the Chester, Lancaster, Cumberland, and Philadelphia County Almshouse records from the date of their entry into Pennsylvania until their death. I supplemented these records, when possible, with the unusually detailed state vital statistics register, 1852–1855, for Lancaster and Chester counties; the United States Census, MSS. population schedules for Pennsylvania, 1850 and 1860, located at the National Archives, Washington, D.C.; and writs of

Habeas Corpus, Freedmen, in the Records of the Supreme and Superior Courts, Record Group 33, Division of Public Records, Pennsylvania Historical and Museum Commission, Harrisburg, Pennsylvania, to note the condition, occupation, and wealth of these manumitted slaves.

Though some manumitted slaves not migrating in cohesive groups fared quite well and were often incorporated into existing black community structures, most were not. Especially revealing is the testimony of Jane Brittanham, a freed slave from New Castle County, Delaware, in Chester County Admission and Examinations, 1843, pp. 7–8, C.C.H.S.

22. For information on the expanding and quite lucrative practice of indenturing Delaware and Maryland bondsmen in Pennsylvania, see the indenture records in Henry Fleming's Record of Marriage Book, C.C.H.S.; the legal cases in the Reah Frazer Papers, Box 12, Division of Public Records, Pennsylvania Historical and Museum Commission, Harrisburg (hereafter cited as Pennsylvania Historical Commission); and the deeds of William Bell of Reading, Pennsylvania, in Deed Books 15–554, 18–408, 22–468, and 30–676 in the Recorder of Deeds Office, Berks County Court House, Reading, Pennsylvania.

23. For details in the case, see the Chester County Almshouse Admissions and Examinations Book (hereafter cited as Chester County Examinations), entry for November 8, 1841, p. 10a, C.C.H.S.

24. James Miller's examination details how Joseph Hannum exploited him. See Chester County Examinations, entry for June 4, 1841, pp. 4–5a, C.C.H.S.

25. In the sample of 100, seventy-eight freemen from Maryland, Delaware, and upper Virginia never held an indenture and worked irregularly.

There are dangers in making an analysis based upon samples of freemen drawn from the almshouse records. Undoubtedly, these records tell us only about those free blacks who never required upward social mobility; the more successful were not in prisons or charity homes. I have, however, not relied on almshouse reports alone; in my larger study of five southeastern Pennsylvania towns, I have found nearly 700 border state freemen, all of whom had experiences similar to my sample of 100.

26. The "Barrens" were areas in southern Chester, Lancaster, and York counties which colonial inhabitants denuded of forest and rendered almost uninhabitable by wasteful farming practices.

27. Again I traced a sample of a hundred fugitives from the Chester, Lancaster, Cumberland, and Philadelphia almshouse records in order to determine their occupational and living experiences in antebellum Pennsylvania. Where possible, I learned who their slave masters had been from Judge Isaac Darlington's Docket Book, C.C.H.S.; from the court testimony in the Reah Frazer Papers, Boxes 9, 18, Pennsylvania Historical Commission; and the legal cases in the Papers of Jasper Yeates (a former Lancaster City jurist) *passim,* Historical Society of Pennsylvania.

The steward of the Chester County Almshouse recorded the presence of twenty-one fugitives in Chester County between 1806 and 1813. The bulk of my sample, however, appeared in the records during the 1830s and 1840s, with very few recorded in the 1850s (see Table II). Most migrated from neighboring New Castle County, Delaware, and Cecil, Harford, and Frederick counties Maryland. Again my larger study indicates that other fugitive slaves from the border states fared as poorly as my sample group in southeastern Pennsylvania.

28. See Charles H. Tillman, *Biographical Sketch of the Life and Travels of John W. Tillman, by his Son* (West Chester, Pennsylvania: Horace F. Temple, Printer, 1896).

Similar living and job experiences are recorded for fugitives sojourning in Columbia in a series of articles run by the Columbia *Herald* between 1903 and 1905, which are held by the Lancaster County historian, John W. W. Loose.

29. Indictment and conviction papers of Elijah Yorke, recorded December 6, 1856, and filed among the miscellaneous papers piled in the basement of Conestoga View, Lancaster, Pennsylvania.

30. Examination of John Craig at West Chester, July 9, 1853, Chester County Crime Folder, C.C.H.S.

31. Examination of James Miller at West Chester, August 10, 1856, Chester County Crime Folder, C.C.H.S.

32. The wording of the arrest papers is most revealing. In West Chester in 1853, Charles Hercules stole two pairs of "crude boots" from John Gladman; Henry Smith "stole a shirt of Soloman [sic] Cooper," William Smith stole clothes out of an old trunk belonging to James Baugh, and Peter Brown stole a buffalo robe for the winter months." See Chester County Crime Folder, *passim,* C.C.H.S.

33. The bulk of the Chester County prison records were unavailable when I wrote this essay; consequently, I have at present, little information on the families of convicted black criminals. I very seldom had the good fortune to find notations in the almshouse admission book columns as I did for Rebecca and "her child Elizabeth" Reed, "in the almshouse because her husband was convicted of murder." See Chester County Almshouse Admissions Book, 1800–1826, entry for December 25, 1821, C.C.H.S.

34. See especially the letter from the Director of the Almshouse, Schuylkill Haven, Pennsylvania, to the steward of the Chester County Almshouse, August 29, 1856, Chester County Almshouse Folder, C.C.H.S.

35. Chester County Examinations, entry for September 20, 1841, pp. 8–9a, C.C.H.S.

36. This generalization is based upon an analysis by occupation of the 155 death certificates in the Commonwealth of Pennsylvania Vital Statistics, Chester County, 1852–1854, Cabinet B, C.C.H.S.; the Records of 147 Cases of Diseases in the Chester County Almshouse, 1841–1842, entered in the Miscellaneous Hospital Book, Cabinet B, C.C.H.S.; and the reports of a midwife in the Lancaster *Intelligencer,* June 1, 1861.

37. A father's death made it especially hard for a black working class girl to move in the "right" circles, to avail herself of the opportunity to meet a suitable spouse, and thus to maintain her previous level of living. Sons of deceased working class fathers usually had a better opportunity to find work and thus maintain their families' previous economic and social position.

38. Testimony of Sarah Benson, taken at the Philadelphia Almshouse and included in the correspondence in the Chester County Almshouse Folder, 1854, C.C.H.S.

39. York County Poor House Book, entry for May 28, 1839, located at the Historical Society of York County, York, Pennsylvania.

40. This case is a particularly good example of the crucial importance of a father's presence in insuring his family's well-being. See Chester County Examinations, January 26, 1843, pp. 23–24.

41. Some black working class families who suffered the loss of a father

used the almshouse as a base in their fight to recover lost status in the black community. Eventually a few such families were able to lift themselves out of poverty either through remarriage or through a shrewd indenture contract made for a son with one of the elite blacks. Particuraly good data exists on the extraordinary efforts of the Derry family in West Chester in the 1850s in the Chester County Admissions and Discharge Book, 1843–1861, *passim,* C.C.H.S.

42. Solitary black entrepreneurs or black artisans employing a helper were particularly hard-pressed by foreign competition in shoemaking, tailoring, blacksmithing, coppersmithing, and especially in carpentry and paperhanging in these three southeastern Pennsylvania cities.

43. In West Chester, the apprentices in skilled labor were increasingly drawn from Irish and German stock rather than, as previously, from Negroes. Especially revealing for the situation in Lancaster and Columbia are the detailed accounts on investment, number of employed, and value of annual productions of each business in the manufacturing schedules of the United States Census. Between 1850 and 1860, black artisans in both towns suffered reverses in the value of their annual production and investment, being replaced for the most part by German tinsmiths, blacksmiths, shoemakers, and chairmakers in Lancaster and Irish shoemakers and blacksmiths in Columbia.

I base my analysis of the contractions in job opportunities in the black skilled trades for West Chester on the indenture contracts placed in Henry Fleming's Record of Marriage Book, C.C.H.S.; and for Lancaster and Columbia on the microfilm copy of the United States Census, MSS. Manufacturing Returns, 1850, the National Archives, Washington, D.C. For statistical tables comparing Irish and black job mobility in Columbia and Lancaster City in the 1850s see Table IV.

44. Compare the report on the Shadd family in Canada in the West Chester *Village Record,* July 6, 1852, with the reports on the Shadd family activities in Benjamin Quarles, *Black Abolitionists* (New York: 1969), *passim.*

45. York County Poor House Book, entries for August 5, 1841, and August 12, 1841, Historical Society of York County, York, Pennsylvania. Compare this account with the experience of an Irish carpenter, who, in 1852, "began to build for himself" in West Chester in George Morris Philips, "An Account of Twenty-One Citizens of West Chester, Pennsylvania . . . ," p. 10, MSS. filed at the Eleutherian Mills Historical Library, Greenville, Delaware.

46. Based on an analysis of the Chester and Lancaster County Almshouse admission books, entries for the years 1837 to 1845.

47. Examination of John Coats, Chester County Examinations, 1841–1851, p. 5, C.C.H.S. Supplementary pauper testimony indicates that the Irish had moved into the quarrying jobs on Nemans Creek as elsewhere.

48. See *supra,* footnote 1.

49. See Stuart Blumin's excellent analysis of this trend in "Mobility and Change in Ante-Bellum Philadelphia," in *Nineteenth Century Cities: Essays in the New Urban History,* eds. Stephan Thernstrom and Richard Sennett (New Haven, Connecticut: 1969), pp. 200–206. For the rise of the merchant manufacturer see John R. Common's pioneering piece, "American Shoemakers, 1648–1895," *Quarterly Journal of Economics* XXIV (1909): 39–84; and George R. Taylor, *The Transportation Revolution, 1815–1860* (New York: 1940).

50. Carlton O. Wittlinger, "Early Manufacturing in Lancaster County:

1710–1840," *Journal of the Lancaster County Historical Society* LXII, no. I (January, 1958):1–38.

51. John W. W. Loose, "The Anthracite Iron Industry of Lancaster County, Pennsylvania: 1840–1900" (unpublished M.A. thesis, Department of Education, Millersville State College, 1967).

52. Wittlinger, "Early Manufacturing, 1710–1840," pp. 1–38; and the United States Census, 1850, MSS. manufacturing schedule for Lancaster City, which notes that two large textile plants in the Southwest Ward of Lancaster employed 447 men and 602 women in 1850.

53. Original Returns of the Assistant Marshal, Schedules for West Chester, Seventh United States Census (1850). MSS. copy on deposit at C.C.H.S.

54. Original Returns of the Assistant Marshal, Schedules for York, Seventh U. S. Census (1850), microfilm copy located at the Historical Society of York County, York, Pennsylvania; Original Returns of the Assistant Marshal, Schedules for Lancaster, Seventh U. S. Census (1850) microfilm copy located at the Lancaster County Historical Society, Lancaster, Pennsylvania.

55. See especially the excellent description in George R. Prowell, *History of York County, Pennsylvania* 2 vols. (Chicago: 1907), I, pp. 760–762.

56. See the commentary in Sam B. Warner, "If All the World Were Philadelphia: A Scaffolding for Urban History, 1774–1930," *American Historical Review* XXIV (October, 1968):27.

57. For example, note the reduction in the number of Negroes employed in coppersmithing in Lancaster City and especially shoemaking in Columbia between 1850 and 1860 in Table III: Number and Percent of Black Workers in Occupations, 1850 and 1860, and the downward mobility of skilled workers who stayed in Columbia, Lancaster, and West Chester in the 1850s in Table IV: Comparative Occupational Mobility in Three Pennsylvania Towns: 1850–1860. Some of my skilled workers never appeared in the 1850 or 1860 Census.

Most white customers of black artisans simply began buying their clothes, farm implements, and shoes and boots from larger, more efficient, retail outlets and contracted for building with construction firms which combined a number of craft operations.

58. See the examination of Smith's wife, Eliza Parker, in Chester County Examinations, pp. 30–31, C.C.H.S.

59. Examination of Harriet Thompson, "formerly Shirl," July 16, 1858, at the Chester County Almshouse, Almshouse Folder, C.C.H.S.

60. See the indenture contracts for West Chester, 1850–1857, placed in Henry Fleming's Record of Marriage Book, C.C.H.S. The same trend is observable in York, Lancaster, and Columbia.

61. Original Returns of the Assistant Marshal, Schedules for West Chester, Seventh United States Census (1850); Eighth United States Census (1860). Tabular returns located at the C.C.H.S. The only blacks in West Chester who were sure of passing on their accrued status and wealth to their sons were the black barbers and oystermen.

62. See particularly Leon Litwack, *North of Slavery: The Negro in the Free States, 1790–1860* (Chicago: 1961), pp. 153–186; David M. Katzman, "Before the Ghetto: Black Detroit in the Nineteenth Century" (unpublished Ph.D. dissertation, Department of History, University of Michigan, 1969), pp. 1–64; and Theodore Hershberg, "Free Blacks in Ante-Bellum Philadelphia: A Study of Ex-Slaves, Free Born, and Socioeconomic Decline," *Journal of Social History* V (Winter, 1971–1972):1–23.

# 5

# The Settlement of Roseto: World View and Promise

## CLEMENT L. VALLETTA

*Clement Valletta presently teaches at King's College, Wilkes-Barre, Pennsylvania. He attended the University of Scranton and earned a Ph.D. in American Civilization at the University of Pennsylvania.*

When they came across from Roseto, Foggia, they settled on the hill north of Bangor in the Slate Belt region of Northampton County. They were *contadini* (peasants), looking for a job and perhaps some land and a home, although at first most wanted to return. By the turn of the century there were some 800 to 900 Italians in Roseto (or "New Italy" town as it was first called), and at least another 600 lived in that part of Bangor that adjoins Roseto.[1] There was laboring work laying rail lines and removing the tops from slate quarries. The Rosetans are remarkable Americans. In the tradition of work and progress, they settled in the wooded area that in 1890 was cut only by a wagon road and a rail line. After six years of opposition, they incorporated their village into a borough in 1912—a historic, Italian-American first. They soon built a fine grammar school named for Columbus; their brass band had an interstate reputation. Within two generations they developed a parochial grammar and high school; they built up the garment industry to a dominant position in the area; and they established Catholic and Presbyterian churches as well as numerous clubs and organizations dedicated to mutual help. Their proudest achievement in their own eyes is the number of "professionists" of the second generation alone—about 150 doctors, dentists, lawyers, pharmacists, religious, teachers, scientists.

The Italian-American is one of the most misunderstood groups in America. Only the Polish and, until recently, the Blacks have been so misunderstood. One is faced with the obligation to those of Roseto or any "subculture" to show what it was like from their experience. Most sociological and historical studies tend to reduce an ethnic group into "social characteristics" of residence, occupation, income, educational levels or else the group is related chronologically to nativist political and economic achievements.[2] These accounts are of great significance, but there is the further obligation to convey and understand the richness of a minority experience *from the point of view of the actual participants.*

The studies of Gans and Whyte attempt to present the quality of a particular ethnic experience—what I shall call world view—in process with American physical, social, and religious life. (There is no assumption that the ethnic group will or must become middle class, living in this or that locale, making a certain income; nor do I assume that the immigrant was exploited or advantaged in America.) Themes of world view are like axiomatic principles of belief that a people live. The people will tell their reasons for doing things (empirical concepts), and these can be seen as reflecting underlying themes. Such presentation of their culture helps to understand their way of life that in its mystery can never be fully understood. It is necessary to present the principles of belief that the *contadini* took with them and established, or not, in the New World. In generalizing, I hope not to distort the reality too much. Ethnic studies may benefit from an anthropological or ethnocultural approach that attempts to show the process of Americanization, the interaction of ethnic world view with a particular region of America. We can begin by discussing a world view that intrigued and mystified Dante, Hawthorne, Barzini, Malamud. . . .

Immigrant family life expressed a whole world of personal desires alive in interpretations of religion and fate, and in everyday events. The *contadino* regarded physical reality as ultimately hostile and not given to what Western, "enlightened" man might regard as causal explanation and mechanistic control. But parental and institutional control was of course necessary. The Rosetans—and other new immigrants of similar background—believed that desires of man, God and other spiritual beings, and fate were the most real explanations of what happened. Authority was family and religiously centered in the intense desires—or to use a shortened expression, the *voli*—of parents and spiritual beings.[3] Imagine, if you will, the similar theme of personal desire, counterpointed by sanction and tradition, in subsequent vignettes and practices.

When a young boy, Carmello (who is sixty-six now) went to his uncle's home in Newark where he expected more kindly treatment than he believed he received at home; his mother was so distraught that he had left that she exclaimed, "May he be eaten by dogs." Two hounds attacked Carmello when he arrived at his uncle's home; so his mother felt responsible because she said that she wished it "with her whole heart."[4]

The immigrant, and even his grandchild, knows that unless the *voli* of a pregnant woman is satisfied, she might give birth to a baby marked by the image of what it was she desired. A child marked with a growth resembling a bunch of grapes supposedly bore the sign of her mother's unfulfilled wish.

It was good to pray to a personal saint and especially the Blessed Mother to intercede, because the wishes of the Blessed Mother would most likely move her Son on one's behalf. Even *malocchio* (evil eye) resulted from the envious, evil, or vindictive—albeit unintentional—wishes of others. Those afflicted had a headache or nauseous feeling, and children might have colic, worms, whooping cough, mumps, measles. A person did not necessarily know he was transferring the evil eye through envy; it just happened if he temporarily had a bad wish. By saying "God Bless You" any possible maliciousness was removed. An old woman who knew the special prayers (and many do today) had the power to remove *malocchio*.

The Italians built their churches in memory of the saint or Blessed Mother who years ago worked a miracle for them. Processions were (and Roseto still has her procession) a traditional way of petitioning and honoring the Patron.

Pious Rosetans walked barefoot or carried a heavy stone in gratitude for a special favor from Our Lady of Mount Carmel, their Patroness. A man of the Enlightenment, Henry Adams, wrote of such belief in his descriptions of the Virgin in *The Education* . . . and *Mont-Saint-Michel and Chartres*. Adams explained the Virgin as a great mystic force, attracting the energies and imagination of medieval believers to build magnificent Gothic cathedrals. Man and women gave their gold and their labor to honor the Virgin. In Roseto, the women of the second generation have given their engagement rings to be melted and set into crowns for Our Lady and Her Son.

"We went all out [an older Rosetan woman said of the procession]. We saved the best flowers from our garden. We had three dresses, one for each day of the celebration. And for Sunday we had white flowers in our hair, and people were religious and walked with a stone, and barefoot; what you did, you did from the heart." They went into debt, if necessary, to buy clothes and food for the celebration. Fear of *malocchio* was removed because the Patroness and Her village sanctioned the *fèsta*. Only one or two old women now walk barefoot in the procession, but the faces of the participants reveal the belief that their ancestors had.

When times were hard, the immigrant knew it was useless to argue with fate. With almost a Greek sense of destiny, Rosetans accepted the inevitable even while they prayed for divine intercession. Streams of classical and Christian beliefs seem to cross their words: "But if it's going to come, sickness and death [an elderly woman said], it's going to come. Was God took my children away; why didn't he take me; they were so young, my husband had to see two sons die. . . ." An older woman tells how her father accepted the imminence of death and would not have a cancerous growth removed since he believed that he "got so much out of life that maybe he was supposed to die from cancer." If there was an accidental death at a slate quarry, they would say *"è 'u destino."* Fate gave warnings in the form of dreams; and dream interpretation has been very much a part of Rosetan life.

The world view of intense personal desire—as you can imagine—is so involved that the boundary between tangible and intangible has traditional boundaries but is beyond ultimate explanation. Such "bifurcation," to use Whitehead's term, between observable and unobservable, is unified by the immigrant sense of divine and earthly will; (whereas the bifurcation between common sense observation and scientific explanation of phenomena in relativity physics, or Freudian psychiatry, for example, is unified only to the mind of the expert—if then). To the Rosetan everything from a headache to death to the behavior of their *paesani* had to do with the *voli*. They observed the desires and activities of one another's families over generations, so that sooner or later the family name carried with it a host of attributes. So you will hear many conversations ended with the exclamation: "What are you going to do, he's a 'Mattino' [or if it is a nationality], he's a Dutchie." The Rosetans felt as much at home in their universe as did feudal man who saw his firmament alive with symbols of good and evil, right and wrong. He knew that a moon turned down indicated the right time to plant rooted vegetables, one turned up meant the time to plant beans, and one in a growing stage warned not to pick the grapes. A violent storm could be calmed by placing a palm outside that was blessed on Palm Sunday. A person with eyebrows growing together might bewitch with the evil eye and they could "blind" the evil eye by wearing sharply pointed amulets shaped like horns or scissors, or like a hand with ring and little fingers extended.

Desires have traditional sanctions even enabled the Italians to live through *la misèria*. The force of will through religion, dreams, familial discipline, and a host of practices (fatuously labeled superstition) gave them strength to order and survive a world of "ignorance," "poverty," and "disease." Ignorance of tradition, poverty of will, and disease resulting from immorality were to be feared much more than ignorance of book learning, poverty defined by income level, and disease from which there is no recourse to God.

Personal desires mattered to the extent sanctioned by what Redfield calls the oral tradition.[5] This aspect of peasant world view simply defines how important words and customs were to an illiterate people. Many men had, at most, three or four years of schooling in Italy, and the women rarely had any schooling at all. Having the power of words, Rosetans passed on to their children sensible and often colorful advice in the form of proverbs and anecdotes. One story tells about Christ and St. Peter who saw a man quietly trying to get his donkey moving. They passed him by and came upon another man who was also trying to move his donkey, but this man was cursing. Christ helped him, and told St. Peter that unless he did, this man would lose his soul. They also had proverbs to enlighten the uninformed, e.g., "A lie goes on one leg, because the truth is right behind it"; "Go slow little one, the way is bumpy."

Values, beliefs, and practices (from child rearing to wine making, gardening, and cooking) were passed on orally from generation to generation. You can still hear a parent saying "I'll teach him and then I lose him." An elderly woman, describing a cherished custom will say, *così si dice* (that's what is said) and that will end debate as far as she is concerned. The *voli* had meaning if sanctioned by one having knowledge, position, and respect enough to pass on tradition. There was a veritable pantheon of demigods and deities who had such respect. From visions, dreams, scripture as well as by signs one knew the pronouncements of God, Mary, fate, saints, the devil. And the demigods were the parents and even kindly priests and padrones who helped the family by saying the influential words. Consider all of this regarding a story that reveals the force of *voli* sanctified by the words of a beloved parent and wife—as told by her daughter-in-law. Since Philomena was her only granddaughter, Mrs. Riscona intended that after her death her jewels would go to Philomena. If her husband did not carry out this wish, Mrs. Riscona said that she would put a curse upon the jewels. On the night of the death of his wife, Mr. Riscona gave the jewels to Philomena. Another informant, also a second-generation woman, tells of her contribution toward the crown of the infant Jesus for the Rosetan Church:

I had raised many ounces of gold, but I still felt I had not done enough for the favor I had received. God had given me my life to raise my son. He was only six weeks old [when she became very ill], and it would have been very unfortunate for him to be raised without a mother. . . . When I gave up my engagement ring, I felt something tear out of me. . . . Of course, I broke down crying . . . and a member came up and said that she couldn't help doing something special too.

Expressed by the oral tradition, immigant *voli* was ordered by a third aspect of world view, implicit in every social group. The peasant occupied at the time of the new immigration a particular class—he seemed to believe it was God's will that he did—that he could not easily transcend. Italian peasants probably had a harder time transcending their status than did Carpathian Russians or Poles. Although the Italian was not quite so harrassed by foreign domination, he had a harder time trying to survive *la misèria*. The place of the Italian was both more fixed and more resented by him than that of most other nationalities of the new immigration, or so comparative ethnographic studies and the novels of Silone and Reymont and accounts by immigrants lead one to believe.

In Southern Italian and Catholic tradition, power and worth descended from the Trinity through the Blessed Mother and the saints, to the pope, to bishops and priests, then to the superior classes (lords and bourgeoisie or about fifteen percent of a given village) and finally to the peasants who made up about eighty percent of the population.[6] Given such a hierarchical view of things, it was not surprising to hear an elderly tailor give his political views. He insisted that Woodrow Wilson was the best president because he was a university professor; and that Eisenhower, a "great general," was a better president than Kennedy and certainly better than Truman who was "ordinary." (I hesitated to mention Johnson or Nixon.) The hierarchical principle naturally applied in the home: "The rooster sings, not the chicken," an elderly cobbler said. And a priest admonished one man not to allow a wife's irreverence because "God gave you the power" to keep authority.

The peasant assumed equality, if not superiority, to other families of his status. He expected his supposed betters to act favorably; if not, he might join with others to "put them in their place." Groups of Rosetans have petitioned the bishop to remove a local priest who flouted his authority. Those professionists who charged too much, they said, had a "sickness" for money. The immigrants believed that on the one hand their status was fixed, but that on the other they could do something about their low position. They could provide their sons with the opportunity to become, as they said, "better than we are"; hence the ironic self-sacrifice of those who ate "bread and onions" to send their sons to professional schools.

The three patterns of world view—hierarchical, oral, and *voli*—have heuristic roots in Italian village life and in the Rosetan settlement, explaining its unique culture. The nature of family life expresses world view in Italy and America, because there were certain similarities. About 90 percent of the immigrants were seasonal laborers, making about eighty-five cents a day at the quarry. Their status was as low in America as in Europe. Although they worked in industry, they each had a tiny farm that was much smaller than in Italy but still provided them with much of their food. Each family raised a pig or two, chickens, perhaps a cow or goat, a large garden, vineyard, fruit trees. Nearby woods provided berries, nuts, firewood, and bean and tomato poles. The soil was rocky and only the peasant genius for cultivating the meager brought results.

Ethnic world view in a context of familial independence means that the Rosetans were quite free of massive institutional reliance in a society as specialized as America was becoming. The Rosetans like others of the old and new immigration were, after all, part of that American citizenry who were independent, self-reliant tillers of the soil, having their homestead and village secured. The Rosetan no less than other historical settlements began democratically. The question of democracy in America is obfuscated, however, by an assimilation process in which "Anglo-conformity, in various guises, has probably been the most prevalent ideology of assimilation in the American historial experience. . . ."[7] But since a democracy is not measured by conformity to anything but its own standard, the ethnic experience might be instructive if studied in and for itself with reference to democratic values—rather than to American and quasi-European ones. Certain assumptions arise: the nativist American culture, with its plutocratic class lines, may have been as Europeanized (though roomier and richer) than the society the immigrant left; the immigrant may have been in his self-reliance and hope of becoming more independent in America an even greater contributor to American democracy than he has been; and if an end of assimilation is the bland upper middle class life described by Reisman in *The Lonely Crowd,* for example, it may be prudent to rediscover our ethnic and democratic roots. We may do this by considering an open-ended—as opposed to a priori—explanation of our ethnic experience, or what is called Americanization:

*Assuming that an ethnic world view involves implicit responses restrained by Old World conditions, these same responses, although controlled by world view, have often found expression in America when restraints were missing and alternatives open.* This approach does justice, I hope, to the Rosetan and American experience, particularly in understanding in Roseto, the rise of Protestantism, political incorporation, industrialization, parochial education, and familial development. One of the most interesting aspects of Rosetan life is the rise of Protestantism. The historical account begins with the journey of an Italian Rosetan who left Bangor in 1887 for New York, where he was converted to Presbyterianism.[8] He returned to New Italy—what was to become Roseto in 1912—in 1890 to distribute copies of the Bible and religious pamphlets written in Italian. This same man persuaded an Italian missionary to come to New Italy. The first meeting place, the story goes, was a shanty located along Columbus Avenue furnished with tree stumps and crudely made benches for pews and an empty beer keg for a pulpit. With help from the Bangor Presbyterian Church, the Rosetans established a church in 1893. Dedication services were held in both languages; and Protestant missionaries from other Italian settlements spoke. The Italians raised $300 for the church, and nativists donated the rest for a total of $1,283.[9] (The Roseto church has received aid from the regional presbytery, until recent years.) There were sixty-four charter members of the Presbyterian Church in 1893, or about 20 percent of the population; however, membership declined to 6 percent in 1924 when the number was 103 members. In the early twenties, about ten Rosetans left the Presbyterian Church to form the Association of Bible Students, which as Jehovah's Witnesses continues until the present.

We can assume that there were reactions to the Catholic Church that found Protestant expression in the New World, particularly since there was no permanent Catholic priest in Roseto until 1897. Even after the Catholic Church was built in 1894, the faithful had to go some fifteen miles to Easton, where an Irish priest dispensed the sacraments. He knew Italian and would go to New Italy to celebrate the mass or administer baptism, but not on Sundays. There were, furthermore, reactions against the hierarchical power of the priest. Belief tales abound about the priest, for instance, who asked the penitent where he hid the stolen ham. Priests lived, as one put it, by the unwritten code, "Do as I say, not as I do." Informants remembered "insults" that they or their parents received from clergy. An informant remembered that his father, who later became Protestant, was "slapped by the priest for doing something wrong during his marriage ceremony." In America such reactions could be institutionalized in the form of conversion particularly in the light of other considerations of world view.

The moral and aesthetic quality of words, central to the oral tradition, was enhanced by Protestant emphasis upon reading Scripture instead of simply reciting prayers by memory. Protestantism implied an oral, paternal, and filial rather than hierarchical, imagistic, and maternal sense of faith. The Italian men were certainly not as enthralled with religion as were their wives; yet the men believed in the need for authority. One can imagine what must have inspired potentially religious men when they read the Bible in their own tongue and realized a direct communication with God:

My father [an elder of the Presbyterian Church reports] was an ardent reader of the Bible. He would have . . . people come to him for advice. He used to sit in the middle of the house, there, and he used to read to us, and I remember when he and my mother used to have spats; he used to quote to her, 'It's better to live in a housetop; than to live in a home with a contentious woman.'

A Jehovah's Witness told of a Bible student who preached beautifully: "Words like 'joy,' 'happiness,' mean something in Italian. Old men could see I had something better. When the minister spoke, he spoke just like music." An elderly Presbyterian woman put it this way, "With the Word, you feel so close to the preciousness of the infinite God."

Informants will also say that the Presbyterian Church is more "democratic," because the ruling elders can have a minister removed. Men relished this kind of power that was openly sanctioned in Presbyterianism while restrained in Catholicism. Even the power of the *voli* has been intrinsic to Rosetan Protestant life. The Catholic asked the Virgin for special favor; the Protestant petitioned her Son. An older woman told about her Protestant belief:

> I accept Her as the Mother of Christ. He was born through her in a special way . . . that's all. She is a plain, ordinary mother like any other mother. I cannot see where she has to be worshipped. I can't see where we have to go through Her for what we want from Christ. He's the One—to think of how He was born, what He came for. He was crucified for us. No man around here would give up what He had to do for us.

I sought an economic reason to explain the conversion, to balance, perhaps, the other approaches. Two elderly informants indicated that about six of the original sixty-four "maybe" changed their faith because the quarry bosses encouraged it. "If you Presbyterian, you up to them," said an elderly man who formally became Presbyterian only five years ago, "if you Catholic, they look sideways." The immigrant would have to have changed much more than his faith to obtain more than a laboring job at the quarry. English and Welsh slaters controlled the skilled and semi-skilled jobs, because they or their ancestors learned the trade in the British Isles, and they were the ones "qualified" to do the important work, they told me. Italians say they were "not allowed to make slate" until the last two decades. "We were," they said, "only good enough to work in the hole or throw out rubbish on the landing."

The immigrants found that they could and had to satisfy their *voli* by using the industrial alternative to acquire a home while keeping close to the land. They needed to earn money to establish the homestead, yet, by their choice to continue a semi-agrarian life, they furthered their original desire to modify the restraint of a peasant, landholding existence in Italy while retaining its virtues in a rural American region. To these ends they had the friendship and all-important help of *paesani*. They helped each other to dig out and build stone foundations for houses that were at first stone, four-room, one-story affairs; build outdoor kitchens and sheds; have their skillful friends over at butchering time and acknowledge them with a choice ham; sympathize in hard times with gifts of labor and some money. Each family gathered its own firewood; made sheets from flour sacks; sewed all but the most "dressy" outfits; repaired shoes; trimmed hair; made wine; and of course grew much of what they ate. Immigrants ingeniously used available materials: native stone in building; slate for roofs, walls, and walks; steel chisels turned into hoes, axes and hammers by quarry blacksmiths; fertilizer from the animals, ashes, and the forest (mulch). The Rosetan blended industrial and agrarian into an identity that in its independence was Italian and democratic; however, this world was destined to change in an increasingly mechanized America.

The immigrant might have committed himself and especially his children to the agrarian more than industrial alternative as other Italians in America had done. But land in Roseto was hilly and rocky as well as expensive for the impoverished immigrant. The long distance from large urban centers prevented him from taking up truck farming as his compatriots did in New Jersey. That the elderly still maintain large gardens and still make wine may indicate their agrarian preferences supported by social security earned while working in industry. There is one eighty-six year old woman, living by herself now, who has a large garden, and makes her wine. "God bless her," as Rosetans would say. The immigrants taught their eldest sons how to carry on their traditions. The younger sons, as might be expected, generally took less interest particularly following their wartime experiences, although there are exceptions to this. While the immigrant's life style was poised between industry and agriculture, he did commit his children to the industrial more than the other possibility. Since he believed the homestead stayed in the family and that adjoining lots were for his children, he had his children work to pay off his and, therefore, their debts. So that although the child would help with gardening and butchering, he was contributing more perhaps by turning in his pay earned in the silk mills, blouse factories, and quarries. (Such second-generation involvement was not always happy and rendered the allurements of mass society more irresistible than the quasi-peasant existence of their parents—but this is to anticipate.) The immigrant himself was ambivalent about his status—wanting to transcend it but not always knowing how. There was, moreover, a stigma attached to those who lived on a few acres in the outskirts of a village. These were the *cafoni;* and Rosetans will still use this term, if jokingly, to characterize the few Italian farmers who live in nearby East Bangor.

The Italian was class-conscious and reacted against any negative identity attached to his peasant status lest he be regarded in America as he regarded the *cafoni* in Italy. But there is even more significance in understanding the egalitarian and competitive reaction implicit in the hierarchical principle. Each Italian was more aware of his provincial and communal background (called *campanilismo,* within earshot of the village bell tower) than he was of his Italian nationality, except of course before nativists. Village loyalty (involving regional differences, poor transportation, ignorance) that made him antagonistic to strangers from different towns in the Old Country, made him competitive enough to want to prove his worth in America as old restraints were missing. All this is illustrated in a series of letters that appeared in the *Stella di Roseto.* A Rosetan wrote the nativist Bangor paper denouncing two Sicilians for knifing each other in Roseto. According to this Rosetan, they were "Sicilian and not Rosetan, and this race of people is not desirable in this country."

Another Rosetan evidently did not like the implications of this, so he wrote the editor of the *Stella*—not to the Bangor paper:

> The Sicilians merit the same respect as all Italians, and there is no need to hate the Sicilians in general, solely because any had committed some crimes. Never! The Italians ought not to be culpable for the action of one, as the Sicilians ought not ever to be held responsible for an act committed by one Sicilian. In Roseto there ought to be harmony and respect without taking into account Sicilians or Rosetans or Biccarese, etc. We are Italians; let us love one another, let us respect one another, let us help one another in turn (*vicènda*) and let us abandon forever, the hatred of race! [He went on to conclude that] we ought to cure the wounded ourselves and not resort to the Americans. . . .[10]

While in Italy the Rosetan may not have been aware of what the Biccarese (those who lived near Roseto), the Sicilians, or Neapolitans were doing; in America he was extremely aware of his comparable status. It was as if he confronted an Italian as well as American pluralism. His identity was fixed in Italy, but was somewhat relative in America to what his more enterprising *paesani* were doing. The movement toward incorporation of the borough suggests how Rosetans helped each other to become strong enough vis-à-vis the "Americans." It may be noted that Roseto accomplished a separate identity much as the Norwegian, Swedish, and German immigrants did in the nineteenth century.[11] Had the Rosetans settled in a large city they might have formed a Roseto club. (Italian groups in Wilkes-Barre and nearby Plains Township have organized cooperatives and halls named after their place of origin—Roma, Umbria —and even a St. Paul's Society named after a church in Calabria.) The Rosetans, unlike most other Italian groups, settled a rural area and established a town on their own while retaining their folk ways.

Their spirit of helping one another was guided by several leaders who understood how to work with immigrant reactions in terms of American alternatives. The first permanent settlers—Nicola Rosato, Lorenzo Falcone, and Giovanni Policelli—must have envisioned a rural life close to Bangor, which was easily reached by a wagon path and a rail line. Falcone sold several lots of land above the rail line to his *paesani*. He operated a hauling business and later diversified his interests. Falcone and Rosato developed the southwestern part of New Italy; Policelli, who was Presbyterian, the central and eastern part. The northwestern half resulted from the increased settlement of the Bangor Ward adjoining Roseto; the establishment of the Catholic Church; and the improvement of the wagon road into Garibaldi Avenue. The first settlement looked like a two-sided sword just showing beyond a board—the two sides representing the rail line and Garibaldi Avenue meeting at a point just beyond Columbus Street. Garibaldi Avenue gradually became the central axis of the town with the Catholic Church to the south and the Presbyterian Church to the north. Philip Sabatino, Roseto's first mayor, was instrumental in having New Roseto Hall along Garibaldi Avenue. Its three stories, it is said by elderly informants, were imposing enough to rival the commercial buildings of Bangor. A shirt company, financed by Roseto money, was housed in the new hall. Thus by 1906 when the leaders made their first effort to incorporate their town, Roseto had made sufficient progress to be regarded by almost any standard as a thriving community.

The one man who opposed this first attempt was ironically the very one who had done most to promote Italian responses in terms of American alternatives. His directing role had the effect of Americanizing the Italians to the extent necessary for them to retain their ethnic values before the outside. The man was Father Pasquale De Nisco, the most honored man in Roseto history: the Knights of Columbus Council, a marble monument, a street, and a housing development all bear his name.

When asked what was the very first thing he had tried to accomplish in Roseto, he answered: "Everything! I tried to improve all their conditions: homes, labor, the church, social conditions—everything—I tried to start it all growing at once, for I knew it would be slow, slow."[12] Born in the province of Avellino in 1860, he studied for the priesthood at the English College in Italy. He was sent to England to serve in an Italian church and then to America, in 1884, where he founded Brooklyn's first Italian church and parochial school. Archbishop Ryan of Philadelphia offered him the Roseto parish which he assumed in 1897. He intended to secure land for a cemetery, parochial school, and eventually a hospital. He first cleared the existing cemetery that was overgrown with briars. He worked with his own hands, thereby allaying negative responses to clergy who usually avoided manual labor. He reinforced his example by offering monetary prizes to Rosetans who most beautified their homes with flowers and shrubbery.

He strove to maintain the integrity of the family by encouraging available educational, aesthetic, and economic opportunities. Separate religious sodalities were organized for male or female, married or unmarried parishioners. He persuaded parents to send their children to college, and soon two boys were graduated from Villanova University.

Developing a friendship with a county judge, De Nisco kept order by having imprisoned two principals in a knife fight, and by having a disorderly house removed from the outskirts of town. He told his following, "You are law-abiding, self-respecting American citizens; build comfortable, substantial American homes fit for American citizens."[13] And those who did, like Lorenzo Falcone, set an example for the rest. De Nisco recommended loans for those hard-working Rosetans who would pay their debts. Rosetans have always had a reputation for paying their debts, as local merchants will say. De Nisco started the Catholic Dramatics Club which staged plays in St. Philip Neri Hall. In those days, informants remember, the prompter was important, "You could always hear him." He umpired baseball games the youngsters had during recess from Sunday School. He encouraged the game, but warned his charges not to step on or pick any of the flowers that were "for all to look at and enjoy." De Nisco opened a school in order to train applicants in the language and laws of America and stressed the beauty and greatness of this country. First and final citizenship papers were handed out in the basement of the church to Rosetans of both faiths, and De Nisco or a well-to-do friend oftentimes paid the cost.

Thus in a variety of ways De Nisco encouraged the egalitarian and competitive reactions of his people toward ends that he, a respected "better," sanctioned and developed from available American alternatives. Since the restraints of *la misèria* were alleviated, mortgage money was available for houses "like the Americans," education could enable children to become better, and the family could be secure, hard working, and even entertained by athletics, dramatics, books from their library, and beautification contests. De Nisco's effort represented an optimum way of integrating responses of world view with the industrial as well as other opportunities. He used his hierarchical powers for the humane and egalitarian ends of obtaining local industry and better pay for workers at the slate quarries. The men made eight cents an hour for a ten-hour day; many had to trade at the company stores between paydays that were three months apart. De Nisco talked quietly with quarry superintendents, pointing out that the men ought to receive more pay, be paid monthly, and not forced to trade at a company store which was illegal, anyway. He was ignored. Collecting a few of the workers' pay books, he went to Philadelphia where with the aid of Archbishop Ryan, he met with the presidents of several slate companies. The owners were ostensibly astonished that only a few cents remained after the company store settled an account; and that the wage was not twenty-five to fifty cents a day higher. But the visit had no effect, except to have an unscrupulous superintendent fired.

In 1903, De Nisco organized and became president of a branch of the A.F. of L., and proceeded to call a strike. The owners retaliated by importing black labor from the South, who upon looking into the depths of the quarries, left with dispatch. But the men became desperate without work. De Nisco borrowed $300 and, standing on the road at dawn, met his members and distributed strike pay. The strike finally ended, providing $1.50 for a nine hour work day. By 1905, De Nisco had secured better wages for the men and had also encouraged local business leaders to organize a shirt company to employ women part time.

These same leaders, Falcone and Rosato among them, petitioned the county for incorporation papers. But De Nisco was opposed on the grounds that too few villagers were qualified to hold office. Elderly informants discount this. They stress rather their desire for political independence from the prejudice of German township supervisors, and for roads, fire and police facilities, a school, and, of course, community prestige. But De Nisco opposed the move and his objection evidently influenced the court: "There are not enough educated Italians in the village at the present time to fill the various offices and . . . if the town is incorporated now, a state of anarchy will exist in six months. . . ."[14] The villagers were divided on the issue; many feared a greater tax burden. By 1911, Ralph Basso believes De Nisco had removed his objection. The first borough secretary (who emigrated at the age of six and received an American education) remembers telling the judge that he "guaranteed" enough qualified people to run the town, "If not, we'll bring you the charter, you won't have to send for it." The villagers had agreed on the need for incorporation and the *Stella* had vigorously supported the move. De Nisco died an untimely death in July, 1911. One assumes he would have supported the leaders and other villagers in 1912, even if he had hoped for more time to have the educated second generation assume leadership. But he had been the de facto mayor, working with an energetic people who soon gained the confidence he hoped to instill in them. Incorporation was, in many ways, the democratic fruition of the settlement.

"When De Nisco died everything died," the borough secretary said. "Now everything is the parochial school." The great influence of the church has continued since the time of De Nisco, since the American church has been very instrumental in Americanizing the immigrant. This has been the experience of Roseto. Both churches have received Rosetan support and participation in social gatherings and religious activities. Both clergy may be facing, however, the challenge of preserving Christianity in a secular age, for as one said, "The people are living a good sensuous existence." To understand the coming of secularism, in the form of big cars, color television, stylish clothes, one has to consider how Rosetans, like most other Americans, have experienced the American Dream. As you might expect, it has been a joint family effort in Roseto.

Close to 500 Rosetans, about 80 percent women, are involved in the blouse industry.[15] Even with the recent competition from foreign goods cutting into the industry, Rosetan families have benefited materially from wives working. But the industry needed stability for everyone to profit. Competition among local apparel contractors was so fierce that only the organizing efforts of the I.L.G.W.U. and the Apparel Contractors Association prevented the contractors from "cutting each other's throats for work." They underbid each other to get contracts from the New York apparel firms until a union manager showed them the folly of their ways in the late thirties and early forties. By about 1950 the union and the association were cooperating over grievances, vacation pay, wage schedules, and even design of plants. Also by this time, Rosetans ran close to thirty factories in the area; and it was this base that has helped to finance the parochial school system.

One of the most successful, older bosses began helping the church when he first heard a priest ask for larger donations:

> I went out and bought a little lamb and chanced it off, and raised $250 and brought it to him. In following years I chanced off calves. The Sisters came in 1942, and we got the Holy Name together, and we hauled stones to build a home for the Sisters. We chanced off a car then. After the Sisters started the kindergarten, we started to think about the school. We got the idea of chancing off a Cadillac—$500 apiece, thirty tickets. . . . With the money we've raised or helped to raise, we've paid off the church and the school buildings.

The parochial school has given Rosetans a sense of accomplishment in their community and pride in their children. Fully two-thirds of the high school graduates go on to some form of advanced education. The school is faced, however, with many of the same problems as elsewhere: paying for quality education during a period of declining religious vocations. Father Leone has used his considerable influence to encourage Rosetans to provide a religious education for their children in the face of rising costs and larger class sizes. The Rosetans seem to enjoy having their own school which usually wins its athletic contests, and they still remember the prejudice they endured not that many years ago at Bangor schools. Rosetans celebrate their children's graduation from high school and college with such large parties that one remarked: "Graduations are like weddings used to be." A graduate is feted by family, *compari,* and friends as well as the boss of his mother's factory; and the monetary gifts make a fine nest egg for the first year of college. Older Rosetans know who among their youth are outstanding, and at the appropriate time will remind them of their Rosetan ancestry and encourage them to uphold the Italian name. Tiny Roseto has had more than its share of genius, and the village elders are aware of this.

But in their moments of reflection parents realize the irony of losing their children to educational and occupational opportunities that the parents, themselves, encouraged their children to pursue. The second generation have had to integrate (or not) Italian tradition with American diversity.[16] We can consider this by summarizing the past and presenting change within the form of tradition, much the way a contemporary iconographer works.

The scene is naturally familial; for who, the immigrant believed, more than one's own blood and kind could allay fears of sickness, untimely death, hunger, old age, loneliness. They appealed with their whole hearts to a special saint, to Jesus, and especially to the Blessed Mother—so much like the Italian mother, herself. To lose another member of the family was the same as losing another self, so a child must replace the other and was so named, compared with the other, and expected to assume his place. Even after death, the other could reach one through dreams or be petitioned and helped in prayer. Time followed the cyclical cosmos of the seasons and the church calendar—eternal as the family was eternal. Desires appropriately sanctioned by words and status ordered reality.

Second-generation parents placed more and more reliance upon extra-familial ways of allaying their fears. They reduced family size and substituted consumer and competitive responses associated with industry and mass society for cooperative and independent ones associated with the land and village life. They have relied upon American society to care for them in their old age, provide jobs for their children, welcome their children regardless where they go or whom they marry, diagnose and treat their maladies. It would seem that the second generation have thrown over the restraints upon their parents and have assumed the modern middle-class alternative as a way of life. But this is not quite the case. They have shown, it is true, much more interest than their parents in competing for possessions and money and in emulating the modern image of success. They will admit they have "spoiled" their children by "giving them too much."

Yet they still cling to their Italian traditions in the hierarchical family structure; they still try to avoid community malediction for their family by admonishing their children with the words, "What will people think"; they still worship through the Madonna and Jesus; and even the few who gamble and the many who follow sports address whatever fate has made them win or lose. The town has become a group of clans (interrelated families), each with a patriarch and matriarch, much like the figureheads of a European nation; a directing prime minister, who is usually a blouse contractor; and a cabinet made up of brothers and sisters, at least one of whom has some advanced education and is in charge of protocol and new ideas. Thus familial forms of the nuclear immigrant family have been extended to the clan made up of the surviving immigrants, their married children, and the grandchildren. Although a study in itself, clans are dominant if there are several brothers having status as contractors or professionists. A male in-law who is not so prestigious may be drawn into his wife's clan. Familial forms have also been extended into the blouse factories, clubs, and organizations. The garment contractors, second-generation padrones, have assumed the active role of patriarchal leaders; the workers react to the boss almost as younger children to an older brother. Bosses say they want to stay "close" to their operation, "work along with their workers"; and they ask a worker "to help me out" and work overtime or even leave another factory. Experienced workers have a good deal of independence and they are often treated as equals especially since they know or are even related to the family of the owner. Bosses are usually active on the town council, and administer the Knights of Columbus Council as well as the other clubs and organizations. The latter are devoted to providing athletic interests for the youngsters. They also will raise monies for victims of disease requiring expensive treatment.

The working wives contribute to the income of the home, regarding it as their aesthetic expression, and mothers make possible advanced education for their children. Husbands enjoy running organizational activity while their wives enjoy the home. Thus the hierarchical pattern of order continues, but has expanded to clan, organizational, and industrial forms with the boss's word and life style determining second and often third generation desires. First generation world view (*voli,* hierarchical, and oral traditions) are retained in *form* in the second generation but order a different *content* (money, possessions, personal appearance, industrial involvement).

First-generation responses of competition and consumerism have been expressed to a greater degree in the second generation as restraints of *la misèria* have been reduced and industrial alternatives accepted. Given the independence, security, and homogeneity of Roseto, world view has been expanded to involve the whole community and its successful image before the outside. But since the content is becoming more and more mass produced, it is probable that in time immigrant world view will also change, unless the third generation returns to the first—according to the forecast of Marcus Lee Hansen.[17]

The young Rosetans have retained the faith of their ancestors; they want to be less "materialistic" than their parents; and they want occupations that offer "personal" involvement. These are early signs that Hansen may be right; but the youngsters may have to start listening to their elders, especially the old-timers, to hear the democratic sound that is too easily mistaken for "irrelevant" rhetoric. Youngsters may learn to appreciate their grandparents'—and often their parents'—independence in raising "natural foods," having strong families and good friends, participation in community decisions, and a feeling that life will continue even beyond an age of nuclearism, secularism, pollution, and spoiled children.

The Rosetans have competed successfully for the riches of American life while preserving their traditions. They have done so in the American spirit of self-help and local rule. I can still hear an elderly Rosetan berating the state for "telling us what to do." But if they are consistent with their history, the Rosetans will find a way—

and a wise leader—to adapt the latest American offerings to their Italian and democratic style.

## NOTES

1. Since Roseto was not incorporated until 1912, exact census figures are unavailable until 1920. Census estimates based upon assessment records list taxable residents in 1913 as 330 (Northampton County archives) and each representing, conservatively, a family of two or three, including boarders. Census records show that Roseto's population has hovered between 1600 and 1800 over the past fifty years. For those interested in a fuller account of Roseto see my dissertation in which Roseto is "Carneta": "A Study of Americanization in Carneta" (unpublished Ph.D. dissertation, University of Pennsylvania, 1968).

2. There is little room for alternative views if it is *only* assumed that the "Italian stock will one day lose its identity in the United States," as in Robert F. Foerster, *The Italian Emigration of Our Times* (Cambridge: 1919), p. 410. Similar presumptions may be found in Lloyd W. Warner and Leo Srole, *The Social Systems of American Ethnic Groups* (New Haven: 1945); for even grosser distortions see Peter Binzen, *Whitetown, U.S.A.* (New York: 1970) or Andrew Greeley, *Why Can't They Be Like Us?* (New York: 1969).

The foregoing lack the depth and sympathy of such studies as Herbert J. Gans, *Urban Villagers* (New York: 1962), or William F. Whyte, *Street Corner Society* ed. 2 (Chicago: 1955).

3. The *voli* is a form taken from Rosetan dialect in which it is usually expressed as *tengo 'nu vulio*—I have a yearning or great wish for something—a particular dish, or for peace and quiet or whatever. Even the third generation will say they have a *voli* for something. As used here to express world view it implies an intense yet simple (and sometimes not so simple) wish or desire.

4. Since most informants were skeptical about being quoted, and since "the name" is so important in Rosetan life, I found it desirable to change names (except of course for historical figures), and to designate first-generation informants as "elderly" and second-generation ones as "older." Where thought relevant, other information concerning sex and occupation of informant is given. By first-generation is meant those born in Italy who did not emigrate until their teens.

5. Robert Redfield, *Peasant Society and Culture* (Chicago: 1956).

6. Leonard W. Moss and Stephan C. Cappannari, "Estate and Class in a South Italian Hill Village," *American Anthropologist* LXIV (1962):299. Only the *cafoni* (the "lower, lower") were beneath the peasant.

7. Milton M. Gordon, *Assimilation in American Life* (New York: 1964), p. 115. This point is also made by E. Digby Baltzell, *The Protestant Establishment* (New York: 1964). Many writers have questioned whether the difference between America and Europe is very great—and hence have wondered about how democratic American institutions have been: Thoreau in *Walden* and "Civil Disobedience" presents a far-reaching critique of an increasingly urbanized and luxury-oriented society that denies its democratic

traditions. A similar critique is made by Whitman in *Democratic Vistas;* Melville in *The Confidence Man;* Twain and Warner in *The Gilded Age;* John Dos Passos in his *U.S.A.* trilogy; John Steinbeck in *Grapes of Wrath;* to mention a few. These writers imply an uncomfortable meaning: to the extent Americanization is, in actuality, an Anglo-conforming and plutocratic experience it is undemocratic.

8. The Rosetan account is given by Ralph Basso, *History of Roseto, 1882–1952*, trans. in collaboration with Francis Copozzi (Easton, Pa.: Tanzella Printing Co., n.d.), pp. 31–33. For the urban experience see F. Aurelio Palmieri, O.S.A., D.D., "Italian Protestantism in the United States," *Catholic World* CVII (May, 1918):177–189. It may be noted that there are Italian Episcopalian Churches in West Bangor and Wind Gap which are near to Roseto. There are, furthermore, Italian Presbyterian and Episcopalian Churches in Pittston, Pa., which suggests that Italian Protestantism is hardly a unique Rosetan growth. The Christian Church of North America is an Italian-American sect with some 20,000 followers in America.

9. *Bangor Observer,* Aug. 3, 1893, p. 2. Membership figures are derived from the rolls of the Presbyterian Church.

10. *La Stella di Roseto* was the Italian newspaper which survived until 1931, but only collected fragments and several copies remain from which this exchange was taken, most probably from an issue published in 1907. After this publication in the *Stella,* the first Rosetan retracted his anti-Sicilian statement in an interview with the *Stella,* in which he indicated his "great respect" for Sicilians, attested by his "cordial hospitality" extended to them in the past.

11. For a general discussion of ethnic attempts to perpetuate their identities see Nathan Glazer, "Ethnic Groups in America" in *Freedom and Control in Modern Society,* eds. Morroe Berger, Theodore Abel, and Charles Page (New York: 1964), pp. 158–173. For treatment of Italian rural settlements, which are fewer than those by the "old" immigrants for obvious reasons, see Luciano Iorizzo, "The Padrone and Immigrant Distribution," in *The Italian Experience in the United States,* eds. Silvano M. Tomasi and Madeline H. Engel (New York: Center for Migration Studies, 1970), pp. 43–77; see also Lawrence Pisani, *The Italian in America* (New York: 1957).

12. Marion H. Carter, "One Man and His Town," *McClure's* XXX (January, 1908), 278. She describes Roseto as a "prosperous, lively little town," having "groceries, markets, dry goods and millinery stores; a druggist's shop, a hotel, a 'Banca Italiana,' cigar and shirt factories." Carter's and Basso's accounts of De Nisco, embellished by county and informant reports, serve as sources.

13. Carter, "One Man and His Town," p. 280.

14. *Bangor Daily News,* Feb. 12, 1906, p. 2.

15. These estimates are based upon records of the local earned income tax office and upon unpublished data from the Joint Planning Commission of Lehigh and Northampton Counties. Commission officials indicate that average Rosetan family income is higher than that of Bangor and that of families in the Metropolitan areas of Easton and Allentown.

16. For a study of the second generation as "marginal" men between two worlds see Irwin L. Child, *Italian or American?* (New Haven: 1943).

17. Marcus L. Hansen, *The Immigrant in American History* (Cambridge, Mass.: 1940).

# 6

# Occupational Mobility of Ethnic Minorities in Nineteenth-Century Warren, Pennsylvania

## MICHAEL P. WEBER

*Michael P. Weber wrote his doctoral dissertation at Carnegie-Mellon University. He has taught at Central Michigan University and is currently in the Department of History at Carnegie-Mellon.*

Interest in the last decade among historians in quantitative studies of geographic and social mobility has produced significant descriptions of the nineteenth-century experience of most Americans. Previously investigations of the nineteenth century dealt with the social origins of members of America's business elite. This valuable research, however, did not provide us with a satisfactory reconstruction of the lives of ordinary laborers and immigrants who lived and worked in nineteenth-century America. Millions of immigrants making the long arduous journey to the United States in search of jobs and a better way of life settled in major American cities such as Pittsburgh, Boston, and Philadelphia. However, while most historians focused their attention upon the social change in these cities, a similar but less spectacular change transpired in hundreds of smaller communities throughout the United States. In fact, the small community under 25,000 people may indeed be more typical of American society during this era than the large city. Although urbanization within the large city affected the lives of millions of persons, no less than 400 new communities of 10,000 or more emerged during the same period. This chapter, part of a larger investigation of social mobility in Warren during the 1870–1910 period, deals with the history of the inarticulate ethnic minorities in one small Pennsylvania town. It traces the changing social position of hundreds of immigrants who arrived in Warren after 1850, searching for opportunity. This entails a study of a single community, yet one hopes it will reveal something of importance about similar types of society and may illuminate the life patterns of immigrant groups in other communities during this era.

From 1810 to approximately 1850 the lumbering industry dominated the economic activity of Warren, attaining its summit between 1836 and 1840. Hard times, the depression in prices, and the bank suspension of 1838 crippled the lumber industry, and, before prices rose again, the supply of timber declined as loggers stripped the land along the river bank of her forests. Dragging the lumber a considerable distance to the river proved difficult and costly; hence, the natural advantage of river transportation declined. The county timber industry never fully recovered. Following its decline Warren residents turned to agriculture, but the presence of rich soil could not overcome other natural obstacles. Burdened with heavy snows, late and early frosts, and rough terrain, agriculture for most inhabitants never exceeded subsistence levels.

During the next two decades—1840 through 1860—Warren exhibited a limited amount of growth and economic progress. The town's "official" biographer, H. L. Schenk, described the period thusly:

> The decades which followed [1840–1860] were not marked by any unusual degree of prosperity. The town kept along on an even tenor . . . slowly increasing in population as a result of being the commercial center of the area. In the destruction of pine forests and in farming, a few of the citizens acquired considerable wealth, but the many . . . barely earned enough to provide shelter and food for their families.[1]

Due, perhaps, to the decline of the lumber industry, the rate of turnover of population within the borough during the first four decades of its existence remained constant. Unfortunately, no record is available of nonpropertied inhabitants. Of the 114 residents owning 300 or more acres in 1832, only thirty-nine remained visible in the borough in 1860.[2] Since persons owning this large an amount of land tend to remain the most stable segment of the population, the rate of turnover appears high. Foreign immigration, however, did not play a large part in this changing population structure. The *Warren Gazette* of 1828 noted the arrival "from Europe of eighty German and French immigrants" and a small number of French immigrants from Alsace arrived in 1840.[3] However, New Englanders, New Yorkers, and Pennsylvanians of English and Scotch-Irish origin continued to maintain population dominance until the 1860s.[4] Of the 1,742 inhabitants of Warren in 1860, only 417 were foreign-born.[5] The major "wave" of immigration hit Warren after 1875 consisting largely of persons of Swedish, Danish, Irish, and Italian origin.

Between 1860 and 1875 Warren experienced almost no economic growth. The population increased by only 276 during the decade and immigration almost completely ceased. Moreover, on February 17, 1870, a major fire broke out in the business section of town. By nightfall twenty-six buildings and residences had been damaged or destroyed. The national financial depression of 1873–74 added to this disaster. The effects of this panic reached Warren, as the editor of the *Ledger* pointed out: "The products of the country have been comparatively worthless during the past two years and the problem is how the businessmen have borne the pressure."[6] By 1875 the community's fortunes seemed destined to retrogression but for the discovery of a far more important and valuable resource—petroleum.

On March 14, 1875—a full 16 years after the discovery of the famous Drake Well at Titusville—David Beaty, a wealthy oil man, struck the first oil deposit in the vicinity of Warren. During the succeeding year oil men flocked to the area, creating a new prosperity. The editors of the *Warren Mail*, capturing the excitement of the era, exclaimed:

Great is oil and desirable is its profits. Who can fathom its mysteries or foretell its coming or going? . . . How the barren hillside blossoms with greenbacks like the leaves of June! Look across the Conewango where we used to go for pious meditations or a lonely drive. Two months have made marvelous changes. . . . You can count from 50 to 100 new rigs and more going up. Loads of coal, loads of timber, loads of boards, loads of old rigs, loads of pipe and loads of tile are constantly crossing. Three or four hundred men are busy as bees. Nearly every house in town is a boarding house.[7]

Oil production, however, failed to maintain this frenzied pace but rather served as the catalyst for the industrialization of the community. Oil refineries and industries producing equipment used in oil production—pumps, rig irons, barrels, and tank cars—contributed significantly to the industrial and urban growth of the community.

By 1910 Warren had completed its transformation from a placid rural village to a dynamic progressive industrial community. Population increased from 2,014 in 1870 to over 11,000—16,000 including surrounding areas—in 1910. Nine oil refineries, six furniture factories, a box manufacturer, two flour mills, several foundries, a cigar factory and various other businesses began operations during the three previous decades. In addition, eleven hotels, six banks, two daily and two weekly newspapers and service to several metropolitan areas via three major railroads signified the growth and progress of Warren as an urban area.

The industrialization and urbanization which occurred from 1870 to 1910 induced a number of significant social changes in the community. Because the discovery of Warren's first oil well—March, 1875—conveniently bisects the 1870–1880 decade, an analysis of the 1870 social order will reveal much about the experiences of ethnic minorities in the preindustrial community.

The changing social position of Warren's ethnic minorities may best be understood by examining in detail the male labor force over the age of eighteen throughout the study.

In 1870, 397 of the 609 persons employed in Warren were native-born Americans. The remaining 212 persons came primarily from

France, Germany, Ireland, and England. As Table I reveals, the majority of the immigrant population in 1870 originated from Northern Europe.

Table 1
Nativity of Work Force—1870

| Place of Birth | No. of Manual Laborers | No. of Nonmanual Laborers | Total No. of Workers | % of Total Work Force |
|---|---|---|---|---|
| U.S.A. | 197 | 200 | 397 | 65% |
| France | 39 | 17 | 56 | 9% |
| Germany | 31 | 19 | 50 | 8% |
| Ireland | 41 | 5 | 46 | 8% |
| England | 16 | 2 | 18 | 2% |
| Denmark | 13 | 2 | 15 | 2% |
| Misc. | 21 | 6 | 27 | 4% |
| Totals | 358 | 251 | 609 | 98% * |

* Total does not equal 100% due to rounding.
*Source:* U.S. Bureau of the Census, *1870 Manuscript Schedules,* Warren Borough.

Of the total work force, 58% engaged in manual labor, whereas 251 or 42% may be classified as white-collar or professional personnel. The role of the immigrant in the 1870 economic structure of Warren becomes clear when one notes that only 51 or 20% of the nonmanual workers were foreign-born. Most immigrants in Warren, with the exception of the Irish, were skilled workers or craftsmen. In particular, French and German immigrants became tailors, bootmakers, gunsmiths, and other self employed craftsmen. Furthermore, a large number worked as carpenters and machinists. The Irish, in contrast, the most recent arrivals to Warren, supplied almost one-third of the unskilled labor even though they constituted only 8% of the work force.[8] Unskilled labor in Warren, as elsewhere, found erratic rather than steady employment. Hence, the unskilled often drifted from job to job throughout the year, often earning less than one dollar per day. Thus one may conclude that the unskilled Irish lived on the brink of poverty and often required assistance to survive the long winters.

Location of residence provides further evidence of the degraded position of the Irish in 1870 Warren. Prior to industrialization the majority of the population lived along the town's main business arteries. Residential and commercial establishments often shared the same building and the town's better homes were erected on the choice "downtown" locations. Wealth and poverty coexisted, at least residentially if not socially. The Irish again provided the exception to this heterogeneous residential arrangement. While no discernible patterns of ethnic segregation existed for French, British, or German immigrants in 1870, thirty-nine of the forty-six Irish immigrants lived in the western sector of town.[9] The west side, which housed the major industrial plants and the railroad depot, already began to acquire the characteristics of a transitional area. Editorials frequently complained of "unsavory characters" seen in this section of town. Minor crimes apparently increased as the west-end residents continually petitioned the borough council for an expanded police force.

The lack of "status" of Warren's Irish-born citizens holds particular significance as one begins to examine mobility during the industrialization after 1875. The plight of these individuals reveals much regarding the openness of American society during this period. However, we would also do well to note the position of other ethnic groups in Warren in 1870. Faulty conclusions appear if one emphasizes only the position of the Irish immigrant. The lack of discrimination against other immigrants is perhaps equally significant. The Germans, French, British, and Danes, primarily skilled craftsmen, participated freely in community affairs. Eight immigrants served on the Warren Borough Council from 1870 to 1875. All came from the above four groups. In addition, almost one-third of these four immigrant groups held some type of nonmanual occupations. With the exception of the predominantly unskilled Irish, other immigrants found acceptance in preindustrial Warren.

An examination of the population growth in Warren during the four decades—1870 to 1910—presents the image of a growing but stable community. A more detailed analysis reveals considerable change in the composition of the population and significant migration both in and out of the community.

Table 2
Nativity of Adult Male Population by Decade

| Birthplace | 1870* | 1880* | 1890* | 1900* | 1910* |
|------------|-------|-------|-------|-------|-------|
| U.S.A. | 65% | 65% | 58% | 66% | 73% |
| Canada | 1 | 2 | 3 | 2 | 1 |
| England | 3 | 3 | 4 | 2 | 1 |
| Ireland | 7 | 6 | 8 | 5 | 2 |
| Scotland | 2 | 1 | 1 | 1 | 1 |
| Germany | 8 | 7 | 8 | 4 | 2 |
| Sweden | — | 3 | 6 | 9 | 10 |
| Denmark | 2 | 3 | 4 | 4 | 2 |
| France | 9 | 7 | 7 | 3 | — |
| Italy | — | — | — | 1 | 2 |
| Others | 1 | 1 | 1 | 2 | 5 |
| Totals | 98% | 98% | 100% | 99% | 97% |

* Total does not equal 100% due to rounding.
*Source: 1870 Manuscript Census,* Warren Borough, *1880 Manuscript Census,* Warren Borough, 1890, 1900, 1910 City Directories, Immigrant Alien Dockets, Naturalization Records, Birth Records.

In 1870, three-fourths of the immigrant working population consisted of persons of English, Irish, German, and French origin. As industrialization progressed, the proportion of each of these groups declined dramatically. By 1890 the combined percentage fell to 64 and the next decade produced a similar decline. In 1900, for the first time in the borough's history, the majority of immigrants now consisted of Swedes, Italians, and Danes.

The Swedish immigrants made the most dramatic increases in the latter part of the nineteenth century. Prior to the borough's industrialization, the few adult male Swedish immigrants residing in Warren constituted less than 1% of the total immigrant population, although more lived scattered throughout the county. Concurrent with the onset of industrialization, an influx of Swedish immigrants migrated to Warren. By 1910, well over one-third of all immigrants living in the community came from Sweden. Working primarily as manual laborers, the Swedes, in contrast with the Irish and Italians, found a hospitable environment in Warren. During the first decade of the twentieth century the ratio of foreign-born workers decreased from a high of 42% in 1890 to 27% of the total labor force. Nevertheless, the changes occurring in Warren produced an increased heterogeneity of the immigrant population. Not only had the four dominant immigrant groups changed, but by 1910 newcomers from eighteen other nations established residence in Warren.

Most of the newcomers entered the labor force as manual workers and with few exceptions remained blue-collar laborers throughout their careers. Fully three-fourths of all immigrants in Warren performed some type of manual labor in 1870, 1880, and 1900.[10] Only in 1890 did the percentage of immigrants wearing blue collars to work drop below 75%. During that year 63% of all immigrants engaged in manual labor.[11] In comparison, over one-half of all United States born adult males performed white-collar work in each decade from 1870 through 1910.[12] In addition to doing mostly manual labor, foreign-born workers also held the majority of unskilled jobs in the community. Immigrants constituted approximately one-third of the adult labor force each decade—see Table 2—yet over one-half of the men classified as unskilled in any period of this study came from the ranks of the foreign-born.

Fortunately for the migrants from Europe, the industrial and urban expansion created needs for semi-skilled and skilled workmen. Comparison of the first occupations held by immigrants with those held by native-born workers reveals considerable opportunities for foreign-born workmen possessing marketable skills.

Table 3
Percentage of Natural-Born and Foreign-Born Workers in Each
Skill Group at the Start of Career

| Skill Classification | 1870* | 1880 | 1890 | 1900 |
|---|---|---|---|---|
| Unskilled** | 12% | 16% | 10% | 24% |
| U.S.-Born*** | 7% | 10% | 5% | 14% |
| Foreign-Born | 22% | 29% | 16% | 44% |
| Semi-skilled | 11% | 13% | 11% | 9% |
| U.S.-Born | 12% | 9% | 8% | 10% |
| Foreign-Born | 9% | 20% | 15% | 8% |

| | | | | |
|---|---|---|---|---|
| Skilled | 36% | 29% | 26% | 26% |
| U.S.-Born | 31% | 24% | 20% | 25% |
| Foreign-Born | 44% | 39% | 33% | 30% |
| | | | | |
| Nonmanual | 41% | 42% | 53% | 48% |
| U.S.-Born | 50% | 57% | 67% | 51% |
| Foreign-Born | 25% | 12% | 36% | 18% |
| | | | | |
| Total # Each Decade | | | | |
| U.S.-Born | 397 | 470 | 413 | 1081 |
| Foreign-Born | 212 | 241 | 330 | 518 |
| | | | | |
| | 609 | 711 | 743 | 1599 |

\* Workers in this cohort had already begun their careers.

\*\* Indicates percentage of the total work force in each skill group.

\*\*\* Indicates percentage of origin working in each skill.

*Source: 1870 Manuscript Census,* Warren Borough, *1880 Manuscript Census,* Warren Borough, 1890, 1900, 1910 City Directories, Immigrant Alien Dockets, Naturalization Records, Birth Records.

Table 3 reveals the relationship between initial occupations of all workers and ethnicity. In each Census group from 1870 through 1910 the proportion of immigrants joining the work force as unskilled laborers remained three or more times as great as the ratio of native-born day laborers. Foreign-born workers experienced a particularly large disadvantage in 1900 as a large number of Italians and Swedish immigrants migrated into the community. Unfortunately, the industrial growth of the community began to decline at the same time, forcing most of these men (44%) into unskilled positions.

Immigrants arriving in Warren possessing skills, however, suffered little disadvantage when compared with native-born Americans. Prior to the industrialization of the community, the ratio of immigrants attaining semi-skilled work nearly equaled the percentage of United States-born laborers who began their careers in this skill group. During the next two decades immigrants joining the work force managed to attain an even larger proportion of the semi-skilled occupations. In 1880 and 1890 foreign-born men were nearly twice as likely to begin work as semi-skilled laborers than native-born men. By 1900 the opportunities for immigrants to attain these minimal skilled positions declined. By this decade only 8% of all immigrants could attain semi-skilled positions compared with 10% of all United States-born workers. This shrinkage in opportunity again appears related to the stabilization of the economy and the changes in the character of the immigration. During the latter part of the nineteenth century as the community rapidly expanded, immigrants experienced considerable opportunities, although never as great as that enjoyed by native-born workers. However, as industrial and urban expansion began to decline, the disadvantages of lacking specific skills and that of being foreign-born became particularly acute.

Skilled workers also felt the effects of the changing industrialization within the community. From 1870 through 1910 a large number of immigrants entering Warren began their careers as skilled craftsmen. In 1870, 44% of all foreign-born workers held some type of skilled position. During the next three decades the percentage of foreign-born workers joining the work force as skilled craftsmen, although declining somewhat, remained significant. In each of the last three decades of the nineteenth century immigrants entering the work force attained skilled occupations more frequently than native-born workers. Nearly four of every ten immigrant workers in 1880 began as skilled craftsmen while only 24% of all United States-born workers attained similar positions. One decade later while the total percentage of all skilled workers in the labor force declined, one-third of all foreign-born workers began their careers as skilled craftsmen. Only 20% of the native-born workers joining the work force in the same decade became skilled workers. Finally, three in ten of all foreign-born workmen joining the work force in 1900 captured skilled positions while one of every four United States-born workmen attained a similar occupation. The above evidence clearly indicates the presence of considerable occupational opportunity for those moving into Warren during the latter part of the nineteenth century.

Occupational opportunity, however, did not extend into the area of the white-collar worker. The striking initial disadvantage (Table 3) of immigrants in the quest for "middle-class" occupations becomes immediately apparent. In 1870 one-fourth of all immigrants held white-collar jobs while one-half of all United States-born men worked with their heads rather than their hands. By 1880 the percentage of

native-born Americans beginning work wearing white collars reached
58% while only 12% of all new immigrants attained such a position.
During the succeeding decade two of every three United States-born
workers initially started their careers in nonmanual positions while
one in three of all immigrants began work as white-collar workers.
The disadvantage of one's birth widened during the next decade as
nonmanual opportunities for all workers declined. Only 18% of the
immigrants starting work in 1900 could secure a nonmanual occupation while one-half of all native-born Americans captured white-
collar jobs.[13]

Although we know little of the actual skills possessed by immigrants starting work in the lower two job classifications—some of
these men may have been craftsmen forced to accept jobs demanding
lesser skills—it seems apparent, however, that skilled newcomers to
the community had little difficulty securing skilled occupations. But
when compared with native-born Americans, immigrants arriving in
Warren were at a distinct disadvantage in both the bottom and top
skill groups. Clearly, foreign-born workers did the majority of the
unskilled work in the community. Conversely, with the exception of
the immigrants arriving in Warren at the height of industrialization
—1880 to 1890—few found it possible to secure nonmanual occupations in their initial endeavor in the work force.

Table 4

Ethnic Differences in Intra-Generational Occupational Mobility, 1870–1910

Occupational Status Attained by Unskilled Workers*

| Year | Unskilled N.B.** | F.B.*** | Semi-skilled N.B. | F.B. | Skilled N.B. | F.B. | Nonmanual N.B. | F.B. | # in Group N.B. | F.B. |
|------|------|------|------|------|------|------|------|------|------|------|
| | | | | 1870 Census Group | | | | | | |
| 1870 | 100% | 100% | — | — | — | — | — | — | 28 | 47 |
| 1880 | 25% | 85% | 25% | — | 25% | — | 25% | 15% | 4 | 13 |
| 1890 | — | 100% | 100% | — | — | — | — | — | 1 | 4 |
| 1900 | — | 100% | 100% | — | — | — | — | — | 1 | 2 |
| 1910 | 100% | — | — | — | — | — | — | — | 1 | 0 |
| | | | | 1880 Census Group | | | | | | |
| 1880 | 100% | 100% | — | — | — | — | — | — | 45 | 70 |

| | | | | | | | | | |
|---|---|---|---|---|---|---|---|---|---|
| 1890 | 32% | 79% | 16% | 4% | 32% | — | 20% | 17% | 25 | 24 |
| 1900 | 16% | 64% | 16% | — | 25% | 27% | 42% | 9% | 12 | 11 |
| 1910 | — | 60% | — | 20% | 25% | 20% | 75% | — | 4 | 5 |

1890 Census Group

| | | | | | | | | | |
|---|---|---|---|---|---|---|---|---|---|
| 1890 | 100% | 100% | — | — | — | — | — | — | 22 | 53 |
| 1900 | 33% | 83% | 33% | 6% | 22% | 11% | 11% | — | 9 | 18 |
| 1910 | 25% | 70% | — | 10% | 25% | 10% | 50% | 10% | 4 | 10 |

1900 Census Group

| | | | | | | | | | |
|---|---|---|---|---|---|---|---|---|---|
| 1900 | 100% | 100% | — | — | — | — | — | — | 153 | 229 |
| 1910 | 50% | 80% | 15% | 4% | 20% | 9% | 15% | 7% | 80 | 107 |

* This table measures the occupational mobility of each unskilled laborer in various stages of his career. Thus, of the 75 unskilled laborers in Warren in 1870 (28 native-born, 47 foreign-born) only 17 continued to reside in the community in 1880. Of the men remaining only 25% born in America continued to work at unskilled jobs while 85% of the foreign-born workers remained in this low skill, low pay classification. By 1890 only five men from the unskilled group remained in Warren (one U.S.-born, four foreign-born). All four immigrants held unskilled jobs; the remaining native held a semi-skilled job, etc.

** N.B. indicates native-born Americans.

*** F.B. indicates foreign-born.

*Source: 1870 Manuscript Census,* Warren Borough, *1880 Manuscript Census,* Warren Borough, 1890, 1900, 1910 City Directories, Immigrant Alien Dockets, Naturalization Records, Birth Records.

If the immigrants felt a disadvantage in securing an occupation, one might expect as they became familiar with American customs and language that they would experience mobility similar to their American-born counterparts. A comparison of the occupational mobility of these two groups, however, reveals that the initial disadvantage experienced by the immigrant workers continued throughout their careers.

Rates of persistence of all workers improved in each succeeding decade of this study. In addition, foreign-born workers left Warren at a slightly greater rate than native-born workers from 1870 through 1910. Most immigrants and native-born Americans did not remain in Warren for more than a single decade. Table 4 reveals a much stronger relationship between one's birth and occupational mobility. Although the numbers from which the above percentages are derived remained small throughout the industrial era, the lack of mobility of foreign-born unskilled workers is dramatic. Native-born unskilled laborers from every census group experienced superior mobility in each decade. Of the forty-seven unskilled immigrants residing in Warren in 1870 only thirteen continued to live there one decade later. Two of these day laborers somehow managed to attain non-manual positions by 1880. None of the others achieved even limited mobility into the semi-skilled classification.

Mobility of the 1880 census group of unskilled laborers presents a more accurate pattern of the relationship between ethnicity and occupational opportunity. Seventy of the 115 unskilled workers joining the work force in 1880 emanated from foreign shores. One decade later only 34% of these men remained while 55% of all native-born Americans from this group persisted. The rate of occupational mobility clearly demonstrates the disadvantages of foreign birth. Fully 79% of all immigrants remained unskilled by 1890 while only 32% of the native Americans achieved no mobility at all. Moreover, 52% of all United States-born menial laborers advanced at least two skill classifications while only 20% of the foreign-born laborers achieved this kind of mobility. In addition, none of the immigrant group managed to attain a skilled position during this decade. By 1900 immigrants from the 1880 census group improved upon this record but only slightly. Nearly two-thirds of all foreign-born workers remained unskilled after twenty years in the community. Conversely, only 16% of the native-born Americans remained day laborers during the same period. Furthermore, 42% of all United States-born unskilled workers managed to attain the security of a white-collar position as compared with only 9% of the immigrant group able to do so. During the first decade of the twentieth century only five of the original seventy workers from the 1880 group continued to live in Warren. Yet three of these men continued to engage in the low-skill, low pay classification while all remaining American-born workers escaped this occupational group. The lack of occupational opportunity for 1880 immigrants is particularly striking, considering that these men arrived in Warren at the onset of industrialization. From 1880 through 1900 jobs remained plentiful and labor was constantly in demand. An analysis of all unskilled workers combined, undertaken in the larger study from which this essay is drawn, revealed that the upward mobility of the 1880 group exceeded all other census groups. Occupational opportunity for workers in the 1880 census group frequently occurred but immigrants in this group rarely enjoyed it.

Occupational advancements by unskilled immigrants joining the work force in 1890 or 1900 present a similar pattern. Only 17% of the immigrants arriving in Warren in 1890 without skills could move even one step up the occupational ladder and by 1900 none achieved white-collar "status." In contrast, two-thirds of all native-born Americans starting work in the same low classification attained a better occupation. Interestingly, only 11% of the native-born workers in this group attained a nonmanual position, suggesting a shrinking of opportunities for all workers by 1900. Only a few unskilled workers joining the labor force in 1890 remained in Warren by 1910. Of this limited number, however, 70% of the immigrants still held unskilled occupations while only one-fourth of the American-born workers failed to achieve some mobility.

During the first decade of the twentieth century Warren's industrial growth leveled off. But a large influx of immigrants mainly from Sweden and Italy arrived in Warren concurrently with the decline in occupational opportunity. Around the turn of the century 229 immigrant workers and their families arrived in the borough. By 1910, 107 of these men (47%) still lived in the community. The disadvantages of foreign birth continued to exist, however, as 80% of all immigrants remained concentrated in the lowest skill classification. During the same decade, only one-half of the native-born day laborers failed to achieve upward mobility.[14]

Conclusively, the impressive mobility of Warren's day laborers, noted in Table 4, did not extend to foreign-born workers who lacked skills. While a few immigrants achieved skilled or nonmanual positions, most found it impossible to move up even one small step into the ranks of the semi-skilled. Stephan Thernstrom, in his study of unskilled workers in Newburyport, Massachusetts, notes similar disadvantages for the unskilled immigrants in that New England city.

Nearly three-fourths of the 1850 Census group of unskilled immigrants in Newburyport failed to move up one skill classification by 1860. In addition, less than 20% of the 1860 and 1870 Census groups experienced even limited mobility.[15] During the same three decades, between 40% and 50% of all native-born laborers in Newburyport enjoyed some type of mobility.[16] Thernstrom concludes, "The immigrant workman in Newburyport was markedly less successful than his native counterpart in climbing out of the ranks of the unskilled in the 1850–1880 period. In each of the three groups at each census, disproportionately high numbers of the foreign-born remained concentrated at the bottom of the occupational scale."[17]

Of course, not all immigrants arriving in Warren during the 1870–1910 period began their working careers as unskilled laborers. An impressively large number of immigrants arriving in Warren each decade possessed skills and initially entered the labor force in the three higher skill classifications (see Table 3). A significant number joined the labor force as semi-skilled workers. Similarly, foreign-born workers were particularly successful in obtaining work as skilled laborers in the latter part of the nineteenth century. A comparison of the mobility experienced by native-born and foreign-born semi-skilled and skilled workers reveals that one's place of birth continued to influence his chances for success.

The relationship between ethnicity and occupational mobility of semi-skilled workers appears in Table 5. All workers initially joining the labor force as semi-skilled enjoyed more frequent mobility than unskilled laborers. Consequently, immigrants who found it possible to secure semi-skilled occupations enjoyed greater prospects for mobility than their unskilled counterparts. However, when compared with native-born semi-skilled workers the disadvantage of foreign birth again becomes clear.

Semi-skilled workers constituted the smallest portion of the labor force throughout the 1870–1910 period. Therefore, small shifts in the occupations of these workers result in a more erratic occupational pattern. However, with few exceptions, the relationship between one's birth and economic achievement remains consistent. Nearly three-fourths of the semi-skilled workers residing in Warren in 1870 left

Table 5

Ethnic Differences in Intra-Generational Occupational Mobility

Occupational Status Attained by Semi-skilled Workers

| Year | Unskilled | | Semi-skilled | | Skilled | | Nonmanual | | # in Group | |
|---|---|---|---|---|---|---|---|---|---|---|
| | N.B. | F.B. | N.B. | F.B. | N.B. | F.B. | N.B. | F.B. | N.B. | F.B. |
| | | | | 1870 Census Group | | | | | | |
| 1870 | — | — | 100% | 100% | — | — | — | — | 47 | 20 |
| 1880 | 9% | 25% | 18% | 63% | 18% | 12% | 55% | — | 11 | 8 |
| 1890 | 9% | 16% | 45% | 16% | 9% | — | 36% | 66% | 11 | 6 |
| 1900 | — | — | 33% | — | — | — | 67% | 100% | 6 | 3 |
| 1910 | — | — | — | — | — | 100% | — | — | — | 1 |
| | | | | 1880 Census Group | | | | | | |
| 1880 | — | — | 100% | 100% | — | — | — | — | 44 | 47 |
| 1890 | 11% | 7% | 39% | 50% | 22% | 29% | 28% | 14% | 18 | 14 |
| 1900 | 6% | 8% | 27% | 50% | 27% | 33% | 40% | 8% | 15 | 12 |
| 1910 | — | — | — | 57% | 83% | 38% | 17% | 14% | 6 | 7 |
| | | | | 1890 Census Group | | | | | | |
| 1890 | — | — | 100% | 100% | — | — | — | — | 32 | 49 |
| 1900 | 11% | 10% | 55% | 62% | 11% | 5% | 22% | 23% | 18 | 21 |
| 1910 | — | 18% | 36% | 36% | 18% | 9% | 45% | 36% | 11 | 11 |
| | | | | 1900 Census Group | | | | | | |
| 1900 | — | — | — | — | — | — | — | — | 107 | 40 |
| 1910 | 4% | 18% | 83% | 56% | 3% | 13% | 9% | 12% | 55 | 16 |

*Source: 1870 Manuscript Census,* Warren Borough, *1880 Manuscript Census,* Warren Borough, 1890, 1900, 1910 City Directories, Immigrant Alien Dockets, Naturalization Records, Birth Records.

the community by 1880. Of the few who remained, 73% of those born in America advanced to a higher skill classification whereas only 12% of the immigrant group attained skilled positions; none were able to achieve white-collar work. Interestingly, during the next decade, native Americans and immigrants from this Census group reversed positions. United States-born workers previously experiencing mobility into skilled and nonmanual positions failed to maintain these newly acquired positions while two-thirds of the remaining foreign-born workers joined the white-collar group. However, semi-skilled laborers from the 1870 census group continued to leave the community and by 1900 the small number remaining renders any further conclusions meaningless.

The succeeding three census groups of foreign-born semi-skilled workers fared no better than those from 1870. Even length of residence failed to improve one's chances for occupational mobility. Well over one-half of all foreign-born semi-skilled workers remained in that classification, or fell to unskilled, throughout the entire length of their work careers in Warren. Conversely, native-born workers from each of these groups frequently improved their positions, particularly after one decade or more in the community. Fully one-half of the 1880 census group born in America advanced at least one position by 1890. One decade later 67% of the workers from this group had experienced some mobility. In addition, 49% were able to bridge the gap into the ranks of nonmanual workers. By 1910 only six of the original American-born workers from the 1880 census group still resided in the community but none of them remained in the ranks of the semi-skilled.

Both American-born and foreign-born semi-skilled workers from the 1890 and 1900 groups experienced less mobility than either of the two previous census groups. Only one-third of the 1890 group of native-born semi-skilled laborers moved up the occupational ladder while 28% of the immigrants from the same period demonstrated similar mobility. During the succeeding decade nearly two out of every three remaining native-born workers from the 1890 group left that classification for a better job, with 45% attaining nonmanual occupations. In addition, the disadvantage of foreign birth decreased as nearly one-half of the immigrants remaining from the 1890 group became either skilled or nonmanual workers. Finally, foreign-born semi-skilled laborers joining the labor force in 1900 apparently suffered no disadvantage as their mobility exceeded that of the native-born workers. However, the increased disparity in rates of persistence distorts the pattern. Six of every ten American-born semi-skilled workers joining the labor force in 1900 continued to live in Warren at the close of the decade. Conversely, only four of every ten immigrant workers managed to persist one full decade. If the least successful most frequently left the community, it seems reasonable to conclude that the higher mobility of immigrants in the 1900 group, displayed in Table 5, is somewhat misleading. Nevertheless, the negative relationship between occupational mobility and foreign birth largely disappeared by 1910. Both immigrants and native-born semiskilled workers from the 1900 group experienced limited mobility. The shrinkage of economic opportunity rather than ethnicity became the most significant factor affecting mobility of semi-skilled workers in the period 1900–1910.

As previously noted, immigrants arriving in Warren, particularly between 1870 and 1890, more often began work in the skilled classification than in any other group. Craftsmen possessing a skill were geographically and occupationally less mobile than their less skilled counterparts. Immigrants beginning work in this classification also held greater occupational security and one might reasonably expect a less negative relationship between one's birth and occupational mobility. Table 6 illustrates that while native-born skilled workers continued to enjoy greater upward mobility than foreign-born craftsmen, the degree of inequity is not as striking as that experienced by the unskilled and semi-skilled immigrants. Conversely, skilled immigrants, particularly from the 1870 and 1880 census groups, fell from that classification with greater frequency than their native-born counterparts.

Table 6
Ethnic Differences in Intra-Generational Occupational Mobility

Occupational Status Attained by Skilled Workers

| Year | Unskilled N.B. | F.B. | Semi-skilled N.B. | F.B. | Skilled N.B. | F.B. | Nonmanual N.B. | F.B. | # in Group N.B. | F.B. |
|---|---|---|---|---|---|---|---|---|---|---|
| | | | | 1870 Census Group | | | | | | |
| 1870 | — | — | — | — | 100% | 100% | — | — | 122 | 97 |
| 1880 | 7% | 4% | 3% | 7% | 73% | 59% | 17% | 29% | 29 | 27 |
| 1890 | — | — | 11% | 12% | 50% | 59% | 39% | 29% | 18 | 17 |
| 1900 | — | — | 8% | 27% | 67% | 36% | 25% | 36% | 12 | 11 |
| 1910 | — | — | — | 29% | 62% | 27% | 28% | 14% | 8 | 7 |
| | | | | 1880 Census Group | | | | | | |
| 1880 | — | — | — | — | 100% | 100% | — | — | 101 | 104 |

| 1890 | 4% | 6% | 4% | 3% | 56% | 72% | 35% | 19% | 43 | 36 |
|------|----|----|----|----|----|----|----|----|----|----|
| 1900 | — | 10% | — | 16% | 58% | 63% | 42% | 10% | 24 | 19 |
| 1910 | — | 12% | — | — | 50% | 50% | 50% | 38% | 10 | 8 |
| **1890 Census Group** | | | | | | | | | | |
| 1890 | — | — | — | — | 100% | 100% | — | — | 83 | 108 |
| 1900 | 3% | 2% | — | 6% | 74% | 79% | 23% | 13% | 34 | 48 |
| 1910 | — | — | — | — | 68% | 71% | 32% | 29% | 14 | 28 |
| **1900 Census Group** | | | | | | | | | | |
| 1900 | — | — | — | — | 100% | 100% | — | — | 268 | 154 |
| 1910 | 4% | 6% | 1% | 4% | 81% | 72% | 14% | 18% | 134 | 71 |

*Source: 1870 Manuscript Census,* Warren Borough, *1880 Manuscript Census,* Warren Borough, 1890, 1900, 1910 City Directories, Immigrant Alien Dockets, Naturalization Records, Birth Records.

In 1870 Warren's 212 skilled workers constituted slightly over one-third of the total labor force. Within one decade only one-fourth of these craftsmen—divided nearly equally between foreign-born and native-born—continued to reside in Warren. Upward mobility of both foreign-born and native-born skilled workers from this group yields interesting but inconclusive evidence regarding the relationship between ethnic background and occupational opportunity. During the decade spanning the onset of industrialization in Warren, 29% of the foreign-born workers from this group managed to attain a "middle-class" occupation. At the same time only 17% of the native-born workers achieved the same leap into a nonmanual position. During the next decade the percentage of immigrant skilled workers attaining non-manual occupations remained constant (29%) while the ratio of native sons achieving white-collar work rose to 39%. This erratic pattern continued through the next two decades as a larger percentage of foreign-born workers attained white-collar positions in 1900 and American-born craftsmen achieved a greater percentage of nonmanual positions in 1910. At least for the 1870 group of skilled laborers, the relationship between one's place of birth and occupational mobility remains unclear.

Two hundred-five skilled workers joined the Warren work force during the decade prior to 1880. The 104 foreign-born workers among this group, however, labored under greater handicaps than the skilled immigrants from the 1870 group. The members of the 1880 census group had little chance to become established in the community before the industrial boom began. Consequently, the relationship between one's place of birth and occupational mobility appears much stronger than with the 1870 group. By 1890, 35% of the remaining American-born skilled workers from the 1880 group had attained some type of nonmanual position. At the same time only 19% of the remaining immigrants joined the ranks of the white-collar worker. During the succeeding decade—1890–1900—almost one-half of all the skilled workers from the 1880 census group left Warren; yet, the gap between immigrants and native sons continued to widen. Only one-tenth of the immigrants from this group held a nonmanual position by 1900 while two-fifths of the native-born laborers no longer worked with their hands. The disadvantages of foreign birth continued to exist through the first decade of the twentieth century although the gap narrowed considerably. By this time the few remaining foreign-born workers from the 1880 group were older and more securely settled. Fully 38% of them managed to achieve a "middle-class" occupation by 1910 while one-half of the native sons from 1880 attained a similar position. The skilled workers first listed in the 1880 Census arrived in Warren at a most fortuitous time. Some industrial expansion occurred in every succeeding decade through 1910. The occupational mobility experienced by native-born skilled workers from this group provides evidence of considerable economic opportunity. Yet, only a few foreign-born skilled workers could bridge the gap into the nonmanual work world.

Foreign-born skilled workers joining the labor force in 1890 fared no better than the 1880 group although native-born Americans experienced limited mobility. By 1900 only 23% of the native sons and 13% of the foreign-born skilled workers from 1890 had attained nonmanual occupations. One decade later 32% of the remaining native-born skilled workers and 29% of the immigrants from this group still in Warren held white-collar occupations. Native-born workers apparently still held some advantage in 1900 but by 1910 the distinction between skilled workers born in America and those born in Europe ceased to exist. Mobility of skilled workers joining Warren's labor force in 1900 also reflects this shrinkage of opportunity for all workers but increasing equality of opportunity for foreign-born workers. While nearly one-half of all the men in this group remained in the community for the full decade, only 16% enjoyed mobility into the nonmanual classification. This decline of opportunities in the nonmanual occupations occurred because of stabilization of the economy rather than from the change in ethnic composition of the skilled labor force in Warren. Only in this decade—1900–1910— did the number of native-born craftsmen entering the labor force exceed the number of foreign-born skilled workers. Immigrants, however, experienced a slightly higher rate of upward mobility than skilled workers from the 1900 group born in America. For skilled craftsmen joining the labor force at the turn of the century, the relationship between ethnicity and occupational mobility was negligible.

The comparison of the career patterns of both native-born American workers and foreign-born laborers suggests the following conclusions:

1) Immigrants upon arrival in the community most often joined the labor force as manual laborers. However, while immigrants performed most of the unskilled work in Warren a large number of foreign-born workers enjoyed considerable success in securing skilled work throughout the 1870–1910 period.

2) American-born workers most often joined the labor force as white-collar workers while only a minority of the foreign-born ever found employment in nonmanual positions.

3) The initial economic opportunity of immigrants most closely reflected the overall economic conditions of the community. During the period of greatest economic expansion in Warren—1880–1900— immigrants had little difficulty securing work in the higher skill classifications. However, when the economic growth of the community declined—around 1900—a much larger percentage of immigrants were forced to accept unskilled occupations.

4) Unskilled immigrants were almost totally immobile throughout their careers in Warren while a majority of native-born Americans beginning work in the lowest classification advanced to higher

positions in each succeeding decade. Even more remote was the prospect of an immigrant beginning work as an unskilled worker and rising to a nonmanual position.

5) Semi-skilled and skilled immigrants fared better than unskilled foreign-born workers, but continued to experience limited mobility when compared with native sons beginning their careers from the same groups. Clearly the remarkable upward mobility of manual laborers occurred largely within the ranks of the American-born.

6) During the periods of economic expansion in Warren occupational mobility existed mainly for the native sons. However, when the expansion declined, primarily during the last decade of this study, the gap between native-born Americans and immigrants decreased. Thus, the advantages of economic growth in Warren applied mainly, but not exclusively, to those workers born on American soil.

Of course not all immigrant groups experienced the same degree of opportunity in nineteenth-century Warren. But when one divides each ethnic group into specific skill classifications, the number remaining after outward migration becomes too small to yield reliable generalizations. But in at least a few aspects we may ascertain the relationship between specific nativity and occupational opportunity. Analysis of the initial occupations attained by specific ethnic groups (Table 7) indicates that certain groups performed primarily skilled and nonmanual work while others were relegated to the less desirable unskilled tasks.

Throughout the last three decades of the nineteenth century, Germans migrating to Warren enjoyed greater possibilities of success than any other group of foreign-born workers. Four of every five German-born workers attained either skilled or nonmanual occupations upon first joining the Warren labor force. The rapid industrialization of Warren created a demand for trained workers, particularly in machine and tool making, and the townsfolk willingly accommodated workers from Germany. As early as 1852 the growth of the German-born population of Warren warranted the building of a German-Methodist church and by 1870 the press regularly reported on the activities of two German-American lodges.[18] The large number of German children in school reflects the financial

## Table 7
### Initial Occupation of All Workers by Nativity

| Birth-place | 1870* Unsk. | Semi-sk. | Sk. | Non-man. | 1880 Unsk. | Semi-sk. | Sk. | Non-man. | 1890 Unsk. | Semi-sk. | Sk. | Non-man. | 1900 Unsk. | Semi-sk. | Sk. | Non-man. |
|---|---|---|---|---|---|---|---|---|---|---|---|---|---|---|---|---|
| U.S. | 28 | 48 | 122 | 200 | 45 | 44 | 111 | 270 | 22 | 32 | 83 | 276 | 153 | 107 | 268 | 553 |
| Canada | 1 | 2 | 4 | 1 | 4 | 6 | 6 | 2 | 3 | — | 5 | 20 | 3 | — | 18 | 13 |
| England | 2 | — | 14 | 2 | 5 | 12 | 14 | — | 3 | 9 | 9 | 16 | 17 | 8 | 8 | 9 |
| Ireland | 24 | 2 | 15 | 5 | 29 | 4 | 7 | 2 | 21 | 12 | 17 | 15 | 33 | 9 | 21 | 16 |
| Germany | 4 | 4 | 23 | 19 | 3 | 7 | 30 | 11 | 7 | 6 | 18 | 27 | 19 | 3 | 16 | 12 |
| Sweden | 1 | — | 2 | — | 5 | 6 | 8 | 5 | 12 | 10 | 20 | 16 | 96 | 9 | 47 | 25 |
| Denmark | 3 | 3 | 7 | 2 | 6 | 3 | 13 | 2 | 2 | 5 | 12 | 17 | 31 | 1 | 24 | 11 |
| France | 11 | 7 | 20 | 18 | 11 | 9 | 12 | 8 | 3 | 7 | 12 | 18 | 7 | 5 | 6 | 9 |
| Italy | — | — | — | — | — | — | — | — | — | — | — | 1 | 20 | 4 | 3 | — |
| Other | 1 | 2 | 8 | 5 | 7 | — | 4 | — | 2 | — | 15 | — | 3 | 1 | 21 | — |
| Totals | 75 | 67 | 215 | 252 | 115 | 91 | 205 | 300 | 75 | 81 | 191 | 396 | 382 | 147 | 422 | 648 |

* The 1870 group held these occupations at the initiation of this study; thus, the indicated occupation may not have been the first task performed by members of this group.

*Source: 1870 Manuscript Census,* Warren Borough, *1880 Manuscript Census,* Warren Borough, 1890, 1900, 1910 City Directories, Immigrant Alien Dockets, Naturalization Records, Birth Records.

security of the German-born population—they could afford to pay for books and a modest tuition—and also the favored position of German immigrants in the community. Beginning in 1874, following a petition by German citizens, the school board hired a full-time teacher to instruct the school's 130 German students in the language of their parents.[19] While no other ethnic group in the town's history received such favored treatment, the diversity of Warren's ethnic minorities contributed to the generally hospitable environment.

The French and British also found considerable occupational opportunity available in nineteenth-century Warren. Ancestors of both groups were among the early settlers to the community and perhaps paved the way toward harmonious environment. Writing in 1887 the town's local historian commented, "It seems quite appropriate that natives of France should at last become occupants and owners, in part at least, of a region which was first explored and honored by Frenchmen. They are good and honored citizens and when Americanized compare favorably with those who came before them."[20] Nearly 68% of the French residents in Warren in 1870 held jobs in the two highest skill groups. One-half of those joining the labor force during the next decade also succeeded in attaining either skilled or nonmanual occupations. Interestingly, the French residents during these two decades demonstrated a greater rate of persistence than Warren's German population. Nearly 40% of the 1870 group of French residents continued to live in the community in 1880 and one-half of the 1880 group remained in 1890.[21] The German migrants, however, in spite of their initial occupational success, left Warren at a more rapid rate. Only 30% of the 1870 group of German workers still lived in Warren by 1880 and less than one-fourth of the 1880 group remained as long as one full decade.[22] Persistence rates of the 1890 and 1900 German residents increased significantly but never exceeded that of Warren's French residents. The reasons for this negative relationship between geographical stability and ethnicity remain unclear but simply suggest that the French residing in Warren had a greater propensity to settle than the Germans.

Warren's British residents, unlike the French or the German migrants, held few nonmanual occupations until 1890. The English migrants, however, apparently possessed some skills and had little difficulty in securing craft work. Three of every four English workers in preindustrial Warren held skilled occupations. One decade later 45% of the newly arrived English workers secured skilled positions and only 16% had to accept unskilled work. During the first full decade, coinciding with Warren's industrialization, the English immigrant fared even better. Fully 45% attained nonmanual occupations upon their initial entry into Warren's labor force, while another one-fourth acquired skilled positions.

Only the Irish, of the major immigrant groups through 1890, reflect any negative relationship between initial occupation and place of birth. Over one-half of the Irish residing in Warren in 1870 worked at the low paying, often temporary unskilled labor. In fact, this group held one-third of all the unskilled occupations while constituting only 8% of the total population. Even the Irish, however, enjoyed some economic opportunity as nearly one-third of the men in the 1870 group worked at skilled occupations and a few held white-collar positions. But during the decade between 1870 and 1880, opportunity for the Irish worker decreased—industrial growth had just begun—as only 30% of the newly arrived adult males from Ireland could attain work above the unskilled classification. Warren's economy continued to grow through 1890, however, and the Irish, although still performing a large share of the unskilled labor, gained a significant number of skilled and nonmanual occupations. Sixty-five Irish workers joined the labor force during Warren's major decade of expansion. Almost one-half of them managed to find employment in either the skilled or nonmanual occupations attesting to the relationship between the expanding economy and occupational opportunity.

Two other ethnic groups—the Swedes and the Italians—although later arrivals to the community, played an important role in the economic development of the borough. Swedish immigrants migrated to several villages around Warren as early as 1850 and although only a few of the Scandinavian families actually lived within the borough's boundaries in 1870, they were apparently considered an asset to the community. As early as 1880 the *Warren Mail* proclaimed:

> The Swedish inhabitants [of the county] have recently built a fine church. It is built in modern style and is a standing monument to the industry and thrift of this intelligent, economical and persevering class of the adopted citizens of our country. The disinterested looker on must . . . be led to the conclusion that the settling of this people in our midst was to our country a godsend. In short, they bid fair at no distant day to become a power for good in our country.[23]

The first significant number of Swedish immigrant families arrived in the borough during the height of the town's industrial growth. The success of the 1890 group of Swedes in attaining initial higher-level occupations indicates the hospitable attitude toward the foreign-born. Over one-quarter of this most recent group of immigrants to Warren attained white-collar jobs upon joining the labor force. In addition, one-third of the 1890 group of Scandinavian workers attained skilled occupations upon initial entry into Warren's work force.

By the mid 1890s as the flow of immigration from Southern Europe began to affect Warren, the town's accommodating attitude toward the foreign-born began to change. The Chicago Pullman Strike of July, 1894, created considerable controversy and some anti-immigrant feelings within the community. In a series of sermons decrying the evils of competition—which he considered the cause of the strike—the pastor of the Presbyterian Church declared, "It [competition] has led to all the horrors of the iniquitous sweating system. It has led some capitalists to import foreign laborers from the lowest classes and thus by competition force the American workmen to accept a lower wage."[24]

One month later, August, 1894, Warren experienced its own labor difficulties when the molders employed by the Struthers Iron Works refused to accept a 20% cut in wages.[25] The management quickly imported a number of Irish workers from Buffalo, New York, to replace the striking workers. Violence occurred and several men were injured as townsmen retaliated by refusing to permit the nonunion employees entrance to the Iron Works. Both local newspapers condemned the violence but agreed that the Iron Works was largely at fault for bringing the "Irish scabs" into the community.[26] The strike continued for several weeks and anti-immigrant sentiment began to crystalize. Letters to the editor reflecting this attitude appeared regularly throughout the month. Finally on August 8 the editors of the *Warren Mail* reversed their previously hospitable attitude toward immigrants. A front page editorial entitled "Restrict Immigration" proclaimed, "The public sentiment in favor of a more rigorous restriction on immigration is gaining strength constantly in all parts of the country. Keep out the agitators, keep out mob leaders, keep out the idle, the vicious, the restless, the turbulent, the disorderly. America has long been the washpot of Europe. Restrict immigration. That is the urgent demand of truly patriotic Americans in this age and generation."[27]

The initial occupation attained by immigrants arriving in Warren after 1895 (Table 7) reflects both the decline in economic expansion and the new attitude toward the foreign-born. Fully 44% of all immigrants joining the Warren labor force in 1900 accepted jobs as unskilled laborers. In addition, the decline in occupational opportunity affected nearly every ethnic group including those who previously enjoyed initial advantages in the community. Almost one-half of the newly arrived German and French groups began working in the lowest two skill groups in 1900. The English and the Irish fared no better with 58% of each group beginning work as unskilled or semi-skilled laborers. However, the greatest burden fell upon the most recent ethnic additions to the community—the Swedes and the Italians. Over one-half of the Swedes joining the work force in 1900 had to accept work as unskilled laborers compared with 20% who did so in 1890. In addition, only 18% of all foreign-born workers secured positions as white-collar workers in 1900 while 51% of the native-born Americans began their careers in "middle-class" occupations.[28]

All groups of foreign-born workers arriving in Warren at the turn of the century experienced greater disadvantages than their counterparts who had arrived before them. The Italians, however, aroused the greatest antagonisms. In a scathing article entitled "No Dago's Wanted" the editors of the *Weekly Democrat* criticized a local leather company for advertising for fifteen Italian families to come to Warren for work. "Just think of it," the editor exclaimed, "fifteen Italian families for Warren. Does anyone believe that Warren wants those families here? If they do they had better get an expression from a few people as I have done. . . . We can tell the Penn Leather Company that we don't want any dagoes in Warren and if that is the class of people they contemplate bringing here we don't care for the industry."[29] Anti-Italian articles—disparaging their "shiftless ways" or their proclivity to violence continued in the press with marked frequency through the first decade of the twentieth century. Twenty-seven Italian-born males joined the Warren labor force in 1900; as one might expect none became white-collar workers and only three could secure occupations as skilled laborers. One decade later nearly one-half of these men still lived in the community but only one Italian worker was able to move up even one step on the occupational ladder.

For the immigrants who entered Warren during the height of industrialization, the community provided impressive economic opportunity in the skilled trades. Only the Irish had difficulty in securing occupations above the level of the unskilled. Conversely, with the exception of the 1880s, middle-class nonmanual occupations were almost exclusively reserved for the native-born American worker. Similarly, immigrants failed to share in the impressive occupational mobility enjoyed by the native-born manual laborer. For most immigrants remaining in the community, the initial occupation they secured upon arrival became their lifelong work. In addition, immigrants arriving in Warren after 1890 experienced particular difficulties. The town's rapid economic expansion declined around the turn of the century. Furthermore, anti-immigrant attitudes created a less than hospitable environment for newly arrived ethnic groups. Economic opportunity declined for all groups but particularly affected the newest ethnic groups in the community, the Swedes and the Italians.[30]

It is futile to speculate on the aspirations of these groups of immigrant workers. However, they clearly did not develop any strong sense of class solidarity. The high rate of outward migration, particularly among the unskilled, prevented any continuity of residence within the community. The transient members of this group obviously could not act with unity to correct common grievances.[31] In addition, unemployed laborers—those most likely to express discontent—were treated severely in nineteenth-century Warren. Local law decreed that vagrants be arrested, forced to work on a chain gang for two days, then evicted from the community.[32]

The impressive success experienced by immigrants in attaining skilled work upon arriving in the community also hindered the development of a proletarian conscience. Warren's highly diversified economy and ethnic composition created varying opportunities for workers in different occupations and at several skill levels. A commonality of interests simply did not exist. Labor organization for the purpose of increasing wages and improving working conditions aroused no more than temporary interest and never involved more than one craft. Even craft unionism had a difficult time surviving in a community of small shops and factories. Only one trade union— the Cigarmakers' Union—had a continuous existence; and they were not listed in the city directories until 1890.[33] Moreover, although immigrants experienced limited mobility, enough unskilled workers did advance up the occupational ladder to give hope to all. Workmen tended to generalize from the familiar experiences within their own community. For most manual laborers of Warren frequent occupational mobility more than justified their belief in America as a land of opportunity.[34] The Chamber of Commerce, perhaps unwittingly, best illustrated the attitude of manual workers in Warren when it declared:

"Labor is reasonably well paid and therefore is contented and prosperous. Laboring men are industrious, frugal and intelligent. They realize that regular employment at fair wages affords the greatest measure of prosperity and hence, *Warren is absolutely*

*free from labor disputes either as to wages, conditions of employ-
ment or other surroundings* which in other localities interfere with
the business of the employer and the wage earning of the em-
ployee."[35]

# NOTES

1. J. S. Schenk, *History of Warren County, Pennsylvania* (Syracuse: 1887), p. 340.
2. *Ibid.*, p. 338.
3. *Warren Gazette*, August, 1828, p. 2.
4. S. P. Johnson, "A History of Warren County," *Warren Directory of 1885* (Warren, Pa.: 1885).
5. U. S. Bureau of the Census, *Ninth Census of the United States, 1870: Population* I, 256.
6. *Warren Ledger*, March 2, 1876, p. 3.
7. *Warren Mail*, August 8, 1876, p. 3.
8. U. S. Bureau of the Census, *Manuscript Schedule, Ninth Census of the United States, 1870: Warren, Pennsylvania.*
9. Tax Assessor's Valuation Lists, Warren Borough, 1870 (Located in the attic of the Warren County Court House).
10. Compiled from: U. S. Bureau of the Census, *Manuscript Schedule, Ninth Census of the United States, 1870: Warren, Pennsylvania; Manuscript Schedule, Tenth Census of the United States, 1880: Warren, Pennsylvania;* 1890, 1900, 1910 City Directories, Warren, Pennsylvania.
11. *Ibid.*
12. *Ibid.*
13. Stephan Thernstrom, "Immigrants and WASPs: Ethnic Differences in Occupational Mobility in Boston, 1890–1940," *Nineteenth Century Cities* (New Haven: 1969), pp. 129–141. Thernstrom reports similar but greater disadvantages for foreign-born workers in securing nonmanual occupations in twentieth-century Boston. He concludes: "Native-born Americans had a distinct advantage in the competition for jobs on the higher rungs of the occupational ladder. . . . Both immigrants and the native-born children of immigrants were far more likely both to begin and to end their careers working with their hands and wearing blue collars."
14. The arrival in Warren in 1900 of a large number of unskilled immi-grants did not alone cause the decline in occupational opportunity. When one compares mobility of immigrants and native-born laborers separately the shrinkage of opportunity shows up in the data for both groups.
15. Stephan Thernstrom, *Poverty and Progress: Social Mobility in a Nineteenth Century City* (Cambridge: 1964), p. 100.
16. *Ibid.*
17. *Ibid.*, p. 101.
18. *Warren Mail*, June 10, 1871, p. 3.
19. Minutes of the regular meeting, May 25, 1874, Warren School Board of Directors, Book 'C,' p. 165. (In the office of the County Superintendent of Schools.)

20. J. S. Schenk, p. 154.

21. Compiled from: U. S. Bureau of the Census, *Manuscript Schedule, Ninth Census of the United States, 1870: Warren, Pennsylvania;* U. S. Bureau of the Census, *Manuscript Schedule, Tenth Census of the United States, 1880; 1890 Warren City Directory,* Warren, Pennsylvania.

22. *Ibid.*

23. *Warren Mail,* March 22, 1880, p. 3.

24. Rev. J. W. Smith, "The Evils of Competition," *Warren Mail,* July 25, 1894, p. 3.

25. *Warren Ledger,* August 3, 1894, p. 3.

26. *Warren Ledger,* August 3, 1894, p. 3; *Warren Mail,* August 5, 1894, p. 3.

27. *Warren Mail,* August 8, 1894, p. 3.

28. It is noteworthy that while immigrants arriving in Warren in 1900 experienced particular difficulties in securing higher level occupations, those who succeeded experienced mobility equal to native-born Americans. This is due largely to the decline of the spectacular mobility enjoyed by earlier American-born workers rather than an increase in mobility by immigrants.

29. *The Weekly Democrat,* June 7, 1900, p. 6.

30. For a more complete investigation of occupational, wealth, and property mobility as well as voting patterns of all of Warren's manual laborers see: Michael P. Weber, "Patterns of Progress: Social Mobility in a Pennsylvania Oil Town, 1870–1910" (Unpublished Dissertation, Carnegie–Mellon University, 1972).

31. Thernstrom, *Poverty and Progress,* p. 159. Professor Thernstrom reports that in Newburyport, "The pressure to migrate operated selectively to remove the least successful from the community." Hence, "Members of this group had no capacity to act in concert . . . stable organization based on a consciousness of common grievances was obviously impossible."

32. Minutes of the regular meeting, April 1, 1889, "Police Regulations," Warren Borough Council, Book 4, p. 134. (Located in Warren Borough Municipal Office.)

33. J. N. Lacy, *Warren County Business and General Directory for 1890* (Warren, Pa.: 1890).

34. Thernstrom, *Poverty and Progress,* pp. 163–165. Thernstrom feels that even though workers in Newburyport—who experienced much less mobility than Warren's manual laborers—"could view America as a land of opportunity despite the fact that the class realities . . . confined most of them to the working classes. . . . These newcomers to the urban life arrived with a low horizon of expectations." Hence, "The typical unskilled laborer who settled in Newburyport could feel proud of his achievements and optimistic about the future." Cf. Clyde Griffin, "Workers Divided: Craft and Ethnic Differences in Poughkeepsie, New York, 1850–1880," *Nineteenth Century Cities,* p. 51. Griffin agrees with the above conclusions by Thernstrom claiming that workers "judged their prospects for advancement more by the instance of success in their own trade than by cases of 'rags to riches' in unrelated occupations. . . . Had Newburyport laborers judged their progress by the models of success exemplified in the Horatio Alger novels, they would have despaired. But their frame of reference was the experience of their own kind in their community."

35. Chamber of Commerce, *Warren, Pennsylvania: The Gem of the Allegheny* (Warren, Pa.: 1913), p. 17.

# 7

# The Rusin Community in Pennsylvania

## WALTER C. WARZESKI

*Walter C. Warzeski is now chairman of the Department of History at Kutztown State College. He did his doctoral dissertation at the University of Pittsburgh.*

Nationalism and religion, which have been two of the main themes of history, are most important in the study of the Ruthenian migration to the United States. The term Ruthenian is a misnomer, having been employed by the Vatican to distinguish those eastern Slavic people who were in union with Rome as contrasted to those who remained part of the Orthodox Church.[1] To be more specific, the group under consideration can be subdivided into two categories, the Carpatho-Ruthenian or Rusin people and the Galician-Ruthenian or Ukrainian people.

Both segments have numerous similarities and hold a great many cultural attributes in common; these include membership in the same hybrid church which has been referred to by several names, e.g., Greek Catholic, Byzantine Catholic or Uniate Church;[2] habitation in the eastern area of the Austro-Hungarian empire;[3] agricultural backwardness and subordination to foreign land magnates;[4] obligation to pay heavy taxes, and subjection to long periods of military

175

service;[5] and responses to the propaganda emitting from agents of steamship, coal mine, and steel mill companies.[6]

The emigration of these Slavic people from their Austro-Hungarian homeland commenced in the 1870s, reached a crescendo in the two decades preceding World War I, and tapered off to an insignificant number during the period between the two wars.[7] By 1933 there were approximately 700,000 Ruthenian immigrants in the United States, who inhabited the anthracite areas near Scranton and Wilkes-Barre, the bituminous coal fields of Ohio, western Pennsylvania, and West Virginia, the steel mill towns near Pittsburgh, the iron ore regions of Michigan and Minnesota, the farm lands of the New England, Middle Atlantic, and Mid-West areas, and the industrialized region near Chicago.[8]

Of the total number of Ruthenian immigrants, approximately 60% of the total number migrated from Carpatho-Ruthenia[9] and are referred to as Rusins. The main focus of this chapter is on this group of people. They inhabited the south side of the Carpathians adjoining the regions of Bukovina and Galicia. The area had been under the jurisdiction of the Magyar people for the preceding one thousand year period.[10] As a result, the people did not possess a national consciousness. They spoke several dialects which were akin to the Ukrainian and Russian language and referred to themselves by a variety of national designations, such as Carpatho-Ruthenians, Ruthenians, Ugro-Rusins, Rusins, Rusnaks, and Russkis.[11] In America they were referred to by such unflattering names as "Hunkies" or "Polacks."

The departure of the Rusins from Ruthenia to the United States was primarily based on economic motivations. It began during the period 1870–1899 and was the beginning of mass immigration from the Habsburg empire. Since the Immigration Commission kept a record of the country of origin and not of race, language or nationality, it is impossible to arrive at an accurate number of Rusin emigrants during this period.[12] The size of the Rusin community must have been large, for the Reverend A. Hodabay who was the Apostolic Visitor for the Ruthenians, in his report of January 11, 1905, specified that 262,500 members belonged to the Uniate Church in the United States. Prior to the migration of Ruthenians, the Byzantine Rite or Uniate Church was not in existence in the United States.[13] The total number of Eastern Slavs who migrated from Austria-Hungary in this same period has been estimated at about one-half million by the Immigration Commission.

As already stated, the main reason for the exodus of Ruthenians was economic. The late nineteenth century witnessed a transition in the Hungarian ruled province from that of a self-sufficing family economy to that of the factory system. This economic change occurred together with various psychological developments. The peasants were agriculturally backward, and although serfdom was eliminated in the province in 1848, as it was throughout the Habsburg empire, the Rusin peasant was unable to maintain a stable standard of living. The economic destitution of the Rusin peasant made it mandatory for the promulgation of much needed economic legislation in the Magyar-ruled province of Ruthenia. When this type of legislation was not forthcoming, the Rusin peasant was that much more prone to take drastic measures such as emigration to the new world.[14]

The United States was viewed as the land of opportunity for the destitute peasant. He was made aware of this by correspondence from Rusins who had already emigrated to the new world. Whereas the American laborer considered conditions in the factories and mines as extremely intolerable and the wages pitifully low, the Rusin considered these same conditions as a tremendous improvement over his peasant lot. Another inducement that encouraged migration to the United States was the availability of free homestead land. To the land-starved Rusin, who tilled an average plot of less than two acres of marginal land, the prospect of a free homestead was the fulfillment of his fondest dreams. These economic inducements, together with various freedoms not enjoyed in Ruthenia, and the opportunities for education and social mobility, and the absence of military conscription, all contributed to his desire to seek a new home in the United States.[15]

Although emigration seemed to be the most sensible course to follow and would provide economic and social benefits to the peasant and at the same time alleviate the overpopulation in Ruthenia, the Austro-Hungarian government sought to restrict emigration. As early as March of 1877, a government decree demanded that the Catholic clergy should preach on the theme of the hardships and the sufferings being experienced by the immigrants in the United States. Stress was to be put upon unemployment, the hunger and starvation, crime and poor living conditions that faced the emigrants.[16] Where the policy of intimidation was not sufficient, the policy of suppression was to be utilized. The border police made it more difficult to leave the country, but this was offset by agents of the steamship and mining companies who resorted to bribes of the police.[17]

A more concentrated effort to forbid emigration, or at least to make it more difficult, was the promulgation of the Hungarian Law of 1903. Besides prohibiting public speeches and advertisements which recommended emigration and providing additional complements of men to the border patrol, it provided the establishment of a government fund to assist emigrants to return to the Magyar-dominated province. This legislation was not any more successful than the previous laws, but it did prescribe categories of people who were prohibited from emigrating. In this respect the restriction of certain categories of people anticipated immigration laws in the United States. The following were prohibited from emigrating:[18]

1. Parents who had not made provisions for their children who were left behind.

2. Male minors who did not have parental consent.

3. Female minors who were unaccompanied by a trustworthy adult.

4. Persons with insufficient means.

5. Criminals and mental deficients.

Despite incurring the wrath of governing officials, large numbers of Rusins were able to emigrate to the United States. The exact date of the first immigrant from Carpatho-Ruthenia is difficult to ascertain because of a lack of documentation, but it took place in either 1877 or 1878 and involved a peasant from the Ruthenian village of Radoczyna.[19] As was the case with other immigrant groups, the arrival of the Rusins was viewed with a great deal of suspicion and hostility by the native and more established groups in America. This hostility was perhaps most vociferously shown by the labor movement, who denounced the new immigrant as a threat to the program of higher wages and better working conditions. The enmity of labor toward the Rusin came about, not because of the new immigrant's acceptance of a lower wage, but because of his scab activities. The newly arrived immigrant was hired by coal mine and steel mill executives to replace workers who were on strike.[20]

This great exodus from Austria-Hungary, which averaged between 20,000 to 30,000 annually during the decades of the 1880s and 1890s, was to reach a sharp upward trend by 1903, reaching 120,000.[21] Most of the Rusin immigrants settled along the Eastern seaboard states. Pennsylvania received the majority of these Rusin people. The eastern area in particular, the Hazleton, Scranton, and Wilkes-Barre region became a center for the Rusin people. From these cities the Rusins migrated to the southwestern regions of Pittsburgh and Allegheny County.[22]

The Rusin immigrants faced a two-fold problem generally not experienced by other immigrant groups. They were members of a relatively small Slavic group and were members of a church community which was strange and unknown to the people of the United States. These two problems were compounded by the general illiteracy of the mass of the people. In order to solve their problems and enjoy a certain degree of security and fellowship, the Rusins joined larger Slavic groups, particularly the Slovak and the Polish communities. This association with other ethnic Slavic groups failed to solve their uniquely religious problem, namely that of their Uniate religion. To solve their religious situation the Rusins began to organize their own churches. The first was in Minneapolis in 1878 and was followed by the creation of a parish in the Scranton area.[23]

The central thread of the Rusin community in Pennsylvania is interwoven with church affairs. Therefore, in order to understand the Rusin people it is necessary to develop the history of the Uniate Church in Pennsylvania. The creation of Uniate parishes did not solve the religious situation, for now it was necessary to procure priests to staff the churches. Since there were neither Uniate priests nor Uniate Seminaries in the United States, it was necessary to seek those priests from either Carpatho-Ruthenia or Galicia. The first Uniate priest in the United States was Ivan Volansky, who arrived in December of 1884 and presented himself to the Archbishop at Philadelphia. Volansky was of Galician origin, and he was sent to minister to the Ruthenians at Shenandoah. Through his efforts a church was built in 1886. This church, St. Michael the Archangel, was the first Uniate Church in America.[24]

During the next four years, Volansky's efforts resulted in the construction of Uniate churches in the Hazleton, Kingston, and Olyphant areas of the Commonwealth. He did not neglect the intellectual and cultural attributes of the Uniate community, for on August 15, 1886, the first issue of *America,* a biweekly newspaper was published. The success of this, the first Ruthenian newspaper in the United States, was apparent by the decision taken in 1887 to begin weekly publication. Besides seeking to inform the Rusin populace, *America* also sought to formulate the social and economic tenor of its readers. In the latter category it became embroiled in the labor disputes in the anthracite industry and as a result lost a great amount of its circulation and ceased publication in 1898.[25]

There are today two Ruthenian publications that trace their origin to the last decade of the nineteenth century. The older of the two the *Amerikansko Ruski Vistnyk* or the *American Ruthenian Herald* has undergone several name changes but is still being published near Homestead, Pennsylvania, as the *Greek Catholic Messenger.* This Rusin newspaper, which is the oldest active Ruthenian newspaper in the United States, utilizes both the English and a Slavic language in its feature articles. Today, the *Messenger* utilizes Roman script, but formerly it relied on the Cyrillic script to inform its readers of the issues of the day. Its counterpart, among the Ukrainians, is the *Svoboda* or *Freedom,* which began publication in 1893. Many of the *Svoboda* articles appear in the Cyrillic, and like the *Messenger,* it is still being published.[26]

The Ruthenian people in Europe were basically illiterate and looked to their clergy for guidance and leadership. The same situation was to transpire in the United States, for the clergy were not only to minister to the spiritual needs of the Uniates but also to provide social and fraternal guidance. More so than in the other immigrant groups the clergy served as the cohesive unit among the Ruthenian people, especially among those from Carpatho-Ruthenia. It is difficult to ascertain who was the first Uniate priest of Rusin extraction in the United States. One segment indicates that a Nicholas Zubricky, who ministered to the people in the Kingston area around 1887, was the first Rusin priest in America. Another faction insists that Alexander Dzubay and Cyril Gulovich, who were active in the Wilkes-Barre and Freeland areas in 1889, have that distinction.[27] That the number of Rusin migrants to the United States was increasing and that they continually desired to maintain their cultural and religious identity can be attested by the number of Uniate Churches in existence in 1894. By that date thirty Uniate Churches, of which twenty-six could be classified as Rusin, had been built.[28]

The Rusin and the Ukrainian immigrants were to undergo many travails in establishing the Uniate Church in the United States. Although the hostility of the Latin hierarchy was the greatest danger to the Uniate Church at the turn of the twentieth century, other factors leading to a Rusin schism were the active missionary activity of the Orthodox Church, petty jealousies among the people, and the desire to become more quickly Americanized.[29]

The Latin hierarchy, fearful of the effects of the Uniate Church would have upon the laity and disenchanted with the Byzantine clergy who were not required to be celibate, were instrumental in securing the promulgation of a papal decree in 1890 that was detrimental to the Uniate Church. It placed a number of restrictions upon the Ruthenian clergy and its church. It specified that the United States was a missionary area for the Uniate Church, and that Uniate clergy had to secure the permission of their bishop prior to emigrating to the United States. This request would be forwarded to the Sacred Congregation for the Eastern Church in Rome, which in turn would refer it to the American diocese in which the clergyman desired to work.[30] The greatest hardship imposed upon the Rusin church was celibacy. This ban not only applied to newly arrived clergy in the United States but it also required the recall of all married clergy. The Rusins considered these prohibitions to be an infringement upon their rights which were guaranteed by the Uniate agreements.[31]

This papal decree was followed by another distasteful decree in

1895 entitled *Orientalium Dignitas,* which specified that the Uniates should become members of the Latin Church whenever there was a lack of an Eastern Rite Church. The Orthodox Church was to capitalize on these papal decrees, declaring that the papacy was circumventing the Uniate rights and privileges. The Orthodox efforts culminated in a schismatic movement within the Ruthenian Uniate Church in the United States.[32]

The Ruthenians, who remained within the framework of the Catholic Church, held meetings to promulgate a program to combat this schism. The first meeting was held at Shamokin, on May 30, 1901. At this meeting an "Association of Church Congregations in the United States and Canada" was organized. It provided for the creation of three agencies which were to coordinate the affairs of the organization. The association was to be under the leadership of six directors, a Spiritual Council was formed to minister to the spiritual needs of the group, and a permanent secretariat was to keep the records and manage related matters of this agency.

A general convention of the association was convened on March 26, 1902, but the convention was unable to resolve the problems besetting the Uniate Church, and in fact added to the divisive forces among the Ruthenian people. This was caused by the fragmentation of the convention. The radical wing proposed the severing of ties with the Catholic Church. A moderate segment sought to preserve its autonomy by stipulating that Uniate Churches were to be incorporated in the name of the trustee members rather than in the name of the Latin Rite bishop. Near unanimous approval was given two other resolutions. The first called for the appointment of a bishop of the Byzantine Rite for the Uniates in America. The second provided for a subsequent meeting of the organization in 1905. The second resolution was not to be fulfilled, for the Latin Church hierarchy was to prohibit the calling of another convention.[33]

The desire of having an Uniate bishop was foremost among the Rusin clergy. On September 5, 1893, a clerical meeting was held at Olyphant which petitioned the Vatican to appoint a bishop for the Ruthenians in America.[34] The Vatican did not respond to this request until 1902, when Rome named Rev. Andrew Hodobay as the Apostolic Visitor for the Ruthenians in America. The Hodobay Mission, after investigating all phases of the Ruthenian problem, made a report in 1906 which recommended the naming of a Uniate bishop for the United States. However, the Hodobay Mission did not satisfy the several factions among the American Ruthenians. Those from Galicia, who preferred to be called Ukrainians, refused to cooperate, while the Rusins split into two factions, the Preshov and Uzghorod group. As a result Soter Stephen Ortynsky was named bishop for the Ruthenian Church in America.[35]

The selection of Ortynsky, although it was first viewed as a triumph for the Uniate Church, was to fade into the bitterness of despair because of the cleavage that developed within the Ruthenian group. The resulting bitterness of the Rusin and Ukrainian factions has engendered a feeling of suspicion and distrust between these two groups that persists to the present day. The Rusin organization that took the lead against Ortynsky and what they called the "Ukrainian Menace" was the Greek Catholic Union. This fraternal organization's goals were at times the zenith and at times the nadir of the Rusin Uniate Church in the United States. Its professed aim was to help the Uniate Church, but the method of achieving these goals many times was to have the exact opposite effect. This in turn was to lead into schism and witness a correspondent decrease in membership of this church.[36]

This fraternal organization was organized by 1892, largely through the efforts of six of the ten Rusin clergymen who served the several parishes in the eastern seaboard states. These priests sought an organization which would insure the preservation of the Rusin cultural heritage and serve as a social agency for the people. These six clergymen, Alexander Shereghy, Nicholas Stecovic, Augustin Lauryshyn, Nicephor Chanath, Stephen Jackovich, and Eugene Volkaj, met at Wilkes-Barre together with delegates from fourteen of the Uniate Churches. Their charter, which was approved on February 14, 1892, sought the following four goals. First, it was to seek a religious unity among the Rusins. Second, it was to provide a form of fraternal insurance. Third, it was to seek the construction of schools and churches for the Rusin populace. Fourth, it was to provide a feasible method of providing for the care of the indigent, widows, and orphans.[37]

The Greek Catholic Union Organization had as its official newspaper the *Viestnik,* which was published in the Rusin language using both the Cyrillic and Latin type. During its formative years the newspaper was the mainstay of the Uniate Church in seeking to combat the defections which had severely crippled the Eastern Rite in the United States.[38] The Union played a leading role in securing the Hodobay Mission to the United States and the subsequent naming of a bishop for the Uniates.[39]

The Union, together with other Rusin elements, was opposed to Ortynsky on several counts. He came from Galicia and was identified with the Ukrainian element; he did not possess full episcopal jurisdiction for he was merely the vicar-general for the Uniates within Latin Rite dioceses; and he had to enforce the *Ea Semper* decree.[40]

The combined Ruthenian clergy, the Rusin as well as the Ukrainian, met at a synod held in Philadelphia on October 15–16, 1907. There they learned the full impact of the papal decree which had been promulgated the previous June 14th. The decree placed a great many restrictions upon the members of the Byzantine Rite. It stipulated that the clergy must be celibate and forbade the dispensation of the sacrament of confirmation. The Uniate Church was placed under the jurisdiction of the Apostolic Delegate, thus severing episcopal ties with bishoprics in Galicia and Ruthenia. Other requisites affected marriages, salaries, stipends of the clergy, and the organization of the Uniate Church.[41]

A number of Rusin clergymen, disenchanted by their Galician bishop and the conditions of the *Ea Semper* decree, organized a coalition which adopted an opposition policy against Ortynsky. Rather than an attack upon the bishop's policies directly, they concentrated their attack upon the papal decree. This Rusin clerical cabal met on December 19, 1907, at Wilkes-Barre and included the following Rusin priests: Nicholas Chopey, S. Jackovich, A. Kossey, J. Szabo, G. Chopey, T. Obushkewicz, A. Kaminsky, T. Vasovscik, M. Bendas, and F. Szabo. These priests drafted a proposal to the Apostolic Delegate seeking a nullification of the *Ea Semper* decree.[42]

Despite the rivalry between the two ethnic factions within the Uniate Church, the opposition toward Ortynsky and the disenchantment caused by the papal decree, the growth of the diocese continued during the next two decades. With the consolidation of the diocese, educational facilities were secured for the education of both the laity and the clergy. Besides promoting the culture of the people and their church, a start was made in promoting the Americanization of the people.[43] By the end of the first decade of the twentieth century, the Ruthenian Church consisted of 140 churches, the majority being located in the eastern states with Pennsylvania having 80. There were 118 priests to staff these churches; of this total 62 had migrated from Carpatho-Ruthenia and only 8 were born in the United States.[44]

Ortynsky, whose episcopal see was at Philadelphia, was unable to handle the problems of his diocese. These problems revolved around the twin issues of social and religious compositions of the people and the church. These perplexing situations could be further subdivided into one affecting the clergy and the other the laity. The clerical question focused on their refusal to become Americanized. They refused to learn the English language and conducted their liturgies in the Old Slavonic and Ruthenian dialects. The clergy procrastinated on becoming citizens, refused to associate with the Latin Rite clergy, and abetted the movement for lay control of the church. This lack of vision on the part of the clergy not only hindered the vitality of the church, but also retarded the social acceptance of the Rusin immigrants by the other ethnic groups in America. The clergy, who had a very limited outlook, only served the immediate needs of the people and the church, rather than seeking the establishment of a viable church in America. This desire to remain static prevented the Uniate Church from being able to combat the inroads made by both the Latin Rite Catholic Church and the Orthodox Mission in the United States. The result was periodic schisms that threatened the very existence of the Uniate Church, as well as the Rusin social community in America.[45]

The laity appeared to be an even greater mystery for the first Uniate bishop in America. The attitude, the make-up, and the aspirations of the people were both baffling and unpredictable to Ortynsky.

Part of the riddle was due to the Rusin's inability to decide whether they were to be permanent residents of the United States or whether they would return to Ruthenia. This segment of the problem was to be solved by the advent of World War I, and the young people's disinclination to return to their homeland in Europe. The Rusin attitude toward the control of the church was not as easily solved. In Europe the church was subsidized by the government, while in the United States there was a separation of church and state. The Rusins assumed that if they were the only support of the church, they should control the physical attributes of the organization.

Ortynsky not only had to combat the problems of indifference and hostility on the part of people and clergy but also the growing propaganda activities of those who opposed the papal decree. In the forefront of this attack was the Greek Catholic Union. The organization, which had a total membership in excess of 28,000 in 1909, became a very potent instrument in the ensuing struggle.[46] The fraternal newspaper was under the editorship of Paul Zsatkovich, who directed a personal vendetta against the Uniate bishop. The campaign which began as a protest against the papal decree now became an attack upon the mental competence of the bishop.[47]

The change from a passive to a vigorous attack upon the bishop resulted from Ortynsky's order to change the articles of incorporation of the churches from the control of a lay board of trustees to that of complete control by the episcopacy. The *Viestnik* countered by advising its members to refuse compliance and not amend their charters. Furthermore, the newspaper urged the withholding of the annual 5% diocesan assessment. This latter provision was meant to severely limit the economic resources available to the bishop. Subsequent issues of the *Viestnik* in January of 1908 featured attacks upon Ortynsky because of his Ukrainian background. He was accused of attempting to impose the Ukrainian culture upon the rite and subsequently undermining the Rusin cultural elements.[48]

During the fall of 1909, the attacks upon Ortynsky became more vindictive. The Executive Council reiterated its anti-Ukrainian stand and demanded a person of Rusin ancestry assume the position of bishop for the Uniates. The Council ended its broadside by declaring that the Rusins had nothing in common with the Ukrainian faction and therefore sought an end to the Ortynsky leadership of the church.[49] The impasse with the Uniate bishop resulted in a schism in 1909 and a loss of 10,000 members to the Orthodox Church.[50] The *Viestnik* attacked the honesty, the political activity, the mental and physical condition, the education, and even the moral aspects of the bishop's life.[51]

The Rusin clergy was divided into those that supported and those that resisted the policies of the bishop. The clerical faction opposed to Ortynsky had an organizational meeting at Harrisburg on November 5, 1908, and they joined a coalition of laymen which met at Johnstown on January 12, 1910.[52] At a subsequent meeting held on August 30, 1911, at Scranton, which was attended by forty-four priests, a radical plan was adopted to impede the work of Ortynsky. The bishop countered by suspending all the priests who were in opposition to his episcopacy. This action by Ortynsky aggravated the situation and made wider the gulf that separated the supporters of the bishop and his vilifiers.

It was not until 1913 that peace was restored within the Ruthenian Church. It was to come about from an unexpected quarter, that of the papacy. Rome issued two decrees, that of May 28, 1913, gave Ortynsky full episcopal power, and the other decree of October 27, 1914, guaranteed the clergy and the people their right to worship according to the rights granted under the Uniate agreements of 1596 and 1646.[53] Ortynsky, in turn, made concessions to the Rusin clergy by appointing the chancellor and the vicar-general from within this group and lifting the suspension of the forty-four priests provided they pledge their obedience.[54]

The outward restoration of peace did not bring about harmony but merely a change in direction of the attack. Instead of Ortynsky, the new target for the *Viestnik* was the Rusin clergy who collaborated with the bishop, namely John Hanulya and Valentine Gorzo. Hanulya, who was the editor of the *Ruthenian,* a newspaper ostensibly written for the Rusin *intelligentsia* was accused of being a *Ukraphil,* while Gorzo's competence was questioned.[55]

The unexpected death of Ortynsky on March 24, 1916, restored unity to the Ruthenian Church. The papacy appointed two adminis-trators to handle the affairs of the Uniate Church[56]—Gabriel Mar-tyak for the Rusins and Peter Poniatyshyn for the Ukrainians. This was only a partial solution for neither was given the powers or jurisdiction of a bishop, and once again the Ruthenian people and their church were under the Latin Rite jurisdiction.[57] This in turn led to new schisms. Whether it was pride, jealousy, disappointment or some other cause, it is difficult to ascertain, but it did result in the defection of Alexander Dzubay, one of the leading Rusin clergymen, to the Orthodox faith in 1916. This new controversy was to embroil the Greek Catholic Union, for at their 14th con-vention, held in May, 1916, Dzubay was endorsed as the best quali-fied clergyman for the office of bishop.[58] Except for the Dzubay affair and isolated instances of churches going into schism, the Martyak period was relatively quiet and peaceful. It was to be a period of consolidation of the customs and traditions of the Rusin people and the implanting of them upon the American scene. A number of social and educational concepts were begun. A parochial educational system was undertaken, a teaching order of nuns, the Basilians, was incor-porated into the diocese, and the system of Americanization was executed.[59] More than these beginnings was the regeneration in the life of the Rusin people. Greater pride was taken in their churches and cultural heritage. This was due to two factors—the creation of an autonomous Ruthenia and the stability of the Rusin Church in America. For the Rusins their church was more than a spiritual center; it embodied the whole gamut of their cultural life. It was to be the focal point of assimilation, and like other immigrant groups it was to undergo several stages of development. The migrants sought to build in America a replica of their existence as experienced in Europe. Since they were basically illiterate, the church and the clergy were to guide their destinies. Those born in the United States, or second generation Rusins, were even more tenacious than their parents in keeping with the old world mores. The forces of assimi-lation were to change this trend in subsequent generations, and would lead to a revulsion against the old ways and becoming truly Americanized.[60] This trend occurred in the late 1920s and had not dissipated until the 1960s. Since that period a Rusin self-consciousness has once again manifested itself, but because of the high mobility of American life it has not been very effective.

It was the second generation that took the lead during the Martyak administration. This group, for the most part, comprised natural born citizens of the United States, but their attachment to the European heritage can be seen by their refusal to modify any of the old customs, beliefs, or traditions. This was to cause new problems in the affairs of the Uniate Church under the new bishop, but in the Martyak period it was a basis of stability. It was, however, in the political sphere that the solidarity of the American Rusins with their Ruthenian counterparts may most closely be ascertained. This development, which occurred in the post World War I period, saw the incorporation of an autonomous Ruthenia into the Czechoslovak Republic, not through the activities of Europeans but through the efforts of American citizens of Rusin descent.[61]

It would be useful at this juncture to trace very briefly the history of Carpatho-Ruthenia. Prior to the twentieth century the area had been ruled for approximately 1,000 years by the Magyars, who constituted one of the two segments of the Austro-Hungarian or Dual Monarchy. During the Revolution of 1848, the first sparks of Ruthenian nationalism had surfaced. This was a belated attempt to gain autonomy by switching their allegiance from Hungarian rule to that of Austrian control. They petitioned the Habsburg rulers for the recognition of the Ruthenian people as a distinct nationality, asked for the introduction of the Rusin language in the educational system, and desired partial autonomy in domestic affairs.[62] These fond hopes or aspirations were thoroughly crushed by the *Anschluss* of 1867, which created the Dual Monarchy.[63]

The collapse of Rusin autonomy was followed by an intensified policy of Magyarization which attempted to circumvent all non-Hungarian elements in this appendage of Hungary. The Carpatho-Ruthenian province was to be the scene of domestic chaos brought about by the unenlightened policies of the Hungarian rulers, who brought about chaos in the economic and religious life of the people. The peasant's holdings were insufficient to meet the needs of the growing population, their methods of cultivation were primitive; there was a complete absence of attempts by the government to improve methods and productivity. Spiritually the province was to be wrecked by schismatic movements that threatened the very existence of the Uniate Church in the first decade of the twentieth century.[64]

Further national feeling in Ruthenia was almost thoroughly lacking until the advent of the First World War, and it did not manifest itself until the end of that struggle. During the war, the Russian army temporarily penetrated the Carpathian mountain area[65] and was welcomed as liberators, very much as they were welcomed into the area during the Revolution of 1848. During the course of the war, President Woodrow Wilson formulated his famous Fourteen Points, which became the focal document for the restoration of a just and lasting peace. For the Rusin people in the United States, as well as other immigrants from the Dual Monarchy, Point Ten, which provided for the self-determination of the people of Austria-Hungary, was of particular interest.[66]

Never before in the history of the world, nor ever since, have the emigrants from Europe played such a significant role in the shaping of their former homelands. The national aspiration of the larger ethnic groups in the United States was to be rewarded with the establishment of independent nations as witnessed by a Poland, Czechoslovakia, or a Yugoslavia. The American Rusins were cognizant of the fact that the area of Ruthenia was too small and the number of people was too insignificant to justify an independent existence, but they sought autonomy within a larger state. To the Rusin leaders in the United States, the appeal of Thomas Masaryk was enormous and when he approached them, they consented to the incorporation of Carpatho-Ruthenia into the newly constituted state of Czechoslovakia.[67]

It would not be an exaggeration to state that the inclusion of Carpatho-Ruthenia in the Czech state resulted mainly from the action of the American-Rusin populace. In the political area this was the most important contribution and the central unifying action on the part of these hyphenated Americans. This action resulted because of the inability on the part of the Ruthenian leaders in

Europe to decide which nation they sought to be aligned with and the feeling of the diplomats in Paris that Czechoslovakia must act as one of the counterweights on the east to impede another *Drang nach Osten* by a revitalized Germany.

Largely through the collective efforts of the Greek Catholic Union and members of the Uniate Clergy an American Carpatho-Rusin Council was formed at Homestead, Pennsylvania, on July 23, 1918. This organization was in response to Thomas Masaryk's plan of uniting Ruthenia to the Czech republic, which he voiced at the signing of the Pittsburgh Agreement in June of 1918.[68] The newly elected members of the Council included Julius Gardos, George Komolos and Reverend Nicholas Chopey. There was less than unanimity within the Council in the course of action to be followed. The clergy, which was Magyar-oriented, favored Oscar Jaszi's proposal of Rusin autonomy within the Hungarian kingdom.[69] The Rusin laity generally was opposed to this solution but in turn could not immediately agree upon a counter-program. Instead they proposed three alternative solutions—complete independence, which was completely unrealistic and impossible to implement; a union of Ruthenian people of Bukovina and Galicia, which stirred parochial sentiments; and autonomy, or inclusion within another state.[70]

It was at this jointure, that the work of Gregory Zatkovich, a Pittsburgh attorney, was most significant. After being chosen the spokesman of the Council, he conferred with President Wilson[71] and began negotiations with Masaryk on the future of Carpatho-Ruthenia. This was climaxed by the inclusion of Rusins into membership in the mid-European nations and the signing of the Declaration of Common Arms at Philadelphia on October 26, 1918.[72]

Zatkovich's negotiations with Masaryk led to the adoption of the "Scranton Resolution" by the Council on November 12, 1918. The resolution favored the inclusion of an autonomous Ruthenia in the newly proclaimed Czech republic provided that all areas with a Rusin majority (of the populace) be part of the autonomous province.[73] Before the "Scranton Resolution" could be considered binding, it had to be voted upon by the Rusin Uniate Churches in the United States.[74]

The discussion and the actions taken by the Rusins in America were unknown to both the Czech officials negotiating at Paris and to the several Rusin Councils in Ruthenia who were undertaking the same question. In order to rectify this situation the Council in America decided to send an American Rusin delegation to the Paris Peace Conference. Three delegates were chosen, including Zatkovich as the main conferee, Julius Gardos, the president of the G.C.U. and the Council, and Reverend Valentine Gorzo, the head of the United Societies who was forced to withdraw from the delegation prior to their departure for Paris. The Council also provided a fund of $12,000 which was to be used to finance the expenses of the two delegates at Paris. (Any remainder was to be utilized for humanitarian purposes in Ruthenia.) Zatkovich, while serving as the representative of the Council, was to be paid a monthly salary of $500.[75]

With the approval of the Paris Peace Commission, Ruthenia was formally included in the newly created Czechoslovak Republic by the treaty of St. Germaine-en-Laye on September 10, 1919. Masaryk, who was elected the president of the republic, created a five member "Directorium" which was given the authority to organize the province of Carpatho-Ruthenia, and he appointed Zatkovich, who was one of the members of the Directorium, as its president.[76] This group was directed to unravel and solve the many vexing problems facing the province. The most crucial and unfortunately insoluble issue was the western boundary involving Slovakia. The negotiations between Czech and Rusin officials were useless and were to bring about charges and countercharges before the League of Nations during the ensuing two decades.[77]

With the solution of the Ruthenian problem, albeit not to the satisfaction of the Rusins, the attention of the Uniate Church in America was directed toward the acquisition of a bishopric. The people, through their clergy as well as fraternal organizations, expressed the hope of securing a bishop for their rite. The Greek Catholic Union at its sixteenth convention held at Trenton, New Jersey in 1920 and at its next convention held at Youngstown, Ohio, two years later petitioned religious leaders in Europe and America concerning a bishop for the Rusin Uniates. The securing of a bishop, which appeared to be a rather simple issue, was wrought with inherent difficulties that appeared to be insurmountable. Besides the geographical and ethnic factors, the character and the jurisdiction of the Uniate diocese had to be considered. Should there be one Ruthenian diocese or a separate diocese for the Rusins and another for the Ukrainians? Should the bishop be of American or European extraction? Since most of the Uniate clergy were married, would a non-celibate priest be acceptable as the new bishop? Would one or both of the two administrators appointed after Ortynsky's death be named to the status of bishop?[78]

Rome finally acknowledged the Uniate request by naming, in 1924, two bishops for the Uniates in America. For the Ukrainian segment, a Galician priest, Reverend Constantine Bohachevsky, was selected as bishop with his diocesan see at Philadelphia; for the Rusins, a Ruthenian who was an administrator at the seminary at Uzhorod, Reverend Basil Takach, was chosen with his diocesan see to be located in New York City. The episcopal seat for the Rusins was never in New York but was first located at Uniontown and later transferred to Munhall, a suburb of Pittsburgh.[79]

The acquiring of a bishopric was viewed as a great accomplishment by the Rusin Uniates, and during the next five years an outward peace and tranquility seemed to prevail in the Rusin community. Outside of the religious sphere this calm was most manifest in the Greek Catholic Union which basked in the limelight of having been in the forefront of the settlement of the Ruthenian problem in Europe and the religious problem in the United States.[80] This outward peace was shattered by the promulgation of the *Cum Data Fuerit* decree by Pope Pius XI in 1929.[81] The decree was divided into four component parts each dealing with a special category. These included a chapter concerning the Bishops of the Uniate Church, the clergy, the laity, and mixed-rite marriages. More specifically, those who opposed the decree attacked the provisions enforcing celibacy, the trusteeship system, and the ban against interference in church affairs by the fraternal organizations.[82]

The pronouncement of the decree had a profound effect upon both the people and the Uniate Church, Where, during the previous five years, peace and tranquility seemed secure, the next decade was to be marked by unrest and schismatic revolts. Caught in the middle were the clergy, more than 85% of whom were married, who were not certain whether they should fight for their rights or remain loyal to their church. This last schismatic movement had profound effects upon the organization of the Rusin Church and its people. Families were split as to their acceptance or their rejection of the papal decree. The loss of membership by this greatest of schismatic movements among the Rusin Uniate is difficult to ascertain because of the unavailability of adequate records. Conservative estimates place the loss at about 20,000 while others place the number at approximately 100,000.[83]

Whole congregations went into schisms, and a number of Rusin clergymen were charged with disobedience. Tried by ecclesiastic courts, they were found guilty, were excommunicated and relieved of their clerical office. Six priests excommunicated by the Pope were Orestes Chornak, Stephen Varzaly, Constantine Auroroff, Ireneus Dolhy, Peter Molchany and John Soroka.[84]

The Greek Catholic Union was to begin its active role in the celibacy struggle at its 1930 convention held at Binghamton, New York. The action taken by the G.C.U. was not without any ulterior motives. The directors, faced with financial problems that threatened the solvency of the organization, used the celibacy issue to divert attention from their financial plight. The depression and its subsequent bank closings were to bring great hardships upon the Union. The insolvency of the bank of Johnstown and its subsequent closing were particularly hard, for the G.C.U. had $200,000 of its funds invested there. This was followed by action of the state of New York, which in June, 1931, forbade the collection of premiums in that state by the G.C.U. The state of Pennsylvania, taking similar action in 1932, demanded that the Union must revise its premiums according to the "American Experience System" or cease to do business in the state. The new rates raised the premium for older members to an almost prohibitive level.[85]

There were a number of groups who either directly or indirectly fostered the schismatic movement. To summarize, these included the officers of the G.C.U.; those who desired the incorporation of church property by lay trustees, those who fostered intrigues among various groups of clergy especially over parish assignments, those who were dissatisfied with Takach's episcopacy, and those who believed their inherent religious rights were violated by the *Cum Data Fuerit* decree.[86]

The event that triggered the battle against the papal decree of 1929, sometimes referred to as the celibacy controversy, was the refusal of Bishop Takach to ordain three married seminarians to the priesthood. This event was the outward manifestation of the struggle, but the underlying cause was the failure of both the laity and part of the clergy to submit to ecclesiastical discipline. The refusal to ordain the married seminarians precipitated an editorial campaign in the *Viestnik* that became violently anti-Takach in tone. In an editorial entitled "With Justice Towards All and Malice Towards None," a trio of married seminarians, Basil Brenyo, Michael Cybercy, and Joseph Mihaly, were portrayed as righteous individuals doing battle for their rite and national heritage.[87]

The Greek Catholic Union by this time had overtly become embroiled in the celibacy controversy. The decade of the 1930s was rampant with schismatic movements among the Rusin Uniates. A number of priests had led the way into schism and had been excommunicated, and the *Viestnik,* through editorials by Peter Zeedick, Stephen Steranchak, Michael Yuhasz, and Reverend Stephen Varzaly, best exemplified the disobedience and defiance against church authorities.[88]

The celibacy schism was the last and the most serious controversy involving the Rusin Uniates in the United States. The seriousness of this religious split was compounded by the opposition of the clergy as well as the laity. Efforts aimed at curbing the opposition of lay organizations might have been successful if the clergy steadfastly supported their bishop, but this was not to be the case. The difficulty of the Rusin clergy was not necessarily their opposition to the papal pronouncement but their ambivalent attitude toward the decree. This irresolution was also manifest in the bishop who waited until the summer of 1931 to take action against the editor of the *Viestnik.*

A great many of the clergy were caught in the middle of the controversy. Since they were married, celibacy was an alien concept to them, and although they were opposed to celibacy they were bound by their religious vows to support their ordinary. This dichotomy is best exemplified by Reverend Joseph Hanulya, who although remaining loyal to the Uniate Church showed his consternation with celibacy in an article entitled, "In Defense of the Sacrament of the Holy Matrimony of Our Married Priests."[89] In the article Hanulya asks whether marriage administered prior to ordination is valid or merely sanctions priests' wives as "legalized mistresses."

As the controversy continued, the arena of action expanded, and the passions of the people were heightened to an almost explosive force. Those supporting the bishop gathered around the fraternal organization, the United Societies and its newspaper the *Prosvita,* while those in opposition looked to leadership from the Greek Catholic Union and its organ, the *Viestnik.* The struggle was to reach a climax with a series of court cases that ensued in the period prior to and during World War II.[90] The court cases involved a great many churches of the Byzantine Rite, including the Rusin Cathedral Church of St. John located in Munhall,[91] St. John the Baptist Church of Bridgeport, Connecticut,[92] whose case was finally decided by the Connecticut Supreme Court in 1944, and St. Peter and Paul's Church of Ambridge, which was won by the dissidents.[93]

The judgments of the courts in these church cases varied, although the Uniate Church was victorious in more actions than the dissident factions. The Rusins, regardless of whether they were loyal or disloyal to Bishop Takach, agreed upon certain rights which they believed were guaranteed to them by the Union of Uzhorod of 1646. This union was a compromise entered into by the Rusin clergy of Ruthenia with the Latin Rite Church of the Austrian Habsburgs. Among the privileges afforded the Rusins were these: they would be allowed to freely practice their rite, they would be allowed to select their own bishop, and they would be able to enjoy certain ecclesiastical rights.[94]

Although it is impossible to state one major premise upon which the church cases were adjudged, the one that was often utilized questioned the source of authority under which the church was incorporated. It must not be assumed that a victory in a court case was ipso facto a defeat for the other faction. Equally as devastating as the court cases to the Rusin people were the polemics that were entered into by the editorial staffs of the *Prosvita* and the *Viestnik*.

The *Prosvita* was the newspaper of the United Societies which was an offshoot of the G.C.U. organized on March 29, 1903. It had been formed, according to its board of incorporators, because of the inability of the Greek Catholic Union to provide good leadership. Ten years later the bylaws of the organization were amended with the proviso that the United Societies was to work for the best interest of the Uniate Church.[95] The first editor of the *Prosvita* was Reverend V. Balogh, who served in that capacity from 1919–1933. He was succeeded by Reverend A. Papp, who became the leader of the pro-celibacy faction during the later stages of the controversy.

The *Viestnik,* which was anti-celibacy, had the far greater circulation and was to be the staging area for the Komiteta Oborony Vostoenoho Obrjada (Committee for the Defense of Our Faith—to be referred to as the K.O.V.O.).[96] After its organizational meeting the K.O.V.O. called for a Rusin Religious Congress, which was held in Johnstown in June of 1933. The Congress called for high ranking clergymen to attend all meetings of the K.O.V.O., provided for a joint clerical lay group to handle all financial affairs of the diocese, designated that the laity was to help choose the bishop, and made provisions for a newspaper to disseminate information.[97] This meeting was followed by a K.O.V.O. convention which met in Pittsburgh July 26–28, 1933. A committee of K.O.V.O., the Religious National Congress of the Carpatho-Russian Greek Catholic Church of America headed by Stephen Steranchak, drafted a letter to Pope Pius XI. The K.O.V.O. convention adopted the twelve resolutions and disseminated the letter among the Rusin people. Among the resolutions were these:[98]

1. The Uniate Agreement of 1648 was binding on Rome.
2. Celibacy and Latinization must be stopped.

3. Bishop Takach must be recalled.
4. Penalties enacted against those fighting celibacy must be revoked.
5. Ordination of married seminarians must be allowed.
6. The new bishop elected by the clergy must be an American.
7. Pittsburgh Exarchate must be represented in the Congregation for the Oriental Rite.
8. The term Ruthenian must be replaced by "Carpatho-Russian."
9. Local autonomy in financial matters must be acknowledged.
10. Church property must be incorporated in the name of the congregation.
11. Lay control of salaries of priests must prevail.
12. Papal authorities must comply with this request within sixty days or else the K.O.V.O. would break with the Catholic Church.

Once these demands were approved by the K.O.V.O., there was no turning back. Awaiting a reply from the Vatican, the organization continued its propaganda war. Time and time again a review of the celibacy issue made its way into the various Rusin newspapers. One pamphlet entitled *Nase Stanovisce* (Our Stand) reviewed the whole controversy and emphasized that celibacy would destroy the Uniate religion in America. It further charged that the Rusins had to guard against the twin encroachments of Ukrainization and Latinization.[99]

Finally, in July of 1934, Rome replied to the K.O.V.O. demands in a letter to Takach through the Apostolic Delegate in the United States. The Vatican reviewed the history of the Uniate Church in America and warned against the independent and schismatic movement of the K.O.V.O., emphasizing the need of the clergy to attest their loyalty and fidelity to the church.[100] The letter requested the Rusin bishop to send detailed information of his diocese to Rome and vigorously prosecute those clergymen who were in opposition to the Vatican.[101]

By the mid 1930s the celibacy struggle not only had completely fragmented the Pittsburgh Exarchate but had effectively disrupted the G.C.U. organization. It was apparent to the leaders of both groups that peace had to be restored if the Rusin community was to remain viable. In 1936 a series of articles in the *Viestnik,* entitled "Our Fight of Self-Defense,"[102] took a more conciliatory tone toward Takach and the celibacy issue. Rather than make demands, the articles sought reforms. These requests could be subdivided into two categories, those for Europe and those for the United States. The former are not germane to our study, but the latter are rather interesting for they underlay the whole reform movement of the Catholic Church in the 1960s. The reforms sought included these:

1. An archbishopric for the Rusins.·
2. A seminary.
3. A pension plan for the clergy.
4. Parochial education, including supplies.
5. The vernacular in the mass.
6. Annual diocesan meetings.

Within the G.C.U. organization itself a new approach was manifested by the election of John Sekerak as the new president at the Wilkes-Barre convention in 1936. This did not necessarily herald a new peace proposal by the G.C.U. for on September 6, 1938, a delegation consisting of Peter Zeedick, John Sekerak and George Ferrio departed for Rome to once again present their case to papal authorities. Again nothing of great or lasting importance was realized by this journey.[103]

The restoration of peace and the end of the enmity between the bishop and the fraternal organization took place gradually over a period of four years. With the elevation of Michael Roman as editor of the *Viestnik* in October of 1937 a drastic change in the tone of the newspaper took place. Peace was finally restored and was punctuated by the appearance of Bishop Takach at the twenty-third convention of the G.C.U. held at Harrisburg from June 24 to July 3, 1940.[104] The results of the celibacy struggle are difficult to adequately gauge. That it hurt the Rusin Uniate Church is quite evident. Conservative estimates place the loss in membership at twenty thousand,[105] while impartial observers place the number at two or three times that figure.[106] If the successful struggle for the creation of a Carpatho-Ruthenia demonstrated most dramatically the unity of the Rusin Uniate community, the celibacy fight was to show most effectively the fragmentation of the unity. However, even though the Rusin community was badly splintered by the latter struggle, it showed a remarkable resiliency that made it possible to regain the vitality that it has kept to the present day. The celibacy struggle was the "time of troubles" for the Rusin community, and, although it came near to bringing catastrophe to the people, it ended with a stronger community of interest and a new dedication for the Rusin people.

Before the celibacy struggle had been concluded, the interest of the Rusins had already been turned to events transpiring in Europe. The Munich agreement, the Vienna Award, the Hungarian takeover, and finally World War II saw the death of autonomous Ruthenia, the creation of a Ukrainian Piedmont, and following the war the absorption of Ruthenia by the Soviet Union as the Zakarpatska Oblast. Unlike the period following World War I, the American Rusins could do little to affect a change for Ruthenia.[107]

Nevertheless, Rusin leaders in the United States sought to halt or at least to delay the incorporation of Ruthenia by the Soviet Union. On one hand the American Rusins sought a legal redress of this injustice, and on the other, large amounts of food, clothing, and money were sent to alleviate the hardships of the people in Ruthenia. In reference to providing help to their European brethren, the G.C.U. and the United Societies formed a *Komitet Pomosci* (The Aid Committee) which raised in excess of $3,000 for relief and was responsible for shipping 10,000 tons of food and clothing to Ruthenia.[108] Another $26,000 was contributed by the Rusin Uniate parish churches. Due to the Soviet incorporation of Ruthenia, this aid was withheld from the Mukachevo Diocese and only the region of Presov, which remained part of Czechoslovakia, received American Rusin financial assistance.

In seeking to avert the Soviet Union's complete domination of the area, a petition was addressed to the United States State Department reviewing the complete history of Ruthenia and protesting the Soviet incorporation. A similar petition was sent to the American representatives to the United Nations.[109] This memorandum which was signed on April 23, 1945, was followed by the sending of a Rusin delegation to the State Department. The delegation was unable to secure a satisfactory redress of its grievances and made plans to hold a Carpatho-Ruthenian Congress.[110] This meeting, which was held at Munhall on August 14, 1946, authorized the drafting of another formal protest to Secretary of States James F. Byrnes. The State Department replied that since the incorporation of Ruthenia was an internal problem of the Czech state, the government of the United States was powerless to intercede.

With the inability of the Rusins to materially affect the course of events in Europe, their attention was once again focused on events at home. World War II brought about peace and the end of schismatic movements within the Uniate Church. Bishop Takach, having emerged the victor after a decade of religious strife, now was afflicted by physical maladies. To ease his tasks, provision was made for the selection of an auxiliary bishop. The man chosen to assist the aging bishop was Reverend Daniel Ivancho. Soon after his consecration at St. Paul's Cathedral in Pittsburgh, he began to exercise full episcopal powers and succeeded to the bishopric with the death of Takach on May 13, 1948.[111]

Ivancho's episcopacy signaled a new era for the Rusin Uniate Church in America. Being a natural born American, he attempted to conduct the affairs of the diocese along the lines of the other American bishops. He envisioned the Uniate Church as being the leader of a Rusin renaissance in the United States. To accomplish this monumental task, Ivancho set forth a list of priorities, of which the construction of a new cathedral and a seminary were uppermost. Since the Uniate Church did not possess the financial resources necessary for these two projects, Ivancho turned for assistance to the G.C.U.[112]

This fraternal organization responded by selling the assets of its buildings and land at Elmhurst, Pennsylvania, which formerly housed an orphanage. Half of the sale price of $329,011.14 was turned over to the diocese to help finance the construction of the seminary. In 1952, the G.C.U. decided to give the other half of the funds to the

Rusin Church. During the decade of the 1960s the organization further aided the seminary by authorizing the payment of hundreds of thousands of dollars for this purpose.[113]

The winds of change were bringing about important consequences upon the Byzantine Rite in the United States. As the decade of the 1960s came to an end, the Rusin Uniate Church was finally and formally constituted as an organization which was canonically free of the Latin Rite hierarchy and equal to its Ukrainian counterpart. This development did not take place without its share of pitfalls and disappointments for the laity and the clergy of the Rusin-Americans. In retrospect, although the decade began with a feeling of tranquility among the people and an increase in the influence of the Pittsburgh Exarchate, it was also an era of tension and anxiety. The new source of trouble was an abortive rebellion of a segment of the clergy against their bishop, together with the fear that the diocese would be absorbed and become part of the Ukraine metropolitan area of Philadelphia. This was the nadir of the Rusin plight which was to be transformed dramatically into a new zenith for the Rusin Uniates. Instead of losing their autonomy, the Pittsburgh Exarchate was elevated to the status of Metropolitan district. It was formally referred to as the Arch-eparchy of Munhall[114] and had jurisdiction over the two suffragan eparchies of Passaic, New Jersey, and Parma, Ohio.[115]

The establishment of the Munhall Arch-eparchy was the culmination of the American Rusin aspirations of the preceding half century. This was not accomplished without periods of travail, even though the former Pittsburgh exarchate continued to grow both materially and spiritually during the decades of the 1950s and 1960s. Each of these decades was to have moments of great trauma for the Rusin diocese. These problems which were so immense and seemingly unsolvable threatened the very existence of the Rusin Uniate Church in America.

Much of the drama involved the resignation of Bishop Daniel Ivancho and the subsequent appointment of Nicholas T. Elko as the new exarch of the diocese. This seemingly normal transition of authority had many undisclosed perils to the stability of the diocese.[116]

The appointment of Elko brought a degree of stability to the imperiled Uniate Church but left unanswered the reason for the resignation of Ivancho. The cloak of secrecy involving these events did not begin to fade away until the close of the 1960s, and then only by inference. The disclosure of the resignation of Bishop James P. Shannon as auxiliary bishop of the archdiocese of St. Paul–Minneapolis[117] and his subsequent marriage[118] was carried by the newspapers and leading magazines in the United States.[119] The Shannon disclosures were accompanied by the notation that he was the second Catholic bishop in America to renounce his ecclesiastical office and marry. The news release did not mention the other bishop by name, merely stating that the Shannon action was antedated by that of an anonymous bishop in 1954.[120] Unless these newspaper and magazine accounts dealt with still another bishop, the anonymous bishop of the 1950s was former Bishop Ivancho. From conversations with knowledgeable individuals concerning the events of 1954, it can be ascertained that Ivancho, who was in ill health, married his nurse and subsequently resigned his office.[121]

Equally as incomprehensible as the Ivancho episode was the consecration of the new exarch, Nicholas T. Elko, who was the vicar general of the Rusin diocese. Elko had the support of several Latin Rite bishops who recommended that he be appointed the new exarch. Elko's consecration took place in Rome on March 6, 1955,[122] and was conducted according to the ritual of the Western Rite rather than that of the Oriental or Byzantine Rite.[123]

These rather unusual and unorthodox events were both disquieting and disconcerting for the Rusin clergy and laity during the 1950s. However, these setbacks were only momentary, for the exarchate was to prosper and grow, indicating once again its great resiliency. The growth of the exarchy continued throughout the decade and showed it to be the largest Byzantine Rite diocese in the United States. This growth took place during the Rusin preoccupation with a neo-Ukrainian peril, which once again surfaced during the 1960s. This "Ukrainian phobia" which has so dominated the Rusin people and their church was not to be abated by the official Catholic census figures. According to these census figures, the Byzantine Catholic population in the United States was 582,524. Of this total number the membership of the Ukrainian eparchies was as follows: Philadelphia 161,665, Chicago 20,456 and Stamford 87,610; the remainder of 312,793, which comprised almost 54% of the total, was part of the Pittsburgh Exarchate.[124]

These figures bolstered the Rusin contention that the exarchate be subdivided into several dioceses and that the creation of a metropolitan see was mandatory. On this premise they were to be partially successful, for in a letter dated July 31, 1963, and addressed to Bishops Nicholas T. Elko and Stephen J. Kocisko, the Vatican announced the creation of two eparchies, Pittsburgh and Passaic, with the elevation of the two named bishops as their eparchs. The two new eparchies, created from the former Pittsburgh exarchate, established the first resident dioceses for the Carpatho-Rusin people in the United States.[125]

The statistics for the Passaic diocese showed a total Eastern Catholic population of 94,682 members who resided in the Atlantic coastal states from Maine to Florida, including a segment who dwelled in eastern Pennsylvania. The Passaic jurisdiction included Maine, New Hampshire, Vermont, Massachusetts, Rhode Island, Connecticut, New York, New Jersey, eastern Pennsylvania, Delaware, District of Columbia, Maryland, Virginia, North Carolina, South Carolina, Georgia, and Florida.[126] The Passaic diocese was staffed by 69 secular priests, 10 monastic priests, and 68 nuns. The eparchy embraced 74 parishes and 13 parochial schools with a total enrollment of 2,247 students.[127]

The new Pittsburgh eparchy remained under the jurisdiction of Bishop Elko, who had served for eight years as the bishop of the former exarchate. In that period twenty-one new churches had been established, the last one being "Christ the King" in Taylor, Michigan.[128] The most adventuresome but perhaps the least feasible was the Byzantine Rite Church in Alaska. The Pittsburgh eparchy included an eastern Catholic population of over 220,000, most of whom resided in the Pittsburgh–Cleveland metropolitan area.[129]

Conditions within the Rusin Uniate Church in the United States continued to be peaceful, at least outwardly, for the next several years. Although there were occasional snipings between the Latin and the Byzantine rites, a greater cordiality on the part of both groups was manifested in the official pronouncements of both church bodies. Even antipathy between the Uniate and the Orthodox Uniates began to disappear, although conversion to the Orthodox still persisted among the clergy. Not that there was any attempt by the hierarchy or the clergy of either group to meet officially, but the bitter recriminations and hostility held by both had begun to disappear and was replaced by a begrudging recognition, if not an admiration, of each other's accomplishments.

The major discordant factor affecting Uniate and Orthodox interrelations was the role played by the clergy of the two factions. The disenchantment and subsequent changeover of clergy from the Orthodox to the Uniate religion was accompanied with great publicity in the fraternal and religious newspapers. The reverse was true in regard to defections to the Orthodox cause as portrayed in Orthodox publications. Several of the Orthodox clergymen seeking admission into the Catholic Church were aided by the Latin hierarchy rather than by their Uniate counterparts.

This Orthodox Church disfavor was first made manifest in 1965 by the announcement that two Orthodox priests had been received into the Catholic Church. The action of Catholic authorities was undertaken by Archbishop, later Cardinal, John Krol of the Philadelphia Latin Rite Archdiocese. The Passaic eparch who had jurisdiction over the area was disregarded in favor of the Latin hierarchy. The two Orthodox priests were Reverends Andrew C. Musko, pastor of St. John's Greek Catholic Orthodox Church of Allentown, Pennsylvania, and Andrew Zapotcky, pastor of several churches in the Fords, New Jersey, area.[130] Both men had been ordained Orthodox clergymen, Musko by Metropolitan Theophilus in 1935 and Zapotcky by Metropolitan Philapovsky in 1937. Musko remained at St. John's Church, where trouble soon ensued over ownership of the church. The Common Pleas Court of Lehigh County ruled in favor of the adherents of the Uniate Church with the stipulation that the Orthodox factions would be permitted to utilize the church for their services. Specific hours were established for the Catholic services and other hours for the Orthodox liturgy. This was at best merely a temporary expedient, for on several occasions police have had to restore order and tranquility. As of June, 1971, the problem had not been solved and litigation proceedings were being heard in the higher courts of the Commonwealth.[131]

Earlier in the year, a lesser known incident transpired in the same region. Two Orthodox priests, who were part of the American Carpatho-Russian Orthodox Greek Catholic diocese sought admittance into the Catholic Church. Another Latin Rite bishop, Joseph McShea of the Allentown Catholic diocese, acting as the Apostolic Visitator, accepted the petition of the two clergymen. The newly accepted priests were Ivan D. Dornic of Monongahela, Pennsylvania, and Andrew Kertis of Clymer, Pennsylvania.[132]

The Passaic eparchy was to have another Orthodox priest added to its clergy. Once again it was through the action of Archbishop Krol, who received Reverend Michael B. Sisak of Ambler, Pennsylvania, into the Catholic Church. Sisak's changeover was witnessed by Bishop Kocisko, and, although Sisak was under the jurisdiction of Krol, he was assigned to work in the Passaic eparchy.[133]

Except for these unpleasant incidents, relations with the Orthodox Church proceeded without the recriminations that were so common in the past. The belated acceptance of the Uniate-Orthodox situation by the Rusins was followed by other favorable events in the middle 1960s. One such incident involved Bishop Chornock, who formerly was the prime antagonist of the Uniate Church. The official diocesan newspaper ran as one of its feature stories an article lauding Chornock. This story was in reference to his promotion to the position of Archbishop of the Carpatho-Russian Orthodox diocese of Johnstown, Pennsylvania. The installation took place at the Holy Trinity Greek Orthodox Cathedral in New York City. Chornock, who at the time was eighty-two years of age, was head of a diocese comprising 100,000 members, most of whom were former Uniate Catholics.[134]

Not all of the events of the 1960s were to be pleasant for the Rusin Uniate Church. In the middle of the decade, factionalism had broken out in the Uniate Church of St. John Chrysostem, which is located in the Greenfield section of Pittsburgh. A faction of this parish began court proceedings in 1964 accusing Bishop Elko and the pastor, Rev. Andrew Pataki, of interfering with the management of the church and its property. On August 18, 1967, Judge Frederick G. Weir of the Common Pleas Court of Allegheny County ruled that St. John's, also known as "Russka Dolina," was under the jurisdiction of the Pittsburgh Byzantine bishop.[135]

The seemingly tranquil state of affairs in the Pittsburgh eparchy was shattered by disclosures made public in 1967. Once again a state of uncertainty and a feeling of danger engulfed the Rusin population which professed the Uniate religion. It dealt with the long unexplained absence of Bishop Elko, who had been ordered to Rome in early 1967. This action was predicated by charges drawn up by a group of young Uniate clergymen against Elko. After a stay of six months in Rome, during which time the charges were investigated by a special commission without any decision being rendered, Elko decided to make his position known in a public letter to the *Pittsburgh Press*. In his position paper, Elko stated that a philosophical conflict within his diocese had brought about the papal inquiry. The Uniate bishop disclosed that thirty-five young priests had signed a protest petition against him. The two main arguments presented in the petition were that he leaned too much toward the Latin Rite and that he refused to accept phenomenological existentialism—which is the study of man as he is in society rather than as he ought to be.[136] The *Press* further disclosed that the philosophical issue had led to a realignment of faculty in Duquesne University's philosophy department. Elko further stated that Vatican authorities were conducting a survey of the Pittsburgh eparchy prior to the rendering of their decision.

The severity of the problem could be ascertained by the disclosure that there was no indication when or if the Byzantine Bishop would return to Pittsburgh.[137] Instead, rumors persisted that the group of priests seeking Elko's ouster—Elko stated there were originally 37 priests who signed the petition but that two withdrew—had advanced one of their group as a potential candidate for the bishopric. Dissatisfaction of the younger clergy could be seen by the resignation of the former chancellor Reverend John Martin, who left the Uniate clergy and joined the Carpatho-Russian Church. Martin was later to be named the auxiliary bishop to assist metropolitan Chornock. Martin's defection did not aid those seeking the ouster of Elko, for it eliminated the strongest candidate among the young clergy from consideration as Elko's successor.[138]

In October of 1967, a special Vatican commission was established by Pope Paul VI for the purpose of investigating the controversy between Bishop Elko and the recalcitrant priests of the Pittsburgh Eparchy. The commission, which consisted of a cardinal and two bishops, began its work on November 10th. The delay was due to a bishop's conference, which was held at Vatican City during the month of October. The appointment of the commission removed the case from the jurisdiction of the congregation for the Oriental Church, which usually handles matters dealing with the Byzantine Rite.[139]

By December 1967, the displeasure of both the clergy and the laity of the Pittsburgh Eparchy had become very pronounced. Rumors were persistent that the two Rusin eparchies would become suffragan dioceses under the Ukrainian Metropolitan See at Philadelphia.[140] Furthermore, some of the clergy were thoroughly dissatisfied with the chancellor of the diocese, Monsignor Rosack, who was cast in the unenviable position of seeking to solve the problems of the diocese without having any of the episcopal powers to do so. The Oriental Congregation had received petitions signed by approximately 9,500 lay people expressing concern over Elko's long absence and seeking his early return.[141] Bishop Elko was reached by transatlantic telephone in December, 1967, and the context of the conversation was carried in one of the Pittsburgh newspapers. By this time organized attempts to secure public support for his return had been organized. Members of the Elko family had visited several of the parishes to have their presence felt, but not one official act of enlisting support by the family had been reported. Elko claimed that he had received over 1,000 letters and cablegrams from supporters during the preceding five months. He complained that during his year-long forced stay in Rome, he was not allowed to communicate officially with his diocesan personnel or laity. To further compound the issue, no official charges against Elko were made public, and instead, Vatican sources indicated that he did not stand in disfavor with the papacy.[142]

The controversy which had become overly heated was headed toward a solution with the disclosure that Bishop Stephen Kocisko of Passaic was to succeed to the Pittsburgh Eparchy and Elko was to be consecrated a titular archbishop. This solution was reached after an extensive investigation of the eparchy had taken place. Bishop George J. Biskup of Des Moines, Iowa, had met with a great many of the diocesan priests, and his recommendations were discussed by the commission and dispatched to Rome.[143] The appointments of Kocisko and Elko were conferred on December 22, 1967, and were to be effective immediately.[144]

The installation of Bishop Kocisko as eparch of the Pittsburgh Byzantine diocese finally terminated the Elko matter. That the former bishop remained within the bounds of the Catholic Church was seen in his appointment at Titular Archbishop of Dara and his designation as the prelate in Rome for the conferral of sacred orders in the Byzantine Rite. The Pontifical Commission further acknowledged the spiritual and priestly integrity of Elko. However, the commission concluded that it would be inopportune for Elko to return as the bishop of the eparchy because of the existing conditions.[145]

The installations of Kocisko as eparch on March 5, 1968, signalled not only the restoration of peace within and without the Rusin eparchies but also initiated a period of consolidation unmatched in the history of the Rusin Church in America.[146] The naming of an eparch for the Passaic diocese was disclosed by Archbishop Luigi Raimondi, who announced that Monsignor Michael J. Dudick was the new bishop of Passaic.[147] The installation of the new eparch of Passaic took place on October 24, 1968. That a new era within the Rusin dioceses had begun was made clear in Dudick's installation remarks as he asked for and demanded a closer cooperation, not only between the Latin and Byzantine Rite, but also between the Rusin and Ukrainian Catholics.[148]

That the Ukrainian threat, namely that of absorbing the Rusin dioceses, was dispelled came with the announcement that Bishop

Kocisko was elevated to the position of a metropolitan or archbishop and that the eparchy of Pittsburgh was to be established as the Arch-eparchy of Munhall. The official announcement was dated April 2, 1969, with the ceremonies listed for June 11, 1969.[149] Simultaneously with the announcement creating the Munhall Archeparchy was the discloseure that the Pittsburgh Byzantine diocese was to be split with a portion designated as the Parma Eparchy. The Reverend Emil J. Mihalik was consecrated bishop and installed as the first eparch of Parma on June 12, 1969.[150]

According to spokesmen of the Rusin people, the future of the Byzantine Rite lies not in the old homeland but in the new world. If this assumption is correct, the Rusin Uniate Church has taken gigantic steps forward to insure its existence as a strong moralistic force among the people. However, the question that remains unanswered is whether in a dynamic society such as ours, a hyphenated small group (American-Rusins) can maintain their cultural identity through a likewise hyphenated religious organization, the Byzantine Catholic (Uniate) Church.

## NOTES

1. The Catholic Church is divided into a Western and Oriental Church.
2. Carl F. Wittke, *We Who Built America, The Saga of the Immigrant,* ed. 2 (Cleveland: 1964), pp. 431–433.
3. George M. Stephenson, *A History of American Immigration, 1820–1924,* (New York: 1964), p. 88.
4. *Ibid.,* p. 89.
5. *Ibid.,* p. 89.
6. Yaroslav Chyz, "New Immigration" in Francis Brown and J. S. Roucek, *One America, The History, Contributions and Present Problems of Our Racial and National Minorities* (New York: 1945), pp. 127–134.
7. Maldwyn A. Jones, *American Immigration* (Chicago: 1960), pp. 198–199.
8. Carl F. Wittke, *We Who Built America,* pp. 433–434.
9. Yaroslav Chyz, "New Immigration," p. 129.
10. Hugh Seton-Watson, *The Russian Empire, 1801–1917* (London: 1967), p. 50.
11. Wasyl Halich, *Ukrainians in the United States* (Chicago: 1947), p. 12.
12. Ambrose Senyshyn, "The Ukrainian Catholics in the United States," *Eastern Church Quarterly* VI, no. 8 (October–December, 1946), pp. 439–441.
13. According to the "Dictionary of Races" *Senate Documents,* 61st Congress, 3rd Session (Washington, 1911), IX, 118.

14. Stephenson, *American Immigration*, p. 89.

15. "Emigration Conditions in Europe," *Senate Documents*, 61st Congress, 3rd Session (Washington: 1911) XII, 270.

16. Emily G. Balch, *Our Slavic Fellow Citizens* (New York: 1910), pp. 135–137.

17. Peter Roberts, *Immigrant Races in North America* (New York: 1910), pp. 27–38. John R. Commons, *Races and Immigrants in America* (New York: 1927), p. 180. Edward A. Steiner, *The Immigrant Tide, Its Ebb and Flow* (New York: 1909), p. 207.

18. Baron Louis de Sevay, "The Hungarian Emigration Law," *North American Review* CLXXX, no. II, 115–122.

19. Frank B. Clarke, *Old Homes of New Americans* (New York: 1913), pp. 5–50.

20. United States Immigration Commission "Reports," 61st Congress, 3rd Session, Senate Document No. 747 (Washington: 1911) I, 37–39.

21. Stephenson, *American Immigration*, pp. 89–90.

22. J. Davis, *The Russians and Ruthenians in America, Bolsheviks or Brothers* (New York: 1922), pp. 22–50.

23. *Greek Catholic Messenger*, May 13, 1934, p. 1.

24. D. Attwater, *The Catholic Eastern Churches* (Milwaukee: 1935) I, 86; Ivan Ardan, "The Ruthenians in America," *Charities* (December 3, 1904) :248.

25. J. P. Chase, "Ukrainian Milestones in America," *Ukrainian Life* (August, 1941) :6–7.

26. See the files of the *Viestnik* (1892–1972), and the *Svoboda* (1893–1972).

27. *Prosvita Kalendar* (McKeesport, Pennsylvania: 1920), p. 214.

28. Isidore Suchocky, "The Ukrainian Catholic Church of the Byzantine-Slavonic Rite in the U.S.A.," trans. by C. Berdar, *Byzantine-Rite U.S.A.* (Philadelphia: 1958), pp. 250–51.

29. F. H. Sampson, "Eastern Rites in the West," *America* (October, 1949) : 695.

30. The Pittsburgh Exarchate relinquished the practice of utilizing foreign-born priests in 1950.

31. Sochocky, "The Ukrainian Catholic Church," pp. 256–257.

32. Stephen Gulovich, "Rusin Exarchate in the United States," *Eastern Churches Quarterly* VI, no. 8 (October–December, 1946) :463–472.

33. M. Roman, "Istorija Greko-Kaft Sojedinenija," *Golden Jubilee* (Munhall, Pennsylvania: 1942) :46–50.

34. S. Gulovich, *Windows Westward* (New York: 1947), p. 133.

35. Senyshyn, "The Ukrainian Catholics in the United States," pp. 443–444.

36. See Kenneth S. Latourette, *The Great Century* (A.D. *1800*–A.D. *1914*) *Europe and the United States of America* vol. IV, *A History of the Expansion of Christianity* (New York and London: 1941) :107, 122.

37. Michael Roman, "Istorija Greko-Kaft Sojedinenija," pp. 38–44.

38. The defectors joined the Orthodox Church. The Orthodox Church nearly doubled its membership from 129,606 to 249,840 during the period 1906–1916. See Bureau of Census, *Religious Bodies* II (1926) :516–518.

39. See *Viestnik*, March 1, 1906 and April 14, 1906.

40. V. J. Pospishil, *Interritual Canon Law Problems in the United States and Canada* (Chesapeake City, Maryland: 1955), pp. 27–28.

41. D. Dunford, *Roman Documents and Decrees* II (Chicago: 1907), pp. 79–86.

42. *Viestnik,* December 26, 1907, p. 1.
43. Senyshyn, "The Ukrainian Catholics," *Eastern Churches Quarterly* VI, no. 8 (1946):447–451.
44. Andrew Shipman, "Greek Catholics in America," *Catholic Encyclopedia* V:743.
45. Gulovich, "Rusin Exarchate in the United States," pp. 467–468.
46. *Ibid.,* and Andrew Shipman, "Ruthenians and Their Rite," *Catholic Encyclopedia* XIII:277–280.
47. *Viestnik,* January 6, 1908, p. 1.
48. *Viestnik,* January 16, 1908.
49. *Viestnik,* October 29, 1908, p. 1.
50. Gulovich, *Windows Westward,* p. 135.
51. See *Viestnik* files, 1909–1912.
52. Sochocky, "The Ukrainian Catholic Church," p. 267.
53. Gulovich, *Windows Westward,* p. 136.
54. Ortinsky, Pastoral Letter of August 25, 1913.
55. *Viestnik,* February 25, 1915 to March 15, 1915.
56. *Pastoral Letter of the Ruthenian Church* III, no. 4 (May 17, 1916).
57. Gulovich, "Rusin Exarchate in the United States," p. 479.
58. Byzantine Slavonic Rite Catholic Diocese of Pittsburgh, *Silver Jubilee 1924–1949* (Pittsburgh: 1949).
59. George Gulanich, *Golden–Silver Jubilee* (Uniontown: 1946), pp. 31–85.
60. Oscar Handlin, *Immigration as a Factor in American History* (Englewood Cliffs, N.J.: 1959), pp. 76–77.
61. Walter Warzeski, *Byzantine Rite Rusins in Carpatho-Ruthenia and America* (Pittsburgh: 1971), pp. 127–128.
62. C. Macartney, *Hungary and Her Successors, The Treaty of Triavon and Its Consequences* (London: 1937), pp. 199–200.
63. O. Jaszi, *The Dissolution of the Habsburg Monarchy* (Chicago: 1929), p. 108.
64. R. W. Seton-Watson, *Racial Problems in Hungary* (London: 1908), pp. 322–323.
65. J. B. Heisler and J. E. Mellow, *Under the Carpathians, Home of a Forgotten People* (London: 1946), pp. 115–116.
66. U. S. Congress, *The Congressional Record* LVI, Pt. I (Washington: 1918), pp. 680–681.
67. T. Masaryk, *The Making of a State—Memories and Observations, 1914–1918* (New York: 1927), pp. 255–257.
68. *Ibid.,* p. 257.
69. H. Seton-Watson, *Eastern Europe Between the Wars 1918–1941* (Cambridge, Mass.: 1946), pp. 179–180.
70. K. Krofta, "Ruthenes, Czechs, and Slovaks," *Slavonic Review* XIII (1934–1935): 622.
71. Macartney, *Hungary and Her Successors,* p. 215.
72. Twelve ethnic groups signed the document. These included: Czechoslovaks, Poles, Yugoslavs, Ukrainians, Uhro-Rusins, Lithuanians, Rumanians, Italian Irredentists, Unredeemed Greeks, Albanians, Zionists, and Armenians.
73. Z. Zawadowski, *Rus Podkarpatska* (Warsaw: 1931), p. 11.
74. Macartney, *Hungary and Her Successors,* p. 215. (The percentage vote for inclusion in Czechoslovakia was 67% of the churches.)
75. Interview with G. Zatkovich, Pittsburgh, Pa., August 5, 1961.
76. Gregory Zatkovich, *The Tragic Tale* (Pittsburgh: 1926), pp. 1–5.

77. R. W. Seton-Watson, *Treaty Revision and the Hungarian Frontiers* (London: 1934), pp. 39–42.

78. Interview with J. Hanulya, Cleveland, Ohio, June 14, 1959. Married clergy were not eligible for the office of bishop in the Uniate Church.

79. Gulovich, *Windows Westward*, pp. 137–138.

80. Michael Roman, "Istorija Greko-Kaft Sojedinenija," pp. 59–62.

81. Sacred Oriental Congregation, *Decree on the Spiritual Administration of the Greek Ruthenian Ordinariates in the United States of America* (Rome: 1929).

82. Gulovich, "Rusin Exarchate," p. 481.

83. Interview with J. Hanulya, Cleveland, June 14, 1961.

84. Cardinal Tisserant, letter of October 29, 1936, to Bishop Basil Takach.

85. Roman, "Istorija Greko-Kaft Sojedinenija," pp. 64–66.

86. Gulovich, "Rusin Exarchate in the United States," pp. 482–483.

87. J. M. C. Cheresnya, "With Justice Towards All and Malice Towards None," *Viestnik* (August 27, 1931).

88. See the editorials of the *Viestnik*, 1931–1937.

89. *Viestnik*, February 11, 1932.

90. Although the celibacy struggle has long since ended, the Rusin Uniate Church has been embroiled in court cases to the present.

91. Basil Takach vs. Peter Molchany, *Supreme Court of Pennsylvania*, no. 15 (March, 1935).

92. *Prosvita*, February 24, 1944.

93. Moneta vs. Varnar, *Supreme Court of Pennsylvania*, no. 22 (March, 1940).

94. See the document, "Union of Uzhorod," in Warzeski, *Byzantine Rite Rusins*, pp. 272–273.

95. Alexander Papp, "O Nas Pro Nas.—O Nasom Sobraniju," *Kalendar Sobranija 1938* (McKeesport: 1938), pp. 38–44.

96. "K.O.V.O. Organization," *Viestnik*, July 7, 1932.

97. *Viestnik*, June 15, 1933.

98. Stephen Steranchak letter of August 14, 1933 in the *Viestnik*, October 3, 1933.

99. Zeedick and Smor, *Nase Stanovisce* (Homestead: 1934), pp. 37–72.

100. Luigi Cardinal Sincero letter of July 23, 1934 to Apostolic Delegate G. Cicognani and transmitted to B. Takach.

101. B. Takach letter "De Statu Dioecesis," April 12, 1934.

102. "Our Fight of Self-Defense," *Viestnik*, issues of June 4, 11, and 18, 1936.

103. Zeedick-Sekerak-Ferrio, "Report of October 10, 1938" in *Viestnik*, October 20, 1938.

104. M. Roman, "Convention," *G.C.U. Messenger* (December 19, 1940).

105. Gulovich, "Rusin Exarchate in the United States," p. 481.

106. B. Y. Landis, *1963 Yearbook of American Churches* (New York: 1963), pp. 41, 251.

107. Andrew Gyorgy, *Governments of Danubian Europe* (New York: 1949), p. 104.

108. "Collection for European Relief," *Queen of Heaven* XX, no. 6 (June, 1946): 8–10.

109. George Michaylo, *A Memorandum in Behalf of Podkarpatska Rus to the State Department of the United States of America and Representatives of the United States at the World Security Conference* (Munhall, 1945), 9–11.

110. M. Roman, "D'ijatelnost' Karpatorruskoho Kongressa," *Kalendar, 1947* (Munhall, 1947): 68–69.

111. Gulovich, *Windows Westward,* pp. 141–142.

112. D. Ivancho, "Address of June 28, 1948 to the G.C.U. Convention," *Messenger* (July 22, 1948) : p. 1.

113. See *Kalendar,* 1955, pp. 39, 40 and *Kalendar,* 1962, p. 32.

114. The clergy of the Metropolitan see are striving to change the name of its designation to that of the Pittsburgh Metropolitan district. Interview with Reverend Andrew Dzmura, Allentown, April 12, 1971.

115. Papal Document, "Quandoquidem Christus," of May 13, 1969, original in the Munhall Metropolitan Chancery. Copy in author's possession.

116. *Messenger,* December 30, 1954, p. 1.

117. *New York Times,* May 30, 1969, p. 27; "Bishop Shannon's Resignation," *America* vol. 120 (June 14, 1969) : 678.

118. "Bishop and Mrs. Shannon," *Newsweek* vol. 74 (August 25, 1969) : 76.

119. See *New York Times* coverage May 29, 1969 to June 5, 1969 and J. B. Sheerin, "Loss of Bishop Shannon," *Catholic World* vol. 210 (October, 1969) : 3 and "Shannon Case," *Commonweal* vol. 90 (May 5, 1969) : 531–532.

120. "Burden of Responsibility," *Time* vol. 93 (June 6, 1969) : 88.

121. For the purposes of not disclosing sources still active within the Byzantine Rite, only the interview with Rev. John Pipik, who is now deceased, shall be included. Interview with Rev. John Pipik, Pittsburgh, June 3, 1964. Ivancho's activities after 1954 are rather hazy. Rumor had it that he took up residence in Florida and operated a motel, this venture was not too successful. Another persistent rumor holds that the marriage was floundering and the former bishop sought admittance to a Catholic friary to once again take up his clerical activities. This rumor has since been proven completely untrue, and as of July, 1972 the marriage is intact. The Munhall Archeparchy refuses to confirm or deny these allegations.

122. *Messenger,* Dec. 30, 1954, p. 1; "Byzantine Catholic Diocese of Pittsburgh," *Kalendar,* 1962, p. 77; *Byzantine Catholic World,* August 11, 1963, p. 10.

123. Interviews with Rev. John Kallock, Pittsburgh, July 20, 1961, Rev. John Pipik, Pittsburgh, July 24, 1961, and Rev. Andrew Dzmura, Pittsburgh, July 24, 1961.

124. *The Official Catholic Directory, Anno Domini,* 1963, pp. 623–628.

125. *Byzantine Catholic World,* August 11, 1963, p. 1.

126. *Pittsburgh Post Gazette,* August 1, 1963, p. 5.

127. *Byzantine Catholic World,* August 11, 1963, p. 1.

128. *Byzantine Catholic World,* May 3, 1961, p. 1.

129. *Hazelton Standard-Speaker,* August 3, 1963, p. 1.

130. *Byzantine Catholic World,* August 29, 1965, pp. 1, 15.

131. See the *Allentown Morning Call* and the *Allentown Call Chronicle* file of 1965–1971.

132. *Byzantine Catholic World,* January 3, 1965, p. 2.

133. *Byzantine Catholic World,* August 13, 1967, pp. 1, 19.

134. "American Carpatho-Russian Church Primate Elevated to Metropolitan," *Byzantine Catholic World,* January 9, 1966, p. 1.

135. J. Weir, "St. John Chrysostem Greek Catholic Church et al. v. Elko et al.," *Pittsburgh Legal Journal,* vol. 115, November 1, 1967, 391–413.

136. *Pittsburgh Press,* June 11, 1967, Sec. 3, p. 2.

137. *Pittsburgh Press,* June 11, 1967, p. 2.

138. Martin was chancellor of the diocese during the year 1964.

139. *McKeesport Daily News,* December 12, 1967, p. 5.

140. Interview with Rev. Andrew Dzmura, Pittsburgh, December 26, 1967.

141. *McKeesport Daily News,* December 12, 1967, p. 5.

142. Art Glickman, "Elko Stays in Exile," *Pittsburgh Press,* December 10, 1967, p. 1. In 1967 Archbishop Elko was named auxiliary bishop of the Cincinnati Latin Rite diocese. In 1972 Elko as auxiliary bishop was working in the Columbus, Ohio, area. Elko was not given jurisdiction to assume the powers of bishop following the death of the Archbishop in 1972.

143. Interview with Reverend Andrew Dzmura, Pittsburgh, December 26, 1967.

144. Stephen J. Kocisko letter to the Pittsburgh Eparchy of December 27, 1967, reprinted in the *Byzantine Catholic World,* Jan. 7, 1968, p. 2.

145. *Byzantine Catholic World,* February 11, 1968, p. 1.

146. "Bishop Kocisko Installed as Eparch of Pittsburgh," *Byzantine Catholic World,* March 10, 1968, p. 1.

147. *Byzantine Catholic World,* September 1, 1968, p. 1.

148. "Bishop Dudick Consecrated in Passaic," *Byzantine Catholic World,* November 3, 1968, p. 1.

149. *Greek Catholic Union Messenger,* March 15, 1969, p. 1.

150. *Greek Catholic Union Messenger,* May 22, 1969, pp. 1, 12.

# 8

# Pennsylvania: Focal Point of Ukrainian Immigration

## BOHDAN P. PROCKO

*Bohdan P. Procko holds degrees from Albright College, Columbia University, and a Ph.D. from the University of Ottawa. He is presently Professor of History at Villanova University.*

Because of serious social, economic, and political hardships, large numbers of people from Eastern Europe, particularly from the Austro-Hungarian Empire, began to migrate to the new world in the second half of the nineteenth century. Most of them came to the United States, introducing new and unfamiliar cultures, traditions, and languages into American society. Conditions in Eastern Europe following both World Wars tended to continue and even expand the migration of peoples. Consequently, for over a century now, Americans of various Eastern European origins have been contributing their cultures and customs to the new world.

Any attempt to write about the early Ukrainian immigration to the United States must constitute only a rough outline, for neither the United States immigration records nor the immigrants themselves provide the historian complete data for a thorough history.[1] In general, four periods can be distinguished in Ukrainian immigration to 1924: the first before 1877; the second from 1877 to 1899;

the third from 1900 to 1914; the fourth since 1914. In the first period only scattered individuals began arriving, at least as early as the 1860s.

One of the most picturesque of the early Ukrainian immigrants was a political exile from the Russian empire, Agapius Honcharenko, an Orthodox priest originating from the Kiev region of the Ukraine, who arrived in January of 1865. It was Father Honcharenko who celebrated the first Russian Orthodox Liturgy in the United States; established the first Cyrillic press and published the first newspaper, *The Alaska Herald—Svoboda,* for Russian-speaking settlers in Alaska following its purchase by America in 1867; printed *The Russian and English Phrase Book* in 1868 for the United States Army in Alaska; and authored *The School and Family Russo-American Primer,* the first American school book published specifically to facilitate teaching English to the Russian-speaking Alaskans.[2] In October of 1867, Honcharenko had left New York City for California, where he was to remain (except for thirteen months in Alaska) until his death in 1916. Thus, he had only limited relations with the large-scale immigration which began in the second period and which was to be concentrated in the state of Pennsylvania. It is with this considerable influx of Ukrainian immigrants, which began in the late 1870s and which greatly expanded between 1900 and 1914 and was to decline following the outbreak of World War I in 1914, that this essay is concerned. The center of gravity for the entire period was Pennsylvania.

Ukrainian mass immigration to the United States commenced in the year 1877 or 1878 after agents of Pennsylvania mining companies in the anthracite region of the eastern part of the state succeeded in recruiting workers from Transcarpathia in Hungary "to replace employees that they found hard to deal with, and especially the Irish, with cheaper and more docile material."[3] Quickly the news spread to the neighboring Lemkivshchyna in Austria's Galicia. Thus it was from the mountainous border districts between Transcarpathia and Galicia—the territories of present day Western Ukraine and at the time under the political control of Austria-Hungary—that the mass Ukrainian immigration originated.

The early Ukrainian immigrants from Lemkivshchyna, as well as the *Rusin* immigrants from neighboring Transcarpathia, became generally known in America as Ruthenians. The name is a Latinization of Slavic *Rusini,* derived from Kievan *Rus',*[4] which was commonly used in the 19th century by the immigrants from both Galicia and Transcarpathia. Because the national consciousness of many of the so-called Ruthenian immigrants did not fully develop until the current century, the term Ruthenian found its place in the American immigration records, thus adding to the confusion about the national origin of the immigrants so listed. The term should not be used in reference to modern-day national-political groupings. The national name *Ukrainian* is used by the descendants of the Ruthenian immigrants from Austrian Galicia and Bukovina, while most of the American descendants of the immigrants from Transcarpathia in Hungary (the southern slopes of the Carpathian mountains) accept the name *Rusin.*[5] Although the ancestors of the Transcarpathian Rusins were anthropologically and linguistically related to the ancestors of the Ukrainians, cultural and political differences have developed between their descendants because of the dissimilar socioeconomic and political fortunes of the Rusins under Hungarian control and of the Ukrainians under Austrian rule. This essay is concerned with the Ukrainian immigration from Austrian Galicia and Bukovina and the subsequent one from the Russian empire.

The Ukrainian immigrants of the 1870s and 1880s were entirely of the peasant class whose economic condition was so hopeless that the tales of the opportunities in America were sufficient to prompt the more adventurous among them to seek a new life. That the extreme subdivision of land was the main cause of emigration from Galicia was undisputed, according to Professor Balch, a leading authority in the first decade of this century.[6]

Virtually all of these early immigrants from Lemkivshchyna were Eastern Rite Catholics who became generally known in America as Greek Catholics. Although technically correct, the term has proved to be very misleading in the United States and Canada and therefore its use is not desirable.[7] It is often associated either with the Greek Orthodox Church or with the Greek nation. The facts are that these people were and are in communion with the church of Rome and they are neither of the Greek nationality nor do they use Greek as their Liturgical language. The generic terms "Byzantine Rite Catholics" or "Eastern Catholics of the Byzantine Rite" are acceptable. The national terms "Ukrainian Rite" and "Ukrainian Catholics" are more popular today. Easternmost Galicia and Bukovina did not contribute to this immigration until the 1890s.[8] The Ukrainian immigration from the Russian empire remained relatively insignificant until World War I; there was, therefore, little representation of the Ukrainian Orthodox among the early mass immigrants. Immigration reports indicate that in the twelve fiscal years from 1899 to 1910 inclusive, 98.2 percent of the Ruthenians admitted to the United States came from Austria-Hungary.[9]

According to Nestor Dmytriv, a very active Ukrainian Catholic priest in immigrant affairs after 1894, the early immigrants from Lemkivshchyna came mostly from Novy Sanch, Horlytsi, and Krosno counties. They settled, in groups, primarily in Pennsylvania coal communities like Shenandoah, Shamokin, Mount Carmel, Hazleton, Lansford, Freeland, Olyphant, and Mayfield.[10] Almost all of these in the beginning worked in and about the coal mines.[11]

Upon their arrival, the Ukrainian immigrants were confronted with serious cultural and linguistic problems not faced by their earlier counterparts from the countries of western Europe. This proved to be particularly serious since the Ukrainian immigrants of the 1870s and early 1880s did not have any representation from the educated classes (until the arrival of their priests), a representation that might have made the period of transition less difficult by providing a more qualified leadership. Lacking proper leadership when it was badly needed, the immigrants often fell prey to unscrupulous agents of one sort or another.[12]

The unfamiliar and even hostile surroundings gave rise to a yearning for their own familiar institutions, in particular their own church, which had been the center of their social life in Europe. It was the Ukrainian and Rusin immigrants in Shenandoah in 1884 who made the first attempt to obtain a priest from Europe. They petitioned the Ukrainian Metropolitan of Galicia, Sylvester Sembratovich, Archbishop of Lviv (Lvov), for a priest to minister to their religious needs.[13] The Archbishop replied by sending Reverend John Volansky, who thus became the first Ukrainian Catholic priest in the United States and under whose leadership began, in 1884, the formal organization of Ruthenian Catholic churches. Their own churches became the nucleus around which other Ukrainian institutions and cultural traditions began to sprout in the New World. Until the arrival of their own priests and the organization of their own churches, the Ukrainian immigrants attended the Latin Rite churches, particularly those of their European neighbors like the Poles, Slovaks, or Hungarians. Those that remained in the Latin churches eventually lost their national identity.

By the fall of 1886 the first Ukrainian Catholic church in the United States, which was started the previous year, was finally completed in Shenandoah and dedicated to St. Michael the Archangel. Father Volansky's missionary work was not limited to Shenandoah alone, since a great number of Ukrainian and Rusin immigrants had settled throughout the coal regions of Pennsylvania and a substantial number had found their way to many other states. Having fixed his residence in Shenandoah, Volansky traveled to most of the important Ukrainian and Rusin colonies from New York to Colorado, ministering to their religious needs.

Father Volansky received much needed assistance with the arrival of Rev. Zenon Liakhovich and young Vladimir Simenovich in March 1887. Father Liakhovich was the first celibate Ukrainian priest in the United States; he became the first Ukrainian priest to be buried on American soil after his untimely death in November 1887. Vladimir Simenovich, a university student from Lviv, is considered to have been the first educated Ukrainian layman to settle in the United States. Thus, with the help of other leaders, by the time that Father Volansky returned to Galicia in June 1889, other churches had been built in Kingston, Freeland, Olymphant, and Shamokin, all in Pennsylvania, as well as in Jersey City and Minneapolis.[14] At his Shenandoah parish he had organized the first Ruthenian choir, established the first reading room and library and the first Ukrainian evening school in the United States. In addition,

Volansky founded the first Ukrainian newspaper, *America,* the initial issue of which appeared on August 15, 1886. He was also the prime organizer of the fraternal organizations and of the cooperative general stores which were founded for the benefit of the Ruthenian workers and their families.

An interesting tribute to the first Ukrainian Catholic missionary and his dedicated work was supplied by a Shenandoah reporter in an article about Rev. Volansky in 1887.

> Although young, barely more than 30 years of age, tall and slim, though compactly built, and fairly good looking, Father Volansky has no superior as a worker. He scarcely permits himself any rest, so thoroughly is his soul in his work. If life and health stands the test, his religious standing and that of his church will in a decade or two of years rank high and firm in America, and he will then be able to enjoy with ease the honors he will have richly earned.[15]

From 1889 priests began to arrive from Hungary's Transcarpathia, the first being Alexander Dzubay. They quickly outnumbered the Ukrainian priests. Thus in 1890, of the ten Ruthenian priests in the United States, only three of them were Ukrainians from Galicia; the remaining seven were Rusins from Hungary's Transcarpathia. All, except two, settled in and served the coal communities of Pennsylvania.[16] When the first Ukrainian book was published in the United States (an almanac for 1897 edited by Rev. Nestor Dmytriv) it listed only five priests from Galicia.[17] The Ukrainian population at this time is extremely difficult to estimate. The early parishes that these priests served were characterized by mixed congregations of Ukrainians and Rusins from different sections of Austria-Hungary. As previously stated the immigration records merely add to the confusion about national origin by their reliance on the "umbrella" term Ruthenian for both the Ukrainians from Galicia and the Rusins from Transcarpathia. In addition, some Ukrainians were listed as Austrians, Hungarians, Poles, Slovaks, Russians, etc. The leading Ukrainian newspaper *Svoboda* (Jersey City, New Jersey), as well as the leading Rusin newspaper *Amerikansky Russky Viestnik* (Munhall, Pennsylvania), provide us with loose estimates of Ruthenian immigrant population in the mid-1890s ranging between 200,000 and 300,000.[18] Considering that the immigration statistics indicate a steady growth of immigration up to World War I, and taking into consideration the immigration figures which indicate that during the twelve fiscal years 1899–1910 inclusive 147,375 Ruthenians were admitted to the United States,[19] it would appear that the estimate of 200,000 immigrants in the mid-1890s, after twenty years of ever-increasing immigration, is a responsible one.

The arrival of priests from Transcarpathia, unfortunately, led to shameful disputes between the Ukrainian and Rusin immigrants, who had previously generally cooperated in mixed church congregations and other organizations. It is important, at this point, to provide the reader with a brief background to the conflicts among the Ruthenian immigrants and their priests, without which it is extremely difficult to understand the reasons for the organization of separate churches and institutions beginning in the early 1890s.

Broadly speaking, the Ukrainian immigrants from Galicia were divided into two major factions, the "Ukrainians" and the "Moscophiles." The Ukrainians stood for the interest of the Ukrainian peoples distinct from the Russians and desired to develop the Ukrainian language, literature, and nationality along their own individual lines, in contrast to the Russian. The Moscophiles imitated all things Russian and looked toward Moscow as the seat of Slavic culture.[20] The Rusins from Transcarpathia were divided into three distinct factions: those Rusins who were sympathetic to the Hungarians, those who claimed cultural communion with Russia, and those that claimed cultural communion with the Ukrainians.[21] To a great extent the conflicts among the Ukrainians and Rusins, as well as those among the Ukrainian immigrants themselves, were inherited from factional differences which were born in Europe.

In the 1890s neither the Ukrainian nor the Rusin priests displayed the necessary tact, patience, and understanding towards each other's views; consequently, as a result of various misunderstandings, the Ukrainians under the leadership of Rev. John Konstankevich left the common federation of the fraternal brotherhoods that had been organized in Wilkes-Barre in 1892, and formed the Ruthenian

National Association (Rusky Narodny Soyus) in Shamokin on February 22, 1894. It is the oldest and the largest Ukrainian American institution in the United States today. The newspaper *Svoboda* (Liberty), organized and first published by Rev. Gregory Hrushka on September 15, 1893, became the official organ of the Soyus on May 30, 1894.

Between 1895 and 1898 seven young celibate Ukrainian Catholic priests, imbued with the spirit of Ukrainian national revival, arrived from Galicia. While seminarians in Lviv, they had formed themselves into the so-called "American Circle" with the hope of doing missionary work among the Ukrainian immigrants in America after their ordination. They were to play an unusually important role in the cultural and national development of the Ukrainian immigrants in the United States.

Early in 1896 these young priests made specific appeals and recommendations for the formation of their own Ukrainian church administrative organization which would control the priests and their activities, bring order to their church in America, and protect it from the Russophile propaganda of the Russian Orthodox Mission.[22] Finally, on May 30, 1901, clerical and lay delegates met in Shamokin and formed an association of the Ruthenian Church Congregations in the United States and Canada headed by a general committee of three priests and three laymen. The stated goal of the association was "to obtain good priests, to see that in every parish there be order, schools, choirs, reading rooms, and that the poorer chapels obtain the services of a priest at least from time to time, etc."[23]

Although only fifteen parishes and ten priests accepted the administration of this general committee,[24] it was the first serious attempt to introduce lay control over the church, a principle which troubled the Ukrainian Catholic Church in the United States for many years to come.

The height of the movement was reached at the second convention held in Harrisburg on March 26, 1902, where the official name of the association became the Ruthenian Church in America.[25] The characteristic feature of this organization, which lasted until the arrival of the first Ukrainian bishop and the settlement of the religious matters that were canonically the prerogative of the bishop, was its radicalism towards the Latin bishops in particular and towards the hierarchy of the Church in general.[26]

The internal conflicts and the misunderstandings with the hierarchy provided the Russian Orthodox Mission, beginning in 1891, an opportunity to disseminate their beliefs among the Ukrainian Americans. By the opening of the current century, the chief problem facing the Ukrainian Catholics was combating the Russian Orthodox propaganda financed by the Tsarist Government, which saw in the Ukrainian Catholic Church in the United States an important element of the Ukrainian movement.[27] The Russian Mission's proselytizing brought considerable results. By 1901 there were no less than 2,448 Ukrainians from Galicia who had converted to Orthodoxy.[28]

The seemingly unending differences with the Latin bishops and the resultant spread of the anti-Roman feeling among the Ukrainian "radical" priests, which reached its climax in 1902, also provided open opportunity for proselytizing by the Episcopalian, Presbyterian, Baptist, and other Protestant groups. The Presbyterians were the most energetic in their colportage work among the Slavic immigrants at this time.[29] Thus, for example, in the first decade of the current century Presbyterian congregations were established in Pittsburgh, Newark, and New York, and a Baptist congregation was organized in Scranton.[30]

The appointment, in 1907, of Monsignor Soter Ortynsky, O.S.B.M., from Galicia, as the first bishop for the Ukrainians as well as for the Rusins, had the unintended effect of intensifying the problems. Nevertheless, despite the bitter opposition, Bishop Ortynsky succeeded during his episcopate in establishing several important and long lasting institutions for the Ukrainian Catholics in the United States.

In 1908, Bishop Ortynsky bought an Episcopal church in the 800 block of North Franklin Street in Philadelphia which, after refitting, was consecrated as the Cathedral of the Immaculate Conception. The adjoining building became the Bishop's permanent residence. The immediate area surrounding the Bishop's cathedral and residence, the quadrangle formed by Brown, Seventh, Parrish, and Eighth Streets, was soon to become the center of the religious life of the Ukrainian Catholics in the United States, as the town of Shenandoah was its original center in the mid-1880s. Here were located many of the institutions and organizations founded or supported by the Bishop and the homes housing many of the people having direct relations with these institutions.

In 1911, partially with his own personal funds, the bishop established an orphanage at Seventh and Parrish Streets in Philadelphia.[31] The Sisters of St. Basil the Great (O.S.B.M.), whom the bishop obtained from Galicia to direct the orphanage, arrived in the United States on December 2, 1911. To help support the sisters and the orphanage the bishop founded a church supply store, a printing press, book store, and a rug and carpet shop, all in close proximity to the bishop's residence.

In 1912, Ortynsky founded one of his most successful organizations, a Catholic mutual insurance association, the Providence Association. The headquarters of the new organization was moved from New York to Philadelphia in 1914, partly because it was felt that without its own publication the growth of the association would be limited. In Philadelphia, however, the Basilian Sisters had published the weekly newspaper *America,* which became the official organ of the association, since 1914. The move to Philadelphia provided the impetus for the Providence Association to expand into the strong national organization of Ukrainian Catholics which it is today.

It was not until May 28, 1913 that the Papacy conferred full and ordinary jurisdiction upon Bishop Ortynsky by creating an independent Byzantine Slavic Rite Exarchy (vicariate) with its seat in Philadelphia, serving an estimated 500,000 Ukrainian and Rusin Catholics, the vast majority of whom were concentrated in Pennsylvania.[32]

It must be remembered, however, that despite Bishop Ortynsky's successes, internal conflicts as well as Russian Orthodox proselytizing among the Ukrainian Catholics intensified rather than abated during his episcopate. Thus, for example, the number of Ukrainian Catholics seceding to the Russian Orthodox Church increased, reaching its apogee in 1916, the year of Bishop Ortynsky's death. The importance of the Ukrainians in the growth of the Russian Orthodox church in America is not to be overlooked. According to a Russian Orthodox source, 43,000 Ukrainians and Rusins were registered members of the Russian Orthodox Church in America in 1914, out of a total membership of 100,000.[33] Virtually all of the 43,000 were former Catholics who passed into Orthodoxy because of the quarrels with the Latin hierarchy or with Bishop Ortynsky (or other internal conflicts) and the increased propagandizing activities of the Russian Orthodox Church. According to the census of religious bodies in the United States, prior to the fall of the Tsarist regime in 1917, the Holy Synod of the Russian Empire spent $77,850 annually from the Tsar's treasury for the support of the Russian Orthodox Mission in America.[34] The Mission's activities were aimed primarily in the direction of the Ukrainian Catholics.

With the outbreak of World War I, for the first time the Ukrainians in the United States found themselves in a position of leadership in the affairs of their people as a whole. Thus as a result of events taking place in the European lands of their origin during the war, the first impetus was provided for the founding of national political organizations among the Ukrainian Americans. It was in 1914 that the leading organization of the Ukrainian Americans, the Ruthenian National Association (Soyuz), officially changed its name to the present Ukrainian National Association. Even the least politically conscious now embraced the national name "Ukrainian" in place of the old name "Ruthenian."

On November 1, 1916, delegates from the Ukrainian Catholic clergy, the Soyuz, Providence Association, and Zhoda Bratstv (founded in Olyphant, Pennsylvania, in 1913) organized the Ukrainian National Alliance. The Alliance was an organization of political and humanitarian character that became the unofficial intermediary between Ukrainian aspirations and the government in Washington.[35] The role of the Alliance in publicizing the Ukrainian national desires and providing material aid to the victims of war should not be underestimated. A major part in this work was played by the American Ukrainian Catholic Church through Father Poniatishin, who became its administrator after the death of Bishop Ortynsky in 1916.

The greatest accomplishment of the Ukrainian Alliance was its work leading to the proclamation of a Ukrainian Day by President Wilson in 1917.[36] The designation by the President of the United States of April 21 as a special day for the collection of funds to aid the Ukrainian people suffering as a result of the war was considered by Ukrainian American leaders to be their finest accomplishment since the beginning of Ukrainian immigration to the United States.[37] Apparently, this was the first time that the name "Ukrainian" was used in a United States government document.[38] From this time on the old name "Ruthenian" began to pass rapidly out of use among the Ukrainian Americans and the national name of "Ukrainian," growing in use since the turn of the century, promptly replaced it in American usage.

After the armistice in November of 1918 the Ukrainian Alliance, now reconstituted as the Ukrainian National Committee, started action towards Washington's recognition of an independent Ukrainian state. The committee prepared a memorandum to that effect for President Wilson, who headed the American Peace Delegation in Paris. Through Congressman James A. Hamill a joint Resolution was introduced in Congress on December 13, 1918 which, if it had passed, would have recommended that the American Delegation in Paris apply Wilson's self-determination-of-nations principle to the Ukrainians.[39]

The Ukrainian Committee also sent a delegation to the Peace Conference in Paris to assist the official Ukrainian delegation. The motive was to aid the Ukrainian cause by influencing the official American Delegation. The Ukrainians failed to realize their political aspirations at the Peace Conference; consequently, the Ukrainian National Committee lost prestige and soon was dissolved. However, during nearly five years of important activity, through its ties with similar organizations of other stateless peoples, its various deputations, memoranda, petitions, publications, and letters, the Committee had publicized the Ukrainian aspirations before the American government and public.[40] Writing many years later, Father Poniatishin stated that never before or since have Americans of Ukrainian descent been so united and active in aiding the national organizations of their people in Europe. Through its work the Committee gained respect and influence not only in the American press, educational circles, humanitarian and political organizations, but also among the political and military leaders in Washington who turned to it as the spokesman and representative of Americans of Ukrainian descent for information regarding Ukrainian matters.[41] Major forces behind this work were the Ukrainian Catholic Church and the Ukrainian National Association. According to Poniatishin, "The Church and the Soyuz actually created the Ukrainian national movement in America and educated the masses in it. Were it not for the Church and the Soyuz the greatest portion of our immigrants would have been scattered among Polish, Russian, Hungarian, and other Churches and organizations, and would have been lost to the Ukrainian nation. They are two great fortresses of Ukrainian national consciousness in America."[42] In essence, Poniatishin felt it was the result of the united efforts of the Church and Soyuz during the war years that Americans of Ukrainian descent began to understand that an appreciation of their national heritage was an important sign of cultural maturity.

The temporary division of the Ruthenian Catholic Church in the United States into administrative halves, following the death of Bishop Ortynsky in 1916, became permanent in 1924 when the Papacy created separate exarchies (vicariates) out of each administration. Father Constantine Bohachevsky from Galicia was appointed Bishop for the Ukrainian Americans who since 1916 had been under the administration of Rev. Poniatishin. Bishop Bohachevsky's See was to be Philadelphia, the seat of the late Bishop Ortynsky. The Ukrainian exarchy comprised 144 churches, 102 priests, and 237,495 members. Sixty of those churches were located in Pennsylvania which had two-and-a-half times as many as New York, the state with the second largest aggregate in the country.[43]

Unfortunately, the 1920s were characterized by serious internal conflicts among the Ukrainian Americans. The decision of the Allied Council of Ambassadors on March 15, 1923, that Galicia be permanently attached to Poland also affected the conditions among the Ukrainians in America. Many Ukrainians fearing Polish rule left for the United States, thus creating in America the first purely political Ukrainian immigration. Some of these political exiles found it difficult to accommodate themselves to American conditions.

In the strictly religious sphere, prior to the war, the Ukrainian religious life in the United States centered almost exclusively in the Catholic Church. It has been pointed out, it will be recalled, that since the 1890s the Russian Orthodox Mission had considerable success in converting Ukrainian Catholics to Russian Orthodoxy. In 1916, partially due to the impetus given to Ukrainian national consciousness by the events of the war, there now began a Ukrainian Orthodox movement in the United States which attempted to gain adherents from the Ukrainian Catholic communities.[44] With the fall of the Tsarist regime, the Russian Orthodox Mission lost its material support from Petrograd; some of the Russian Orthodox priests who were of Ukrainian origin now tried to form their own diocese and obtain their own bishop. When on February 13, 1924, Archbishop John Teodorovich arrived from the Soviet Ukraine to become the first bishop of the American Ukrainian Orthodox Church he received substantial support from Ukrainian Catholics who opposed the administration of Bishop Bohachevsky. The Archbishop's strongly democratic and patriotic sentiments also made a strong impression on the politically disturbed Ukrainian patriots in exile.[45] The spark grew into a conflagration lasting nearly ten years before a new and brighter era was to be introduced—a contemporary era wherein Ukrainian Americans of different religious faiths and political views would finally display a willingness to cooperate for the attainment of their common goals.

## NOTES

1. The work of Wasyl Halich, *Ukrainians in the United States* (Chicago: 1937), is still the most useful study of the Ukrainian Americans in the English language.

2. For a recent study on Honcharenko see Theodore Luciv, *Father*

*Agapius Honcharenko, First Ukrainian Priest in America* (New York: Ukrainian Congress Committee of America, 1970). For other interesting first-hand illustrations of less illustrious Ukrainian pioneers see, e.g., Julian Chupko, "Obrazky z Ameryky," *Svoboda* (Jersey City), March 19, 1896, pp. 1–2 (continued on pp. 1–2 of the next two issues).

3. Emily G. Balch, *Our Slavic Fellow Citizens* (New York: 1910), p. 238. This classic work, which was reprinted by the Arno Press and the *New York Times* in 1969, provides considerable information on the early Ukrainian immigration.

4. See, e.g., Oscar Halecki, *Borderlands of Western Civilization* (New York: 1952), p. 34.

5. For an instructive account of the Rusin immigrants see Walter C. Warzeski, "Religion and National Consciousness in the History of the Rusins of Carpatho-Ruthenia and the Byzantine Rite Pittsburgh Exarchate" (unpublished Ph.D. dissertation, University of Pittsburgh, 1964).

6. Balch, p. 138. For a useful discussion of economic and other causes of emigration by a very active Ukrainian pioneer see John Ardan, "The Ruthenians in America," *Charities* XIII (December 3, 1904): 246–252. In addition, the United States Immigration Commission's reports also contain useful statistical information concerning the causes of emigration from Austria-Hungary and the characteristics of that immigration to the United States. See, e.g., U. S. Senate, *Emigration Conditions in Europe,* Doc. No. 748, 61st Cong., 3d Sess., 1911, XII, 361–384.

7. Father Gregory Hrushka, a Ukrainian Catholic priest who came to the United States in 1889 from Galicia, was the first to realize how misleading the term was and strongly recommended that it be dropped from use as early as 1893. See his "Poznaimo Sia," *Svoboda,* October 15, 1893, p. 1.

8. Julian Bachynsky, *Ukrainski Immigratsia v Ziedynenykh Derzhavakh Ameryky* (Lviv: J. Bachynsky and Ol. Harasevych, 1914), Vol. I, 88. This is a valuable study of the early Ukrainian immigration.

9. U. S. Senate, Reports of the Immigration Commission, *Dictionary of Races or Peoples,* Doc. No. 662, 61st Cong., 3rd Sess., 1911, IX, 118.

10. Nestor Dmytriv, "Pershi Roky Emigratsii Ukraintsiv v Zluchenikh Derzhavakh piv. Ameryky," *Kalendar Provydinia,* 1924 (Philadelphia: Providence Association), pp. 161–162. Father Dmytriv also lists Jersey City, New Jersey, Yonkers and Troy, New York, and Ansonia and New Britain, Connecticut, as important centers of early Ukrainian immigrant groups. A useful statistical skeleton of the source and distribution of the new immigration (also its political, economic, and educational characteristics), based on the report of the Commissioner of Immigration, is provided by an editor for the U. S. Census Bureau, Kate Holloday Claghorn, in "Slavs, Magyars, and some others in the New Immigration," *Charities* XIII (December 3, 1904): 199–205.

11. The effects of the new immigrant labor on the anthracite region of Pennsylvania is discussed in detail by Professor Frank J. Warne, *The Slav Invasion and the Mine Workers* (Philadelphia: 1904). Unfortunately, however, Warne applies the term Slav to all non-English-speaking immigrants from Southern and Eastern Europe, consequently the work contributes only limited information regarding the Ukrainians.

12. *Ibid.,* pp. 113–116, Warne comments on the most common exploiters of the Slavs in the anthracite region of Pennsylvania. The social, economic, and educational problems of the Slavs in general are also profitably discussed by the Congregational minister and scholar Peter Roberts in "The

Slavs in Anthracite Coal Communities," *Charities* XIII (December 3, 1904) : 215–222, and by Mary Buell Sayles, a tenement house inspector, "Housing and Social Conditions in a Slavic Neighborhood," *ibid.*: 257–261. The above authors, incidentally, are examples of early American scholars and writers deeply interested in the problems of the new immigrants from Eastern Europe. The December 3, 1904 issue of *Charities* represents an early attempt by an American journal to provide a comprehensive and authoritative coverage of the new immigrants.

13. The immigrant's signed petition cited in *Svoboda*, October 10, 1894, p. 1 (article entitled "Pro Rusku Emigratsiiu").

14. John Voliansky, "Smomyny z davnych lit," *Svoboda*, September 5, 1912, p. 4.

15. *Evening Herald* (Shenandoah, Pennsylvania), May 30, 1887, p. 4.

16. H. J. Heuser, "Greek Catholics and Latin Priests," *American Ecclesiastical Review* IV (March, 1891) : 197–198 (footnote).

17. *Pershy Rusko-Amerykansky Kalendar* (Mount Carmel, Pennsylvania: Ruthenian National Association, 1897), pp. 168–169.

18. See e.g., *Amerikansky Russky Viestnik*, March 6, 1894, p. 1; *Svoboda*, October 10, 1894, also December 5, 1895.

19. U. S. Senate, Reports of the Immigration Commission, *Dictionary of Races or Peoples*, 1911, IX, 118. The estimated 500,000 Ruthenians in the United States as shown by a chart on page 118 indicating the number and distribution of those immigrants in 1897, is difficult to substantiate. It might be a typographical error.

20. See e.g., Andrew J. Shipman, "Greek Catholics in America," *Catholic Encyclopedia* VI (1909) : 748. Shipman was one of the first American authors to become intimately associated with the Ukrainian immigrants at least as early as the mid-1890s. The high esteem with which Shipman was held by the Ukrainian Americans is illustrated, for example, by a long biographical article on him in *Svoboda*, September 8, 1910, p. 4, in which he is given full credit for informing the American public about the Ukrainians.

21. Stephen G. Gulovich, "The Rusin Exarchate in the United States," *Eastern Churches Quarterly* VI (October–December, 1946) : 463.

22. *Svoboda*, March 5, 1896, p. 1, also May 14, 1896, p. 1, illustrate the strong tone of these appeals.

23. *Ibid.*, June 6, 1901, p. 2; June 13, p. 2, June 27, p. 2, provide additional information by leading priests of the Association.

24. *Ibid.*, June 6, 1901, p. 2.

25. *Ibid.*, April 10, 1902, p. 2 and May 14, p. 4, contain an extended report of the Convention's radical discussions and resolutions.

26. The radical views of the association of the Ruthenian Church in America are well illustrated in the association's booklet *Unia v Amerytsi* (New York: T.R.T.A., 1902).

27. Numerous articles in *Svoboda*, particularly during 1901–1902, illustrate the bitterness of the struggle.

28. *Unia v Amerytsi*, 1902, p. 20. The same figures are given by the Russian Orthodox *Kalendar Pravosl.*, 1901, cited by A. Levkov in *Svoboda*, April 11, 1901, p. 4.

29. Warne, pp. 101–102. The report of the Board of Home Missions of the Presbyterian Church to the Chairman of the Immigration Commission, dated New York, November 22, 1910, illustrates the extensiveness of their colportage work among the new immigrants, including the Ukrainians. See U. S. Senate, Reports of the Immigration Commission, *Statements by Socie-*

ties Interested in Immigration, Doc. No. 764, 61st Cong., 3d Sess., 1911, XXIII, 297–301.

30. Conde B. Pallen, ed., A Memorial of Andrew J. Shipman (New York: 1916), pp. 96–99.

31. In 1954 St. Basil's orphanage was finally moved to its new quarters at West Lindley Ave. in North Philadelphia.

32. The Official Catholic Directory, 1914 (New York: 1914), p. 823.

33. Pravoslavnii Russko-Amerikanskii Kalendar, 1915 (New York: Svet, 1914), p. 119.

34. U. S. Bureau of the Census, Religious Bodies: 1926, II (1929), 514.

35. A letter from a second Assistant Secretary in the State Department to Rev. Peter Poniatishin, chairman of the Ukrainian National Committee, dated December 16, 1918 (in reply to Poniatishin's letter of November 18, 1918) indicates that the State Department was glad to utilize the Committee as a medium through which to acquire information regarding the Ukraine, but that it was not prepared to recognize it as an official spokesman of the Ukrainian people. Letter in the archives of the Ukrainian Museum in Chicago.

36. U. S., Statutes at Large, XL, part 2, 1645–1646.

37. According to Father Poniatishin, upon whose shoulder rested the responsibility of obtaining the Ukrainian Day proclamation, the Ukrainian Americans are indebted to Congressman James A. Hamill, President Wilson's secretary, Joseph P. Tumulty, attorney William J. Kearns, and a half-dozen other Senators and Congressmen, who understood their aspirations and through whose influence the Ukrainian Day became a reality. See Svoboda, April 3, 1917, p. 3.

38. See Poniatishin's "Ukrainska Sprava v Amerytsi," Yuvileiny Almanakh Svobody, 1893–1953 (Jersey City: Ukrainian National Association, 1953), p. 76.

39. U.S., Congressional Record, 65th Cong., 3d Sess., 1918, LVII, Part I, 434.

40. The Committee's significant role in its attempts to bring aid to the Ukrainian people in Galicia might readily be gleaned from, e.g., a letter from the Department of Foreign Affairs of the Western Ukrainian Republic in exile, dated from Vienna, November 10, 1921, and signed by Gregory Myketey, officially thanked Father Poniatishin and the Committee which he headed for taking the first politico-diplomatic action to inform the United States government and President Wilson about the Ukrainian viewpoint concerning Galicia. The above letter is in the archives of the Ukrainian Museum in Chicago.

41. Poniatishin, "Ukrainska Tserkva i U. N. Soyuz," Propamiatna Knyha Ukrainskoho Narodnoho Soyuza, 1894–1934 (Jersey City: Ukrainian National Association, 1936), p. 294.

42. Ibid., p. 299.

43. Catholic Directory, 1925, pp. 750–754.

44. See, e.g., Rev. Peter Poniatishin's letter dated September 30, 1916, published in Catholic News, October 7, 1916, and reproduced in Svoboda, October 28, 1916, p. 3.

45. The Archbishop's views are extensively reported in Svoboda, February 19, 1924, p. 3, by a representative of that paper who interviewed the Archbishop.

# 9

# The Origin and Development of the Italian Community in Philadelphia

## RICHARD N. JULIANI

*Richard N. Juliani is Assistant Professor of Sociology at Temple University. He completed his undergraduate studies at Notre Dame and holds a Ph.D. from the University of Pennsylvania.*

Although individual Italians had been in Philadelphia since before the Revolutionary War, there is no evidence of any sizable Italian population in the city until the middle of the 19th century.[1] In December, 1853, Bishop John Neumann, himself a German immigrant, established St. Mary Magdalen de Pazzi as the first national parish for Italians in the United States.[2] The sacramental records, particularly for baptisms, provide the only existing social data on this first Italian community in Philadelphia.

The majority of these early settlers came from a section of Northern Italy, beginning at Genoa, stretching down the Ligurian coast 35 kilometers to Chiaveri and reaching inland 55 kilometers to Tortona in the region of Piedmont and 51 kilometers to the town of Bobbio in Liguria. Italians had also come, however, from other sections of the Kingdom of Sardinia and nearby regions of Northern Italy, as well as, in a handful of cases, Naples and Sicily, far to the

South. The occupational information for parents in the baptismal records suggests that this early Italian settlement was composed mainly of musicians, merchants, and industrial and outside laborers.

It is impossible to know exactly why these early immigrants left their homeland for Philadelphia, but several factors are worth noting. The baptismal records show clearly that these families were mainly from the cities and larger towns of the North, and near the coast, which were less locked into the feudalism and the traditionalism which marked the small towns and peasant villages of the Southern regions. The area along the Gulf of Genoa also had a tradition of commercial enterprise, and inhabitants who were probably well accustomed to travel. The baptismal records, in fact, reinforce this point by revealing a predominance of occupations in which travel was common. Furthermore, the area around Genoa was a center for revolutionaries advocating the republican cause in the mid-nineteenth century, many of whom had to flee Italy to escape punishment after the temporary defeat of the nationalist movement in 1849.

It is similarly difficult to know what ultimate plans these early migrants had for themselves after their arrival in Philadelphia, but naturalization records for the city show 374 Italians initiated citizenship proceedings in the years before 1881.[3] Moreover, the Italian colony which gathered around St. Mary Magdalen de Pazzi Church consisted conspicuously of families, a fact which ordinarily denotes permanent settlement in a new land. But, most important, although many Italians undoubtedly moved westward with the rest of the American population, the establishment of the church itself unequivocally signifies a permanent Italian community in Philadelphia.

Actually, very little is known about this first group of Italians in Philadelphia. It would be particularly interesting to know what role they may have had in the mass immigration of later years. Perhaps these early settlers, as in other cities, not only became the *prominenti* of the "Little Italy" which emerged in later years, but also functioned frequently as brokers and mediators between the Italian community and the larger social order. In providing these services, it is not clear whether the *prominenti* were leaders and protectors *or* exploiters in their relationships with the Southern Italians who came afterwards. Similarly, it would be worthwhile to know if these early Northern Italians were more easily assimilated into American society than the *contadini* of Southern Italy in later years. Unfortunately, no one knows enough about the Italians of Philadelphia, at present, to answer these questions in a satisfactory manner.

In contrast to later conditions, these early "adventurers" represent a rather unique phase in Italian migration to the United States. They came as families; many of the men sought citizenship; and political motives may have been as important as economic ones for this group. But the most significant aspect of their uniqueness was the fact that these Northern Italians were genuine pioneers in a sociological sense. Unlike the masses of later decades, they had no "Little Italy" waiting to materially aid and to emotionally comfort them. To the contrary, these families were on a social and cultural frontier, and they were the pioneers of the Italian settlements in this country. Their presence, eventually, provided a distinctive "Italian" character to sections of the city, originating the institutions and identity which were the social foundations of the Italian-American community in Philadelphia. Thus established, the community could function as a magnet for later Italian immigrants, particularly the masses which were to come from the Southern regions.

Mass immigration to the United States from Italy came only after the tremendous shift from sailing ships to steamships which revolutionized international trade and travel.[4] Ironically, Philadelphia, which was the destination for the first steamships to carry immigrants to the United States, never became a major port of entry during the steamship era for immigration originating in Mediterranean countries. By the 1880s, when the great competition between German and British companies began, ships carrying immigrants from Mediterranean ports were more likely to arrive at New York, Boston, or New Orleans. Cargo ships regularly arrived in Philadelphia from Mediterranean ports, but carrying only small numbers of Italian passengers. Passenger ships carrying large numbers of immigrants also arrived, but they virtually always originated in Northern European ports. Finally, in 1909, steamers from Mediterranean ports began to arrive regularly at Philadelphia. Between

1909 and 1915, when the war ended all service, and between 1919 and 1925, several companies, mainly Italian, had runs between Mediterranean ports and Philadelphia. But this service only accounted for a grand total of 86 landings in Philadelphia, while similar ships made 2,668 arrivals in New York City during the same period. The immensely greater importance of New York as the primary port of entry for Italian immigrants is evident from the fact that from 1890 to 1930, the staggering total of 6,065 Mediterranean passenger ships arrived at that port.

Figures for the actual number of immigrants arriving at United States' ports also show Philadelphia to have had a limited role, with the peak years being 1910–1914.[5] In the fiscal year ending June 30, 1909, only 14,294 immigrants from all countries entered at Philadelphia. But in the succeeding five years, the number grew greatly: 37,641 in 1910; 45,023 in 1911; 43,749 in 1912; 59,466 in 1913; and 56,857 in 1914. During the last of these years, of the 68,837 alien passengers (immigrants and nonimmigrants), most were from Russia (29,000), Italy (19,000), Austria (13,000), and the British Empire (5,000), and no less than 95% of the Italians were supposed to have been from Southern Italy.[6] By late 1914, however, the outbreak of World War I was already reducing immigration. In 1915, only 1,379 passengers arrived at Philadelphia; 948 of them had come on two trips of the Ancona of the Italia Line in April and June, before being sunk later the same year. Before immigration ceased altogether, many Italians rushed back to their homeland to enter military service. In terms of the actual number of immigrants, Philadelphia arrivals were between 3% and 12% of the New York volume during the years 1880–1916, varying between 5% and 7% during the peak years, 1910–1914. For the 37 years between 1880 and 1916, Philadelphia always ranked behind New York as an immigrant port as well as behind Boston, except for six years, and Baltimore, except for 16 years. While we cannot determine exactly what part Italian immigration had in these matters, one respected writer has concluded:

Among the ports of destination in the United States, New York leads, far outdistancing Boston, while Philadelphia, New Orleans, and Providence receive Italians but intermittently.[7]

A great emphasis upon the limited role of Philadelphia as a port of entry can obscure the fact that, despite relatively light direct immigration, the Italian community was steadily growing. It is essential to stress that fact that, even when direct service existed, many Italians bound for Philadelphia preferred to disembark at New York. In 1909, when direct service to Philadelphia was established, it was more as a response to the large Italian community already there, than as a cause for some future one. But it is not possible to know precisely the size of the community at any time. The figures vary considerably; no estimate appears totally reliable. In 1850, only 200 Italians were supposed to be in Philadelphia; by 1890, the figure was 6,799.[8] In 1897, Koren claimed that the Italian colony in Philadelphia numbered over 20,000, and was exceeded only by New York City and Brooklyn.[9] Another writer noted only 17,830 from the census of 1900.[10] An Italian language newspaper said over 80,000 in the city and another 20,000 in the suburbs in 1906.[11] A church historian, in 1909, maintained that the Italian population was almost 50,000.[12] Foerster, the author of probably the best study of the Italians at the time, claimed the population to have been 45,000 in 1910, about the same as Chicago, and second only to the enormous population of 340,770 Italians in New York.[13] Even the relatively conservative U.S. Census caught up to the higher estimates by reporting 76,734 Italians in 1910 and 136,793 in 1920 for Philadelphia.[14]

Although the greatest concentration of Italians in the Delaware Valley has always been in South Philadelphia, other colonies had also emerged in the area. Within the city itself, Italian settlements could be found in many neighborhoods: Manayunk, West Philadelphia; North Philadelphia, Frankford, Nicetown, Mayfair, Germantown, Chestnut Hill; Richmond; and Southwest Philadelphia. Outside of the city, visible Italian communities were found in Norristown, Bristol, Stafford, Chester, Conshohocken, Coatesville, Marcus Hook, Narberth, and Bridgeport. In neighboring counties of New Jersey, Italian colonies existed in the pine barrens of Vineland, Hammonton, and Landisville, and in the industrial centers of Camden and Trenton.

In less than 50 years, Italy changed from a society without any significant overseas migration to, perhaps, the most significant source of the mass immigration to the United States at the beginning of the 20th century. Numerous factors in Italy produced this great change: a tremendous growth in the population; a slowly growing economy and occupational system; rising aspirations and discontent with traditional living standards; and the erosion of the customary peasant community which had kept the people "in their place," both socially and physically, for centuries. Two broad types of Italian emigrants appeared on the American scene. First were the "birds-of-passage," the young, male, migratory laborers who regularly crossed the Atlantic in pursuit of working opportunities during the late 19th century, but who also, in increasing numbers, began to remain permanently in America. With this shift, a second type of migrant followed, namely, the conscious, deliberate expatriates, certain from the start that their departure from the homeland would be permanent. By the early 20th century, the latter type, frequently women and children, grew in numbers and significance, until they exceeded the "birds-of-passage," whom they often came to join, thus, reuniting families and "normalizing" communities. As the Italian-American community appeared, it facilitated this shift in the character of immigration even more, becoming the most decisive and determining element in the history of Italian immigration to the United States.

Italian settlements, however, undoubtedly varied from place to place. Consequently, it is not enough to attempt an explanation of Italian immigration in terms of conditions in Italy alone. In this regard, it is necessary to examine some of the more outstanding and influential dimensions of the character of Philadelphia as they impinged upon Italian immigration, particularly in the 20th century. Several factors are useful in understanding the Italian experience in Philadelphia: transportation patterns; the image of this particular city; industry and job opportunities; housing and property ownership; the *padroni* and the *prominenti;* the character of Italian settlements; and the development of ethnicity.

As previously noted, Philadelphia never approached New York as a port of entry for Italian immigrants during the steamship era. Yet, among the hundreds of thousands who entered by way of New York City, there were many Italians who intended to reach Philadelphia. The Italians who came to Philadelphia did so because they consciously wanted to go there, and not simply because their ships happened to dock there. Most Italians, destined for Philadelphia, regularly landed at New York, and completed their trips by train.

It is difficult to say how much knowledge of Philadelphia the ordinary Italian had when he left his homeland, but even in peasant villages some immigrants knew and admired Philadelphia for its historical role as the cradle of American independence and liberty. Some men also felt that Philadelphia offered better job opportunities than other cities. In fact, some immigrants knew only one thing about Philadelphia: that it was easy to get a job there. On the other hand, other men knew practically nothing about Philadelphia. Despite the information provided by returnees and the letters sent back by friends and relatives still there, most Italians probably had only negligible knowledge of Philadelphia, vague or exaggerated in many cases. However, in time, many Italians learned one compelling fact which was sufficient to draw them to Philadelphia—their people were there. Often the latter stimulated immigration in more active ways by returning to Italy and regularly "escorting" new immigrants back to America, and by "sponsoring" others either by providing passage money or steamship tickets. These relationships also meant that new immigrants were regularly arriving with very specific destinations. Immigrants frequently arrived bearing a precise address —such as a boarding house located at a particular intersection in South Philadelphia, where their *paesani* (literally "kinsmen") who had previously provided them with the means to come now waited to greet them.

The *paesani* already there provided a wide range of services for the newcomer to Philadelphia. Often the *paesani* met new arrivals at the docks in New York, or at the train stations in Philadelphia. The newcomer would be brought to a *paesani* boarding house to live with old friends or relatives from his home town (*paese*). Housing for Italian individuals and families invariably began in boarding houses, usually of a specific *paese* character and clientele, which honeycombed South Philadelphia. In some blocks, almost every house, even though only three or four rooms large, held a family or two to five working men in every room. The single room was the entire living space provided for each group in the house, and used for all purposes—cooking, eating, and sleeping. A study of housing conditions at the time reported 104 single room "housekeeping apartments," containing nearly one-third of the Italian families of the area, in a single block.[15]

In addition to these smaller dwellings, perhaps 25–30 larger establishments were connected to area restaurants, although still with a regional character, such as Corona di Ferro, on South 10th Street, for immigrants from Chieti and Pescara, and Palumbo's, on Catharine Street, for immigrants from all Abruzzi. Here the immigrant could find a room at a modest cost as well as a meal for a nickel. Immigrants from all parts of Italy could be found at the Giannini Hotel at 7th and Fitzwater Streets, operated by a Tuscan family which also owned Verdi Hall, a popular theater on Christian Street.

As in other cities, the migration chains and resettlement patterns based upon the *paesani* principle produced in Philadelphia not one monolithic Italian community, but an elaborate proliferation of "Little Italys." In addition to the cleavage between northern and southern Italians, the social organization of Italian neighborhoods was based upon even more complicated and specific *paesi* loyalties. The *paesani* principle was reflected in the number of *societe* (mutual aid societies) found in Philadelphia; one informant, active for many years in Italian-American civic affairs, claimed that 435 societies existed among the Italians in Philadelphia at some time. Based mainly upon *paesani* relationships, every town had its own society, if it had enough immigrants in Philadelphia. However, mutual aid societies could be based upon other interests. Some societies were organized around occupations; the barbers' society still exists today.

Other societies grew out of religious devotions; one *paese* had separate societies for St. Lucy, St. Rosalie, St. Anne, and the Holy Cross. Even very small towns had several societies in Philadelphia, reflecting different factions in the *paese,* or the reactions of vain and ambitious men who, frustrated by the failure to gain control of existing societies, simply formed new ones.[16] Multiple memberships in the societies were common for many individuals. In sum, the societies were basically organizations which were designed to protect mutual interests and to provide leisure activities. Although most societies are now extinct, their former members continue to express sincere pride, gratitude, and deference when discussing the *paesani* who aided them.

By the turn of the century, the Italian immigration to Philadelphia, as for so many other cities, was greatly dominated by natives of Southern Italy. By World War I, the Italian community still centered about the area of Fitzwater, Catharine, Christian, and Carpenter Streets, between 7th and 9th Streets, quite near to St. Mary Magdalen de Pazzi Church, and the historical origins of the Italian area. Immigrants from all the regions of the *mezzogiorno*— Campania, Calabria, Basilicata, Apulia, Abruzzi, and Sicily—were creating a rapidly growing settlement, both within the older boundaries and on their fringes. With rather vague knowledge of what awaited them, but willing to relocate alongside of relatives and friends already in Philadelphia, new waves of Italian immigrants continued to follow the *paesani* chains of migration.

Once arrived in the city, however, the immigrants often found a rather difficult situation. For instance, living conditions were often terrible. At times, the rats and bugs made it impossible to sleep inside the houses. Plumbing facilities were still generally outside of the homes, and stagnant water collected in backyard puddles. The boarding houses were often overcrowded. Faulty oil heaters constantly smoked up the insides of some houses, allowing no one to breathe. Ironically, working conditions which had lured so many Italians to Philadelphia turned out to be very poor in many cases. Some men found themselves working longer hours for less money in Philadelphia than they had in Italy. Many men made barely enough to pay for their lodging. Working days which lasted from dawn to late at night commonly produced $5.00 and $6.00 weekly wages for some men. Many men wanted to go back to Italy immediately after discovering these conditions, but were unable to save even enough money to afford the return fare. An Abruzzese who had worked at many jobs since his arrival in 1911 succinctly summarized the feelings of many of his fellow-immigrants: ". . . the Italian people were slaves." In contrast to popular images of Italy as a land of misery, hardship, and poverty, and of the United States as a land of opportunity, wealth, and abundance, the actual conditions for most immigrants show a more complicated situation in either country. In fact, for many immigrants, resettlement in this country, in certain respects, resulted in a deterioration of personal conditions.

Making this situation even more difficult, the Italians had to cope sometimes with tensions and physical violence resulting from internal group conflict as well as from other nationality groups. While the situation never was entirely clear, apparently, immigrants from the different regions of Italy deceived and cheated one another, fought with each other, and generally retarded the advance of the Italians as a group. With the passage of time, regional hostilities and conflicts receded, but the Italians never succeeded in establishing a comprehensive unification to further their political and economic interests. More clear, however, was the antagonism of Italians, in general, with other ethnic groups with whom they were thrown into conflicts over housing and jobs. The Italian section of South Philadelphia was surrounded by neighborhoods occupied by other kinds of people. East of South 4th Street to the Delaware River, the area almost entirely Jewish, smaller pockets of other Eastern Europeans could also be found. South of Washington Avenue were more Jews, and beyond them, much farmland. West of Broad Street was a large area populated by several groups, but conspicuously by the Irish. Although the boundaries of the Italian section changed over time, there were always distinct lines which could not be crossed without risking violence, particularly from the Irish. By World War I, the Italians had penetrated the Jewish areas to the south as far as

Dickinson Street and Tasker Avenue, and the Irish and German sections west of Broad Street. In the 1920s and 1930s, Italian families spread throughout South and Southwest Philadelphia, moving into new homes as far down as Bigler Street, now the southern edge of residential Philadelphia. The continuous invasion of Italians often resulted in violence with older groups in these areas. Elderly immigrants today recall the knife and organized crime as the means by which the Italians obtained fear and respect from other groups. While these explanations are undoubtedly oversimplified, nevertheless the annexation of territory by the Italians from the Irish, Jews, and Germans was not achieved only through peaceful means.

But the hostility and conflict between Italians and other nationalities over living space frequently acquired an added dimension when the same groups confronted each other at work. For example, as the Italians moved in massive numbers into the factories of the clothing industry in Philadelphia, they ordinarily found the Jews already there, both as working tailors and as plant owners and shop managers. In the construction industry, the crews of unskilled laborers who toiled in the building of streets, homes, and subways of the city were often entirely Italian or Polish, but the owners, supervisors, and foremen—the hated bosses—were usually Irish. To make matters even worse, the Italians also discovered that all the police in the city seemed to be Irish.

Italian immigrants in Philadelphia did not confront only hardship and violence; the economic growth of the city offered numerous opportunities for workers. The Italians, born into rather unpromising conditions in their homeland, discovered an unprecedented and almost unimaginable situation. At the beginning of the era of mass immigration, in the 1870s and 1880s, many Italians had already gone to the mining communities of Northern and Western Pennsylvania. Great rock and stone deposits in the Delaware Valley were also beginning to bring Italians to work in the quarries near Philadelphia. The largest contingent of unskilled Italians at this time in the Philadelphia area came to work as track laborers for the railroads. These men went to Conshohocken, Norristown, Coatesville, Downington, and West Chester, as well as to Germantown and South Philadelphia within the city, where the Reading and the Pennsylvania companies had large yards. In the case of South Philadelphia, because of the nearness of these yards to St. Mary Magdalen de Pazzi, the arrival of the newcomers renourished the roots of the earlier Italian community. Simply by following their *paesani,* the Italians also pursued the flow of working opportunities. By the 20th century, many immigrants still depended, directly or indirectly, on the railroads, either in terms of the relatives who had preceded them to Philadelphia, or in terms of first jobs with the same companies by the later immigrants themselves. In most cases, the *paesani* already here enabled other individuals to immigrate themselves, frequently by providing passage money, but also by aiding them to find jobs. Before the war, thousands of Italians had come to the United States in this way and had worked for the railroads. However, for most men railroad employment was merely temporary, until something better was available and they could "move up." But the railroads had provided an early foundation for the subsequent working careers of a great number of these men.

After World War I, the growth of other industries provided the immigrant with a wider range of attractive jobs than ever before. Many former railroad workers became general laborers for construction companies as city expansion created a great need for new homes, streets, bridges, and subways. Later, the same men climbed into semi-skilled and skilled crafts as bricklayers, masons, carpenters, plumbers, and electricians.

Another important industry, concentrated in Philadelphia, which provided a new and huge source of opportunities was the manufacturing of wearing apparel, particularly men's suits, coats, and hats, and women's shoes. Without knowing much else about the city, many immigrants learned before departing from Italy that tailors, hatters, and shoemakers could easily find well-paying jobs in Philadelphia. John B. Stetson Company was the largest hat maker in the world. The city was a great center for the production of women's shoes. Clothes factories had 600–700 men shops. The manufacturing of clothing, hats, and shoes actually had much in common at the time, because each involved the cutting and stitching of materials by hand.

These occupations also shared another aspect which contributed to their popularity among immigrants—their prestige value. The Italians in Philadelphia retained an Old World distinction between skilled artisans, parts of a small middle class in peasant villages, and unskilled *contadini* (farm laborers). Becoming a tailor or shoemaker meant not only greater income, but significantly higher prestige as well. Many immigrants took the first chance to leap out of the ditches and into the shops of the clothing and shoe industries, which was, surprisingly, not too difficult to do. Because the assembly line process broke work down into detail labor, many immigrants, although called "tailors" or "shoemakers" really performed very limited functions, such as basting collars in men's suit jackets or lasting leather strips in women's shoes, particularly those men who had learned their skills in American factories. Immigrant workers themselves recognized this distinction also, referring as "real tailors," for example, only to those men who had learned the craft in Italy, and who could perform the entire productive process, from first measurements and cutting of patterns to the finishing touches before purchase by a customer.

In addition to the large industries, Philadelphia offered many other job opportunities, on a smaller scale, to Italian immigrants. For instance, some men found work in wood factories and furniture plants, including the Victor Talking Machine Company in nearby Camden, New Jersey. Victor, which later became RCA-Victor, not only employed many immigrants, but became an important impetus for the establishment of a satellite Italian community in South Camden for many former Philadelphia residents. As the Italian community in Philadelphia expanded through the natural increase of families after World War I, immigrants and their children found their way into a wide range of work settings—cigar factories, theater bands, restaurants, milk companies, food importing, barber shops, bakeries, banks, insurance firms, street-car manufacturing, grocery stores, and the government (particularly at the U.S. Quartermaster's

Depot, in the last case). Many Italians were employed in personal services in small shops, barbering, tailoring, and shoe repairing, both within Italian neighborhoods and outside of them throughout the entire city.

Another important feature of the occupational system in Philadelphia was the opportunity for the immigrant to move freely within the job market. In a very fluid situation, the immigrant could "shop around," moving easily from job to job with changing conditions, as one industry contracted and another expanded. Similarly, many men were able to hold two or three jobs at the same time. The tailor who was also a musician in the evening and on weekends in a movie house band was common among the Italians. In these cases, the individual earned a modest income on one job while learning another skill, perhaps a higher-paying, more respectable trade. Thus, the immigrant explored various career possibilities, or used one job as a means to advance himself to a better one, or simply to maintain income during hard times.

The clothing industry, in particular, allowed a peculiar integration of work and home as well as a great increase in family productivity and income. The manufacture of men's clothing was basically performed in three different settings. Much work was done in large factories in which detail workers on an assembly line mass-produced "ready-made" trousers, suits, and overcoats. In smaller, custom shops, the more expensive, individually tailored suits were made for more affluent customers. But both of these kinds of shops sent out work to individual tailors, working in their own homes. The custom shop and the "home shop" permitted, by their privacy, greater flexibility in the organization of work. Italian women and children could enter the clothing industry in a discreet and convenient process, much to the material benefit of their families. This arrangement permitted young boys to begin apprenticeships at an early age, enabled women to make economic contributions to their families, and provided some families with the means to open their own custom tailoring shops later on.

Even tailoring had its drawbacks, however, for instance, the annual slow season, from June to September. But the nearby farms of South Jersey provided alternatives during these months, and many families became fruit and vegetable pickers each summer. Particularly, they went to Hammonton, Vineland, and Landisville, which already had permanent Italian colonies, to harvest berries, potatoes, onions, and tomatoes. But the slow summer season was not a crisis for the families of many tailors in Philadelphia who regularly anticipated and prepared for it. Despite such risks, employment in Philadelphia industries generally represented a great opportunity for the immigrant, particularly in comparison to what was available in his hometown in Italy. While some men changed jobs repeatedly, many others found rewarding jobs with a single employer, remaining there for more than 40 years in some cases. Whether he changed jobs frequently or stayed many years with one employer, the Italian immigrant generally earned far more in wages in this country than he could have done in the severely depressed village of his birth.

The *paesani* principle, once again, operated to enable the immigrant to easily find work in Philadelphia, but usually in cooperation with the industrial system and its needs. *Paesani* relationships were the means by which unemployed, immigrant workers were brought into contact with the increasing manpower needs of growing industries. New arrivals were often brought to the bosses by *paesani* already employed in the same places. Often a "moving up" process was involved, by which men, as they secured better jobs, would enable *paesani* already here, or even bring relatives or friends from Italy, to fill the newly vacated position. Thus, the *paesani* relationship also functioned by locating work opportunities for newcomers, but mainly because they congruently fitted into the labor needs of certain, growing industries.

Another particular advantage of Philadelphia for immigrants was the nature of its housing supply and property ownership arrangements. As previously noted, immigrants typically first lived in the ubiquitous *paesani* boarding houses. Few houses in Philadelphia were originally built as tenements, but many were being used in this manner.[17] The small, single-family homes were often arranged into courts, appropriately designated as "horizontal tenements," because living conditions in these crowded alleys, quite common in some sections of Philadelphia, were strikingly similar to the large tenements of other cities. In the "horizontal tenements" of Philadelphia, families shared courts, passageways, water supply fixtures, and toilet facilities. The lack of janitors and caretakers and the dividing of responsibility among tenants resulted in neglect and the accumulation of dirt. Dinwiddie found the worst possible conditions in the adequacy of the water supply, sanitary accommodations, light, and ventilation in these buildings and courts. Few homes had yards, and they were very small. Unsurprisingly, the death rate was much higher here than among the general population. Of the districts she studied, Dinwiddie found the greatest crowding of families in the Italian section. Many families lived in "father, son, and holy ghost" homes, three story structures, consisting only of three rooms, one on top of another. Some civic organizations did attempt to correct these conditions. In the late 19th century, the Octavia Hill Housing Association was formed to provide decent and inexpensive housing for the poor and working classes of Philadelphia. In 1903, the Association opened the Casa Ravello, a four story brick building at 7th and Catharine Streets, containing thirty apartments of two and four rooms, staffed by two physicians and several nurses, and even providing recreation space on the roof for resident families. In 1911, the Association purchased 25 houses on East Rittenhouse Street in Germantown for the families of Italian laborers employed by the Reading Railroad Company. In physical terms, the families in housing provided by the Association apparently fared much better than they would have in most *paesani* boarding houses.

Immigrant families remained in rented housing only until they had saved enough of their earnings to purchase their own homes. In this respect, Philadelphia was a very favorable setting for a quick transition from apartment to home. From its early years, city housing has been noticeably marked by small, sturdy structures designed for single-family occupancy.[18] Thomas Holme, the first Surveyor General of William Penn's colony, permitted only brick and stone as permanent construction materials, a principle which has been maintained. Conveniently, large deposits of rock were available in the nearby tributaries of the Delaware and the Schuylkill Rivers, and brickyards and stone quarries became important enterprises in the area. Penn contributed to these trends by prohibiting all conditions of industrial apprenticeship or serfdom, and by establishing a system of land rent contracts unique to Pennsylvania. The latter enabled the settler to build on leased land, which remained in the family as long as his descendants paid the rent. This system enabled the newly arrived working man, with limited wealth, to become a home owner through a very modest investment.

From 1890 to 1930, home ownership in Philadelphia increased dramatically. In 1890, only 22.8% of city homes were owned by the families in them, a relatively low rate compared to other cities. But this figure grew steadily over the next 40 years. By 1920, home ownership reached 39.5%, second only to Baltimore among 11 cities with a population over 500,000 in the nation; by 1930, Philadelphia reached 51.8%, highest among the 14 largest cities in the United States.[19] Some factors increasing home ownership in Philadelphia were nationwide conditions, such as the tremendous growth of industry with its accompanying prosperity and rising personal incomes after World War I. But the growth of building and loan associations was a factor of particular importance in Philadelphia. From 1916 to 1926, the number of these associations in the city nearly tripled from 1,242 to 3,428; their assets increased from $178,336,000 to $743,-312,000. Moreover, at the end of the period, 1920–1925, as home ownership climbed from 39.5% to 45.5%, 70.9% of the owned homes were mortgaged.[20] Many banks had adopted the "Philadelphia plan" of home financing, which permitted a borrower to amortize a second mortgage while the first loan was continued without reduction. By 1929, over three-quarters of the city building and loan associations allowed the financing of second mortgages. Baltimore was the only other city with this program. The plan was a major factor in making Philadelphia truly a city of homes, and also in enabling many working class families of moderate incomes to purchase those homes.[21]

While probably unaware of these conditions before they arrived, Italian immigrants soon learned of them. By 1902, two-thirds of the homes in the Italian section of South Philadelphia were reported to be owned by Italians.[22] Consequently, Italian home owners began displacing the Irish and Jewish families who had settled earlier in South Philadelphia. Some Italian families were moving into new homes, built on the old farms which remained even into the 20th century in the lower end of the area. Most Italians, however, purchased older properties, closer to the original immigrant community, made substantial and impressive renovations in their homes, and produced an enormous change in the character of private homes in Philadelphia. In the first 20 years of the 20th century, numerous innovations became standard features of Philadelphia homes. In the first decade, electricity, central heating, steam and hot water heating, sanitary plumbing of vitreous china, gas ranges, and hardwood floors and trim became regular aspects of most homes. In the next decade, the two-story row home appeared, with front and back yards; concrete driveways; basement garages in the rear; fronts trimmed with dress brick, tile, and stucco, or stone; enclosed porches; tile bathrooms with built-in tubs and showers, pedestal washstands, low-tank water closets, and plate glass mirrors.[23] The Italians not only contributed to these changes, but settled into these homes to enjoy the fruits of their labors. Families who have lived in the same homes for over 40 or even 50 years are surprisingly common in South Philadelphia.

New or remodeled, the homes into which these families moved were substantially better than anything else in which they had previously lived. After the villages in Italy and the boarding houses here, when he bought a Philadelphia home, in many cases, the immigrant may have believed that he was moving into a small palace. Moreover, the pride and prestige of home ownership, so difficult to attain in Italy, enabled many immigrant families to feel that they had, indeed, joined the aristocracy.

A final institution which deserves some examination is the *padrone* system. In 1864, the U.S. Congress passed a law permitting industrial agents to recruit immigrant laborers by contract in their native countries. The Foran Act in 1885 repealed the earlier law, prohibiting any further recruitment of contract labor. Subsequently, less formal means were used to recruit immigrant laborers for American industries. Much disagreement has marked the study of the role of contract labor in stimulating immigration from Southern and Eastern Europe. Early writers, particularly Koren in his influential study of immigrant banks, placed great importance on the *padrone* system.[24] A very recent writer reached a similar conclusion in a study which presented the *padrone* system as the central mechanism of Italian immigration to America.[25] However, other scholars have expressed more skeptical and cautious views on the importance of contract labor and the *padrone* system.[26] Erickson concluded that no evidence ever showed that American industry actually imported many Hungarians or Italians.[27] Similarly, Nelli claims that a formal *padrone* system may have lasted until the 1880s, but only on a very limited scale. After the Foran Act, Nelli writes that the *padrone* system persisted, but had evolved into an informal operation, conducted by private agents. By the late 19th century, Nelli maintains, the agent no longer needed to recruit in Europe, but merely to meet the immigrant at the port, in order to hire him, mainly as a laborer for the railroads, construction companies, and city departments. But the federal investigations of the time, while documenting many violations of the contract labor laws, never conclusively demonstrated that the *padroni* had actually induced much migration, and by 1907, the Dillingham Commission could find only isolated cases of the *padrone* system.[28]

Undoubtedly, some form of *padrone* existed in Philadelphia in the years of mass migration from Italy to the United States. Koren had noted an intimate connection between the *padrone* system and immigrant banks, and Philadelphia had 25 Italian banks in 1897, mainly concentrated near South 7th Street.[29] A souvenir book, published in 1908, on the 225th anniversary of the founding of Philadelphia, contained advertisements for several Italian firms providing an interesting variety of services. The V. D'Ambrosio Company at 8th and Fitzwater Streets, founded in 1886, which claimed to be the oldest Italian bank in Philadelphia, also was a real estate office and steamship agency. The Italo-American Company (Serafini and Ciaverelli Company) at 9th and Christian, engaged in general banking, steamship tickets, real estate, and foreign exchange. The Banca Calabrese

(Frank F. Bilotta Company), at 7th and Christian, advertised only in terms of building and contracting. G. Tumolillo, established in 1887, on South 8th Street, was a banker and broker. Frank Di-Berardino, on Christian Street, with branches in West Philadelphia and in Pittsburgh, advertised as a steamship ticket agency. Cesare Romano, banker, broker, and steamship agent on South 8th Street, also advertised as the proprietor of the Pottstown Trap Rock Quarry and Crusher, bluntly stating: "Laborers Furnished for Railroad, Reservoir, Grading, Etc." The advertisement for C.C.A. Baldi Brothers and Company read: "Real Estate Brokers and Conveyances, Mortgages Negotiated, Money Loaned, Houses Bought and Sold, Rents and Interest Collected, Estates Managed." A separate advertisement for C.C.A. Baldi and Brothers, with two offices on South 8th Street, identified the firm as an Italian exchange bank, buying and selling foreign money, and as the representative of the Banco di Napoli.[30]

Charles C. A. Baldi began as an interpreter and labor gang leader for the railroad in Manayunk, but became, unquestionably, the most successful and powerful Italian businessman in Philadelphia. But his wealth and influence were not attained without making great enemies of other *prominenti*, leaders of rival firms and factions. One very bitter passage in a generally acrimonious study of the Italians in America characterized Baldi in a manner which reflected this factionalism:

In one of our large cities there is a man of great cleverness, an outstanding example of the common type, who has graduated through all the stages of cicerone,[31] lemon-vendor, undertaker, coal-dealer, banker, real estate agent and proprietor of an Italian newspaper, *L'Opinione*. Among the Italians he has passed for a Roman Catholic; in the American residential district where he lives, he is a member of a Protestant church. He has been able to capitalize his reputation, without holding great office, as to be the colonial boss, so that no Italian considered that he could accomplish anything without recourse to his influence. Although evidently his first thought is for himself, he himself really believes that he is giving his life for his people. It may be said that another faction, enthusiastic over Americanism, is fighting his leadership with the definite slogan, and perhaps ideal, of disinterested community service.[32]

In addition to these activities, Baldi owned the first Italian radio station in Philadelphia, and was the first Italian member of the Board of Education. Baldi supplied workers for mines, farms, labor gangs, and city departments, recruited from the newly arrived immigrants, often in return for their pledge that they would, after becoming citizens, support the Republican political machine of the Vare brothers. Many elderly Italians remember Baldi with great respect and admiration for providing valuable services to the Italian community, and are quick to offer his name when asked to identify the *prominenti* of earlier years. The influence of the Baldi family, for instance, is reputed to have aided many young Italian-Americans gain admission to a local medical school. Perhaps Charles C. A. Baldi provided other *prominenti* with certain standards which, in fact, greatly benefited many Italian immigrants and their families.

As for actually *stimulating* immigration, by the early 20th century, the *padroni* of Philadelphia no longer appear to have had any substantial role. Immigration, itself, was not being *directly* abetted by the *padrone* system. But many Italians had relatives and friends already here, who aided later immigrants with information, passage money, housing, and jobs, as well as emotional support. Frequently, these earlier immigrants, of an older generation in many cases, had worked as track laborers on the railroads, and afterwards their *paesani* came to join them. This earlier wave of immigrants could have been recruited by *padroni,* but we cannot be certain. However, it is clear that the earlier immigrants were involved in family relationships and friendships which both attracted and enabled so many more Italians to come to Philadelphia later. In this way, if it established a necessary foundation for the *paesani* principle as the primary immigration mechanism, then the earlier *padrone* system may have been indirectly, but profoundly, involved in the mass immigration of later years. The *padrone* system did not entirely disappear in the 20th century, but evolved into a different kind of structure, serving different functions, largely restricted to services provided after the immigrants reached the city.

By the 20th century, Italian immigrants came to Philadelphia in great numbers, partly because of the good jobs which they knew to be available. In a complementary manner, the industries of the city had a growing supply of cheaply paid, but eager workers. In contrast to the overseas recruitment of contract labor, the newer system had great advantages for industry, being cheaper, simpler, and legal. Although the new system of recruitment often relied upon other Italians or Italian-Americans who spoke the immigrants' language to serve as interpreters and job-brokers, it did not always eliminate the excesses and abuses of the past for immigrant workers. For instance, immigrants who obtained work from Italian agencies had to pay the *bossatura* the placement fee, while the agencies also collected a commission from the industries. Sometimes, the agencies hired less men than they reported to the companies, hence gaining more money than was paid out. The agencies thus collected from both the hiring industry and the immigrant, an old practice once a prominent feature of the 19th century *padrone* system. Moreover, local politicians reportedly sponsored gambling on weekends to further recover the earnings of the workers. If workers eventually found it necessary to borrow money, the immigrants remained, then, in debt to the employment agency and to the political machine.

Despite these practices, in Philadelphia the *padrone* system by the early 20th century was not extremely abusive and exploitative. Elsewhere the situation may have been different, but in Philadelphia, apparently, the "bosses" quickly discovered that they could accumulate wealth, power, and prestige, while remaining within the law, and legitimately rendering broad services to the immigrant population. In 1913, the late Judge Adrian Bonnelly, then an immigration inspector for the federal government, was assigned to investigate the persistence of *padrone* practices in the Eastern states. Bonnelly's findings led to the indictment of several *padroni* in upstate Pennsylvania and in New York, but his report contained nothing but praise for Italian leaders in Philadelphia. In fact, Bonnelly felt that the latter deserved some recognition from the government for their services to the Italians in Philadelphia.[33]

In retrospect, although the exact character of the *padrone* system in Philadelphia remains somewhat unclear, Koren's conclusion is plausible: "Here also the bosses have intrenched themselves, but do not appear to carry things in such a high-handed manner as in New York."[34] Koren provided several reasons to account for this difference. First, since few immigrant ships went directly to Philadelphia, many Italians, after living elsewhere, came to the city with the intention to settle permanently. Second, the Italian section had few tenements but many smaller homes occupied by their owners. Third, city politicians quickly reached the Italians, encouraged naturalization, and organized them into clubs. While not totally obviating the role of the bosses, Koren maintained that these processes, nevertheless, did give Italians greater prominence and power. In employment, for example, the Italians achieved a monopoly in street cleaning through the control of this work by the Societa Operaia di Mutuo Succorso. Although the organization also was controlled by the bosses, still their power was milder than in other cities.[35]

In commenting on the failure of the Dillingham Commission to obtain evidence of *padrone* practices in 1907, Nelli offers some very general reasons which reflect changes in the immigrant community perhaps everywhere: the large influx of Italians to America after 1890; the more stable nature of later Italian immigration; an increased familiarity with the English language and with American labor practices on the part of Italian immigrants; and a general rise in the economic status of immigrant workers in this country.[36] Clearly the same changes were evident in Philadelphia at the beginning of the 20th century. In short, local conditions seem to have produced a "softer" *padrone* system in Philadelphia than in other areas to begin with. In addition, the *padroni,* themselves, discovered quite early the need for various services in the immigrant community which were also within the law. This situation, along with the development of a settled Italian population whose own interpersonal relations began to serve as the primary mechanisms for chain migration, encouraged the replacement of the *padrone* system by the *paesani* principle as the basis of the social organization of immigration as well as of the immigrant community in Philadelphia.

From the 1880s on, the Italian settlement in Philadelphia was not a single "Little Italy," but a collection of *paesani* communities, somewhat distinct from one another, especially in the eyes of the individuals and families who lived in that section of the city. In Italy, the cultural value known as *campanilismo* had tended to restrict all activity for the individual to within the area in which he could still hear the church bells of his village. Initially, by the nature of their immigration and resettlement, the Italians had merely transferred the concept of *campanilismo* from the villages of peasant Italy to the neighborhoods of the urban United States.[37] While relationships between families in any particular Italian village were frequently marked by hostility and antagonism, the peasant ordinarily had a much stronger dislike of outsiders.[38] Ironically, the disliked and distrusted *forestiero* (stranger) may even have been a person from the nearest neighboring village.[39] In a society with such an under-developed sense of national consciousness, as traditional Italy, if a person was not a *paesano,* it mattered little whether he was from a nearby village or another country.

This attitude of intense loyalty of the individual to the *paese* and his corresponding dependence upon *paesani* became an important principle of social organization in immigrant life with several major consequences. First, the *paesani* relationship frequently provided the social basis for the immigration process itself. For countless Italians, the *paesani* who had preceded them were a chief aspect of the goals of their own immigration to America. With very little left for them in the old country, and if their "people" were already here, the immigrants had sufficient reason to go to this country. More instrumentally, often the *paesani* also provided later immigrants with information, passage money, and encouragement. Second, after arrival in the United States, the immigrants normally relied upon *paesani* relationships for the material means of physical safety and survival in the new society—housing, jobs, friendships, religion, recreation, and a familiar language. Third, in the long run, perhaps the primary function of the *paesani* relationship was more psychological in nature. His *paesani* and the social institutions of their ethnic community permitted the immigrant to adjust successfully to a new and alien society without demanding a total break with his past. In short, the *paesani* community allowed the immigrant to retain his personal identity and values. The emotional continuity with the past, which this experience provided, made life tolerable for the immigrant.[40] These circumstances were so generally apparent among those who came after the 1880s that it is quite appropriate to designate these years as the *paesani* period of Italian immigration.

But if Italian immigrants had to adjust to anything, it was because they did not live entirely in the *paesani* community. Most immigrants, especially the men at work and the children at school, were forced to live in two different social worlds at the same time. The *paesani* dimension did not contain the totality of the immigrant's existence; hence, the cultural and social institutions of the Italians alone cannot adequately explain immigrant experience. For this reason, it is necessary to explore, in addition to the internal character of the immigrant community, the nature of the larger, external social order of the city around it, not only to understand the adjustment of individuals to a new society, but also the actual experience of immigration itself. In terms of immigration as a social process, the *paesani* principle represents a fundamental mechanism, but it, too, operates within a surrounding milieu, consisting of more general conditions in both the "sending" society and the "receiving" society.[41] These conditions are the parameters within which "migration chains" operate. The migration chains are interpersonal networks which can serve to facilitate migration only if they are embedded in favorable contexts in both societies. In the case of Italian migration to Philadelphia, in the preceding pages, we have attempted to describe the interaction between interpersonal relationships and more general societal conditions.

Finally, after the decision to come to Philadelphia, the immigrant had to answer another important question: whether or not to remain there permanently. But the choice to remain in the city as a permanent resident was not the simple outcome of a single, specific conscious decision for most immigrants. Rather than any "decisive moment," the immigrant who remained in Philadelphia had passed through a series of personal experiences which "trapped" him. Many men had intended to stay in Philadelphia only for a temporary period, or had no definite plans for the future. For many, in the beginning, living and working conditions were much more difficult than the immigrants had anticipated; for some men, it was worse than life in Italy. Most men never succeeded in gaining the great wealth which they had sought in America; and some men failed to save even the passage money to travel home again. Similarly, the outbreak of World War I stranded other men in the United States. In addition to the many immigrants who did return to Italy over the years, if it had been possible many more Italians would have done the same thing. But while before World War I poverty seemed to be the major factor in keeping many immigrants from returning to Italy, after the war prosperity became the important factor in keeping them in Philadelphia. Even if he came originally as a "bird of passage," merely being in the relatively favorable social and economic climate which Philadelphia offered exposed the immigrant to these "traps." Despite the early hardships and difficulties in the city, a formidable range of opportunities opened up before the immigrant, such as the chance to secure a steady, well-paying job in a respectable trade, and the chance to purchase his own home. In these years, Italy could hardly have offered comparable opportunities for wealth and respect to so many of her native sons. Furthermore, any prolonged stay in urban America probably raised the level of expectations and aspirations of many Italians in regard to material standards of living. Afterwards, many immigrants would have found life impossible in the remote and depressed villages of Italy from which they came. Consequently, the opportunities extended to the immigrant in Philadelphia became more valuable than whatever amenities and rewards a return to the old country offered. Subsequently, for many men, the death of their parents in Italy, the taking of wives in the United States, and the birth of "American" children became sufficient causes to eradicate any persisting ties with the old country.

Ironically, the *paesani* principle, which played such a significant part in bringing immigrants to Philadelphia, and in achieving their resettlement and adjustment, also became a major casualty of the same changes. The term *paesano* originally meant someone from the same *paese,* or village, but, as the Italian community in Philadelphia evolved, the localistic, insular ideas of the residents had less functional value, and began to expand into more nationalistic ones. The exigencies of survival—making a living, owning a home, finding a wife, and raising children—encouraged immigrants, more and more, to see themselves simply as "Italians." Moreover, neither their own children nor non-Italians could ever quite recognize the importance of the traditional *paesani* distinctions. Oddly, the immigrants in the United States, while being "Americanized," became "Italian" also, before their former countrymen in Italy did. Today, for example, the younger generation of Italian-Americans commonly regard *paesano* as meaning any other person of Italian descent.[42]

The original establishment of a large Italian settlement in Philadelphia resulted from the interaction of social conditions in Italy; interpersonal conditions among the immigrants themselves; and local circumstances in this particular city. The end product was an ethnic community which permitted the immigrant to retain his native culture and original self-identity, while it also provided for him the material opportunities and advantages of American society. In sum, he had the best of two worlds, and no one knew this fact better than the immigrant himself. Although he never forgot his homeland, the immigrant realized that he would be better off, in the long run, staying in Philadelphia, even when he found hardship and need in this country. As one Sicilian so succinctly summarized his own life and experiences: "It is better to be a poor man in South Philadelphia than a rich man anywhere else."

## NOTES

1. Howard R. Marraro, "Italo-Americans in Pennsylvania in the Eighteenth Century," *Pennsylvania History* (July, 1940) : 1–8 ; see also the criticism of this work by Giovanni Schiavo, *Four Centuries of Italian-American History* (New York: 1952), p. 11.

2. The date of the founding of the church is somewhat arbitrary because various events can be associated with the beginning of the parish. For instance, the previously Methodist chapel on the site was purchased by Bishop Neumann in 1852, although the cornerstone for the new church was not laid until 1854, and the dedication of the new church came in 1857.

It is not clear when services for Catholics were first held, but the first sacrament in the church records was a baptism in December, 1853, the date which I have chosen to consider as the origin. Also, the location of the church was in Moyamensing Township until February, 1854, when the area was consolidated with the city.

3. *Index to Records of Aliens' Declarations of Intentions and/or Oaths of Allegiance, 1789–1880 in United States Circuit Court, United States District Court, Supreme Court of Pennsylvania, Quarter Sessions Court, Court of Common Pleas, Philadelphia.* Compiled by Works Projects Administration, Project No. 29837. Sponsored by the Pennsylvania Historical Commission (Harrisburg, 1940), 11 vols. It is well to note that the Free Library of Philadelphia has bound these volumes under another title: *Maritime Records, Port of Philadelphia.*

4. Maldwyn Allen Jones, *American Immigration* (Chicago: 1960), pp. 103–104. The data for this section are largely obtained from the *Morton Allan Directory of European Passenger Steamship Arrivals: 1890–1930,* 1931.

5. U.S. Department of Commerce, *Statistical Abstract of the United States, 39th Number, 1916* (Washington, 1917), p. iii.

6. "Alien Influx of the Year," *Philadelphia Public Ledger,* July 2, 1914, p. 10.

7. Anna Maria Ratti, "Italian Migration Movements, 1876 to 1926," Chapter XV in *International Migrations,* vol. II, edited by Walter F. Willcox (New York: National Bureau of Economic Research, Inc., 1929), p. 458.

8. Sr. M. Agnes Gertrude, "Italian Immigration into Philadelphia," *Records of the American Catholic Historical Society of Philadelphia,* 58 (1947), pp. 137–138.

9. John Koren, "The Padrone System and Padrone Banks," *Bulletin of the U.S. Department of Labor* no. 9 (March, 1897), p. 123.

10. Sr. M. Agnes Gertrude, "Italian Immigration into Philadelphia," p. 138.

11. *La Colonia Italiana de Filadelfia al L'Esposizione di Milano,* Officine Tipografiche del Giornale *L'Opinione,* Philadelphia, 1906. Quoted in Hugo V. Maiale, "The Italian Vote in Philadelphia between 1928 and 1946." (Ph.D. dissertation, University of Pennsylvania, 1950), p. 7.

12. Joseph L. J. Kirlin, *Catholicity in Philadelphia* (Philadelphia: 1909), p. 504.

13. Robert F. Foerster, *The Italian Emigration of Our Times* (Cambridge, Mass.: 1924), pp. 328–329.

14. Sr. M. Agnes Gertrude, "Italian Immigration into Philadelphia," p. 138.

15. Emily Dinwiddie, *Housing Conditions in Philadelphia* (Philadelphia: The Octavia Hill Association, 1904), pp. 19–20.

16. Rudolph J. Vecoli, "Contadini in Chicago: A Critique of the Uprooted," *The Journal of American History* LI (December, 1964):413.

17. These conditions are well documented in the brief, but excellent, early social survey by Dinwiddie, *Housing Conditions in Philadelphia,* pp. 4, 15–23. Also see: Fullerton L. Waldo, *Good Housing That Pays* (Philadelphia: 1917), pp. 33–35, for the source of the material presented here.

18. Henry McCulley Muller, "Urban Home Ownership: A Socio-Economic Analysis with Emphasis on Philadelphia" (unpublished Ph.D. dissertation, University of Pennsylvania, 1947), p. 74. This paragraph is largely based on Muller's study.

19. *Ibid.,* p. 78.

20. *Ibid.,* p. 77.

21. F. J. Shoyer, "Importance of Building and Loan Associations in Making Philadelphia the City of Homes," *Real Estate Magazine,* August, 1925, p. 16.

22. Foerster, *The Italian Emigration of Our Times,* p. 375.

23. Muller, "Urban Home Ownership: A Socio-Economic Analysis with Emphasis on Philadelphia," p. 75.

24. See, for example, in addition to the work by Koren previously cited: Edward Everett Hale, "The Padrone Question," *Review of Reviews,* August, 1894, pp. 192–193; S. Merlino, "Italian Immigrants and Their Enslavement," *The Forum,* April, 1893, pp. 183–190; and Frank J. Sheridan, "Italian, Slavic and Hungarian Unskilled Immigrant Laborers in the U.S.," *U.S. Bureau of Labor Bulletin,* Number 72, September, 1907, pp. 403–486.

25. Luciano Iorizzo, "Italian Immigration and the Impact of the Padrone System" (unpublished Ph.D. dissertation, Syracuse University, 1966).

26. Charlotte Erickson, *American Industry and the European Immigrant, 1860–1885* (Cambridge, Mass.: 1957) and Humbert S. Nelli, "The Italian Padrone System in the United States," *Labor History* V (Spring, 1964).

27. Erickson, *American Industry and the European Immigrant, 1860–1885,* p. 68.

28. Nelli, "The Italian Padrone System in the United States," pp. 153–167.

29. Koren, "The Padrone System and Padrone Banks," p. 128.

30. Philadelphia: *Its Founding and Development, 1683 to 1908,* Official Historical Souvenir (Philadelphia: Joseph and Sefton, 1908), pp. 259–261, 372.

31. *Cicerone* means "guide."

32. Phillip M. Rose, *The Italians in America* (New York: George H. Doran Company, 1922), p. 82. The factionalism in the Italian community in Philadelphia is evident in newspaper accounts of the period. See, for example: "Italians at Meeting Repudiate Bossism," *Philadelphia Public Ledger,* October 5, 1917, p. 3.

33. This information was obtained in an interview by the author with Judge Bonnelly in 1969.

34. Koren, "The Padrone System and Padrone Banks," p. 123.

35. *Ibid.,* p. 123.

36. Nelli, "The Italian Padrone System in the United States," pp. 153–167.

37. John S. and Leatrice D. MacDonald, "Chain Migration, Ethnic Neighborhood Formation and Social Networks," *Milbank Memorial Fund Quarterly* XLII (January, 1964) : 82–91.

38. Vecoli, "Contadini in Chicago: A Critique of the Uprooted," p. 406.

39. Joseph Lopreato, *Italian-Americans* (New York: 1970), p. 104.

40. This conclusion is derived largely from the interpretation of immigrant life by Vecoli. See: Vecoli, "Contadini in Chicago: A Critique of the Uprooted," pp. 404–417.

41. In the present essay we have not provided any adequate discussion of conditions in the "sending" society which generated emigration. However, for an examination of such factors, and in particular how they were experienced and perceived by Italians who came to Philadelphia, see: Richard N. Juliani, "The Social Organization of Immigration: The Italians in Philadelphia" (unpublished Ph.D. dissertation, University of Pennsylvania, 1971), especially Chapter IV, "Italian Conditions before Emigration."

42. This change is primarily psychological; it represents a new self-

identification. In sociological terms, it also permits corresponding behavioral changes, but mainly in terms of individual behavior. For instance, Italians of different regional backgrounds found it possible to intermarry, to work together, and to share the same neighborhoods. But Italians in America still find it difficult to achieve the concerted, organized effort of a political movement. A priest recently revealed the persistence of this problem when he told the author that the "home-mass" of the new Roman Catholic liturgy was a complete failure in his Italian parish. None of the families can accept the idea of having other families, with whom they are not close friends, come into their homes for these services. We might suspect that the "amoral familism" of peasant life persists as the "peer-group society" of urban, working-class Italians. See: Edward Banfield, *The Moral Basis of a Backward Society* (New York: The Free Press, 1958); and Herbert J. Gans, *The Urban Villagers* (New York: The Free Press, 1962).

# 10

# The Croatian Immigrants in Pittsburgh

## GEORGE J. PRPIĆ

*George J. Prpić is Professor of History at John Carroll University, Cleveland, Ohio. He received his Ph.D. degree from Georgetown University and he is the author of* The Croatian Immigrants in America.

Certain reevaluations should be done in discussing the Croatian immigrants in the United States. First of all, contrary to the opinion of numerous American historians of immigration, the Croatians are *not* a typical "New Immigration" ethnic group. Thousands of them were settled in our West, South and in the coastal towns of the East long before the 1880s.[1] The Croatians from the Adriatic regions founded their "New Dalmatias" in California as well as in the Mississippi Delta by the 1850s.

When Ivan Ratkaj, S.J., the first Croatian missionary in this hemisphere, arrived in Mexico in 1680 there were already numerous Croatian settlers from Dalmatia and the Republic of Dubrovnik in Latin America. His countryman Ferdinand Konšćak, S.J., died in San Ignacio, Lower California in 1759 after a lengthy career as missionary, pioneer and explorer who paved the way for the conquest of northern parts of California. The Croatian priest Joseph Kundek died in Jasper, Indiana in 1857. He was a missionary, colonizer, founder of several towns, civic leader, and writer.

It is interesting to note that Father Kundek visited Pittsburgh, Allegheny County and parts of Pennsylvania in the spring of 1841. He reported his visit in a letter written in Jasper, Dubois County, Indiana, dated May 24, 1841, and addressed to his superior, the Prince Archbishop of Vienna, Austria. He covered the entire distance of some 500 miles between Jasper and Pittsburgh—on horseback! During his trip and visit he administered to the spiritual needs of Irish and German Catholics. He paid another visit to Pittsburgh three years later.[2] Joseph Kundek was probably the first Croatian to come to Pittsburgh and spend some time there.

## WHO ARE THE CROATIANS

When Kundek visited Pennsylvania of course nobody knew about the Croatians. Unfortunately, even many years afterwards there is still too much confusion and lack of knowledge about the ethnic identity of this nationality.

The Croatians belong to the South Slav group of nations along with the Slovenians, Serbians, Montenegrins, Macedonians, and Bulgarians. The South Slavs are only a part of the large Slavic family which is an Indo-European linguistic group. The Slavs are a mixture of peoples and races. They all speak languages that have developed from the Old Slavic language. Today different Slavic peoples use their distinct languages resembling each other to a smaller or larger degree.

The South Slav peoples have developed during the last thirteen centuries under different influences and circumstances. Each of these peoples developed their own distinct literature, using their own literary language. Thus, for instance, the Croatians have used their own Croatian language during the past five centuries of printed literature. The Croatian scholars and writers in the homeland insist that their language is a distinct language which should be properly called Croatian.

As in case of other Slavs, the national consciousness of the

Croatians was weak in some parts of their country before the 1890s. This is understandable since Croatia—after periods of complete independence—was partitioned and ruled until 1918 by Germans, Hungarians, Venetians and Turks.[3] Thus many Croatian immigrants came under their local names: Slavonians, Istrians, Dalmatians, Bosnians, Herzegovinians and others. Before the 1920s the confused U. S. Immigration authorities listed them mostly as Austrians, Hungarians, and even Italians. To make these statistics even more confusing, the immigration authorities lumped together the distinct nationalities like Croatians and Slovenians, and put together such provincial groups as one category: Dalmatians, Bosnians, and Herzegovinians.[4] Since the U. S. Immigration and Naturalization service (under the Justice Department) lists the immigrants in its *Annual Report* not by nationality but rather by the country of birth, we will never be able to determine the exact number of Croatian immigrants in this country.

Before 1918 the Croatians were coming to Pennsylvania and other parts of America from the following Hapsburg provinces: the Triune Kingdom of Croatia-Slavonia-Dalmatia (autonomous Croatia); Istria, and Bosnia-Herzegovina. Some came from the diaspora in southern and western Hungary, and even from Italy and the Kossovo region in the Balkans. Since 1920 a great majority of the Croatians have come from Yugoslavia, which between 1918 and 1929 was officially called the Kingdom of Serbs, Croats and Slovenes; after 1929 Yugoslavia, and now is known as the Socialist Federal Republic of Yugoslavia. From the latter they came in recent years either directly or indirectly through Germany, Italy, and even Argentina and other countries of first residence in exile.

After the last war—according to realistic estimates—some 50,000 of them have arrived. While Cleveland, Ohio, has the largest concentration of the post-1945 newcomers, a considerable number of them have settled in and around Pittsburgh.[5]

Numerous American historians and sociologists refer to the Croatians as a "race." The Croatians—like other Europeans—usually call themselves a people, a nationality, or a nation when applied to them in Yugoslavia or abroad. They often use the term "Iseljena Hrvatska"—"Croatia in Exile" for more than two million of their people now living in foreign countries.

The migration from Croatian lands is a more than five centuries lasting process, thus an old phenomenon of their history. The first mass exodus of the Croatians was caused by Turkish invasions, by foreign oppression, and by a variety of political, economic, social, and even religious reasons. It was partly induced by the migration of their Slovenian neighbors between 1860s and 1890s. However, the underlying direct or indirect cause of all their migrations was the lack of national sovereignty. The largest number of political refugees came to this country after 1945.

The maritime character of the Croatian nation was another significant factor contributing especially to their early emigration to different continents. Their immigration to Pennsylvania and the Midwest has been going on for more than a hundred years.

These migrations to America progressed in waves, according to certain periods: early immigration before 1815 and 1860s; another wave between 1860s and 1890s. Then came the periods: the 1890s to 1914, the 1920s and 1930s; followed by the post-war wave which also could be divided in several sections according to the immigration legislation in the United States: war refugees and political victims; displaced persons; immigrants after 1952, 1956; refugees; people with Yugoslav passports; relatives of the citizens and residents of the United States; and even individuals on parole or illegal immigrants who legalized their status later.[6]

What kind of people were these immigrants from Croatia who have made their home in and around Pittsburgh? The answer to such a question is important for a better understanding of the history and contribution of this nationality.

The anthropologists agree that the Croatians are among the tallest people in Europe, averaging five feet, nine inches. The sociologist John R. Commons—who otherwise as a writer showed his racist tendencies and denounced the "New Immigrants"—regarded the Croatians from southern Dalmatia and Herzegovina as "the finest specimens of physical manhood coming to our shores." He also described them as "a vigorous people." Other writers praised the Dalmatians as giants among the people, described them as veritable "Slavic Apollos," dark-skinned, graceful in their movements, and as "the only Slavs who are thorough seamen." They and their Croatian brethren from other provinces were depicted as "sturdy, vigorous people," skilled fishermen, bold sailors, capable traders, a splendid type, markedly fine in their carriage.[7]

Similar compliments were expressed by several other writers. One of them calls the Croatians "a very estimable people," who work hard, and "esteem liberty and have much self-respect." They have an inborn sense of beauty and wear costumes that are "among the most exquisite in Europe." They love music and song.[8]

Louis Adamic, who knew well the Croatians in Allegheny County, remarks in his writings that the Croatians are patient, but their patience is more defensive than real. They are "subdued, ponderous, truly peasant," particularly those from inland Croatia. They are essentially people of the soil, in their way of life slower, more easygoing than their compatriots from Dalmatia; they were "grubbers with toil-eager hands, inured through centuries to sparse living and endless hardship."[9]

Miss E. E. Ledbetter describes the Croatians as people "of excellent physique," who have "broad forehead, the well-placed eyes, and the general cast of countenance which we associate with our most intelligent types. They also have an alert mind and a 'keen intelligence'; it is impossible to watch them without respect even though one does not understand their language."[10]

To an American physician employed by the Immigration Service, many Croatians coming to Pennsylvania looked "as if they were dying of consumption, but they are tougher than wire."[11] Contemporary observers also describe them as men of their word, generous lenders of money, aesthetically inclined in spite of the fact that roughly thirty-five percent of them were illiterate. The illiteracy of so many Slavic immigrants of that time was a product of foreign rule and its policies. With extensive education, it was feared, the suppressed Slavs might become more rebellious. A great number of these peasants learned to write and read in this country, since they were intentionally denied schools in their homelands.

A great number of these immigrants came here with the intention to stay only a few years, earn some money and return. In numerous cases what was first considered a "temporary exile" turned to permanent life in the new homeland.

Oscar Handlin calls these East European immigrants the "uprooted." They were uprooted from their native soil, tradition, homeland, relatives and friends. They traveled to a far, foreign, and quite different country. They spoke no English. They were scared and bewildered, puzzled and shocked by the transatlantic voyage, the treatment at Ellis Island, the reception at the destination of their long trip. They were happy if they could join here their relatives, friends or natives of the same village or town. From the sunny fields of their villages these tillers of the soil went straight into dark pits of Pennsylvania mines and red-hot infernos of the steel mills. This change was too striking and many found it difficult to adjust themselves to this new life. The adjustment process was for all of them an agony, a great deal of suffering and misery. But still, in spite of all hardships, America was to them a "Promised Land." "Pennsylvania" was to become in the course of time a familiar word in their Old Country.

## PITTSBURGH AND THE EARLY IMMIGRANTS

During the 1850s and 1860s thousands of Croatian immigrants, predominantly from the Adriatic regions, established themselves in numerous places of the West, South and eastern coast of the United States.

In 1867, Max Schamberg, a German philanthropist and a friend of Croatian people, opened a "Croatian Bank" in Pittsburgh, then still a small town. It assisted the Croatian immigrants who were slowly coming to the Allegheny County. This group was laying down the foundation for what was to be the largest Croatian immigrant colony in this country. In 1901 this bank, employing about twenty people, was bought by the First National Bank of Pittsburgh.[12]

Even though Pittsburgh became a considerable industrial center already during the Civil War, it was to become a huge industrial area in subsequent decades. In 1872 Westinghouse opened a new plant in East Pittsburgh. In the year of economic panic, 1873, the Edgar Thompson Works were founded. The well-known Homestead Works started in 1880. In 1882 Carnegie and Frick founded a big enterprise, which in 1901 became the famous United States Steel Corporation. All along the rivers new industrial centers were arising one after another. They needed thousands of workers. A large labor force could be supplied only by thousands, even tens of thousands, of immigrants coming now from East and Southeast Europe and also from Italy. The East European arrivals were mostly from Austria-Hungary and Russia; partly also from independent Balkan states.[13]

A great number of Austro-Hungarian immigrants were Poles, Slovaks, Ukrainians and Ruthenians, Croatians, Slovenians, and Serbs. As the so-called "New Immigration" period started in 1882, the number of immigrants was increasing with each year. Most of the Croatians came between the late 1890s and 1914. They were so numerous that they were outnumbered only by Poles and Slovaks among the Slavs. Pittsburgh and Allegheny county contained the largest concentration of the Croatian people in America.

In the beginning of this century the industrial giant known as Pittsburgh enjoyed national and even international prominence. During the "Slavic invasion" the skilled workers in Pittsburgh's industry were generally the Anglo-Saxons, Germans and Irish. As an American writer remarked "when Slavs came to the mills in the 1890s and 1900s they replaced the Irish and the Germans," who either stayed on better paid jobs in the steel industry or became policemen, politicians and city hall employees.[14]

Pittsburgh became, in the course of years, a typical steel mill town with a large number of Slavic people. In and outside the city the homes of the workers were clustered about mills along the rivers. They were clinging to the bluffs of the South Side, scattered over Greater Pittsburgh, from Woods Run to the East End. The U. S. Immigration Commission, established in 1907, in its volumes of now famous *Reports*—that paved the way for the immigration restriction—paid a great deal of attention to Pittsburgh, its industries and its workers. A large amount of valuable information on conditions of workers, their homes, the boarding houses, literacy and illiteracy, social conditions, and related problems was extensively discussed in the Immigration *Reports*. Even though these documents were biased, filled with distorted facts, and designed to prove the "inferiority" of the new immigrants, they still present an excellent source on the history of Pittsburgh and Pittsburghers particularly before World War I.

The period of 1900–1920 was the most significant in the life of a great number of immigrants. It was the heyday of their life and activity; it was in a way a "Golden Age" of their political action in regard to their homelands. In the beginning of 1909, "roughly speaking, one-quarter of the population of Pittsburgh was foreign-born." And as the contemporary observer remarked: "the foreigner is nowhere more at home than here, and nowhere has he been more actively welcomed by employers." Here "the conflict of customs and habits, varying standards of living, prejudices, antipathies, all due to the confluence of representatives of different races of men, may be witnessed. . . ."[15]

Up the Monongahela valley were the milltowns: Homestead of Pinkerton "fame," Braddock with its record-breaking mills and furnaces. Here was Duquesne where the unit of weight was a hundred tons, and here was McKeesport, home of the "biggest tube works on earth."[16]

Today in this age of advanced technology, automation and electronic devices, it is difficult to imagine under what conditions the former peasants of East Europe were working in Pittsburgh's mills decades ago. An open-hearth helper tapped fifty tons of molten steel from his furnace. Here were the vesselmen and the steel pourers, rollers and hookers. Five- and ten-ton steel ingots plunged madly back and forth between the rolls. The men worked here "in hoop mills and guide mills, where the heat is intense and the work laborious." Here were the ladles of molten steel, piles of red hot bars, straightening presses at the rail mills.[17]

A visitor in a steel mill saw "only faces reddened by the glare of fire and hot steel, muscles standing out in knots and bands on arms, clothing frayed with usage and begrimed by machinery."[18] These are the gloomy pictures, realistic images of the immigrants' past, frequently ignored by our historians when they describe the immigrant's contribution to the American industry.

The bosses knew the Slavs chiefly "as sturdy, patient and submissive workmen." Their fellow American workmen hated and despised them largely "because of this patience and submissiveness at the outset to work at any wages and under any conditions."[19] Such an attitude reflects the prejudice and ignorance on the part of the American workers. They themselves—or their father also worked as newcomers for any price and under any conditions. The Slav by his nature is not submissive. He is patient even then when he resents injustice. If some Slavs were willing to work "at any wages" it was because they had no other choice, did not want to starve, and many of them considered their life in America as just a temporary visit. They were willing to endure anything, just to earn enough money and either return to Europe, or if they decided to stay, to bring over with their earnings another member of their family.

The same writer who mentioned the "submissiveness" of Slavs describes also in praising words other traits of these people: their readiness to help their countrymen. Their "generosity shows itself amid the most adverse circumstances." As in those days most of the workers were idle a few months of the year, the landlords kept their boarders even when they were jobless. They were all united by mutual suffering and difficulties. To the oldtimers they were all "greenhorns." They lived in "hunky towns" paying high rents for small miserable apartments or houses. They were discriminated against by industrial companies, the landlords, the merchants, schools and even non-Slavic parishes. In addition, the reporter for the *Charities and the Commons* observed in Pittsburgh in Slavic neighborhoods police brutality at its worst.[20]

EARLY CROATIANS AND THE FOUNDING OF THE
FRATERNAL MOVEMENT

How and why the first Croatians came to Pittsburgh is difficult
to prove. Perhaps they heard from other Slavs about the opportunities; perhaps they read about them in some newspaper. There
were not too many of them before the end of the 1880s. It is certain
that in 1882 there were in Old Allegheny (present North Side)
the following Croatian pioneers: Juraj Grgurić, Juraj Les, Janko
Les, Blaž Sečenj and Josip Buneta. They were natives of Jaska, a
town south of Zagreb. Later on so many people from Jaska would
concentrate on East Ohio Street that it became known among the
Croatians as Jaska Street.[21]

Josip Šubašić, who was born in Vukova Gorica near Karlovac
arrived in Millvale in 1884. Fluent in German, he became a machinist for the City Water Works, later moved to Allegheny City and
bought a house. He is most likely the first Croatian immigrant to
acquire a home in Pittsburgh. Soon afterwards more newcomers
arrived. Among them were: Franjo Žibrat, Trivun Lazić, Kruno-
slav Maljević, Josip Novaković and Josip Štibuhar.[22]

A very prominent immigrant from Croatia lived for a while in
East Pittsburgh, from early 1888 until the end of 1889. This was
Nikola Tesla, the great inventor, a real electrical genius. His many
inventions ushered in the modern industrial age in America. His
total contribution to the American technology and civilization is
tremendous. In Pittsburgh he worked for George Westinghouse
from who he received one million dollars for his inventions. To save
Westinghouse from financial ruin Tesla generously sacrificed over
ten million dollars in royalties that he was supposed to receive from
Westinghouse according to a written agreement.[23]

Tesla was an Orthodox immigrant from Croatia and he was one
of the first educated people to come from Croatia. However, most
of his countrymen flocking to Pittsburgh had little or no education.
A great majority of them were peasants, farmers who were ill-
prepared for hazardous jobs in factories and mines of Pennsylvania.
They knew no English and experienced innumerable problems in

getting adjusted to the American life. While the first immigrants were mostly single or married men, in the course of time wives, children, or fiancees from the old country came in great numbers. Most of them came on prepaid tickets sold through the steamship agencies. By 1893 some 9,000 Croatians lived in Pittsburgh and vicinity.

Unlike other nationalities they had no fraternal or beneficial organizations to provide for injured or sick members and to pay the funeral expenses. At this time the Croatians in California and Louisiana already had their beneficial organizations to provide for cases of emergency. A. G. Škrivanić founded and published since 1891 the first Croatian paper in eastern parts of the United States named *Napredak* (The Progress) in Hoboken, New Jersey. Škrivanić urged his fellow Croatians to organize. Another publication, *Chicago,* printed in Chicago, Illinois by Nikola Polić since 1892, also appealed to the Croatians to found an organization suited to their needs. Zdravko Valentin Mužina, an educated young man who worked for Polić, came to Pittsburgh in December of 1893. Along with Petar Pavlinac and Franjo Šepić, prominent Croatians, he worked towards organizing his countrymen in Pennsylvania. On January 4, 1894 the first issue of the first Croatian paper in Pennsylvania was printed. Its name was *Danica* (the *Morning Star*); its editor was Z. V. Mužina. In this issue he appealed to his countrymen to organize. Thus on January 13, 1894 a Croatian Workingmen's Beneficial Association "Starčević" was founded in Old Allegheny. The name honored the well-known Croatian politician and father of modern Croatian nationalism, Dr. Ante Starčević.[24]

Mužina became the first president of this society. On September 2, 1894 fourteen delegates of the already existing Croatian societies met in the Slovak Majak Hall, 116 South Canal Street, Allegheny City and established a national organization, the Croatian Union of the United States ("Hrvatska Zajednica u Sjedinjenim Državama"). It had in the beginning only 600 members; its assets were $42.00. Its purpose was "to assist members during sickness and assist their families after death." *Danica* was its organ. Some twenty-five new lodges were subsequently founded, most of them in Pittsburgh and vicinity. This was the beginning of a real fraternal movement among the American Croatians. Out of the Croatian Union grew later the Croatian Fraternal Union, the largest Croatian organization in America. Pittsburgh became the center of Croatian fraternalism.[25]

## THE CHURCHES

Many lodges of the fraternal organizations in America were named after saints; thus for instance in Pittsburgh were St. Vitus, St. Cyril and St. Methodius, St. Elias, St. Nicholas and St. John the Baptist before the turn of the century. The pioneers of fraternal organizations were mostly religious and even pious people. But there were no priests of their nationality to take care of the spiritual needs of thousands of these workers and their families. It seems paradoxical that the country that had sent out missionaries to several continents as early as 1600s did not send any to its own people in America. The same men who organized the first fraternal societies were instrumental in bringing the first priest from Croatia to Pittsburgh. Through the intervention of Bishop Josip Juraj Strossmayer, the well known Croatian patriot and promoter of culture and arts, the first priest arrived at Pittsburgh on August 7, 1894. He was Rev. Dobroslav Božić of Sutjeska, Bosnia. On Sunday, August 12, 1894, he said his first Mass for the Croatians in the crypt of St. Paul Cathedral. Under the leadership of Z. V. Mužina the first Croatian church in these parts of the country, St. Nicholas was organized and then opened on January 27, 1895. It was dedicated by the Bishop, and the historic event was attended by several thousand Croatians and their guests. This was a great day for the Croatians. It was on East Ohio Street, on the North Side ("Jaska Street").[26]

In August of 1898 Father Božić left for Steelton, Pa. In December 1898, Rev. Franjo Glojnarić, who came from Croatia, took over the St. Nicholas parish. Because of the influx of Croatians a new parish and church were established at nearby Bennet (now Millvale) and also named St. Nicholas. It was dedicated on January 5, 1900.[27]

These and other churches in Pennsylvania and in various parts of this country were founded considerably late and when there were here already very many Croatian immigrants. Too few priests came from the old country and those that came had to undergo all sorts of internal frictions and tensions with the parishioners.

Father Božić was a very able and versatile man. During his stay in Pittsburgh he published two newspapers. One was *Novi Svijet* (*New World*) whose first issue appeared on December 20, 1897. The other was named *Puco* (*The Shooter*), the first issue of which appeared on March 15, 1898. As in case of most early Croatian publications, these two were short-lived.[28]

Meanwhile the Croatians were flocking to various nearby communities. Their settlements were spreading all over Pennsylvania. They were now better organized and as a community were financially stronger. The two St. Nicholas parishes at North Side and Millvale started to build new churches, rectories and other necessary buildings. Rev. Bosiljko Bekavac, a Croatian from Bosnia joined the St. Nicholas (North Side) parish in time for the dedication of the new church on September 7, 1901. After some troubles with the parishioners Father Bekavac was replaced by Rev. Dr. Ljudevit Lauš. The conflict within the Millville parish (St. Nicholas) went so far that on August 12, 1906 a group of Croatians, assembled under Rev. Ilija Gusić in Mato Šegina Hall, established a short-lived Croatian Catholic Independent Church. Rev. Gusić later on made peace with church authorities and after a while returned to Croatia.[29]

In Rankin, close to Pittsburgh, a new Croatian colony arose. At the invitation of the people the first priest arrived here on August 2, 1902. He was Rev. Dr. Mato Matina, a very learned man, excellent writer and scholar who was persecuted by the Hungarian authorities in Croatia. The Croatian Saint Mary church in Rankin was dedicated on August 14, 1904 and consecrated by the Right Reverend Ricardo Phelan, Bishop of Pittsburgh. Dr. Matina left the parish already the next year for Chicago where he died on May 22, 1905.[30]

The first Croatians were settling down at McKeesport as early as 1886. A Croatian society "Saint George" was founded in 1894.

It was not before March 11, 1907 that the first mass was said in the new Croatian Sacred Heart Church in McKeesport for the parishioners from this and adjacent communities. Numerous troubles that characterized the early existence of all Croatian parishes, also developed here. Rev. Ferdinand Duić arrived here in May of 1907.[31]

These immigrants lived here under peculiar circumstances. Everything was quite different from the old homeland. There was freedom and opportunity for those who endured the hardships. As for the American Church, it was controlled by the Irish and Germans. These Slavic newcomers were not welcomed by the Irish and German parishes (although there were exceptions). Because of the lack of English and prejudice many Croatians either joined some Slavic parishes or completely stopped attending the Sunday masses if they didn't have their own parish. When the first priests were arriving in Pennsylvania, numerous Croatians already did not care for their Church, or were nonbelievers. A considerable number would later become radical members of the labor unions, join the Socialists or other leftists. The Church in Croatia claimed that it could not send more priests for the lack of them. When some of them came they found here *different* former peasants from their native land. They were not willing any more to respect the traditional authority of the priest. Too few priests came and too late. In proportion to their numbers, the Croatians erected considerably few parishes in this country, some 35-odd. Compared to the number of Slovenian or Slovak parishes, it should have been at least 120 parishes.

As Pittsburgh was not too far from New York, a great number of the newly arrived immigrants from Croatia took the train to Pittsburgh to join their numerous countrymen. Or they stopped at Steelton which was even closer to New York, or went to other places. Many individuals from other states—attracted by the news of plentiful work—also found their way to this rising and thriving community of their countrymen. Few could afford to buy a railway ticket all the way to the West and the Pacific where thousands of their brethren were doing extremely well.

# THE DEVELOPMENT OF A LARGE AND THRIVING COLONY

The Croatian colony in Allegheny County was in some ways a transplanted homeland. Social, religious, cultural, political and other activities were increasing. Additional publications appeared. More people learned to read and write. They became more interested in the politics of America and the old country. They resented being listed by American authorities as Austrians and Hungarians. Croatian leaders organized several meetings with Pittsburgh's journalists to explain to them who the Croatians were and what they as a nation wanted. On January 28, 1895, Dr. Theodore Teodorović, a visitor from Zagreb lectured at a reception for journalists on Croatian history and goals for the future. For that same year, Zdravo V. Mužina published an almanac, called *Hrvatsko-Amerikanska Danica,* probably the first Croatian almanac (*kalendar*) in this country.[32]

Josip Marohnić, a printer born in Hreljin, came to America in 1894 and soon joined the Croatians in Pittsburgh. He established the first Croatian book store where he sold thousands of books from Zagreb and soon some of his own production; he established a successful printing business. He issued various pamphlets, booklets of general information, spellers, dictionaries, collections of poems, and on January 1, 1899, the first issue of a humorous monthly, *Brico* (*The Barber*). Marohnić became a distinguished citizen of Pittsburgh, a political and cultural activist, and a man whose name will always be remembered in the history of the American Croatians.[33]

At the time of its second convention in 1895 the Croatian Union (popularly known as Zajednica) had some 1,000 members. After its third convention in Cleveland (September, 1896) it convened again on June 21, 1897, in McKeesport. Seventy delegates (representing almost 8,000 members) attended this fourth convention and changed the name of the organization to Narodna Hrvatska Zajednica (National Croatian Society). *Danica* by now ceased its publication. The organ of the Zajednica was Škrivanić's *Napredak*. He moved to Pittsburgh and printed his paper until 1904 when the new organ, the *Zajednicar,* was inaugurated. It is still in existence, now a twelve-page weekly in both English and Croatian, the largest Croatian paper in this country. A great deal of Croatian history in this country and in Pennsylvania has been preserved over the many years in the columns of this paper.[34]

In 1901 there were some 13,000 Croatians in Pittsburgh and close to 40,000 in the State of Pennsylvania. By 1902 the N.C.S. had some eighty-five lodges in this state alone and spreading all over the country. Marohnić counted in his Census some 136 Croatian settlements and groups in Pennsylvania.[35] The number of Croatians kept rising until 1914.

The Steel Mill on 28th Street employed 1500 Croatians; 600 of them worked for the South Side Iron and Steel Co.; Clinton Iron Works employed some 500; Carnegie, on 28th Street, about a thousand and a small mill, some 400; Black Diamond had a thousand Croatian workers; Iron City Steel Co., some 200; Carbon Steel Co., 600; McConway and Co. Steel Works about 600; Carnegie Bridge Works, 300. They also worked for Ritter and Conley Iron and Steel Co., Thomas Carlin Sons, H. J. Heinz and Co., and others.[36]

It was difficult, dangerous and exhausting work. A worker who was pulling ingots out of the open hearth furnace had to wear heavy gloves, asbestos and steel boots, and was wrapped in wet rags.[37] In Pennsylvania mines the work was even more dangerous and the toll very high. In 1907, the historic year of the highest peak of U. S. immigration, more than 3,000 miners were killed on their jobs, a significant part of them in Pennsylvania. The death rate of the American miners was two and a half times as high as the British rate.[38]

During the 1900s the foremen and highly skilled workers in steel were making around $8.00 a day. Crane drivers earned $4.00 daily. However, the mass of immigrant laborers—organized in groups each speaking one language—were paid only around $2.00 a day. In Pittsburgh almost a quarter of all such laborers earned between $2.50 to $5.00 per day, and only five percent above $5.00. A great number of them worked only during nine months of a year, some only six. A yearly earning of $500.00 was considered as good. When they were employed, they worked twelve hours a day, seven days a week, including the Labor Day and Fourth of July. Among some 70,000 steel workers in Allegheny County, there were approximately 200 fatal accidents a year and countless accidents less serious. It was not before the 1930s that the steel industry was successfully unionized.[39]

These and other circumstances compelled the immigrants to get as much protection as possible from their fraternal organizations. The Croatian Zajednica—as they always called their main fraternal organization—kept growing over the years. Another convention was held in Allegheny City, September 29 to October 7, 1902, in the German Masonic Hall. Among other decisions, it established a fund for promotion of Croatian schools in America. It also sent financial aid to political victims in Croatia. Internal struggle developed within Zajednica. The leader of the opposition was the well known Croatian businessman, owner of the steamship agencies, newspapers and banks, Franjo (Frank) Zotti. The leaders of the Zajednica were now Pavlinac, Škrivanić, and Marohnić. The opposition published for a while the paper *Hrvat* (The Croatian). G. A. Škrivanić started to publish in 1903 a daily, *Hrvatska* (Croatia). A few issues of *Hrvat u Americi* (The Croatian in America) appeared in Rankin. In McKeesport another paper *Velika Hrvatska* (Great Croatia) appeared for a short while in 1902.[40]

In 1906 Franjo Zotti did gain control of the Zajednica at the convention in New York (September 24 to October 6). When the depression of 1907 hit the country, Zotti's bank and several other Croatian banks declared bankruptcy. Thousands of Croatian workers lost their savings, and Zotti was promptly overthrown in 1908 from the leadership of the Zajednica.[41]

Numerous new organizations were founded in and around Pittsburgh. One of them was the short-lived Croatian Catholic Union whose organ was *Hrvat*. The Croatian Fraternal and Beneficial Association "Sloga" was established in May, 1905. Singing societies "Javor," "Sloga" and "Berislavić" were established. A variety of activities undertaken jointly with other Croatian colonies in America were of cultural and political nature. The leadership of the

Zajednica, especially under Marohnić's presidency, sided with the patriots in Croatia, and aided them with thousands of dollars. The American-Croatian press—with some exceptions—was anti-Hapsburg and openly sided with Serbia during the Balkan Wars of 1912–1913. In 1910 *Zajedničar,* the organ of the N.C.S., became a weekly newspaper. Its editor was a priest, Nikola Gršković, a very good writer, journalist, and politician. He espoused the cause of the South Slav unity after the destruction of Austria–Hungary.

During the Eleventh Convention of the Zajednica in Kansas City (Sept. 9–24) a political movement, Croatian Alliance (Hrvatski Savez), was founded. Its president became Rev. Nikola Gršković. Several of its leaders were from the leadership of the Zajednica.[42] Among the politicians in Croatia who received financial aid from the N.C.S. was Stjepan Radić, the imprisoned leader of the rising Croatian Peasant Party. Radić would become one of the leading politicians in Yugoslavia, the leader of the Croatian people. His name was frequently mentioned in the American-Croatian papers. Along with his brother Ante, Stjepan Radić wrote a great deal about the Croatian immigrants, and was in correspondence with them. His book *Hrvatski Politički Katekizam* (Croatian Political Catechism) was published by Hrvatski Savez in Cleveland. The center of the activities of this organization was in Pittsburgh. In fact Pittsburgh became the center of the Croatian immigrant political activity in America and as such influenced even the events in the homeland.

An athletic and patriotic organization called Sokol (Falcon) which was originally founded in Croatia upon a Czech model and was similar to the German *Turnvereine* made its way to the American Croatian colonies. It started in Chicago in 1908 and soon had numerous branches; one of them was founded in Pittsburgh in July of 1912.[43]

In the late fall of 1912, a twenty-three-year-old Pittsburgh Croatian, a member of the Croatian Alliance, Stjepan Dojčić, came to Zagreb. On the birthday of Francis Joseph, August 18, 1913, in front of the cathedral in Zagreb, Dojčić tried to shoot the royal commissary Baron Ivan von Skerlecz, who escaped injury but another official was killed. For many weeks afterwards, this revolutionary act of a young returned immigrant made headlines in Austro-Hungarian, European and American-Croatian presses. During his trial in September, Dojčić declared: "Five thousand Croatians in America are ready to follow my example." He was sentenced to ten years in prison. Such acts of violence were firmly denounced by Stjepan Radić who considered them as very harmful to the Croatian cause in the Habsburg Empire. In a pamphlet directed to the thousands of his compatriots in America, Radić appealed to them to refrain from such activities.[44]

While N. Gršković and his collaborators made publicity for the case of Dojčić and collected funds for his defense, numerous Croatians were opposed to such activities. Several priests, including Dr. M. Kajić of Johnstown and Msgr. M. D. Krmpotić of Kansas City, opposed the policies of the Alliance. Instead of a union with Serbia in a future South Slav state (Yugoslavia), they expressed their view that Croatia and Slovenia should become autonomous states under the Hapsburg dynasty or become completely independent.


## WORLD WAR I

In Pittsburgh, according to Professor Gaži, who did extensive research on the Croatian in Allegheny County before 1914, "the Croatian Alliance dominated the whole colony."[45] Bitter feuds developed between the sympathizers of the "Yugoslav Idea" and those who advocated a separate and free Croatia. On April 26, 1914, at a Pittsburgh meeting the Alliance called on all Croatians to join the struggle against the Hapsburg Monarchy. As Gaži remarks:

The leaders of both groups had their minds concentrated on Europe, living physically only in America. The daily life and destiny of their brothers around them did not in the least concern them. The Croats of Allegheny County faced a new economic crisis and a series of strikes at the beginning of 1914. The workers of Westinghouse Co. in East Pittsburgh ceased work and other strikes followed.[46]

The beginning of World War I found the Croatians, as well as the rest of the South Slavs in America, split by political divisions and bitter feuds. Their press, too, was divided. Several papers, notably Zotti's popular *Narodni List* (*National Gazette*), a widely read daily, were pro-Hapsburg and against establishment of a Yugoslavia. Numerous colonies with a great number of people, especially the Croatians from the Adriatic regions, remained loyal to Austria; all of them, however, adamantly opposed the oppressive Hungarian policies in Croatia.[47] The coming of the great war meant also the end of an era in the history of the U. S. Immigration. Because of the beginning of hostilities in Europe, the last full year of peacetime mass immigration to America was the year of 1913. Never again would numerous thousands of Slavs and East Europeans come to Pittsburgh. The American Croatians found themselves at a historic crossroad. With the passing of the great war they were forced to make their final decision: to stay in America and to get more involved in the American life.

In March of 1915, a Yugoslav National Council was organized at a large gathering of the South Slavs in Chicago; its president was Rev. Niko Gršković. This Council supported the South Slav Council in London, headed by Dr. Ante Trumbić, a Croatian politician in exile. These councils, supported by the South Slav emigrants in South and North America worked for establishment of a South Slav state. While most of them envisaged this union of equal partners as a monarchy under the Serbian Karageorgevich dynasty, some elements in America—including Socialists—advocated a republican form for future Yugoslavia. Disunity on the final goals was evident also at the huge assembly of some 2,000 South Slav delegates in Pittsburgh in mid-July, 1915. They sent a telegram to President Wilson, expressing their loyalty to the United States and condemning the Austro-Hungarian rule in their mother country.[48]

Partly to impress the Americans and arouse public opinion, another great congress of the South Slavs convened in Pittsburgh on November 29 and 30, 1916. Some six hundred and twenty delegates claimed to represent 500,000 South Slavs in the United States and Canada. The National Croatian Society, with headquarters in Pittsburgh, was also represented. It had now some five hundred lodges and around 40,000 members. The Croatian League claimed some hundred and ten branches and around 10,000 members. The chairman of the Congress was Niko Gršković. The present delegates recognized the South Slav Committee in London as the spokesman for all the South Slavs from Austria-Hungary. They also sent a telegram to President Wilson, hailing him as "the defender of the rights of small nations."[49]

The opponents of the South Slav movement in America, a group of Slovenian and Croatian priests, also met in Pittsburgh on November 19, 1916, composed a Memorandum for President Wilson, in which they declared that the South Slav question should be solved by establishing a free Croatian-Slovenian state under Hapsburg sovereignty. They handed in this memorandum to the President in Washington a few days later.[50] The same group also published a pamphlet in English entitled "Our Declaration" (and a Croatian version "Naša Izjava") denouncing the establishment of Yugoslavia as an attempt to create a Greater Serbia. *Narodni List,* Zotti's daily from New York—the most widely read South Slav publication at the time—supported the anti-Yugoslav group and declared itself in favor of an independent Croatian and Slovenian state. After the signing of the Corfu Declaration in July, 1917, between Dr. Trumbić of London and Premier N. Pašić of Serbia, the tensions and disunity in the South Slav movement in America were intensified. Rev. Gršković quit the priesthood in the same summer to devote his energies fully to the work in the office of the Yugoslav National Council in Washington. After President Wilson finally shifted his position from first suggesting reforms in Austria-Hungary (as he expressed it in his Fourteen Points in January, 1918) to his stand in May, advocating a destruction of the Hapsburg Empire, the victory of the South Slav cause was secured.

An indication of the President's friendship occurred on July 4, 1918, when at his invitation thousands of the South Slavs, many from Pittsburgh, marched through the streets of Washington, D.C. Many Croatians wore their national costumes. They were all greeted by Wilson in front of the Capitol.[51] In late October Austria-

Hungary disintegrated. On December 1, 1918, the new South Slav state, officially known as the Kingdom of Serbs, Croats and Slovenes, was proclaimed in Belgrade. America recognized the new state the next year. Had it not been for the activities of the South Slavs in America, especially the Croatians in Pittsburgh, and above all President Wilson's support, the new state would not have become a reality. Within a short time the events that took place in Yugoslavia caused most of even ardent supporters of the Yugoslav idea to be disappointed. A few years later the representatives of the Croatian organizations from Pittsburgh and other cities would denounce the royal dictatorship in Belgrade.

## NOTES

1. Adam S. Eterovich of San Francisco has undertaken a great amount of research on the Croatian and other South Slav immigrants in the West and the South already during the 1700s and early 1800s and published these discoveries under R. & E. Research Publishing Co., San Francisco. See also Bibliography in George J. Prpić, *The Croatian Immigrants in America* (New York: 1971).

2. Anon., "First Croatian Missionary in Allegheny County," in Boniface Sorić (ed.), *Croatian Almanac 1948* (McKeesport, Pa.), pp. 133–143.

3. For historical development of Croatian people see: Louis Adamic, *The Native's Return* (New York: 1934) ; F. H. Eterovich (ed.), *Croatia: Land, People, Culture* (University of Toronto Press, 1964 and 1970), 2 vols.; Stanko Guldescu, *History of Medieval Croatia* (The Hague: 1964) and *The Croatian-Slavonian Kingdom: 1526–1792* (The Hague: 1970) ; Francis R. Preveden, *A History of the Croatian People* (New York: 1955, 1962). Also numerous works by the foremost Croatian historian, now living in Chicago, Dominic Mandić.

4. Emily Greene Balch, a great friend of Slavs, complained bitterly about this confusion in her excellent book *Our Slavic Fellow Citizens* (New York: 1910), p. 247. Miss Balch wrote a great deal about Croatians and other Slavs and was well acquainted with the conditions of the ethnic groups in Greater Pittsburgh area before World War I. Her book and many of her articles still present a very good source for historians dealing with the immigrants in Pennsylvania.

5. On the number of these immigrants see George J. Prpić, *The Croatian Immigration to America After 1945* (Cleveland: 1967), p. 21. Also by the same author, "The Croatian Immigrants in the United States of America," in F. H. Eterovich and Christopher Spalatin (eds.), *Croatia: Land, People, Culture* (University of Toronto Press, 1970), II, pp. 394–478; and also respective references in the book by the same author *The Croatian Immigrants in America*.

6. For causes of Croatian immigration see the well-written chapter in

Stjepan Gaži, *Croatian Immigration to Allegheny County: 1882–1914* (Pittsburgh: Croatian Fraternal Union, 1956), pp. 7-20; and in Prpić, *The Croatian Immigrants in America,* Ch. IV, pp. 89-102.

7. Immigration Commission, *Dictionary of Races or Peoples* (Washington, 1911), p. 47; J. R. Commons, *Races and Immigrants in America* (New York 1920), p. 81; E. A. Steiner, *On the Trail of the Immigrant* (New York, 1906), pp. 26, 180-181; S. F. Orth, *Our Foreigners* (New Haven, Conn., 1920), pp. 171-72; and E. G. Balch, *Our Slavic Fellow Citizens,* p. 193.

8. R. H. Markham, *Tito's Imperial Communism* (Chapel Hill, N.C.: 1947), p. 9.

9. L. Adamic, *A Nation of Nations* (New York: 1944), p. 239.

10. Ledbetter, *The Jugoslavs of Cleveland* (Cleveland: 1918), p. 25.

11. Balch, *Our Slavic Fellow Citizens,* p. 157.

12. Sorić, *Centennial,* p. 33.

13. Leland D. Baldwin, *Pittsburgh, the Story of a City* (1938), p. 326; George E. Kelly, *Allegheny County: A Sesqui-Centennial Review* (Pittsburgh, 1938); Gazi, *Croatian Immigration to Allegheny County,* pp. 21-23; Peter Roberts, *Wage Earning Pittsburgh* (New York, 1910).

14. Peter Robert, "The New Pittsburghers: Slavs and Kindred Immigrants in Pittsburgh," *Charities and the Commons* XXI, January 2, 1909, pp. 533-552.

15. Roberts, "New Pittsburghers," p. 533.

16. *Ibid.,* p. 533.

17. *Ibid.*

18. *Ibid.*

19. Alois B. Koukol, "The Slav's a Man for a 'That'," *Charities and the Commons* XXI, January 2, 1909, p. 589.

20. *Ibid.,* p. 595. For life of Slavs—including the Croatians—in Pittsburgh, see Barbara Holsople, "The Slavic People," in *Ethnic Groups in Pittsburgh (The Pittsburgh Press Roto),* 1971 (n.d.), pp. 9-12, where the writer discusses the history of the Croatian Cubelic family.

21. Gaži, *Croatian Immigration to Allegheny County: 1882–1914,* p. 24; Holsople, "The Slavic People," p. 10.

22. Gaži, *Croatian Immigration to Allegheny County: 1882–1914,* pp. 24-25.

23. Prpić, *The Croatian Immigrants in America,* p. 347. J. J. O'Neill, *Prodigal Genius* (New York: 1944), pp. 79-82. In words of G. Westinghouse, the fate of his company depended on whether Tesla would give up the contract. He did!

24. Sorić, *Centennial,* p. 65; Gaži, *op. cit.,* pp. 26-29.

25. Sorić, *Centennial,* p. 53; Prpić, *op. cit.,* pp. 125-127.

26. Bosiljko Bekavac, "Hrvatska katolička kolonija u Pittsburghu, Pa." *Naša Nada Kalendar za 1927* (Gary, Ind.: Croatian Catholic Union, 1926), pp. 95-115; and also by Bekavac, "Prva hrvatska župa u U.S.A. u North Side, Pittsburgh, Pa." *Naša Nada Kalendar za 1930,* pp. 57-92. Sorić, *Centennial,* pp. 43-45.

27. B. Bekavic, "Povijest hrvatske župe u Millvale, Pa." *Danica Koledar za 1929* (New York, 1928), pp. 161-195.

28. Prpić, *The Croatian Immigrants in America,* p. 130.

29. Gaži, *Croatian Immigration to Allegheny County: 1882–1914,* pp. 36-37.

30. *Ibid.,* pp. 37-38. Also B. Bekavic, *Spomen Knjiga o 25-godišnkici*

opstanka Hrv. Rimokatoličke Crkve Marije Pomoćnice (Rankin, Pa., 1928).

31. Frano Karavanić, Spomen knjiga tridesete obljetnice župe i dvadesete obljetnice škole (McKeesport, 1937). Sacred Heart parish established a grade school in 1917.

32. Prpić, The Croatian Immigrants in America, p. 132.

33. Danica, January 31, 1895; Croatian Almanac for 1948 (McKeesport), p. 109.

34. Sorić, Centennial, pp. 53–55; Prpić, The Croatian Immigrants in America, p. 133; Gaži, Croatian Immigration to Allegheny County: 1882–1914, p. 41.

35. J. Marohnić, Popis Hrvata u Americi (Allegheny, 1902), especially pp. 99–106.

36. Napredak, November 21, 1901.

37. Holsople, "The Slavic People," p. 10.

38. Philip Taylor, The Distant Magnet (New York: 1971), p. 202. The author quotes extensive documents.

39. Ibid.

40. Gaži, Croatian Immigration to Allegheny County: 1882–1914, pp. 43–44.

41. Ibid., pp. 45–46; more on Zotti in Prpić, The Croatian Immigrants in America, pp. 204, 210, 211, 238 and 400.

42. Prpić, The Croatian Immigrants in America, pp. 178–182. The Constitution and bylaws were printed in Pittsburgh under the title Pravila Hrvatskog Saveza, 1913.

43. Ibid., pp. 179–180.

44. Ibid., pp. 166–168. S. Radić, Javna politička poruka probudjenoj seljackoj braći naročito u Americi (Zagreb, 1913).

45. Gaži, Croatian Immigration to Allegheny County: 1882–1914, p. 49.

46. Ibid., p. 50.

47. G. J. Prpić, "The South Slavs," in The Immigrants' Influence on Wilson's Peace Policies, Joseph P. O'Grady, ed. (Lexington, Ky.: 1967), pp. 173–203, which quotes extensive sources and discusses in detail the Croatian political activities during World War I in Pennsylvania and the United States.

48. H. B. Z., Kratki pregled povijesti Hrvatske Bratske Zajednice (Pittsburgh, 1949), pp. 33–48, 180; Franko Potočnjak, Iz Emigracije: U Americi (Zagreb, 1927), pp. 27–61, 115–125; Victor S. Mamatey, The United States and East Central Europe (Princeton: 1957), pp. 114–118; this excellent book includes detailed discussion of South Slav activities in America during World War I. Prpić, "The South Slavs," pp. 176–182.

49. Prpić, "South Slavs," pp. 184–185.

50. Ibid., p. 185.

51. Hrvatski Glasnik (Pittsburgh), July 6 and 20, 1918; Prpić, "South Slavs," pp. 194–195.

# 11

# The East European Jew Comes to Philadelphia

## MAXWELL WHITEMAN

*Maxwell Whiteman is currently consulting archival historian at the Union League of Philadelphia. He has taught at Dropsie College and has authored numerous works on ethnic history. He has coauthored* A History of the Jews of Philadelphia.

Long before the Russian May laws of 1882, East European Jews had found their way to Philadelphia. Most Philadelphians were aware of a small community that had settled in the industrial section of Port Richmond dubbed "Jewtown" and "Jerusalem." The sight of a Russian Jew, although still strange, was no longer unfamiliar. This group, coming mostly from Poland and Lithuania, kept itself apart from the older community. Confined within a quarter-mile area not far from the Delaware River, engaged in peddling along the water front, they planted a Yiddish cultural world of their own. They observed all the dicta of traditional Judaism, maintained their own synagogue, rejected the so-called attempts at Americanization by opposing the installation of English-speaking religious schools, and scoffed at the charitable aid offered by the established community.[1] They found a comfort in their own milieu which could not be had among the descendants of early American families or the

287

immigrants of the antebellum period whose American-born children had already carved a niche for themselves.

It was in the midst of this interreaction that the Port Richmond community learned of the worsening plight of Russian Jews from the Baltic to the Balkans, from Warsaw to Odessa.

The impact of what had been known to only a few people became a public matter when the *Philadelphia Record* of September 8, 1881, spread the news before its readers that a large number of immigrants fleeing Russia were bound for Philadelphia. The report stirred a multitude of feelings among Philadelphia's Jews. Some regarded the news as sensationalism. Others refused to believe it. One segment of the population comforted itself in the assumption that Philadelphia was to become a center for the redistribution of the newcomers and that the city would not be overburdened with immigrants similar to those who lived in "Jerusalem." The United Hebrew Charities representing the consolidated Jewish societies of Philadelphia remained silent. A week after the news story, a cable from the *Alliance Israelite Universelle* of Paris confirmed the report. Four hundred Jews, assembled at Lemberg, were on their way to Philadelphia by way of an English port.[2] Any doubts held by the Philadelphians on the coming of the immigrants were quickly but not satisfactorily dispelled, even though Philadelphia was the American office of the *Alliance Israelite* and the reports were official and irrefutable.

The news should not have come as a surprise. Throughout the seventies the American press had pointed continuously to the unhappy conditions of Russian Jewry, the decay of Czarism, and the growing revolutionary movement. Following the Paris Commune and the rise of Bismarck, the eyes of American Jewry focused on events in Germany. An alarming revival of anti-Semitism was evident. It was a topic for constant discussion in the German language press published for American Jews.[3] Their ties were still with Germany; but as the scene shifted from West to East, from the anti-Jewish temper of a newly unified Germany to the uncontrolled wrath that flared in the interior of Russia and Roumania, Jews of German descent were aroused from their apathy. A detailed account of mass Russian brutality, published in the influential *Times* of London, was widely reprinted in the American press.[4] It enforced upon the minds of those who still doubted the fate of Russian Jewry the recognition of the rapidly changing conditions.

One of the first Philadelphians to express public concern was Alfred T. Jones, the Boston-born editor of the Philadelphia *Jewish Record*. As one of the founders of Philadelphia's first Jewish-sponsored hospital and its first president, he had been confronted by the problems of organizing communal facilities in the face of severe emergencies. His affiliation with the United Hebrew Charities made him better able to judge the potential of the parent philanthropic society. Through his newspaper he undertook to muster the forces of Philadelphia's 10,000 Jews and approximately 15,000 others scattered throughout the state. His deep interest in municipal reform, his masonic affiliations, and his general community activity placed him in an excellent position to organize an effective working unit where none had existed.[5]

The news published in the *Jewish Record* was designed to win support for the immigrants, to create a favorable atmosphere for the Russians, and to present an authentic picture of their harrowing experiences of the previous six months. For weeks Jones described in detail the unprovoked outrages committed in southern Russia. First it was the pogrom in Odessa, then the pillage in Kiev, and the destruction wreaked upon the Jews of Elizabethgrad. Hundreds of Jewish towns and villages in the Pale of Settlement that lay scattered between the larger cities had met a similar fate and, where their Jewish residents had not been murdered, they were driven to despair. It was made clear that the violence was condoned by the Russian government which looked indifferently on the panic and terror that it deliberately instigated.[6] As the story of horror unfolded, Jones successfully reached the hearts of his readers. But his audience was not yet prepared to go beyond sympathy. Jones pleaded not only for good will, but for funds and jobs. Furthermore, he pressed for the organization of a committee of Philadelphia Jews to deal with the reality facing the new immigrants and to plan for the arrival of the mass transport of immigrants announced by the *Alliance*. He chastised the city's Jews for their indifference, for their failure to take quick action in aiding the immigrants who were reaching Philadelphia by way of New York and Baltimore, cities which were eager to divest themselves of as many immigrants as possible. Thrust on their diminishing resources, the newcomers were bound to become a public burden.[7]

During the first week of October, 1881, a combined meeting of the officers of the Philadelphia branch of the *Alliance* and the United Hebrew Charities was held at Reform Congregation Keneseth Israel. Its purposes were to raise a fund for the immigrants, establish procedures for an employment committee, and to find suitable housing.[8] Immediate attention was required for those arriving daily. The greatest number was penniless and without relatives. A few found their way to "Jerusalem" in Port Richmond; and a few, shunning all help, founded a small community of Lithuanian Jews in the area of Fifth and Lombard Streets in the southern section of the city.[9]

In organizing the employment committee, Jones was joined by Arnold Kohn, who became its head. As a penniless boy of twelve, Kohn had emigrated to the United States from Württemberg, Germany, and began his business career as a match hawker. He later trudged through the South as a country peddler and finally followed the Union Army as a wartime sutler. He never forgot his own difficult ascension which brought him into the clothing trade.[10] Kohn was motivated by personal experience. But it would be difficult to say that his zeal was typical of other Jewish immigrants from Germany.

In the fall of 1881, the number of men who responded to the looming crisis was small. Kohn was eager to find employment for the newcomers by establishing a separate committee for immigrants whose special task would be unrelated to the work of the United Hebrew Charities. He learned quickly that his ideals were not held by oth s, that one man alone could not find employment and housing for thirty to forty immigrants each week. Adding to these frustrating conditions was the fact that the immigrants spoke a language that neither Kohn nor the committee understood. When Kohn threatened to resign unless he received ample support,[11] others finally joined in the voluntary work. The committee was also dismayed to learn that those who had settled in "Jerusalem" prior to 1880 and met with some financial success were reluctant to mingle with Jews of German background or the descendants of old American families.[12] As the program of the new committee proceeded, its leaders were more eager to attract recent immigrants to its work, but with few exceptions Russian Jews stood in the background. In fact, few knew what they thought, or sensed their deep concern.

Against this background, Jones appealed to the Jewish clergy to address their congregations on the subject of aid to the immigrants. "It is important that in every city in the Union prompt action be taken for the reception and location of these emigrants of whom forty-eight are expected in New York this week, 116 next week and others to follow. . . . It is now time that the Israelites of this city moved in the matter."[13]

These figures were large by comparison with the number of Jewish immigrants who had come to New York or Philadelphia during any single week of the 1870s, and they were real evidence of the changing character of European immigration. Young single men were followed by family units; village groups left en masse and the pathfinders were quickly followed by other friends and relatives. Between the spring and autumn of 1881, tens of thousands of destitute Jews made their way to Brody on the Russian-Austrian frontier. Rumors that the agents of the *Alliance* would supply them with the necessary funds to continue their journey to America brought them to this Galician city. But the stunned *Alliance* was unprepared to meet the first gigantic influx of emigrants. Its agents provided the best they could in food and temporary shelter before they were dispatched in small groups to the port cities of Germany on their way to the United States. The Russians could not be held back.

Jones realized the significance of this mounting problem when he lamentably reported that Rabbi Henry S. Jacobs of New York had attempted to dissuade the *Alliance Israelite* from directing 1,400 immigrants to the United States. Neither Jacobs nor anyone else could have held back the immigrants, or even induce the *Alliance* to limit the number. No argument could alter the plans of the *Alliance;* there was no turning back those who were bound for the port cities of Germany on their way to England or the United States. Other Jewish editors did not share Jones' views, but observed that the new immigrants were "not of a character calculated to elevate the status of the Israelites in America."[14]

Fear of the new immigrant was no longer limited to nativists, but was shared by Jews as well who thought that their own status would be harmed by the strangers. Jones was as critical of this attitude as he was concerned with how the immigrants would be received upon their arrival. Ignoring prejudgment of the immigrant, he went on to say: "We of Philadelphia have earnest work to do and a holy duty to perform. These refugees are sent here and will continue to be sent against a distinct understanding as to the limit in numbers that we are able to provide for, and yet we cannot attach any blame to the New York committee, who may have by this time six hundred emigrants on their hands, all to be fed, lodged and clothed. The censure of any should apply to the committee of the 'Alliance' in Paris, who have gone beyond their instructions received from this side."[15]

The *Alliance* was in no better position to control the westward flow of immigration than the Americans were able to convince them to stop it. Well-meaning New Yorkers were as confused as well-intentioned Philadelphians. Unable to foresee that the United States was soon to witness the greatest Jewish immigration in history, Jewish leaders of both cities thought in terms of assisting tens, perhaps hundreds, but not tens or hundreds of thousands. They envisioned an orderly immigration of small groups, seldom more than 150 persons a month, a number that could be distributed among smaller inland cities where they could be absorbed gradually. A controlled immigration would fit the established program of the charitable societies, but a number larger than this would disrupt the well-ordered societies that were consolidated after the Civil War and overnight drain the resources of organized Jewish charity.

But the masses of Jews fleeing southern Russia and Roumania continued westward in the face of obstacles far worse than those envisioned by Philadelphians. The Russian Jews were determined to reach America. "Shipments" of immigrants, stated the *Alliance,* could not be stopped. A titanic current had been set in motion by the corrupt Czarist government which could not be restrained by letters of the Americans pleading that large numbers of Jews not be sent to their cities. Alarmed by the upsurge, the Americans intimated their desire to reship the immigrants to Europe, but were quickly deterred by an overwhelming fear that the Jews of the United States would be looked upon by their brothers in Russia as thinking them unworthy to be received. It was also feared that such conduct would be grist for the German anti-Semites as well as the Russian pogromists. Months before the steamer Illinois sailed up the Delaware Bay with her hundreds of Russian refugees, the Philadelphia committee realized that the influx of Jews from Russia was beyond the control of any force on the soil of Europe or on the American side of the Atlantic.[16]

In an effort to accommodate himself to reality, Jones insisted that, "We must procure employment for those now here and that right speedily, and it is the indisputable duty of every Israelite in Philadelphia . . . to act as if they were members of the Committee on Relief. Surely the thriving Israelites of this city and of other cities in this state can provide work for these suffering people! It appears incredible to the casual observer, that 25,000 Jews in Pennsylvania who are trading and manufacturing people, would find it difficult to employ a hundred men, able and willing to work for a bare subsistence."[17]

Although Jones devoted considerable space in the *Jewish Record* to the important work of the employment and relief committee and in describing the condition of Russian Jews, he did not stand alone among the Philadelphia newspapers. For months the *Philadelphia Press* published vivid accounts of the crimes of the Russian government against its Jewish subjects. One of the local non-Jewish editors proposed to Jones that a public protest meeting ought to be held condemning the Russian outrages. Jones deferred publicizing the suggestion in the hope that a spontaneous movement of all Philadelphians, especially non-Jews, would arise in such a protest. But he was naive in his belief. For the time being, he was disappointed by Jews and non-Jews as well. In fact, one outstanding Jewish minister opposed the idea, stating that "he would not raise a finger to promote it." Torn by indifference and a growing opposition from many quarters, Jones asked: *"Is it because the three millions of human beings likely to be swept out of existence by barbarous hordes claiming to be Christians are merely Jews? Again we ask, are their (the rabbis') sympathies only to be lavished on the Southern Negro, or those of their faith when persecuted by the followers of Mahomet?"*[18]

Finally, the weeks of editorializing, the worsening conditions of the immigrants, and the reality of facing a mass of impoverished strangers reached a climax. The turning point took place early in 1882 when a group of the most influential Jews of Philadelphia met to take action. Their meeting coincided with the news that the steamer Illinois was approaching American shores and the announcement that others were rapidly following.

Under discussion were specific preparations to meet the first major tide of immigrants. The *ad hoc* committee requested Mayor Samuel G. King of Philadelphia to use the dignity of his office on behalf of aiding the immigrants. The Mayor responded quickly, issuing an invitation to the city's leading citizens with the request that they help devise means to relieve the exiles upon arrival. State Senator Horatio Gates Jones, a warm friend of Pennsylvania Jewry, called to order the first meeting on February 13, presided over by Mayor King. William B. Hackenburg, a prominent and influential Jewish layman, was named secretary; and Anthony J. Drexel of the banking firm assumed the position of treasurer of a fund-raising committee consisting of fourteen members, five of whom were Jews. At the suggestion of John Wanamaker, Philadelphia's leading Presbyterian and department store entrepreneur, the committee was authorized to call a town meeting at the first opportunity.[19]

With Europe feeling the pinch of mid-winter, the immigrant pace had slowed. Those who were assembled to go to Philadelphia were sent across the North Sea to Liverpool. There, after some further delay, they boarded the steamer Illinois in the first days of February and embarked for Philadelphia. A total of 360 persons comprised the final ship's list of Jewish refugees: eighty-six women, eighty children, and the remainder adult males. Poorly clothed, inadequately fed, weary from travel and endless delays, they settled down for a three-week journey across the Atlantic. Other than one birth, the death of an infant, and a minor accident on shipboard, the winter sea voyage was a quiet one. On Thursday, February 24, 1882, at 7:20 A.M., the Illinois reached the Capes on schedule. Information that the ship had touched the Delaware was telegraphed to Philadelphia, stating that it would reach the landing station between one and two o'clock in the afternoon. As soon as the committee was informed, a select group boarded the river steamboat Juno and sped down the Delaware River to welcome the Illinois. At three-thirty P.M., the Illinois arrived at the Christian Street wharf opposite Old Swedes Church, nosed her way in, dropped anchor, and was made fast. Hundreds of jubilant spectators from all walks of life gazed up at the pleased and excited faces of the Jews who had fled the whip of the Czar. The long journey had ended.[20]

By order of the captain, the Jews were the first to disembark. Men and women descended the gangplank carrying whatever worldly possessions they had. Kosher tin utensils, packs of rags that served for clothing, canvas bags and wicker baskets containing a motley assortment of articles were visible. Occasionally a bearded elderly Jew struggled with a bundle of folio volumes, his only possessions. Many were only the owners of the clothing they wore. It was a scene that repeated itself innumerable times in the decades that followed.

Relief, confidence, and hope inspired them, as their feet touched the soil of the "Free States," as they called America. The plans of the city committee now went into action. After a brief delay, the Pennsylvania Railroad made available a special train of cars to transfer the immigrants to its West Philadelphia station, then located at 32nd and Market Streets. Everyone was made comfortable, proper food was supplied, and an abundance of milk was served. About eight o'clock in the evening, the refugees reached the old depot where they were received with a social grace that astonished the haggard ill-clad strangers. Extensive preparations were made for dinner, bathing facilities were supplied, and a corps of barbers and a staff of nine physicians were in constant attendance. A temporary school was set up for the teaching of "American," and an employment committee with a Yiddish-speaking aide interviewed men for jobs. Within twenty-four hours, forty-nine of the newcomers, some with and some without families, were sent to their future employers throughout the state. Some were dispatched to as far west as Trinidad, Colorado. Five remained in Philadelphia, and twenty-five were sent to nearby Norristown. The following week, twenty-five more were sent there. Within three weeks, more than a third of the arrivals were gainfully employed and the railroad depot continued to be the temporary home of the others. A pattern for the redistribution of immigrants was established.[21]

Immediately after the arrival of the Illinois, a series of meetings were held in the offices of Mayor King, of John Wanamaker, and of Moses A. Dropsie, founder of the university which bears his name. The committee drafted a text for five thousand circulars under the title of *An Appeal for the Russian Refugees,* approved the re-publication of 15,000 copies of the London *Times* report on Russian Jews, and ordered that both items be distributed throughout the city and state. The local press, without cost to the committee, issued an appeal for funds. But the most important step was the call for a town meeting on March 4, 1882, at the Academy of Music.[22]

The meeting was opened by the articulate general, Charles H. T. Collis, who had fought in the major campaigns of the Civil War. His advocacy of humanitarian causes was a matter of common knowledge. The Hon. John Welsh, former United States Minister to England and the man chiefly responsible for the success of the great Centennial Exhibition, presided over the meeting at which the Governor of Pennsylvania, members of the legislature, and lead-ing Christian clergymen were in attendance. Forty-five of the most influential leaders of Philadelphia, many of them prominent in the affairs of The Union League, added emphasis and prestige to the meeting by their presence. An overflow audience at the Academy condemned the Russian destruction of Jewish life and property. John Wanamaker read the resolution which he had helped prepare pro-testing Russian conduct and calling upon the President of the United States, the Senate, and the House of Representatives to take such action as would reflect the spirit of the meeting. A copy of the published declaration, issued under Wanamaker's name, was forwarded to His Excellency the Russian Ambassador at Washington.[23]

Six months of persistent work by Alfred T. Jones had proved effective. And the results came in the overall response by the general community, by non-Jews, and by the city's elected officials. It was a remarkable culmination of events, a peak in the social expression of the city's leadership, and one which was never again reached in local immigrant history. No similar welcome was to be extended to another immigrant arrival and no other East European or Mediterranean people had the benefit of a comparable reception. No other port city could boast the citywide movement that protested against Russian barbarism.

By 1891, when national immigrant quotas were first considered, these episodes were vague memories. Many of the men who had joined in the Academy protest were thinking of the more than 41,000 Jews[24] who had passed through the port of Philadelphia, to say nothing of the still greater number of Slavs, Italians, and Greeks. Serious consideration was taken to curb and to reduce immigration and, when possible, to return immigrants to the port of their origin for a multitude of reasons.

Although there was not to be another shipload of immigrants that approached the number carried by the Illinois until the fall of 1884, a steady stream of Jews continued to arrive from the vast Russian empire. Regardless of the fact that they came from Lithuania and Latvia, Poland and the Ukraine, Roumania and Volhynia, the image of a "Russian Jew" emerged as a composite figure among many Americans. What most Americans did not know was that Poles and Ukrainians, with whom Jews shared the same geographic areas, were unwilling to accept them and that the policy of the Czarist government shrewdly took advantage of Roman Catholic and Greek Orthodox contempt for Jews. Contempt was opportunely transformed into pogroms as unemployment swept Eastern Europe. A disoriented grain market led to increased unemployment. Wages were drastically cut, and the Ukrainian peasants who turned to the villages in quest of jobs saw in Jews a competitive infidel enemy. Economic upheaval impoverished tens of thousands of Jews.[25] Forced to live on their inner resources, be it in Riga or Radomysl, Minsk or Mohilev, Berditchev or Bratislav, Kishnev, Odessa, and Zhitomer, names unforgettable in the spiritual history of the Jewish past, they fled in accordance with the ebb and flow of Czarist-inspired terror. The enlightened assimilationist, the new Jewish revolutionary, the moderate Socialist, and the traditionalist Jew shared the same fate.

Within two years, this dynamic people who were resourceful in every way except in escaping the wrath of anti-Semitism, were now looked upon as undesirable immigrants. Many of those who rejoiced when the Jews arrived on the Illinois were relieved to learn that immigrants were being returned. While some commentator decried this turn in events, others wrote that "when citizens induce such helpless, ignorant creatures to come here as those who not long ago filled the old depot in West Philadelphia, they must not be surprised if they suffer peculiarly."[26] In a harsh outburst of criticism, the Philadelphia *Times* described the route of fifty-two Jews who were returned from New York to Hamburg and then from Hamburg back to Philadelphia. If they were unwanted in New York, why should they be received in Philadelphia? Simon Muhr, a prominent clock maker and jeweler under whose auspices they were received, was particularly condemned even though Muhr was successful in obtaining employment for the entire group. Immigration commissioners assailed the procedure of reshipping immigrants especially since news reached the city that 3,000 penniless Roumanian immigrants were being assembled at Hamburg for Philadelphia. Paupers among them would be returned. The American consuls at Hamburg and Liverpool promised that assisted immigrants would be stopped as soon as detected. This was no easy task, for the English, American, and German steamship lines were concerned only with collecting their fares and not probing into the financial status of their passengers.[27]

In the midst of this public argument, Jacob Judelson, an immigrant from Mariampol in Russian Poland who had settled in Philadelphia in 1879, proposed that a society for the protection of immigrants be organized. His proposal went unnoticed. But the Jews of Philadelphia were confronted with a serious problem. Their *ad hoc* committee was still in a loose state of affairs, although it had provided for 5,000 immigrants at an expenditure of $37,000 since the spring of 1882. Resentment and hostility were apparent among some Jews who believed with Stephen Remak that, "The question of assisted immigration to this country is becoming a very serious one, for the off-scourings of the slums of Europe are being unloaded upon us. America is becoming a sort of dumping-ground for the paupers and criminals of all countries. This was stopped in the case of the Chinese, but the Chinese are angels compared with the malodorous gangs that are unloaded from every steamer from European ports. The cheapness of the passage, once a blessing, has become a curse."[28] Remak, a Jewish nativist, born in the poor district of Posen, Prussian Poland, was at this time a prominent member of the Philadelphia bar.[29] But the voices of the Remaks, although not silenced, were soon overwhelmed by the feverish efforts to turn the *ad hoc* committee into an immigrant association.

Two weeks after Remak's pronouncement, Alfred T. Jones, Simon Muhr, Moses A. Dropsie, Mayer Sulzberger, Louis Edward Levy, and three other prominent Jews met to act on Judelsohn's original plan. They called a mass meeting at the old Wheatley Dramatic Hall in the southern section of the city on September 21, 1884.[30] Its purpose was to deal with all aspects of Jewish immigration, from the hour of arrival until the immigrant was securely settled. The community was criticized by Dropsie for failing to take action at an earlier date, but Dropsie was mistaken in the belief that the Jews of Philadelphia had no earlier immigrant aid society. Actually, an immigrant and mutual aid organization had been in existence since 1784.[31] However, its machinery was designed to provide for a handful of people, not for thousands. As the "compassionate, the children of the compassionate," Dropsie declaimed in Hebrew, Jews had been tardy in fulfilling their ethical commitments and could not afford to lose another day. Adverse anti-Jewish reports prompted by the reshipment of immigrants were inimical to the advancement of a healthy Jewish community. Dropsie condemned as evil the instance of the fifty-two Roumanian Jews who had been forced to return to Hamburg at the behest of the United Hebrew Charities of New York. But he cautioned the audience of five hundred, many of whom could not understand English, to "disperse themselves through the city, and not settle down in one quarter clinging to habits which have engendered prejudice." He spoke with regret of those who kept taverns and admonished other immigrants to avoid such occupations that could "bring disgrace upon them and their coreligionists."[32] Dropsie was repeating an old theme which had been current among American Jews in their search for acceptance and respectability. He had been raised in precisely the kind of neighborhood which he now deplored. His father had lived among the Dutch and German Jews who came to Philadelphia after the Napoleonic wars, operated a pawn shop, an occupation looked upon with disdain by Jews of colonial descent. But Dropsie's new status as a gentleman of the bar and a developer of the city's transportation system compelled him to moralize on the future conduct of Jews.[33] The concept of distributing Jews in order to reduce their visibility among non-Jews was not only a local view, but one which spread across the nation.

Dropsie was sound and foresighted in his other suggestions, urging a functional employment agency "without distinction to creed or race" and the careful consideration of "paupers" which was still an undefined term for unwanted immigrants.

Following the mass meeting, steps were taken to formalize the organization. At the second meeting, attended by the local rabbinate, one rabbi opposed anything beyond an employment committee, in the fear that an official immigrant association would only attract more immigrants. When it was disclosed that the immigrants were forming a society of their own, differences were soon resolved in order to avoid having two separate societies raising funds for the same purpose. The new body was named the Association of Jewish Immigrants of Philadelphia.[34]

In the late fall of 1884, a constitution was drafted and approved. Jones was elected president along with three officers and a board of twelve. All of the men proved themselves to be seriously devoted to the problems of immigration and moved forward to build one of the best immigrant aid societies in the United States. The background of the board was divided equally between American-born Jews and men who came to the United States at an early age.[35]

With a fresh enthusiasm and a zeal for organization, the new society emphasized protection of the immigrant. Protection had a broad definition. It meant establishing an apparatus for meeting immigrants at the landing station, clearing them through the port of entry, providing health services, obtaining shelter, and seeing that they were properly fed.

Locating and claiming baggage, a minor procedure under ordinary circumstances, was a matter of major psychological importance. The worldly possessions of the immigrants were involved. Baggage frequently preceded its owner from the home town to the port of debarkation. Here, baggage officers and ship captains, often working in collusion, played evil sport with their passengers' belongings. Baggage was allegedly lost or delayed and could be recovered at an additional cost. Harassing problems resulted at once. And frequently they were not settled until the immigrant arrived in Philadelphia.[36]

To compound these troubles, the immigrant faced a variety of medical tests. Diseases of the eye and pulmonary afflictions were cause for prompt deportation.[37] If a ticket agent failed to pay the legal head tax included in the cost of passage—fifty cents in 1875 and four dollars in 1906—the immigrant was penalized by a second payment. If a family was large, the cost of the head tax could deprive them of their only funds. Penniless immigrants were defined as paupers and subject to deportation.[38] To aggravate the conditions of entry still more, employment skills had to be defined. A religious functionary, whose services were vital to the traditional Jewish community, was looked upon as a dreg; a street hawker as a parasite; and a peddler as a public nuisance. Overnight, as warnings rippled through to detained immigrants, many who never worked in the clothing industry described themselves as skilled in the needle trades.[39]

To meet these problems swiftly and properly, the Association engaged the services of Moses Klein, a Hungarian immigrant with an intimate knowledge of most European languages. But Klein was more than a linguist, he was an imaginative and tireless worker. He so impressed the United States Commissioner of Immigration at Philadelphia that he was appointed interpreter at the local port.[40]

Klein was present at each ship arrival. He traced and retrieved delayed baggage or rescued it from waterfront thieves. At the behest of the Association he obtained medical counsel to make certain that eye inflammations were not diagnosed as trachoma and that a cough was not reported as tuberculosis. When necessary, he intervened in legal proceedings that could lead to deportation and the breakup of families.

Immigrants were directed to suitable lodging houses and advised of thieving innkeepers who thrived on the uninformed. Decent homes and furnished rooms were secured wherever possible to prevent further crowding into the immigrant slums. By 1890 a permanent wayfarers' home was established to replace an earlier temporary shelter. It was especially attractive to Orthodox Jews, for Kosher food laws and all Jewish holidays were observed. The wayfarers' home in the Society Hill area was used by those remaining in the city until Klein could locate friends or relatives or notify those interested in their arrival in other cities. Those bound for other points had the opportunity to rest before they proceeded with a supply of food and fresh clothing made available by the Association. Railroad tickets were obtained for those traveling to other cities where none were received from the shipping agency.[41]

The Association procured employment for many and started others in small businesses. Two major sources of employment were in the clothing and cigar trades. In both the immigrant was misused. But here the work of the Association ended, not through unwillingness, disinterest, or fear of challenging the notorious sweatshop system, but because its energies and resources would have been soon depleted. With the exception of the bloody cloakmakers' strike in the summer of 1890 when the Association intervened, no attempt was made on behalf of the immigrant workingman. The most sympathetic record of that summer's strike and the harrowing conditions faced by the immigrant was reported by Louis Edward Levy, the Association president, in his own newspaper, *The Sunday Mercury.*[42]

Housing, employment, and the degrading circumstances of both

opened an unexploited field for Christian missionaries, Jewish impostors, zealous social workers, and civic reformers. They swarmed
into the immigrant quarters to improve or prey upon their unsus-
pecting subjects. But for an occasional convert, the missionaries
were failures. Jews whose vocation it was "to rob, swindle and
mislead" were not always thwarted; the ideals of many social workers soon turned to contempt; and the reformers who built neighborhood settlements that survive under other auspices fled after a brief
venture with the immigrants.[43]

Protection, as a word and as a major theme, was incorporated
into the name of the Association. The most harassing problem that
forced conventional Jewish agencies to squirm was the rapid increase
of prostitution where it had not existed before. Unconscionable
Jewish impostors, using their linguistic ability, pounced upon the
newcomers. Robbery, cheating, and petty theft were minor, compared to the induction of young women into nearby whorehouses,
often on the day of their arrival.

Faced by the combination of unanticipated and terrifying circumstances, Joseph Ehrlich, the agent who succeeded Moses Klein in
1890, recommended a formula which demanded identification of all
males who presented themselves as relatives of immigrant women.
After 1900 the procedure was instituted by immigration authorities.
But the unwholesome conditions of the immigrant ghetto produced
circumstances where victims were ready made. Jews, Poles, and
Italians were most susceptible. Each were the targets of their own
countrymen. The Association led a movement to crush this traffic so
far as possible. Co-operation from Jewish and civic agencies was
weak and their activity was limited to the water front. A multi-
lingual literature was distributed throughout the immigrant community and members of the Association plunged into the work of
undoing the conditions that brought it about. Eventually the waterfront activity came under control, but prostitution among immigrants
was not stopped. Where it was unknown to them in the countries of
their origin, it became prevalent in the country of their choice.[44]

That it was possible for the Association to assume these enormous
responsibilities was owing to the courageous stand of its leaders. The

older Jewish charities were overburdened and ideologically unprepared to face the immigrants in spite of their willingness to do so. Their numerous agencies and their emerging bureaucracy were unharmonious with immigrant temperament. Their ante-bellum attitude was no longer conducive to post-bellum urban philanthropic needs. The Association found it necessary to disregard the malignant attitude toward the Russian Jews, to ignore the benign indifference of others, and draw upon the resources of those Jews of German origin who defied organizational conformity.[45] Out of this ferment came the men and ideas that led ultimately to a sweeping reorganization of the Jewish philanthropic structure in Philadelphia.[46]

While an internal communal debate over the future of Jewish charitable conduct was carried on, the Association expanded its activity at home and abroad. Rapport with passenger ship agencies was improved, a closer relationship was established with the Pennsylvania Railroad whose vessels of the American Line brought tens of thousands of immigrants to Philadelphia, and a spirit of warm cooperation was developed with other agencies concerned with the plight of immigrants. Above all, the conduct of the Association was one of respected integrity with health officials and the Commissioners of Immigration. Abroad the Association established official connections with Jewish immigrant societies in St. Petersburg, Paris, London, and Hamburg.[47]

In fields no less sensitive or sophisticated, the Philadelphians were active in combating anti-immigration forces and in influencing national legislation that was injurious to all immigrants. Long before special Jewish agencies arose to combat restrictive laws, the Association worked vigorously in public and adroitly in private to dilute their harshness. The public record is in contemporary printed sources, the private negotiations are still hidden in the correspondence between Senator Boies Penrose and Governor Samuel Pennypacker and Judge Mayer Sulzberger.[48]

In the first three decades of its history the Association successfully modified attitudes toward immigrants and won the support of a divided and sometimes hostile community. It curbed the destructive influences of abrasive social movements and involved the rabbinate in the delicate work of immigrant accommodation to a new culture. It softened the contempt for Yiddish, for Zionism, and the seemingly strange ways of Russian Jews. It established an incomparable record of immigrant life recording in statistical detail the name, the country of origin, age, and occupation of each ship arrival. The Association for the Protection of Jewish Immigrants became a major Philadelphia institution with innumerable patrons, members, and financial contributors. Its work continued without interruption until the close of the First World War, the death of its remarkable president Louis Edward Levy, and its final absorption into the Hebrew Immigrant Aid Society.

## NOTES

1. Of the many accounts of "Jerusalem" or "Jewtown" the most informative are by Moses Freeman, *Fifty Years of Jewish Life in Philadelphia* (Philadelphia, 1929), pp. 10–16, and David B. Tierkel, "Jerusalem in Philadelphia" in the *Philadelphia Jewish American,* Nov. 13, 1908. [In Yiddish]

2. *Jewish Record,* Sept. 16, 1881. The *Record,* published between April 16, 1875 and June 25, 1886 was the only Philadelphia paper devoted to Jewish interests at this time. It is a valuable source for the study of the beginnings of Russian Jewish immigration. See note 5 for Alfred T. Jones, its editor.

3. *Die Deborah,* Nov. 8, 1872, *passim;* edited and published in Cincinnati, Ohio by Isaac Mayer Wise, this intriguing source of Jewish news and its hostile attitude toward East Europeans has not been studied.

4. *An Account of the Outrages Perpetrated on the Russian Jews. The following narrative was furnished to the London Times by its special correspondents, and only contains an account up to January 1, 1882, since that time the outrages have been continued.* (No Imprint).

5. Alfred T. Jones (1882–1888) is described by Henry Samuel Morais, *The Jews of Philadelphia* (Philadelphia, 1894), pp. 332–333, and more recently in Maxwell Whiteman, *Mankind and Medicine, A History of Philadelphia's Albert Einstein Medical Center* (Philadelphia: 1966), pp. 13, 31; 54–55. Population figures published in the *Jewish Record,* Nov. 25, 1881, vary with those published in *Statistics of the Jews of the United States compiled under the authority of the Board of Delegates of American Israelites . . .* (Philadelphia, 1880), p. 15, which approximates the Jewish population of Philadelphia at 12,000.

6. *Jewish Record,* Sept. 2, 16, 30, 1881, for detailed accounts of the pogroms and outrages committed on the Jews of Russia.

7. *Ibid.,* Sept. 23, 1881.

8. *Ibid.,* Oct. 7, 14, 1881.

9. Tierkel, "Jerusalem in Philadelphia," and *Jewish Record,* Oct. 21, 28, 1881.

10. Morais, *The Jews of Philadelphia,* pp. 281–282, for a brief sketch of Kohn's activity.

11. *Jewish Record,* Nov. 18, 1881.

12. *Ibid.,* Nov. 4, 1881.

13. *Ibid.,* Sept. 23, 1881, *et seq.*

14. *Ibid.,* Sept. 9, 1881.

15. *Ibid.,* Nov. 15, 1881.

16. *Ibid.,* Nov. 25, 1881, which contains a summary of news, editorial comment and text reprinted from the Jewish and general press.

17. *Ibid.*

18. *Ibid.,* Feb. 10, 1882, where Jones in an editorial, "Why is Philadelphia Silent?" discusses public disinterest, private apathy and hostile views of the rabbinate.

19. State Senator Horatio Gates Jones was a strong advocate in the eighties for the repeal of the Sunday Laws; William B. Hackenburg was president of the Jewish Hospital Association and Anthony J. Drexel was the head of a prominent banking firm. *Russian Refugee Meetings & Minutes of the Meeting of the Citizens of Philadelphia held at the Mayor's Office on Wednesday, February 15, 1882.* MS. in the possession of Maxwell Whiteman. A preliminary circular dated Feb. 13, 1881, calling the meeting, was issued by the Mayor's office.

20. All of the Philadelphia newspapers reported the landing of the Illinois. The most complete account appeared in the *Jewish Record,* Mar. 3, 1882.

21. *Jewish Record,* Mar. 3, 1882 for these and similar details.

22. *Russian Refugee Meetings,* Feb. 23, 27, 1882, for the meeting in Wanamaker's office and the resolution to publicize the mass meeting in the city's newspapers. A. J. Drexel, *In Aid of the Refugees,* undated card soliciting funds from Philadelphians.

23. Charles H. T. Collis, soldier and lawyer, is described in *Biographical Encyclopedia of Pennsylvania of the Nineteenth Century* (Philadelphia, 1874), pp. 129–230. A record of John Welsh's activities is in J. Thomas Scharf and Thompson Westcott, *History of Philadelphia 1609–1884* V. I (Philadelphia, 1884), pp. 721, 842, 846. See the *Public Ledger* and the *Philadelphia Evening Bulletin,* Mar. 6, 1882 for front page accounts of the mass meeting.

24. The figure of 41,000 Jewish arrivals is based upon the annual compilations prepared by the Association for the Protection of Jewish Immigrants from the fall of 1884 to the spring of 1891.

25. No modern history in English has produced a thorough study of this period. Jesse D. Clarkson, *A History of Russia* (New York, 1961), pp. 330–335 contains a useful summary; David Footman, *Red Prelude, The Life of the Russian Terrorist Zhelyabov* (New Haven, 1945), pp. 29–30, points to the influence of economic conditions on the fate of Jewry and Konni Zilliacus, *The Russian Revolutionary Movement* (New York, 1905), pp. 168–176, explores the legal and religious influences that contributed to the pogroms.

26. *Public Ledger,* Aug. 8, 1882.

27. *Philadelphia Times,* Sept. 6, 1884. Morais, *The Jews of Philadelphia,* pp. 287–289, for Simon Muhr.

28. The few facts that are known about Judelson are in Morais, *The Jews of Philadelphia,* pp. 131–132. *The Philadelphia Times,* Sept. 6, 1884 published Remak's statement and Muhr's defense.

29. Morais, *The Jews of Philadelphia,* pp. 405–406, for Stephen S. Remak.

30. *Ledger and Transcript,* Sept. 22, 25 and Oct. 6, 1884, provides accounts of the formation of the Association. *Minute Book, Association of Jewish Immigrants,* Oct. 9, 1884, *passim.*

31. For the beginnings of Jewish mutual aid see Edwin Wolf, II and Maxwell Whiteman, *The History of the Jews of Philadelphia from Colonial Times to the Age of Jackson* (Philadelphia: 1957), pp. 136–137; 264–265.

32. *Minutes of the Mass Meeting* [at Wheatly Dramatic Hall] Sept. 21, 1884, where Dropsie's address is recorded.

33. Cyrus Adler, *Lectures, Selected Papers, Addresses* (Philadelphia, 1933), pp. 43–64, for the only reliable account of Dropsie.

34. *Minutes of the Mass Meeting,* Sept. 30, 1884.

35. The following officers were elected to serve during the first year: president, Alfred T. Jones; vice-president, Jacob Miller; treasurer, Simon Muhr; secretary, Charles Hoffman. The directors were: A. M. Frechie, Louis E. Levy, L. W. Steinbach, M.D., Joseph S. Simsohn, M.D., Max Rosenthal, Max Sessler, Leopold Krause, S. L. Guinsberg, A. Kessler, N. Lowenburg, N. Leiken and L. Levine.

36. *Second Annual Report of the Association of Jewish Immigrants . . .* (Philadelphia, 1886), pp. 5–6, and Joseph Ehrlich to the Association for Jewish Immigrants, Phila., Nov. 27th, 1891, MS. detailing the problems of baggage.

37. Whiteman, *Mankind and Medicine,* pp. 130–133, for diseases of the eye affecting immigrants.

38. *Memorial of the Steamship Companies carrying Emigrant Passengers to the Port of New York . . . Protesting against the Proposed Increase in the Head-Money* (New York, 1874), p. 6, for background on head tax at the port of New York. Maldwyn Allen Jones, *American Immigration* (Chicago: 1960), pp. 262, 269, for changing rates in head tax.

39. *Third Annual Report of the Association of Jewish Immigrants . . .* (Philadelphia, 1887), pp. 9–14, where these and other clashing internal problems of the Jewish societies are openly discussed.

40. Morais, *The Jews of Philadelphia,* pp. 135, 142 and 354, supplies brief data on Klein, who was agent from 1884 to the end of 1889. He was a pioneer Zionist, a contributor to the English-Jewish and Hebrew press and a strong advocate of agrarian life. He expressed these ideas in his work *Migdal Zophim (The Watch Tower). The Jewish Problem and Agriculture as its Solution* (Philadelphia: 1889).

41. The Wayfarers Home, *hachnosas orchim,* first occupied the house at 430 Lombard St. It was officially organized Nov. 16, 1890 and chartered Apr. 29, 1891. It moved to 218 Lombard St. and opened its doors Oct. 18, 1891. It was completely under the sponsorship of women of the immigrant community who worked with the Association. Although it issued annual reports, some in Yiddish, these have not been located for the 1890s.

42. The work of the employment bureau of the Association is to be found in its *Annual Reports,* 1885–1919. Louis Edward Levy (1846–1919) succeeded Jones to the presidency in 1888 and remained in office until his death. His activity as a scientist, inventor and photographer is in *Dictionary of American Biography* XI (New York, 1933), 202–203. The cloakmakers' strike and the plight of the immigrants is described in *The Sunday Mercury,* Aug. 10, 1890, a newspaper published by Levy.

43. Emily W. Dinwiddie, *Housing Conditions in Philadelphia. An Investigation . . . under the direction of a committee of The Octavia Hill Asso-*

*ciation* (Philadelphia, 1904), the *Annual Reports of the Association* and those of the Society of the United Hebrew Charities are valuable sources for examining the social conditions of the immigrant community.

44. Louis J. Cohen, *Jewish Immigration* (n.p., 1909). An unpublished document of 17 pages prepared for L. E. Levy in which a serious attempt was made to examine the extent of prostitution among Jewish immigrants. L. E. Levy to the President and Board of Directors of the Federation of Jewish Charities, Phila., May 10, 1906. MS., 14 pages, in which Levy appraises the problem; Association of Jewish Immigrants Collection, in the possession of Maxwell Whiteman. Joseph Ehrlich became the Association agent on September 18, 1890 and continued in this post until World War I.

45. Documentary evidence of the internal divisions among Jews is found in the published reports of the Association. See, for example, *Third Annual Report*, pp. 11–12, for correspondence between the United Hebrew Charities and the Association.

46. The earliest known proposal in Philadelphia for a "Federation of Jewish Societies"—to avoid a financial drain and a duplication of efforts—came in a statement from Charles D. Spivak, M.D., to Louis E. Levy, Phila., Aug. 14, 1890. It reflected the thinking of immigrants. A second, broader attempt, involving the older community is noted in the *Philadelphia Inquirer,* April 23, 1894, under "Hebrew Charities to be Organized." Not until 1901 did a formal restructuring take place which led to the organization of the Federation of Jewish Charities.

47. Each *Annual Report of the Association of Jewish Immigrants* comments on the fine relationship between the Association and the various public and private institutions involved with immigrants. An extensive correspondence has survived between the Jewish Colonization Association in St. Petersburg, the French *Alliance,* the *Deutsches Central-Komitee fur Russische Juden* and other European Jewish immigrant aid societies in the papers of the Association.

48. The dividing line for this period was in 1906 with the founding of the American Jewish Committee. The unpublished Sulzberger papers bearing on immigration are in the collection of Maxwell Whiteman.

# 12

# The Formation of Ethnic Consciousness: Slavic Immigrants in Steelton

## JOHN E. BODNAR

*John E. Bodnar finished his undergraduate work at John Carroll University in 1966 and is completing his doctoral studies in American history at the University of Connecticut. He is currently in charge of the Ethnic Studies Program at the Pennsylvania Historical and Museum Commission.*

Recent scholars, such as Timothy Smith in his study of lay initiative in the religious life of American immigrants, have suggested that the ethnic and cultural diversity that characterized the American' urban scene during the late nineteenth and early twentieth centuries was carried over from Europe. Attributing the formation of various ethnic and religious communities in Europe to the process of urbanization which brought Croatian, Slovak, Rusin, Serbian, and Polish peasants into cities and towns, Smith suggests that a "variegated pattern of ethnic and religious settlement" developed in Europe from the eighteenth century onward. In fact, Smith concluded that South Pittsburgh and Cleveland, in 1910, resembled two sub-Carpathian towns, Kosice and Presov: "Cultural artifacts of the Kingdom of Hungary's ethnic diversity."[1]

While Smith's linkage of urbanization and the growth of ethnic pluralism is particularly persuasive, his implication that the cultural pluralism found in American cities was largely transferred to this country from Europe tends not only to gloss over the intricate problems that pervaded American immigrant communities but minimizes the extent to which the American system and environment subjected immigrants to circumstances which had not been encountered before. Indeed, as this essay will argue, circumstances peculiar to the American immigrant experience nurtured the rise not only of ethnic or cultural diversity but of an intense ethnic consciousness which continues to permeate American society.[2]

While it is impossible to isolate one particular variable that was most responsible for the rise of ethnic consciousness in America, cultural and religious conflict within the immigrant communities played a leading role in precipitating ethnic identity. Equally as crucial was the economic competition between ethnic groups and the divisions between natives and the foreign-born. While natives, blacks, and immigrants often competed on an economic plane, cultural and religious issues also fostered internecine tensions within the ethnic community.[3]

In discussing the rise of ethnicity in America this study will focus on cultural, religious, and social occurrences which troubled four Slavic immigrant communities in a Pennsylvania steel town. It will not attempt to trace the economic differences which separated the various ethnic groupings in an industrial city. Bordering Harrisburg on the south, Steelton, a town which housed some 14,000 residents in 1910, 4,600 of which were foreign-born, provides us with the setting to compare developments among Slavic immigrants during their crucial years of adjustment.

In 1866 only six families resided in the area now comprising Steelton. It was in that year, however, that the Pennsylvania Steel Company began erecting the first plant in the nation designed expressly for the purpose of making steel. By 1880 the town of Steelton was incorporated and the plant, situated between the old Pennsylvania Canal and the Susquehanna River, began to attract a diverse work force including Negroes from Virginia and Maryland, Germans from nearby Pennsylvania towns, skilled Irish steelworkers from the British Isles, and Italian and Slavic immigrants from Southern Europe.[4]

The bulk of Steelton's Slavic immigrants came after 1880. They were largely South Slavs—Croatians, Serbians, Bulgarians, and Slovenians. The Croats and Slovenes began arriving in the early 1890s. Most Serbs arrived after 1900. Bulgarians were the last to come, some not joining their families in America until after World War I.[5]

By 1893 Croatians and Slovenes were numerous enough to initiate the formation of characteristic immigrant organizations, especially the ever present fraternal society. Slovenians, learning of the presence of an immigrant priest in Joliet, Illinois, through *Amerikanski Slovenec,* brought the Reverend F. S. Šušteršič to Steelton. Šušteršič performed Easter services in 1893 at St. James Irish Catholic Church in what Slovenes called "the most important experience they had yet had since their arrival in America."[6]

The following day Šušteršič invited Slovenians and Croatians to a hall and explained to them the need of a benefit society which offered sick and death payments. At this meeting Šušteršič inaugurated the Slovenian and Croatian Society of St. Nicholas with Miko Mohoreic as president.[7] While the Croatian version of the founding of the society attributes the impetus for organization to two laymen—Josip Verbos, a Croatian, and Marko Kofalt, a Slovene,[8] the salient fact is that, far from bringing over ethnic diversity, the Croats and Slovenes of Steelton were forming united institutions. The alliance, moreover, while often troubled, would remain essentially intact for sixteen years. It would not completely dissolve until ethnic consciousness had increased in the American industrial milieu.

The Croatians and Slovenes did divide their fraternal society in 1895. The Croatians, learning of the formation of a National Croatian Society in Pittsburgh, decided that they wanted to affiliate with an all-Croatian body. The treasury—$268—of St. Nicholas Croatian–Slovenian Society was thus divided among the membership, and Croats in Steelton organized the St. Lawrence Lodge, naming it after the patron saint of the people around Vjvodina, Croatia. The Slovenes retaliated by forming the St. Aloysius Society.[9]

This divisiveness, however, was not enough to prohibit the Croats and Slovenes from forming one church. The religious needs of the early Croatian and Slovenian settlers were served by St. James. On certain feast days, however, many Croats would walk nearly four miles to Harrisburg to attend St. Lawrence Church, since it reminded them of the St. Lawrence Church in Vjvodina. At both St. James and St. Lawrence, numerous immigrants admitted that they could not understand the priest.[10]

It was more than lingual differences, however, which caused Croats and Slovenes to drift away from St. James. Steelton was in many respects an "Irish town." In the steel mills many of the supervisors and superintendents were Irish. The Slavs, of course, held the more menial occupations. If there was not an inevitable source of antagonism here, the fact that Irish foremen would extract weekly "donations" for St. James from the Slavic pay checks, further created a rift between the two. Such donations, as one Croatian woman recalled, "made it hard on our people." A pew rental system that allowed only the wealthier Irish families to sit toward the front of the church caused further consternation among Slavs, who usually stood in the back. It seemed inevitable that forces of ethnic rivalry and social stratification would move the immigrants away from the Irish church.[11]

Since 1896, the Rev. Joseph D. Bozic had been coming from Allegheny City, Pennsylvania, to offer religious services in Croatian. Indeed, on the occasion of his visits the Slavs would decorate a special trolley with American flags to bring him from Harrisburg. By 1898 a joint meeting of Croatians and Slovenes, along with a few Slovaks and Poles, decided to invite Bozic to come to Steelton on a permanent basis. Bozic accepted their invitation in August and by October the first services were held in St. Mary's Croatian–Slovenian Church. The building used was an old Lutheran Church which was purchased for some $1,800, nearly half of which was donated by Bozic.[12]

In fact, Bozic, who arrived in Pittsburgh in August of 1894 and was the first Croatian priest to arrive in America during the "new immigration" period had published *Novi Svijet* [*New World*] and *Puco,* the first humorous Croatian paper in America. Gazi, in his history of the Croats of Allegheny County, claimed that Bozic had a falling out with his parishioners at Allegheny City. There had been a dispute between Bozic and the church committee over who was to control the parish. In Croatia the church had been supported by the state. In America, many Slavic immigrants felt that because they subsidized the church financially, they should also control both the church and the priest. Bozic, prompted by these troubles at Allegheny City, let the Slavs in Steelton know that he would not mind coming there permanently.[13]

While the Croatian-Slovenian Church alliance progressed smoothly for a number of years, a simultaneous process was occurring almost unnoticed. Both groups were slowly building distinct ethnic communities. The St. Lawrence Society, for instance, not only provided useful sick and death benefits but also met a rising demand for social activities. Here Croatians could have meetings, dances, and a place to express themselves where they "felt safe from the American class of people."[14] The first significant social gathering of Croats in Steelton, in fact, was the blessing of a new Croatian flag by the St. Lawrence Society in June of 1895. By 1902, the St. Lawrence Society had constructed a hall of its own and had firmly established itself as a center for Croatian activity.[15]

The fraternal society's activity increased as the influx of Croatian immigrants increased. Whenever a Croat was killed at the steel mill, it was the St. Lawrence Society that "took charge of the body." If Croatians were reported missing, the societies' members would search the "hills in back of town" looking for their fellow countrymen.[16] Such events as the celebration of the Feast of St. Lawrence in August became a significant event among Steelton's Croatians.[17]

The local Steelton papers began to carry for the first time accounts of numerous activities by the Croatians. As the image of an organized immigrant community began to surface, there was a noticeable decline in the use of the term "Huns" or "Hunkey." Indeed, suddenly the local press seemed quite aware of whom these people were. The confusion as to whether they were actually Hungarians, Austrians, or "Slavonics" seemed to be settled. They were clearly referred to now as Croatians. The Croatian flag blessing ceremony in July of 1898 was termed to be "a very creditable demonstration."[18]

The flag blessing ceremonies were among the most popular of the early social activities of the Croats. Early in the morning the members of the St. Lawrence Society would organize and march to St. James Church [this is before the Croatian church was erected]. After the church services, a procession marched down the town's main street with the American and Croatian flags at the head. A band was hired to furnish the music and three hundred members of the Croatian lodge marched in neat dark blue uniforms. The gathering then proceeded to Hess' Island where a picnic was held. Croatians from as far away as Pittsburgh attended, and the *Steelton Reporter* was quick to point out that "the best of order prevailed."[19]

As Croatian activities increased, Steelton inevitably discovered more about who they were and what they felt. In 1903 the St. Lawrence Society initiated an intensive drive to raise funds for the support of widows and children in Croatia whose husbands and fathers had been victims of recent troubles with Austria-Hungary. The *Steelton Reporter* carried an extensive interview with the Croatian pastor, Rev. Francis Azbe, concerning the drive. Azbe explained the alleged oppression of the government of Austria-Hungary toward Croatians. He cited cases of suppression of the press and exorbitant taxes "which tend to keep the inhabitants in absolute poverty." Azbe continued, "We Croatians here are endeavoring to the best of our ability to relieve the sufferings of our fellow countrymen."[20]

By 1903, Croatians were making it known that they desired to be considered as respectable citizens. In August of that year, for instance, an immigrant named August Olshenski was brutally assaulted. Harrisburg newspapers, in covering the incident, reported that the assault took place in the St. Lawrence Hall. This report was quickly challenged by Josip Verbos, president of the Croatian society, who argued that the assault not only did not occur at the Croatian hall, but that the St. Lawrence Society is very careful to whom the hall is rented, that the best of order is always maintained, and that beer and liquor are not sold there at any time.[21]

In 1909, the Croatians began to lay preparations for the establishment of a local Croatian newspaper. Frank Horvath was to be the publisher of *Hrvatski Dom* [*Croatian Home*], and it was to be printed "in the interest of the Croatian workingman." Unfortunately the project never materialized, apparently because agreements could not be worked out between the five local Croatian fraternal groups that were supposed to support the publication.[22]

In the same year, however, the St. Lawrence Society began a school to teach English to the foreign residents. The school was headed by Michael Tenda and lessons in English were given every day to children too young to work. On weekends instructions would be given to those who worked in the mills. Croatian spokesmen expressed the feeling that the school would "give their children a better opportunity for advancement than they had."[23] By 1911, the Croatians had organized several Tamboritzan orchestras and a Croatian "Sokol" which offered athletic activities to the youth. In fact, the frequent gymnastic exhibitions were "of special importance to the several Slavic nationalities" in the town. They offered immigrant children an opportunity at athletic competition which was normally denied them since they were nowhere to be found on the popular football and baseball clubs in Steelton in the early years of this century.[24]

On the eve of World War I, the Croatians were living in an active and thriving ethnic group. The spring of 1912 saw the "most pretentious procession of foreigners ever witnessed in the borough." A mammoth parade was sponsored by St. Mark's National Croatian Society in honor of the blessing of large silk American and Croatian flags which the lodge had just purchased. After the church blessing, more than a thousand Croatians, Serbs, and Slovenes, some from Reading, Lebanon, Philadelphia, and South Bethlehem, marched in full regalia with red shirts, braided jackets, red caps, and black bands. Nearly all of the "foreign societies" in the town took part in the colorful parade. This heightened ethnicity, however, nurtured in America, loomed as a major threat to the Croatian-Slovenian alliance.[25]

While the Croats and Slovenes founded a "Kroation-Slavonic American Political Club" and opened a school in 1903 "to preserve our language," ethnic tensions began to surface between Croats and Slovenes by 1909.[26] The pastor of St. Mary's at that time, Rev. Francis Azbe, was a Slovenian. Croatians, who made up nearly two-thirds of the congregation, became increasingly disturbed by the fact that Azbe continually preached in Slovenian. A delegation of Croats went to Azbe and asked that the services be held more frequently in Croatian but apparently Azbe was unable or refused. One immigrant put it more forcefully, "We didn't want a Slovenian priest." Croatian delegations were sent to the Bishop of Harrisburg and the Apostolic Delegate in Washington. The Croatians asked for Azbe's removal.[27]

The initial recommendation of the Apostolic delegate was that the Slovenes should receive a sum of money from the Croatians to form a new parish. The Croats refused. They also initially refused a request from Bishop Shanahan of Harrisburg to pay the Slovenians $7,000 to buy a lot and form a new parish and assume the debt of St. Mary's. When Shanahan issued a final decree, the Croatians acquiesced and in March 1909, they gave the Slovenians $6,000 from the church treasury, assumed the debt of the parish, and broke from the Slovenians. By May the Slovenes had established St. Peter's Slovenian Church under Rev. Azbe. The Croats remained at St. Mary's, and the separation was complete.[28]

As among the Croatians and Slovenes, the Serbs also suffered from internecine strife. The chief source of trouble was the animosity between the Serbs and the Russians. In 1913, for instance, the Rev. Theofil Stefanovic, pastor of St. Nicholas Serbian Orthodox Church, resigned and returned to Europe. Stefanovic indicated that he was disillusioned with the Serbian colony. He saw little harmony among the Serbs and claimed that contentions between the leaders and himself caused him to leave. The priest admitted that when he came to Steelton in 1907 he knew that the Serbian colony of Steelton was one of the "hardest to manage."[29]

After Stefanovic left, the Serbs were sent a pastor from Philadelphia. Upon his arrival the Rev. M. D. Vukichevich was prohibited from entering St. Nicholas by the church committee. Although Vukichevich brought suit against the committee, he was eventually forced to vacate the pulpit. Several months later a Rev. Jugovic from Pittsburgh read in a Serbian paper of a vacancy in Steelton and volunteered to make a try at bringing peace to Steelton's Serbian colony. Jugovic soon became the third pastor within a year to leave Steelton over a rift with the church committee.[30]

Apparently the issues revolved around more than assertions by the church committee that they could control the pastor and church affairs. Ethnic feelings again became crucial as in the case of the Croatians and Slovenes. In this instance, the Orthodox Church in America was controlled by Russian officials. Serbians were convinced that the Russian officials were uninterested in Serbian parishes. "We did not want a Russian priest," one Serb recalled. "We wanted a Serbian priest."[31] Thus, as long as Serbs were sent priests of Russian extraction, they refused them entrance to the church.

The last of the immigrant groups to arrive in Steelton were Bulgarians from Macedonia. They came largely from the area around Prilep, especially the village of San Sinot. The first Bulgarians arrived about 1901 and after the Illenden Insurrection against the Turks in August of 1903. By 1904 many Bulgarians had decided to send some of their ranks back to Macedonia to secure their wives and children.[32]

To a great extent European politics dominated the affairs of the Bulgarians from the time of their arrival. In 1903, they called a meeting in Steelton to condemn the Czar of Russia for "intriguing" against the Bulgarians in Europe. An appeal to the President of the United States was included in the resolution, requesting him to cooperate with the powers of Europe in a demand to Turkey that she cease oppression of the people in Macedonia.[33]

Like other Slavic settlements, the Bulgarian community was unable to avoid persistent factionalism. Due partially to their interest in European affairs, the Macedonian-Bulgarian church was weakened by inner turmoil. Originally, when the church was organized in 1909, one section of the congregation wanted it placed under the control of the Bulgarian Synod. Another group wanted greater lay control and a closer affiliation with the Serbian Orthodox Synod. In the initial dispute the faction favoring association with the Bulgarian

Synod emerged triumphantly. The controversy not only left a deep division within the Bulgarian community but caused many of the immigrants to leave the Bulgarian church altogether or join the Serbian parish.[34]

In the 1920s a Macedonian Political Organization (MPO) was revived in Steelton. It was concerned ultimately with sending men and money to Europe to create an autonomous Macedonia. These activities disturbed many of the Bulgarians who did not believe their church should serve as a center for European political activity. The MPO was tolerated, however, until 1936 when the pastor, Rev. David Nakoff, decided to disassociate the church from the Bulgarian Synod. This move accomplished only the splintering of the church into three factions: the Nakoff group, the Synod faction who favored adhering to the original church charter, and the MPO. The Synod group, now backed by the MPO, warned Nakoff that if he did not follow the stipulations of the original charter which affiliated the congregation with the Bulgarian Synod, he would be considered a trespasser on the church grounds and be removed.[35]

The Synod adherents, known also by the names of their leaders, the Minoff brothers, brought a lawsuit against Nakoff in 1937 in Dauphin County Court. One of the Nakoff followers contended, "We didn't want to have anything to do with that government [Bulgaria] because we believe the American church belongs to the people." The court, nevertheless, upheld the original charter and the Minoff faction prevailed.[36]

The court decision caused the Nakoff followers to leave the Holy-Annunciation Church and form a separate congregation on Pine Street. When Nakoff died during World War II, his followers lost the leadership that had apparently held them together, and they were able to gain admission back into the Holy Annunciation Church.[37]

Harmony between the factions again proved to be short-lived. In April of 1948, at a church meeting, George Minoff shot and killed Koche Atzeff and Boris Mioff. The incident was a direct result of the persistent factionalism that had ravaged the congregation. It seems that in 1948 the Bulgarians were in search of a new pastor.

Upon learning of the availability of a priest in Bulgaria, they sent the necessary funds to Sofia to bring him to Steelton. They received no reply. When they sent a second request, the priest in Bulgaria wrote back and said that he was having difficulties in coming to America because someone in the Steelton congregation had written "slanderous remarks and untruths" to the Synod which were "interfering with my departure."[38]

A church meeting was called for April 4, 1948, to resolve the matter. At the meeting the old Nakoff faction began by attempting to oust Dimko Minoff from the finance committee so that it would be composed entirely of members of the Nakoff faction. After considerable argument the congregation voted to retain the old finance committee. Then the factions began to argue over the letter from the priest in Bulgaria. The Minoff followers accused the Nakoff people of trying to split the Steelton congregation by severing its ties with Bulgaria. In the heat of the argument the shooting took place.[39] Bulgarians were also faced with peculiar difficulties in a new land.

In many ways World War I proved to be a crucial period for Steelton's foreign population. They were not only stirred by events in their homeland, to which many still hoped to return, but they were also forced to demonstrate their loyalty to a nation they had hardly settled in. They would have to consciously work out their identity. They would have to decide where to draw the line between Old World ties that ran deep and the demands of an America that she have a loyal and devoted citizenry. In the process they would have to work out their ethnic identity. And, when the war had ended, they would no longer be Croatians, or Serbs, or Bulgarians. But neither would they be Americans. They would be Croatian-Americans, Serbian-Americans, and Bulgarian-Americans.

From the outset the troubles that haunted the Balkans and Southern Slavs in the years before World War I proved to be a continual preoccupation for the Slavs in Steelton. In addition to having an obvious interest in affairs of their homeland, the immigrants had many close relatives still living in southern Europe. In 1912, the Steelton Croats, for instance, growing increasingly hostile to Austro-

Hungarian rule in Croatia, called a meeting of Croatians from the different villages that were represented in Steelton. The assemblage condemned "the violence and tyranny that is ravaging Croatia." They called for a Pennsylvania federation of all Croats and Serbs to work for a free and independent Croatia. They wanted "all patriotic Croatians in America to organize a Croatian Political Association" that would collect funds to be sent to the homeland "whenever the need arises."[40]

At the same time the Slavic communities seemed to be going out of their way to affirm their loyalty to their newly adopted homeland. In 1913 the *Harrisburg Patriot* reported that there would be "little stirring to mark the celebration of Independence Day." But the foreigners will have a celebration, the paper noted, "Serbs and Hungarians will have a big day." Indeed, the Serbs planned a huge parade and a series of athletic events with visiting Serbs from Philadelphia, South Bethlehem, and Lebanon joining in.[41]

By 1913 affairs in the Balkans had Steelton's immigrant population quite aroused. The Bulgarian church was conducting "prayers for victory" for the Serbian and Bulgarian armies at Adrianople. Some former Steeltonians, who had been forced to return to serve in the armies of their homeland, were reported killed in action. The Serbian Sokol was giving gymnastic exhibitions in Harrisburg in order to raise funds to send to the Red Cross in Serbia.[42]

As war rapidly approached in July of 1914, tempers flared among Steelton's Slavs. This situation between Croatians, some of whom were still loyal to the Austro-Hungarian government, and Serbs, who were militantly opposed to the government in Vienna, grew somewhat strained in July, 1914. The assassination of the Austrian archduke by a Serb created "bitter feeling" between Steelton's Croats and Serbs.[43] The situation was inflamed when Ivan Kresic, the editor of *Novi Hrvat,* a Croatian paper in New York, wrote a caustic editorial attacking the Croatian pastor, Anton Zuvic, in Steelton. Kresic had been invited to town by the Croatian Sokol to help celebrate the Fourth of July. "When I went there I found our Croatian and Serbian Sokols divided into two bitter factions," Kresic wrote. Kresic then became more blunt. "This was caused by the Rev.

Anton Zuvic . . . who is planting hatred among these people. This is pitiful because he preaches from the pulpit against the Serbians with whom he has nothing to do."[44]

Kresic's editorial immediately stirred the ire of the Croatian population. Many Croatians, like Spiridion Furcich, an immigrant banker, claimed Zuvic was working hard "for the advancement of our people," and he called Kresic an "undesirable." In fact, the tensions between the two groups resulted in the Croatian Sokol abandoning its plans to hold a street parade along with the Serbian Sokols. There was even an incident of a stabbing of a Croatian which resulted from a brawl between Croats and Serbs.[45]

On July 19, members of the Croatian and Serbian Sokols met in Croatian Hall to attempt to mediate their differences. After impassioned pleas by Steve Memonic and Mile Bogdonovic, it was decided to lay aside all past differences and work together "for the mutual benefit of all." Once the war actually did erupt, animosity between the two seemed to be superseded by a consuming interest in the events of the war itself.

With hostilities in Europe, orders were received in Steelton from the Austro-Hungarian consul in Philadelphia to the effect that all subjects of the Austro-Hungarian Empire should be ready at a moment's notice to "take up arms against Serbia." The Austrian consul, von Grivicic, came to Steelton several days after the war had begun and told a meeting of Steelton's Slovenes, Croats, and Serbs that a general amnesty had been given to anyone who had left the homeland to avoid military service. He called on the Slavs to return to fight. There were probably about 800 males eligible for military induction into the Austro-Hungarian armed forces in Steelton. In fact, the *Harrisburg Telegraph* estimated that there were some 30,000 eligible in Eastern Pennsylvania.[46]

The number of Slavs returning to serve in the Austrian army was negligible. In the first week of August about fifty Steelton "reservists" received notices to report for duty with the Austrian forces. Steelton steamship agents reported in that same week that no Serb or Croat had left for Europe. On the contrary, most of the Serbs and a growing number of Croatians and Slovenes not only had no intention of going to war but were, in fact, growing more sympathetic with the Serbian cause.[47]

On August 3, a mass meeting of Slavs was called to formulate plans to aid Serbia. A committee was appointed to collect funds for the Serbian Red Cross. The committee consisted of Serbs (Voja Yovanovic), Croats (Steve Srbic), and Slovenes (Steven Koncar). Following patriotic speeches by the Rev. George Popovic of St. Nicholas Serbian Church, twenty-five young men volunteered for military services with the Serbian forces. Many of the volunteers soon left their jobs at the Pennsylvania Steel Company and headed for Europe. The *Telegraph* expressed amazement that although many of the foreigners were of Austrian birth, "their sympathies to a man seem to be with Serbia."[48]

Activity through the early months of the war went on at a feverish pitch. Countless events and meetings were held to raise money for relief funds in Europe. The *Telegraph* had special stations set up in the town where bulletins on the war were sent and translated. The news was then carried throughout Steelton's immigrant neighborhoods. News of relatives, former Steelton residents, in addition to the progress of the war was anxiously awaited. Kazmir Pozega, a Serbian leader and one of the translators for the *Telegraph,* told an interviewer, "What the United States fought for in 1776, Serbia is fighting for to-day. I do not believe it is just for an emperor to . . . crush a little country that is beginning to cherish dreams of political freedom. That is why I am for Serbia." Apparently most of Steelton's Slavs were "for Serbia" by August of 1914. Indeed, Meter Dragovich recalls a Serbian flag flying over one of the departments at the steel mill for the duration of the war.[49]

With the heightened activity among the foreign populace, local officials in Steelton grew increasingly concerned. Steelton's mayor, "an Englishman by birth," issued an order prohibiting sympathizers with any of the warring European nations from holding street parades or war demonstrations of any kind. The mayor further advised the Slavs to remain quiet and refrain from discussing the war situation with "any adherents of the opposing forces." The mayor even attended a fund raising meeting at the Croatian hall, which was packed "to almost suffocation." After receiving enthusiastic shouts of *"Zivio! Zivio!"* the mayor spoke:

> Steelton is a cosmopolitan town, containing many subjects of every one of the nations now at war. WE ARE ALL MEMBERS OF ONE FAMILY and we should sympathize with our brothers of all nations. . . . You are here in a neutral country. You can have no part in the struggle. Don't let your enthusiasm get away with you. Street demonstrations of any warlike nature are forbidden.
> . . . : Now you are all poor men; we don't want to fine you, for you can use the money in other ways.[50]

Besides the obvious interests in people and events in Europe, World War I influenced Steelton's immigrant population in other ways. The Bulgarians, for instance, were unable to get a priest from Bulgaria and did without one for a while. Things were slack in 1914 at the mill, as many foreign orders had been curtailed. Those that were working were doing so at reduced rates. The steel officials were hopeful that the future was bright since the "war munition's business was immensely profitable."[51]

Anton Zuvic now began to preach to his Croatian congregation the importance of owning their own homes and becoming American citizens. Zuvic felt that the war in Europe had decimated Croatia to such an extent that it would be useless to attempt to return.[52] Apparently Zuvic's remarks had some effect. Real estate exchange lists in 1914 and 1915 showed an unusual number of Slavic names on the list of those buying properties in the first ward which was Steelton's "lower end." In one month alone properties were purchased in the "lower end" by the following individuals: Anton Brinjac, Steve Salinger, Salvatore Manaro, Joseph Paukner, Marko Klensook, Marko Strasinic, Philip Gruic, Peter Ziozar, Martin Cernugle, Marko Kofalt, Joseph Mika and Joseph Verbos.[53] When the war increased production at the mill, work was again plentiful and many were further convinced that it would be better to stay in America. By 1918, moreover, a new generation of Slavs had grown up in America. As Meter Dragovich, who was born in Steelton, expressed it, "I didn't want to go to Yugoslavia."[54]

The immigrants were kept busy throughout the war, as work was plentiful. America's entry into the conflict in 1917 would inject a new problem into the immigrant's life. For if America was to fight in Europe, she had to be certain that her citizens of European origin were completely loyal.

The Bethlehem Steel Company, which had purchased the Steelton works from the Pennsylvania Steel Company in 1916, took a survey of all its workers in 1918 during a Liberty Loan Campaign and revealed that nearly 20% of its 30,000 employees were "foreigners." The study also noted that about four out of every ten of these "foreigners" wanted to return to their homeland after the war.[55] Bethlehem, in Steelton anyway, began to conduct a series of "get together" meetings at the steel plant. In an attempt to stir up patriotism and loyalty among its nearly 10,000 workers at Steelton, Bethlehem brought in military men, like a Lt. Col. Evans of the British Army, who had seen active service at the front. Evans told the some 6,000 workers on the day shift that their cooperation was needed "to make the world safe for democracy." He described the steel worker as a soldier in the thick of the fight. Evans then went on to give a brief account of the life of "American boys" in the trenches and urged his listeners to back up their brothers and friends in Europe with a "100% output." Following this particular address, the Steelton Band played and patriotic songs were sung. Bethlehem felt such meetings not only helped to foster loyalty but stirred up enthusiasm for Bethlehem's President Charles Schwab's plan to build "a bridge of ships" for the war effort.[56]

An "alien squad" composed of ten American soldiers of different nationalities appeared at Steelton High School to raise funds for the Fourth Liberty Loan Drive. The Italian Citizens Society of Steelton and Harrisburg passed a resolution to "stand-by the government and President Wilson during the present crisis." In fact, the Sons of Italy held several parades, with children in military dress, in an attempt to display "American spirit." The Steelton Knights of Columbus formed a committee of forty to carry on a Liberty Loan Drive. Of the forty, all were either Irish or German Catholic. No one elected to take German at Steelton High School in 1918 and 1919. The Jews initiated a Jewish War Fund Drive.

The Bulgarians raised $2,000 for the Third Liberty Loan campaign.[57]

As with other ethnic groups, the Croatians often seemed as anxious to prove their unquestioned loyalty as government and industry were to instill it. The Croatian Sokol held several dances to raise funds for the Red Cross. The Croatian lodges also took an active part in the Liberty Loan Drives. The Croats and Serbs also found time to participate in demonstrations in Washington calling for freedom of the "Southern Slavs" from Austria.[58]

Articulate Croatians in Steelton continually made a point of reassuring the "Americans" that they had nothing to fear from the Croatians. When a group of Serbs wanted to parade with a banner which read, "The Kingdom of Serbs, Croats, and Slovenes," the Croats and Slovenes refused. "The Croatians and the Slovenians are eager to show their appreciation in every possible way for the fact that America is their liberator," said Michael Horvath, "they will never follow a banner of a kingdom."[59] Kasmir Posega, on the 4th of July, 1918, stressed that all foreigners "gradually became Americanized." Posega used the example of the Fothergill School in Steelton. "There you will find children of about eight or ten nationalities, creeds, or religion. They are only *American*."[60]

The Croatian press was especially sensitive to the accusations and implications that immigrants were not completely loyal. One of the strongest statements affirming Slavic loyalty appeared in *Zajedničar* in 1918. The Croatian organ claimed in an editorial, "Foreigners as War Risks," that Slavs had never been properly understood by the "Americans." The paper failed to see how foreigners constituted a risk for America or her industries. It cited the lack of Slavic leadership or participation in recent labor disturbances as evidence of immigrant loyalty. Then the journal confronted the charge that immigrants did not know the English language: "What of it? Their children do. They would know English too if they were given an opportunity. . . . You would have to show us the man who has worked ten and twelve hours everyday in any one of our steel mills, mines, or freight yards, and . . . is brick enough to go to school."[61] After expressing their bitterness toward corporations for not being interested in the education of their foreign workmen, the diatribe concluded that certainly the Slav loved the land of his birth, but "the patriotism of the Slavs in America, with the exception of a few sporadic cases, is beyond reproach."[62]

In January of 1918, the Croatians of Steelton, in what represents an extreme effort by a people to prove they belong in a foreign land, organized the George Washington Lodge. The Lodge's objective and its name point up graphically the manner by which immigrants were attempting to work out their identity. While the lodge was named after an American president and was intended to demonstrate Croatian loyalty, it also aimed to achieve independence for Croatians in Europe from Austria-Hungary. The point is revealed clearly in a letter sent by Joseph Verbos and Lawrence Rudman on behalf of the lodge to Woodrow Wilson.

> The Croatians of Steelton . . . applaud most heartily the declaration of war upon the treacherous Austro-Hungarian government and beg to assure you that in offering our services we are actuated by sentiments of loyal patriotism and a desire of aiding the United States in this struggle for democracy and freedom of small nations, which we hope will mean freedom for the Croatians.[63]

The loyalty crusade hit a peak in the summer of 1918 during the Independence Day parade at Harrisburg. The parade that day was the first recorded instance where Negroes, Italians, Slavs, and native white Americans marched together. Blacks and Slavs had always marched separately on Independence Day and never with the "native" population. The *Telegraph* observed that "what few persons still allow the hyphen to creep in the names of the foreign born were compelled to forget the hyphenated names after seeing the patriotic spirit with which they marched." The paper remarked that the Steelton Bulgarian-Balkan Band and the First Cornet Band [Negro] received much applause.[64] In fact, Governor William Sproul of Pennsylvania condescendingly remarked once the war was over, "When we entered the war . . . we looked upon this great body of foreign-born people as a menace. . . . We have found in the hearts of the foreign-born an unexpected depth of patriotism. They could be a great asset in the future of our state if properly led." Sproul called for an Americanization program in the schools.[65]

The American environment presented the immigrant with unique problems that fostered an ethnic consciousness. Bulgarians argued over the extent they should be tied to Europe. Croatians and Slovenes, who cooperated for nearly two decades rather than carrying over any ethnic rivalries, became more Croatian and Slovenian once in America and eventually parted. The loyalty issue and the events of World War I forced all of Steelton's Slavs to consider the extent to which they were ready to abolish European ties and interests. Ethnicity was not simply part of the cultural baggage of the immigrant. It was also a product of the immigrant communities established in America.

## NOTES

1. Timothy Smith, "Lay Initiative in the Religious Life of American Immigrants, 1880-1950," in *Anonymous Americans,* ed. by Tamara Hareven (Englewood Cliffs, N.J.: 1971), pp. 216, 222, 245-46 n. 26.

2. For views on the development of ethnicity in America see Nathan Glazer and Daniel P. Moynihan, *Beyond the Melting Pot* (Cambridge, Mass.: 1963), pp. 16-17; Thomas N. Brown, *Irish-American Nationalism* (Philadelphia: 1966). Also see Lawrence Fuchs, ed., *American Ethnic Politics* (New York: 1968), p. 144; John Allswang, *A House for All People: Ethnic Politics in Chicago* (Lexington, Ky.: 1971), p. 10. Allswang argues that ethnicity was "reinforced" in America. Victor Greene, "For God and Country: The Origins of Slavic Catholic Self-Consciousness in America," *Church History* XXXV (Dec., 1966):446-60 points out the importance of internal forces within Slavic immigrant communities in shaping consciousness. For additional comments on the rise of ethnic feelings see W. Loyd Warner, and Leo Srole, *The Social Systems of American Ethnic Groups* (New Haven: 1945), p. 52; Milton Gordon, *Assimilation in American Life* (New York: 1964), p. 38; Robert B. Johnson, "The Nature of the Minority Community," (unpublished Ph.D. dissertation, Cornell Univ., 1955).

3. While this essay does not deal specifically with economic variables that led to the rise of ethnic consciousness, the interested researcher can find a growing literature which is quite suggestive on this point. The author's further studies on Steelton will soon show how Slavic immigrants superseded blacks in numerous occupations after 1900 and actually drove black labor downward. See also Caroline Golab, "The Polish Communities of Philadelphia, 1870-1920: Immigrant Distribution and Adaptation in Urban America" (unpublished Ph.D. dissertation, Univ. of Pennsylvania, 1971), Chapter I. Golab traces Polish competition with the Irish, Italians, Negroes, and Jews. Carl Oblinger has noted blacks being driven downward

in the face of Irish immigrant competition in "Like an Iron Fist: Black Communities in Southeastern Pennsylvania Towns, 1780-1860," (forthcoming Ph.D. dissertation, John Hopkins University). See also Stephan Thernstrom and Elizabeth H. Pleck, "The Last of the Immigrants? A Comparative Analysis of Black and Immigrant Social Mobility in Late-Nineteenth Century Boston," unpublished paper for the 1970 meeting of the Organization of American Historians; Paul B. Worthman, "Working Class Mobility in Birmingham, Alabama, 1880-1914," in *Anonymous Americans,* ed. by Tamara Hareven, pp. 172-213; Clyde Griffen, "Making It in America: Social Mobility in Mid-Nineteenth Century Poughkeepsie," *New York History* LI (October, 1970):479-99.

4. William H. Egle, *History of Dauphin and Lebanon Counties* (Philadelphia, 1883), pp. 400-404. George P. Donehoo, *Harrisburg and Dauphin County* (Dayton, 1925), pp. 210-11; "A History of the Steelton Plant, Bethlehem Steel Corporation, Steelton, Pennsylvania," unpublished manuscript in Charles Schwab Memorial Library, Bethlehem, Pennsylvania.

5. U. S. Immigration Commission, *Immigrants in Industries,* Part 2: *Iron and Steel Manufacturing* (2 vols.; Washington, 1911), I, 591; Hygienic Hose Co., *Souvenir Booklet* (Steelton, Oct. 15, 1910), p. 26; *Steelton Reporter,* May 1, 1886, p. 1.

6. *Zacetek Slovenske Naselbine v Steeltonu* [*Beginning of the Slovene Settlement in Steelton*] (Steelton, 1939), p. 5.

7. *Ibid.,* pp. 5-11; *Pozdrav in Castitke* (Steelton: St. Peter's Church, 1945), pp. 19-20.

8. John Verbos, "The St. Lawrence Story," *Zajedničar,* April 8, 1970, p. 4.

9. *Zacetek Slovenske Naselbine v Steeltonu,* pp. 8-10; Verbos, "The St. Lawrence Story," p. 4; Milan Vranes, "Od Sjek 13 u Steeltonu Odrzao Svecano Otvorrenje Svog Novog Doma," *Zajedničar,* April 23, 1969. Excellent accounts of Steelton's early Croatian colony can also be found in "Iz povijesti Hrvi Župe u Steeltonu, Pa." *Naša Nada* (1928), 169-78, and the reports of Janko Kovacevic in the Croatian newspaper *Narodni List,* June 12, 1901, p. 1 and June 15, 1901, p. 1. *Zajedičar* is on file at the Croatian Fraternal Union in Pittsburgh. Both *Zajedničar* and *Narodni List* are on microfilm at the Immigrant Archives of the University of Minnesota.

10. *Spomen Knjižica Četrdeset Godišnjice, 1898-1938, Hrvatske Rimokatolicke Župe Uznesenja Bl. Dj. Marije,* pp. 6-8. Taped interview with Rev. Jerome Kucan, Steelton, June 30, 1971.

11. Taped interview with John Verbos, Steelton, July 12, 1971; taped interview with Mary Jurina, Steelton, June 30, 1971; taped interview with Thomas Benkovic, Steelton, July 11, 1971. All persons interviewed in this study were either immigrants themselves or children of immigrants who lived through the events discussed.

12. *Spomen Knjizica Četrdeset Godišnjice, 1898-1938, Hrvatske Rimokatolicke Župe Uznesenja Bl. Dj. Marije,* pp. 6-8. Taped interview with Rev. Jerome Kucan, Steelton, June 30, 1971; Verbos, "St. Lawrence Story," p. 4; *Reporter,* Apr. 25, 1896, p. 1.

13. *Spomen Knjizica Četrdeset Godišnjice, Hrvatski Rimokatolicke Župe Uznesenja Bl. Dj. Marije,* pp. 8-9; George J. Prpić, *Croatian Immigrants in America* (New York: 1971), pp. 128-29; Stjepan Gazi, *Croatian Immigration to Allegheny County, 1882-1914* (Pittsburgh: 1956), pp. 2-4.

14. Taped interview with John Verbos, Steelton, July 12, 1971; taped interview with Mary Jurina, Steelton, June 30, 1971; taped interview with Thomas Benkovic, Steelton, July 11, 1971. Benkovic was a former president of the St. Lawrence Lodge; *Spomen Knjizica Četrdeset Godišnjice, 1898-*

*1938, Hrvatske Rimokatolicke Župe Uznesenja Bl. Dj. Marije* (Steelton, 1938), pp. 2–6. This account of Steelton's Croatians was written by early Croatian settlers still living in 1938. I am indebted to Rev. Jerome Kucan for his help in securing and translating this document.

15. Verbos, "St. Lawrence Story," p. 4; *Reporter,* Sept. 26, 1902, p. 4; Vranes, "Odsjek 13u Steeltonu Odrzao Svecano Otvorenje Svog Novog Doma," p. 2. Several members of the St. Lawrence Society disliked the site chosen for the new hall and withdrew to form several other lodges of the National Croatian Society in 1901.

16. See, for example, *Reporter,* Mar. 23, 1900, p. 1; Jan. 18, 1901, p. 3; Jan. 10, 1902, p. 4.

17. Taped interview with Thomas Benkovic, Steelton, July 11, 1971; *Spomen Knjizica Četrdeset Godišnjice, 1898–1938, Hrvatske Rimokatolicke Župe Uznesenja Bl. Dj. Marije,* pp. 2–6; Verbos, "St. Lawrence Story," p. 4.

18. *Reporter,* July 2, 1898, p. 4.

19. *Reporter,* July 2, 1898, p. 4; Oct. 5, 1900, p. 1; Sept. 13, 1901, p. 4.

20. *Reporter,* July 2, 1903, p. 1.

21. *Reporter,* Aug. 28, 1903, p. 1.

22. *Reporter,* July 23, 1909, p. 4; taped interview with Thomas Benkovic, Steelton, July 11, 1971.

23. *Zajednićar,* Mar. 30, 1911, pp. 2, 7; see *Reporter,* Nov. 5, 1909, p. 4; Mar. 31, 1911, p. 4.

24. *Reporter,* Dec. 30, 1910, p. 4; Nov. 3, 1911, p. 4; Dec. 1, 1911, p. 4; Jan. 26, 1912, p. 4.

25. *Reporter,* Apr. 26, 1912, p. 4; May 3, 1912, p. 4.

26. Ironically the most accurate account of the founding of the school is in the *Reporter,* Aug. 7, 1903, p. 4; Sept. 11, 1903, p. 1; Sept. 25, 1903, p. 1; Emily Balch, *Our Slavic Fellow Citizens* (New York: 1910), p. 413; quotation is from taped interview with Tom Benkovic, Steelton, July 11, 1971. See also *Reporter,* Mar. 11, 1904, p. 1.

27. *Spomen Knjizica Četrdeset Godišnjice, 1898–1938, Hrvatske Rimokatolicke Župe Uznesenja Bl. Dj. Marije,* p. 5; *Diamond Jubilee* (Steelton: St. Mary's Parish, 1958); *Pozdrav in Castitke,* p. 24; taped interview with Thomas Benkovic, Steelton, July 11, 1971.

28. *Reporter,* Mar. 26, 1909, p. 1; *Pozdrav in Castitke,* p. 24; *Consecration of Iconostas and Fortieth Anniversary of Circle of Serbian Sisters* (Steelton: St. Nicholas Serbian Church, Oct. 12, 1969); *Spomen Knjizica Četrdeset Godišnjice, 1898–1938, Hrvatske Rimokatolicke Župe Uznesenja Bl. Dj. Marije,* p. 9.

29. *Harrisburg Patriot,* July 14, 1913, p. 8; see also *750 Years of the Serbian Church, 1219–1969* (Cleveland: 1969), p. 31.

30. *Patriot,* Feb. 26, 1914, p. 5; April 1, 1914, p. 1.

31. Taped interview with Meter Dragovich, Harrisburg, Nov. 29, 1971.

32. *Fiftieth Anniversary, Holy Annunciation Macedonian-Bulgarian Church* (Steelton: 1959), pp. 1–8; David Nakoff, *A History of the Macedonian-Bulgarian Church of Steelton, Pennsylvania* (Steelton: 1939), pp. 2–3.

33. *Reporter,* Oct. 23, 1903, p. 1; see also Mar. 5, 1905, p. 4.

34. Interview with George Dimoff, Steelton, Oct. 29, 1971.

35. *Ibid.* Also taped interview with Hope Kormuschoff, Harrisburg, Sept. 10, 1971.

36. "Brief for Defendant on Motion for New Trial," Comm. of Pennsylvania vs. George Minoff, O & T Sessions, Nos. 3–4 (June, 1948), Dauphin County Court House, p. 3. *Transcript,* Comm. of Pennsylvania vs. George Minoff, O & T Court, Dauphin County Court House (June, 1948), pp. 245–84.

37. Taped interview with George Dimoff, Steelton, Oct. 29, 1971.
38. Transcript, O & T Court (June, 1948), Dauphin County Court, p. 285; Patriot, Apr. 5, 1948, pp. 1–2.
39. "Brief for Defendant on Motion for New Trial," Comm. of Pennsylvania vs. George Minoff, O & T Court, p. 3; Patriot, Apr. 5, 1948, pp. 1–2.
40. Zajedničar, June 12, 1912, p. 5.
41. Patriot, July 4, 1913, p. 5.
42. Patriot, Jan. 22, 1913, p. 7; Feb. 9, 1913, p. 6; Mar. 3, 1915, p. 5.
43. Zajedničar, July 15, 1914, p. 2; Harrisburg Telegraph, July 10, 1914, pp. 1, 11.
44. Novi Hrvat [New Croatian], July 9, 1914, pp. 1, 3.
45. Telegraph, July 10, 1914, pp. 1, 11; actually the Diamond Jubilee of St. Mary's Church (1958), p. 4 states that Rev. Zuvic was asked to come to Steelton by the Croats because he had become noted for his outspoken advocacy of Croatian independence.
46. Zajedničar, Aug. 12, 1914, p. 1; Telegraph, July 29, 1914, p. 8.
47. Patriot, July 24, 1913, p. 5; Telegraph, Aug. 1, 1914, p. 3; Aug. 6, 1914, p. 1; Aug. 13, 1914, p. 10.
48. Zajedničar, Aug. 12, 1914, p. 1; Telegraph, Aug. 3, 1914, p. 7; Aug. 4, 1914, p. 9; the Telegraph also published a list of all volunteers who left for Serbia.
49. Telegraph, Aug. 5, 1914, p. 7; Aug. 13, 1914, p. 7; taped interview with Meter Dragovich, Harrisburg, Nov. 29, 1971.
50. Telegraph, Aug. 10, 1914, p. 9.
51. Telegraph, Aug. 28, 1914, p. 11; steel's viewpoint is expressed in "Chandler Bros. Stock Prospectus," in the Pennsylvania Steel Company material, Charles M. Schwab Memorial Library, Bethlehem, Penna.
52. Spomen Knjizica Četrdeset Godišnjice, 1898–1938, Hrvatske Rimokatolicke Župe Uznesenja Bl. Dj. Marije, p. 8.
53. Patriot, April 2, 1914, p. 2; April 5, 1915, p. 3.
54. Spomen Knjizica Četrdeset Godišnjice, 1898–1938, Hrvatske Rimokatolicke Župe Uznesenja Bl. Dj. Marije, pp. 8–9; taped interview ith Meter Dragovich, Harrisburg, Oct. 27, 1971.
55. Telegraph, Feb. 16, 1918, p. 7.
56. Telegraph, June 3, 1918, p. 8; June 4, 1918, p. 6; Apr. 23, 1918, p. 16.
57. Telegraph, Jan. 1, 1918, p. 7; Feb. 4, 1918, p. 8; Feb. 21, 1918, p. 10; Apr. 29, 1918, p. 16; July 10, 1918, p. 12; Sept. 3, 1918, p. 12; Oct. 2, 1918, p. 6.
58. Zajedničar, Oct. 8, 1918, p. 6; Telegraph, Oct. 1, 1918, p. 16; Apr. 2, 1918, p. 11.
59. Telegraph, July 5, 1919, p. 18.
60. Zajedničar, July 10, 1918, p. 3; Telegraph, July 3, 1918, pp. 1, 9.
61. Zajedničar, Apr. 17, 1918, p. 1.
62. Zajedničar, Apr. 17, 1918, p. 1; Apr. 24, 1918, pp. 1, 3.
63. Zajedničar, Feb. 27, 1918, p. 2. Actually the letter the Steelton Croatians wrote was rejected for inclusion in Frank Zotti's Croatian paper, Narodni List. Zotti's paper was strongly pro-German and pro-Austrian. Its offices in New York were raided by the Department of Justice in August of 1918.
64. Telegraph, July 5, 1918, p. 5.
65. Telegraph, Jan. 21, 1919, p. 8.